Scientific Standards of Psychological Practice:

Issues and Recommendations

Scientific Standards of Psychological Practice:

Issues and Recommendations

Edited by
Steven C. Hayes
University of Nevada

Victoria M. Follette
University of Nevada

Robyn M. Dawes
Carnegie-Mellon University

Kathleen E. Grady
Massachusetts Institute of Behavioral Medicine

CONTEXT PRESS
Reno, NV

Scientific Standards of Psychological Practice: Issues and Recommendations /
edited by Steven C. Hayes, Victoria M. Follette, Robyn M. Dawes, &
Kathleen E. Grady

284 pp.   Paperback   ISBN-13: 978-1878978-60-8

Distributed by New Harbinger Publications, Inc.

First Printing in Hardback: 1995
Second Printing in Paperback (with minor typographical error corrections): 2007

Library of Congress Catalogibg-in-Publication Data

Scientific Standards of Psychological Practice: Issues and Recommendations /
edited by Steven C. Hayes, Vicrotia M. Follette, Robyn M. Dawes, Kathleen E.
Grady.
    p. cm.
  Includes bibliographical references.
    ISBN-13: 978-1-878978-23-3
  1. Clinical psychology. 2. Standards. 3. Congresses. I. Hayes, Steven C.
    RC467 .S435 1995
  616.89/002/18-dc21

                                                    98116141

Printed in the United States of America

List of Contributors

Henry E. Adams, *University of Georgia*

Larry E. Beutler, *University of California, Santa Barbara*

John D. Cone, *United States International University*

Gerald C. Davison, *University of Southern California*

Robyn M. Dawes, *Carnegie-Mellon University*

Eve H. Davison, *University of California, Santa Barbara*

Ursula Delworth, *University of Iowa*

Victoria M. Follette, *University of Nevada*

William C. Follette, *University of Nevada*

Patrick M. Ghezzi, *University of Nevada*

Kathleen E. Grady, *Massachusetts Institute of Behavioral Medicine*

Gregory J. Hayes, *University of Nevada*

Linda J. Hayes, *University of Nevada*

Steven C. Hayes, *University of Nevada*

Barbara S. Kohlenberg, *Veteran's Administration, Reno, NV*

Arnold A. Lazarus, *Rutgers University*

Samuel Leigland, *Gonzaga University*

Richard M. McFall, *Indiana University*

Ted Packard, *University of Utah*

Michael Pallack, *Foundation for Behavioral Health*

Jacqueline Persons, *Center for Cognitive Therapy, Oakland, CA*

Robert Peterson, *University of Nevada*

Alan Fruzzetti, *University of Nevada*

Stephen R. Reisman, *ServiceNet, Inc.*

Stanley Sue, *University of California, Los Angeles*

G. Terence Wilson, *Rutgers University*

Logan Wright, *Central Oklahoma University*

Robert D. Zettle, *Wichita State University*

Table of Contents

About this Volume

The era of practice standards for psychological work is upon us. Many scientifically-oriented psychologists view this new era with great hope and expectation. Scientific psychologists may finally have an opportunity to do what has been dreamed of for so long: to link practical psychological work to contemporary scientific knowledge.

This volume was a result of a three-day conference held in Reno at the University of Nevada January 6-9, 1995. The conference was organized by the editors of this volume, along with Todd R. Risley. It brought together national leaders in applied psychology to explore the implications of scientific-based standards of practice. The conference attendees addressed such questions as: can we create such standards? Should we do it? How should it be done? What are some of the problems to be solved and pitfalls to be avoided? This volume challenges the discipline to begin to ensure that scientific knowledge is actually used in clinical practice.

The conference consisted of thirteen major addresses followed in each case by general discussion, led by discussion leaders. The revised major papers and discussions are enclosed in this volume.

As the conclusion of the conference, the speakers agreed upon the following list of general conclusions:
1. Practitioners should evaluate interventions with empirically valid and repeated assessment of the problems being treated.
2. Practitioners should consistently apply interventions that are safe, effective, and empirically validated in dealing with the problems clients are trying to solve.
3. Psychology as a field should develop hortatory and minatory scientific standards of practice and revisit these on a periodic and timely basis.
4. Clients should have full informed consent of the scientific basis of the procedures being applied.
5. If a client has had proven procedures applied and they have been unsuccessful or if there are no proven procedures in this particular area, then the practitioner should be especially sure to emphasize point 1 and point 4.
6. AAAPP should appoint a board to help develop both general and specific scientific standards of practice.
7. The process of developing scientific standards of practice should be open to those who believe that particular procedures either are or are not appropriate given the above.

The primary sponsor of the conference was the American Association of Applied and Preventive Psychology, a four-year old association of about 1,600 scientifically-oriented applied psychologists. The conference was also supported by the University of Nevada College of Arts and Science, University of Nevada Graduate School, University of Nevada Department of Psychology, and CONTEXT PRESS.

To our students and the lives they will touch

Chapter 1

What Standards Should We Use?

Larry E. Beutler

and

Eve H. Davison

University of California, Santa Barbara

Imagine that you are a consultant to a community agency that has hired you to help them implement a treatment program. The community agency who employs you plans to develop an outpatient treatment program based on a model that has been endorsed by major national groups and is widely regarded among mental health specialists as the most effective for treating some behavioral disorders. Moreover, similar approaches have been used and advocated by most treatment facilities in the country. The structured program will result in certificates being awarded to those who complete training and will allow them to train others in the use of these procedures.

You are committed to ensuring that the evaluation and intervention procedures that you recommend and implement have been empirically validated in controlled research. In the initial proposal, however, the agency reviews the history of this treatment model but does not include any examples of or references to controlled clinical research on the efficacy of the treatment. You ask proponents of the program if they know any controlled research to support the proposal and they respond quite negatively. One asserts that such research would be unethical because it would prevent some people from receiving this "obviously effective" treatment. Your own review reveals several articles based on correlational methods, but most of these studies do not address the effectiveness of the proposed treatment. Instead, they report patient characteristics that are associated with improvement while undergoing this type of treatment. One of the few studies that does address efficacy, absent control and comparison groups, reports drop-out rates of 90% over the course of treatment. Of those that continued and participated, 70% were reported to have benefited. Other correlational studies report improvement rates as small as 30%, but do not report drop-out rates. Studies of other treatments report efficacy rates of around 70% even when drop-out is considered a failure of treatment. Further library research uncovers three random assignment studies, all on involuntarily admitted inpatient samples. Of the three studies, none found a significant difference favoring the treatment when compared to ward mileau alone or a peer support program.

Would you support the development of a training program to certify mental health workers in the conduct of this treatment? Certainly not if you followed the guidelines developed by the APA Task Force on Promotion and Dissemination of Psychological Procedures (1993), who defined the standard of validity as "two good group design studies, conducted by different investigators,demonstrating efficacy" (p.21) when compared to a control or established comparison treatment. But reconsider the implications of this decision for a moment because this example is not purely hypothetical. It parallels closely what would occur if you were asked to help establish a program for alcohol abusers based on the 12-step model developed by Alcoholics Anonymous (see McCrady & Miller, 1993). Given the public popularity as well as the widespread belief in the efficacy of these programs by both public and professional constituencies, you can expect some repercussions if you rejected the proposal. You will find, for example, that if you want to conduct treatment research on alcohol abuse and plan to exclude those who are in a 12-step program, cooperation from the community will be less than optimal, and non-representativeness may become critical. Most of those who work in the area will doubt whatever nonsupportive results you obtain, and many will argue that it is unwise to exclude training about 12-step models simply because they are so widely used.

This example illustrates some of the complexities that accrue when non-scientific rules of evidence are ignored. When treatments make sense to the public, are adopted and accepted by a large group of practitioners, and enjoy popular support, the value of scientific evidence is likely to take a back seat when questions of a treatment's "worth" are considered. It raises the question of what to do when the findings from scientific research contradict the non-scientific models of discovery and evidence that characterizes the social system in which one works. Can or should contradictory scientific findings be applied independently of the value system of the broader social system? In a multi-value system such as that of our culture, should our criteria of evidence be restricted to a standard based on a scientific demonstration of clinical efficacy, or are there other qualities that combine with evidence from empirical science to warrant the incorporation of publicly valued programs in our instructional curricula?

To make the problem even more complex, it must be understood that there is not a single definition of what constitutes "scientific evidence of validity" with which all good scientists likely would agree. Instead, there are a variety of standards of "proof" that are used by scientists for different purposes, and some of these sets of criteria overlap with the standards applied by non-scientists. The variety of "empirical criteria" opens the door to the possibility that their application may be affected by scientists' predilective beliefs and that they, themselves, may shift their standards in order to support a favored viewpoint or to reject an unfavored one.

While assessment and treatment do not constitute the totality of mental health practice, these are the two areas in which a sufficient body of empirical knowledge exists to lend itself to defining credible standards of practice. Drawing from these two areas, in this paper, we will: (1) identify several of the most commonly used standards of proof, (2) review a few of their strengths and weaknesses, and (3) explore examples from extant psychotherapy and assessment practice in order to see some of the implications of applying these standards. We will start with an example in order to illustrate the role of personal and professional beliefs in the selection of "empirically validated" psychological tests. We will then extend the presentation to explore a variety of evidentiary models and their implications. We will conclude with a series of recommendations for applying rules of evidence.

An Assessment Procedure: An Example

The X Test is an individually administered procedure designed to evaluate personality. It is a rationally derived, omnibus personality test that yields five rationally derived scoring dimensions, within each of which there are a variable number of subscales whose scores are assumed to be continuous. These scores purport to measure, among other things, impulse control, cognitive efficiency, psychoticism, psychological mindedness, aggression, interpersonal cooperation, and severity of distress. The test is interpreted by comparing both separate scale scores with one another and with roughly defined "norms", as well as by a rational rule-governed analysis of score profiles.

There have been a large number of research studies published on the X Test and a recent meta-analytic report of an articulated subset of these studies found that inter-rater reliability (kappas) averaged .86 and that test-retest reliability (r) averaged .85, across various subscales (Parker, Hanson, & Hunsley, 1988). This report also found that (1) correlations of convergence with other personality tests of similar constructs and with diagnostic criteria were moderate and significant ($M = .41$); (2) significant correlations ranging from .30 to .60 were obtained with concurrent or future ratings of impulsivity, hospitalization, imprisonment, and social adjustment; and (3) low or nonsignificant correlations were obtained with concurrent indicators of sexual preferences, mood, and organicity.

In addition, the literature reveals several studies that have reported significant and meaningful correlations between profiles purported to index aggression, cooperation, and various measures of the therapeutic alliance or relationship, and there are several studies that have found that various indicators of psychopathology level or severity are lower at the end of treatment than before. On the basis of these findings, a recent study addressed the validity of this test for predicting retention in and commitment to treatment.

In this latter study (Hilsenroth, Handler, Toman, & Padawer, in press), the authors contrasted the X Test against the MMPI in the prediction of psychotherapy drop-out. Ninety-seven premature drop outs were contrasted with 81 treatment completers, group matched for problem type and severity, from a University outpatient clinic. Various diagnostic conditions, including adjustment disorders, depression, psychosis, and anxiety disorders were represented. Selected subjects were given both tests at the time of admission. Psychotherapy was short-term (six months or less), "psychodynamic" in orientation.

The predictor variables explored were the 10 standard clinical scales from the MMPI and three score profiles from the X Test, representing respectively, *Interpersonal Aggression-Cooperation*; *Accessibility* to internal reserves and problem solving resources; and level of *Psychopathology*. The latter clusters were defined a-priori; the hypotheses arose from a well articulated theory and were bolstered from related research on the XTest. The MMPI was selected for comparison because of its frequent prior use in predictive research on patient factors associated with treatment retention.

The results indicated that the XTest variables were more closely related to retention than any of the MMPI scales. In fact, none of the latter scales were correlated with drop out, while one of the three XTest clusters (Aggression-Cooperation) was quite strongly related to subsequent drop out (e.s. = .60). From this limited information, how would you vote in deciding if this test should be included in a graduate training curriculum in professional psychology? Obviously, the choice is not a simple one. The test seems to have validity for some things and not for others. Some scales are reliable and some are not. Some research is supportive and some is not. From a value laden perspective, one may even question the selection of "drop-out" from psychodynamic therapy as a relevant criteria to predict. But, assuming that you could qualify the use of the procedure, does it meet your standards for inclusion? Would your decision change, however, when we reveal that the XTest is the Rorschach, one of the most frequently used (Sweeney, Clakin, & Fitzgibbon, 1987) and widely accepted, but controversial instruments in the psychologist's assessment armamatarium?

We contend that if the decision to include or exclude a procedure was made purely on the basis of empirical evidence of reliability and validity, most would consider accepting the XTest as a potentially viable instrument for some restricted purposes within training programs. However, it is our experience that the disclosure of the test's "true identity" is likely to invoke a different set of criteria and post-hoc explanations of the findings. Some psychologists, largely those who identify themselves as "empirical" or "behavioral", disproportionately represented among academic practitioners, may now begin to invoke evidence that establish a case for rejecting the measure. They may argue that there is little empirical support for the projective hypothesis, or that the procedure lacks incremental validity, or that there is no empirical support for all of the various scoring and interpretive methods used, or that the psychometric qualities of many of the scales are weak. Largely, in our experience, these are not criteria that are considered in equal proportion for tests like the MMPI, the WAIS, the MCMI, or many other "empirical" tests. And they are more frequently garnered after the disclosure, not before.

On the other hand, we venture to hypothesize that those who work in clinical settings may become more favorably disposed toward inclusion of the test in academic programs once the identity of the instrument is known, also invoking post-hoc justifications that point out the widespread use and acceptance of the instrument, or recalling examples of instances when it was very helpful, or by detailing its improvements over the years. These arguments may also appear after the revelation of the test's identity and may be applied with a vigor that belies claims of objectivity.

Whatever "empirical standard" one accepts for assessing the value of any given procedure may be both changeable and partially determined by personal biases and beliefs quite independently of scientific data. In our specific example, the likelihood of rejecting or accepting the empirical validity of the Rorschach may represent more general attitudes and beliefs regarding the projective hypothesis, the face validity of the instrument, and frequency of use rather than a strict accounting of the psychometric qualities of the procedure and the empirical demonstration of its usefulness. Who among us cannot say that we evaluate ideas with which we disagree just a bit more critically than we evaluate our own, ask just a few more questions, slightly adapt our criteria of evidence, and raise a skeptical eye at a few more of the weaknesses in theory or research?

To the degree that these latter hypotheses are correct, the usefulness of any standard of empirical proof that is developed must be responsive to the values that exist within the society in which it is to be applied (our AA example), and minimally influenced by the personal biases and predilections of those who make the decisions about inclusion and exclusion (our Rorschach example). Thus, a paradox is presented. The standards invoked to decide what procedures reach acceptable levels of scientific validation must be both value consistent (consistent with social values) in order to achieve acceptance, and value free (free from personal biases) in order to be fair. To say this another way, it must be both empirical in nature and compatible with conventionally adopted non-empirical methods of evaluating truth.

In order to seek this balance, we turn now to a review of the major ways in which evidence is evaluated in our culture, and the likely consequences for professional psychology of accepting each of these standards of evidence. These various criteria of evidentiary truth can be ordered along a dimension of replicability and objectivity (i.e., independence of the observer), allowing us to roughly classify them as either "empirical" or "non-empirical" in nature. While this distinction is not perfect, it does provide a starting place by which to compare the various bases of evidence that are frequently invoked and to anticipate the consequences of directing graduate curricula by reliance on them.

Non-Empirical Approaches to Validation

In contemporary graduate training, non-empirical criteria of validity are frequently used to define whether a procedure will be represented in the curriculum. Some of the mechanisms by which curricular decisions are made parallel the criteria used by the lay person in accepting a principle or practice as "valid". The most common of these are "face validity" and "consensual validity".

1. Face Validity—"It looks good and is logical".

The proof of the validity and value of a procedure or principle is often considered sufficient in lay circles if the explanation is logical and "fits" one's personal experience. This is probably the most common basis of assessing the truth of an assertion among the lay public, especially when the felt need that is being addressed is great. For example, Laetrile treatment, natureopathy, and chiropractic are all accepted among lay persons in the face of strongly felt need and face valid explanations, but in the absence of traditional empirical criteria. Likewise, the concept of co-dependency is popularly accepted because people can identify with their own tendencies to take care of others at the expense of themselves. In both of these cases, as in most wherein one lives by this criteria of worth or "truth", the presence of scientific, empirical evidence is usually used after the fact to support the initial viewpoint rather than as a basis of selecting a curricula or to evaluate it.

While this standard is widely used as the basis for developing clinical training curricula, in the areas of measurement and psychotherapy, we have many reasons to doubt the value of this standard. In the area of *assessment*, for example, the use of this standard has resulted in the acceptance of the logic and appeal of phrenology, tarot cards, and astrology as assessment methods. In the arena of *treatment*, "mesmerizing", blood letting, and demonology are or have been accepted because they arose from an internally consistent theory that had persuasive appeal, fit personal experiences, but lacked scientific support.

One problem with using the criteria of face validity derives from the fact that the standard of proof is usually applied to the underlying theory rather than to its application. Thus, many "empirically" derived tests and therapies have little underlying theory, and these procedures tend to fail when the standard of truth is face validity. Tests like the MMPI, for example, possess minimal face validity, and would likely be rejected if this were the only criteria set used to set curricula. Conversely, defiance-based paradoxical interventions may be effective precisely because the logic of the presented theory is rejected by the patient. Prescribing the symptom or symptom exaggeration, for example, capitalizes on the client doing the opposite of what seems logical from the standpoint of the theory presented to them.

Of course, most empirically minded clinicians would probably reject face validity as the basis for education. Lest we researchers and academics become prematurely smug, however, it is worth noting that 40% of the instruments used in clinical research rest entirely or mostly on face validity rather than independent verification of reliability and validity (Lambert, Christensen, & DeJulio, 1983). This point suggests that an unspoken reverence for face validity exists even among skilled and knowledgeable empiricists.

2. Consensual Validity—"Everyone knows it's true".

Based on this set of criteria, a procedure is accepted if it has wide public support or if recognized authorities advocate it. Face validity is often part of the basis for this acceptance, but the standard of consensual validity goes beyond this set of criteria and appeals to the opinions of others, including and especially those of recognized "experts". Some graduate curricular decisions, for example, are justified because credentialing criteria, licensing laws, and practitioners favor and advocate for including certain procedures. This is a form of acceptance that places reliance on expert opinion above empirical evidence.

Inherent in determining the societal acceptance of a procedure or principle by this standard are such factors as the degree to which authoritative opinion is accepted and respected in a society, and the degree to which the proposed procedure or principle "fits" one's personal experiences. When conflicts of values exist in the society, the appeal to authority may be a more or less salient determiner of opinion depending upon both person and situational variables (Centers, Shomer, & Rodriques, 1970; Harvey, & Hays, 1972). In many cases, if acknowledged experts believe something is true, then it is accepted as factual, even when it doesn't fit the experience of the lay person (Cialdini, 1993). The Szondi test, for example, was accepted for many years, on the basis of expert appeal, even though the theory did not make sense to the lay person.

Twelve-step Programs are examples of therapies that have been and are accepted on the basis of the criteria of consensual validity. Likewise, the legal test of malpractice in the use of psychological assessments and treatments relies on a consensual standard of "truth" and is embodied in the concept of the "community standard" against which one's practices are compared. Creative, interesting procedures that are well embedded within and internally consistent with a popularly accepted theory, may capture the imagination of large groups and gain wide acceptance without substantive empirical evidence of value. Thus, if we were to adopt this as the standard of truth in professional psychology, both the Rorschach and psychoanalytic theory would be accepted as being true. Respectively, these procedures enjoy a wide acceptance among practicing clinicians; the Rorschach is more popular than any individually administered psychological test except the DAP and Bender-Gestalt, as measured by its use in practice (Sweeney, Clarkin, & Fitzgibbons, 1987); and psychoanalytic theory is the most widely favored and practiced single theory among clinicians (Norcross & Prochaska, 1988).

More critically, perhaps, Memory Recovery Therapy has been widely accepted because its underlying theory has both face validity and popular acceptance among experts and the public. Witness the struggle between the forces that rely on consensual validation and more objective standards of science, the latter of which asserts the potential damaging effects of Memory Recovery Therapy (Loftus, Gary, & Feldman, 1994; Loftus & Ketcham, 1994) and the former of which argues that the procedures are justified and necessary to assist troubled individuals (Berliner & Williams, 1994; Courtois, 1988).

A multi-national survey of practitioners by Poole, Lindsay, Memon, and Bull (in press) has revealed that over one-fourth of practitioners assume a correspondence between specific current symptoms and disorders, especially PTSD, Borderline Personality Disorder, and Eating Disorder, and the presence of early childhood sexual abuse. This view persists even though there is convincing research to indicate that most adult victims of childhood sexual abuse are indistinguishable from normals and that there is not an isomorphic relationship between a specific trauma in childhood and subsequent symptoms in adulthood (Beutler, Williams, & Zetzer, 1994). Nonetheless, these clinicians report that they would implement procedures to recover these assumed memories within the first two treatment sessions, even though there is some scientific evidence to indicate that these procedures might create rather than recover memories (Loftus & Ketcham, 1994).

As the example of False Memory Syndrome would indicate, a major problem with consensual validity as a standard of evidence is that it favors complex, abstract theories that are difficult to understand except by "experts" and difficult to validate by scientific means. Among other difficulties of adopting this set of criteria is that it defies the principle of parsimony, it assumes that truth invariably follows linear rules of logic, and it reduces truth to a popularity contest based upon the persuasiveness of the most charismatic theoretician (Loftus, 1993).

If consensual validity was the set of criteria that governed curricular decisions, psychoanalytic and haphazard "eclectic" approaches would be among the dominant offerings in training because of their popularity. On the other hand, systematic prescriptive and integrative approaches would be omitted from training solely because these approaches are difficult to define outside of a consistent and accepted theory. Memory Recovery Therapy would be accepted, as would a host of other professionally credible, but scientifically dubious practices.

Empirical Approaches to Validation

Empirical approaches are usually touted as replacements for rational criteria of proof, holding the promise that they are relatively protected from personal biases and prejudices. Empirical approaches rely on external criteria and statistical estimates of probability in an effort to preserve their independence from the observer. The nature of empirical approaches is not consistent, however, and various empirical criteria would be likely to result in quite different decisions about what to include and exclude in graduate curricula.

1. Theoretical Validity

To many scientists, the major objective of research is the validation and disconfirmation of theory. If research does not add to theoretical understanding, it is considered to be of limited value. By this reasoning, if the theory on which a procedure is built is valid, the method is also thought to be; or conversely, if the theory is false, so is the approach. If a set of criteria based on this principle were invoked for the establishment of graduate curricula, only procedures that were founded on empirically supported theories and valid underlying constructs would be taught. This may well have been the tradition and goal that has driven the selection of the psychotherapeutic methods that are taught in graduate training. While the evidence of proof for a theory is, by itself a matter of controversy, the desire to teach procedures that are founded on strong theory has guided many of us in the preparation of course syllabi and lectures.

By this set of criteria, the projective hypothesis probably would be rejected; thus, the Rorschach and DAP would be considered invalid because they arose from this theory. Indeed, projective procedures would be eliminated from the curriculum, more generally, and psychoanalytic therapy and primal-scream therapy would meet a similar fate. Perhaps this would be well and good, given the controversial nature of many of these procedures and the weak evidence of efficacy for most of them. However, this approach to validation fails to consider the possibility that good theory may lead to bad practice, or that effective methods sometimes arise from bad theory. Thus, if implemented, neuro-linguistic programming would be largely accepted even though it has very limited evidence of efficacy, while client-centered therapy and cognitive therapy would be rejected in spite of good evidence of efficacy. Eye movement desensitization would also be rejected as premature, in the absence of theoretical support.

2. Replicability

The criteria of replicability is a common standard by which psychological tests are accepted. This set of criteria asserts that if a phenomenon can be objectively observed on two or more occasions, the observation must be valid. As applied to clinical practice, replicability holds that if the score on an IQ test has been obtained several times, the likelihood of its accuracy and value has been increased. Likewise, it assumes that if the effects of a psychotherapy procedure has been replicated on a number of occasions, it constitutes evidence of the value of the procedure.

This is the criteria adopted by the Division 12 white paper on Empirically Validated Treatments (APA Task Force on Promotion and Dissemination of Psychological Procedures, 1993). Compared to others considered here, it has the advantage of providing the maximal protection against the influence both of subjective bias and of particular settings or locations. Adoption of this set of criteria would (and did in the task force report) support the value of several models of cognitive therapy (CT), Interpersonal Psychotherapy (IPT), behavior therapy, and others. And, as seen earlier, this set of criteria would result in the rejection of widely accepted twelve-step programs, AA itself, and many other widely influential and accepted approaches.

While some may not consider the subsequent (wide-spread?) loss of credibility within the private and professional communities a problem if it occurred in the course of implementing this criterion, there are other potential problems with implementation. For example, this set of criteria does not assess the relative balance of positive and negative findings, nor does it define what constitutes a "sufficient" number of occasions on which replication has occurred. Thus, psychotherapy for pedophiles would be accepted as valid, as was done by the task force report, and so would the Rorschach, both of which have accumulated some positive findings among the extensive list of research publications on these procedures. By the same token, hypnosis (Kirsch, Montgomery, & Sapirstein, 1995; Ruhe, Lynn, & Kirsch, 1993) and paradoxical therapies would be considered among the most validated interventions to teach in graduate school (Shoham-Solomon & Rosenthal, 1986). Outside of clinical psychology, a strict interpretation of this set of criteria probably would also result in the acceptance of extrasensory perception as reasonable if not mandatory phenomena to teach in graduate school, a decision that would probably be rejected by a large share of the academic community.

This approach to validity favors procedures based on the simplest models, applied to the least complex problems, and that embody the most concrete outcomes. It tends to disallow procedures that address complex problems, those that are non-linearly associated with outcomes, interaction effects, and those problems that are multi-dimensional. Thus, by this criteria, behavioral approaches would be favored over abstract, dynamic approaches.

Moreover, the concept of combining or fitting multiple treatments to specific patients would be rejected (and was in the Task Force report) because of the complexity of studying such interactions. Simple formula for assessing replicability have a difficult time adapting to the observations of the large number of well-controlled studies, including prospective clinical trials, that have found patients who are high and low on various measures that are variously used to define the interrelated concepts of impulsivity, acting out, externalization, and extroversion, produce oppositely valenced and significant correlations with outcome when provided either with behavioral/cognitive change procedures (from whatever theory) or with insight/interpersonal/systemic interventions. An interpretation of these observations usually reflect discrete aspects of the therapy, rather than their easily manualized brands, and characteristics of the patients that are neither clearly related to isolated diagnostic groupings nor easily captured in a well defined measurement device (see Beutler & Clarkin, 1990).

Similar problems with the non-specificity of both the measurement and the operative therapy procedures arises when this set of criteria is applied to the observation that a similarly large number of correlational studies, two major meta-analyses, and several randomized clinical trials, have found a patient dimension, variously referred to as "resistance", "oppositionalism", and "reactance", that is predictive of the efficacy of both paradoxical and non-directive interventions. Since such findings suggest the value of strategies that can be applied within any or most treatment models to patients within a number of diagnostic groups, including such observations of ATI (Aptitude-Treatment Interactions) relations in differential treatment effects is overlooked by criteria that looks only at manualized, theory-driven treatment models and diagnostic-related groupings of patients (Beutler & Clarkin, 1990).

3. Incremental Validity

Incremental validity, as a criterion for deciding the value of a given approach, emphasizes the efficiency of the procedure. This approach to verification embodies the principle that "truth is parsimonious". It argues that unless a procedure is better than a minimal intervention or assessment condition, it cannot be justified.

The advantage of this set of criteria is that it requires a baseline of knowledge based upon a concept of "minimal treatment". If a procedure does not add anything to the use of a simpler, easier to apply, or more straightforward standard, it is rejected. Thus, it relies heavily on research in which treatments are disaggregated, comparisons are made with placebo interventions, or contrasts are assessed between treatments and non-specific and cheaply administered alternatives. Among the disadvantages of this criterion it that there is no inherently acceptable definition of what constitutes a "minimal" intervention and considerable disagreement over whether there is a suitable "psychotherapy placebo" (Kazdin, 1980; 1991). To some, the appropriate comparison may be a no-treatment control condition while to others it is a previously validated treatment, a non-specific intervention, or a self-help regimen. Constructing such alternatives assumes either that one knows what constitutes the so-called "non-specific" ingredients in psychotherapy or can disentangle these effects from how treatment is implemented. While these tasks initially appear simple, the fact that such "non-specific" qualities are both poorly defined in previous research (Beutler & Sandowicz, 1994) and are manifested differently in different treatments (Rounsaville, Chevron, Prusoff, Elkin, Imber, Sotsky, & Watkins, 1987), make it virtually impossible to instigate a placebo or non-specific treatment that does not either include or inappropriately exclude aspects of the targeted active treatment. While some may argue that everything must be compared against no-treatment, when a no-intervention or a no-assessment is not possible for ethical, practical, or legal reasons, the definition of what constitutes the "minimal treatment necessary" is virtually impossible to define. In the arena of assessment, for example, one may wonder if the Rorschach yields a sufficiently large increment of knowledge as to justify it over direct questioning about one's impulses, disturbance, and conflicts. While ostensibly a simple question, the absence of reliability, concurrent validity, and predictive validity data on direct questions precludes a simple comparison that includes an accepted "minimal standard".

Applying this set of criteria, most assessment and treatment procedures would fail the test of validity and would be excluded from graduate curricula, either because they were absent research with suitable control groups or because of the absence of research on the topic, altogether.

Conclusions and Recommendations

In the foregoing, we have tried to identify both the five most prevalent sets of criteria by which the profession and the public define "truth" and to outline some advantages and disadvantages of each. Doing so has clarified certain facts that we would like to pose as recommendations for identifying criteria of evidence for deciding when a procedure has achieved the status of scientific validity.

1. No single set of criteria will best address the problems facing those who define "empirical validity". Our deliberations convince us that while the most sound

empirical basis for assessing knowledge is the independent replication of positive findings, we believe that face validity must also be included within the set of criteria. It is important that whatever interventions are accepted, they must make sense both to the public and to the practitioners who practice them.

2. There are other cautionary notes by which to temper the application of the criteria, moreover. For example, in adopting replication as the primary criterion, the amount of replication needed for validation must be balanced by the number of null and negative findings. Both a minimal number of studies and a proportion of positive to total findings may be incorporated into the criteria.

3. We must remember that we, as scientists, are not immune from being strongly affected by our biases and non-empirical leanings. Thus, protection against these biases may require that whatever decision is made is based upon some type of masking of the identity of approaches and methods.

4. Further protection against biases may be afforded by establishing an arbitrated, quasi-adversarial method in which panels of advocates present arguments, these are countered by panels of opponents, and the proceeding is heard by a jury of disinterested but scientifically sophisticated panelists.

A similar multi-leveled standard, using an independent panel that is suitably disinterested in the results of the deliberations, was originally proposed to evaluate the psychotherapies by Klerman (1983; London & Klerman, 1982). An FDA-like process was proposed by which to evaluate the psychotherapies, with proponents and adversaries squaring off to argue their cases. Maybe it is time for the resurrection of such a recommendation. Whatever procedure is used, at this stage of research on psychological interventions, concepts of multi-level evaluation/approval, independence, and multi-dimensional criteria are important to include. We cannot emphasize enough the importance of whatever standard we use receiving acceptance, among both the professional and lay public. This acceptance must be kept in mind in order to buffer the effects of the apparent wide discrepancies that currently separate the practice and the science of our professions.

References

American Psychological Association. (1993). *Promotion and dissemination of psychological procedures.* An unpublished task force report for Division 12, Washington, D.C.

Berliner, L., & Williams, L. M. (1994). Memories of child sexual abuse: A response to Lindsay and Read. *Applied Cognitive Psychology* (Special Issue), *8,* 379-387.

Beutler, L. E., & Clarkin, J. (1990). *Systematic treatment selection: Toward targeted therapeutic interventions.* New York: Brunner/Mazel.

Beutler, L. E., & Sandowicz, M. (1994). The counseling relationship: What is it? *The Counseling Psychologist, 22,* 98-103.

Beutler, L. E., Williams, R. E., & Zetzer, H. A. (1994). Efficacy of treatment for victims of childhood sexual abuse. *The Future of Children, 4*(2), 156-175.

Centers, R., Shomer, R. W., & Rodrigues, A. (1970). A field experiment in interpersonal persuasion using authoritative influence. *Journal of Personality, 38*, 392-403.

Cialdini, R. B. (1993). *Influence: Science and practice* (3rd ed.). New York: Harper Collins College Publishers.

Courtois, C. A. (1988). *Healing the incest wound.* New York: Norton.

Harvey, J., & Hays, D. G. (1972). Effect of dogmatism and authroity of the source of communication upon persusasion. *Psychological Reports, 30*, 119-122.

Hilsenroth, M. J., Handler, L., Toman, K. M., & Padawer, J. R. (in press). Rorschach and MMPI-2 indices of early psychotherapy termination. *Journal of Consulting and Clinical Psychology.*

Kazdin, A. E. (1980). *Research designs in clinical psychology.* New York: Harper & Row.

Kazdin, A. E. (1991). *Research design in clinical psychology* (2nd edition). New York: Pergamon.

Kirsch, I., Montgomery, G., & Sapirstein, G. (1995). Hypnosis as an adjunct to cognitive-behavioral psychotherapy: A meta-analysis. *Journal of Consulting and Clinical Psychology, 63.*

Klerman, G. L. (1983). The efficacy of psychotherapy as the basis for public policy. *American Psychologist, 38*, 929-934.

Lambert, M. J., Christensen, E. R., & S. S. DeJulio (Eds.). (1983). *The assessment of psychotherapy outcome.* New York: John Wiley and Sons.

Loftus, E. F. (1993). The reality of repressed memories. *American Psychologist, 48*, 518-537.

Loftus, E. F., Garry, M., & Feldman, J. (1994). Forgetting sexual trauma: What does it mean when 38% forget? *Journal of Consulting and Clinical Psychology, 62*, 1177-1181.

Loftus, E. F. & Ketcham, K. (1994). *The myth of repressed memory.* New York: St. Martin's Press.

London, P., & Klerman, G. L. (1982). Evaluating psychotherapy. *American Journal of Psychiatry, 139*, 709-717.

Norcross, J. C., & Prochaska, J. O. (1988). A study of eclectic (and integrative) views revisited. *Professional Psychology: Research and Practice, 19*, 170-174.

Parker, K. C. H., Hanson, R. K., & Hunsley, J. (1988). MMPI, Rorschach, and WAIS: A meta-analytic comparison of reliability, stability, and validity. *Psychological Bulletin, 103*, 367-373.

Poole, D. A., Lindsay, D. S., Memon, A., & Bull, R. (in press). Psychotherapy and the recovery of memories of childhood sexual abuse: U.S. and British practioners' opinions, practices, and experiences. *Journal of Consulting and Clinical Psychology.*

Rounsaville, B. J., Chevron, E. S., Prusoff, B. A., Elkin, I., Imber, S., Sotsky, S., & Watkins, J. (1987). The relation between specific and general dimensions of the psychotherapy process in interpersonal psychotherapy of depression. *Journal of Consulting and Clinical Psychology, 55*, 379-384.

Ruhe, J. W., Lynn, S. J., & Kirsch, I. (Eds.)(1993). *Handbook of Clinical Hypnosis.*Washington, D.C.: American Psychological Association.

Shoham-Salomon, V., & Rosenthal, R. (1987). Paradoxical interventions: A meta-analysis. *Journal of Consulting and Clinical Psychology, 55,* 22-27.

Sweeney, J. A., Clarkin, J. F., & Fitzgibbon, M. L. (1987). Current practice of psychological assessment. *Professional Psychology: Research and Practice, 18,* 377-380.

Footnote

Correspondence about this chapter should be sent to the first author at the Counseling/Clinical/ School Psychology Program, Graduate School of Education, Department of Education, University of California, Santa Barbara, California 93106.

Discussion of Beutler and Davison

Psychology's Failure to Educate

Victoria M. Follette and Amy E. Naugle
University of Nevada

"...man is always free to reconstrue what he may not deny. This should be a source of comfort, not of dismay. Moreover, to give oneself over to a reconsideration of his views is not necessarily to abandon the old and embrace the new, nor does a man always need to suppress what is novel in order to conserve what is familiar" (Kelly, 1963, p. xii).

Beutler and Davison describe sets of criteria which are used by both psychologists and the lay public to define "truth." However, as noted by Hayes (Hayes, L., 1993) "...the truth of what we say cannot be evaluated against anything but other things that we say, and not everyone is saying the same thing" (p. 42). She goes on to state that everyone, scientists and the public alike, is choosing between sets of preferred beliefs and that the truth, as such, is never a matter known. This statement need not invalidate our work as scientists. Rather, it serves to remind us that it remains impossible for us to separate ourselves from the system in which we work (Swain, 1993). How then are we to proceed? All science shares the problem of its contextual nature and yet it moves forward on an assumption of "utility-based truth."

Kelly (1963) indicates that all humans (professional psychologists and the public) are equally interested in the prediction and control of their world. Thus, they are led to develop theories or constructions of human behavior that are used to explain realities. As professional psychologists, we are vulnerable not only to our "scientific" theories of behavior, but also to our personal biases and assumptions that shape daily functioning. That is, in this particular scientific endeavor, we are both the knower and the known. This places us in a particularly problematic situation of never being able to detach ourselves from the study of the phenomena of our interest. When we explain behavior and how it changes, we are under many different sources of control, some of which are related to individual philosophical values. Several of the points raised by Beutler and Davison exemplify the contextual nature of psychology and illustrate the difficulty in outlining objective scientific standards. We will address possible solutions for some of the difficulties pointed out by those authors.

Criteria for Workable Standards

One problem is the difficulty in defining how one is to proceed with the scientific development of standards of care. Hayes (Hayes, S., 1993) provides guidelines for developing a systematic scientific approach that is not dogmatic. His suggestions are also germane to the development of practice standards in the field of psychotherapy. For example, he argues against goals that cannot be clearly defined and/or measured. Psychotherapy outcome is especially vulnerable to such goals. Therefore, it is incumbent upon the scientist-practitioner to define standards for care and treatment outcome that can be explained and evaluated. Ideas such as improved well being or higher self-esteem would be operationalized into measurable outcomes. Additionally, short, medium, and long term goals would provide direction for the therapist-client dyad in assessing progress and evaluating outcome. Finally, it is important to compare the performance of different courses of action for the same treatment problem. It may be that two treatments are similarly effective but require vastly different amounts of time to achieve the same end. For the sake of efficiency, and to eliminate suffering quickly, the shorter intervention should be preferable. However, in that long term goals are also important, it is important to examine relapse rates. Thus, a treatment which works quickly but has a significant relapse rate may not be as valued as an approach with more long lasting effects.

Replication

The criteria requiring replication should indeed include, as Beutler and Davison suggest, not only positive findings, but also those that are not supportive of a particular approach. However, the issue of replication is a complex one. First, when one requires independent replication, it is assumed that the scientist is independent of the results in the different studies. However, the absolute independence of such findings does not seem likely given the nature of the construct (Swain, 1993). If direct replication is used (Kazdin, 1982), the intervention is conducted under the exact same set of conditions, as nearly as is possible. However, pure independence under this set of constraints is difficult to attain.

Failures to replicate are useful in that they give us important information in describing the specific cases in which the intervention may or may not be useful. As Beutler notes, it may not be which treatment works, but more specifically which treatment will work for which person. However, the fact remains that we should have some agreement about when enough failures to replicate should lead us to discard a particular theory or intervention. Unfortunately, this does not seem to be the case and one can note many therapeutic and assessment procedures that persist in their use despite the lack of supporting evidence. An important development for our field would be some agreement regarding a priori decisions about what would lead us to abandon a particular approach as unsupported by the data. Meta-analyses provide some help for combining research in a way that allows for a more comprehensive evaluation of treatments, however it also has difficulties. Differences in opinion regarding the required quality of the data set for inclusion in the analysis, as well as small effect sizes, have limited the utility of the information derived from this procedure.

Face Validity or Heuristics

The question "what standards should we use" is a complicated one. On the one hand, psychology professes to be a science and therefore the standards of practice for psychologists should be consistent with scientific values. Yet, as we mentioned, the interest in the subject matter of psychology is not limited to the profession of psychology. The behavior and interactions of people are frequently the topic of conversation among members of the lay community. Not uncommonly, people form impressions about their friends and colleagues, construct their own causal analyses about why these people act in particular ways, and do not hesitate to offer strategies about how to change their behavior. While the lay and professional versions of psychology may appear to be mutually exclusive, it is not clear that they need be. The authors elaborate on this point in their discussion of different types of validity. They propose that the criteria for empirically valid treatments must also have face validity, that is be logical and make sense to both consumers and therapists. We do not entirely disagree with this point.

Beutler and Davison make clear that neither we as scientific psychologists nor the community at large are immune from values or biases. Although the authors offer recommendations for protecting against certain biases, some of their suggestions may lead to yet other biases that have been elaborated in the extensive literature on inferential strategies and heuristics. We repeatedly rely on biased assumptions to guide how we conduct psychotherapy, approach science, train psychologists, and will continue to do so in our effort to develop standards of psychological practice. Likewise, similar biases will serve as guides for the public community in requesting particular services, and in determining what is "logically" seen as the most effective intervention. The question regarding the relative appropriateness or effectiveness of particular psychotherapies is burdened by the problem of uncertainty and inconclusive data.

Despite a rapidly expanding psychotherapy outcome research literature, which is increasingly sophisticated in methodologies, there is relatively little conclusive evidence about the relative efficacy of different therapies. While there is demonstrated effectiveness for therapies in relation to wait list controls, data has not shown the superiority of any one treatment. Moreover, outcome research has not adequately answered Gordon Paul's famous question regarding "what treatment, by whom, is most effective for this individual with that specific problem, under which set of circumstances?" (Paul, 1967, p. 111). Additionally, outcome studies have frequently targeted clients with circumscribed problems that do not reflect the complexity of the type of problems seen in clients who generally present for outpatient psychotherapy.

Given that we do not have conclusive evidence about what works, both practitioners and clients turn to interventions that are intuitively appealing. The literature on heuristics addresses how it is people make decisions in the face of uncertainty (Tversky & Kahneman, 1982). Cognitive and social psychologists have addressed the problems in relying more on primitive intuitive strategies and less on appropriate inference strategies and when making judgments (Nisbett & Ross, 1980). In this instance we are interested in how it is these heuristics influence the selection and utilization of particular types of therapy. As Beutler and Davison indicated, Alcoholics Anonymous is identified by both therapists and clients as an effective component in treating alcoholism not because it has empirically been shown to be effective. Rather, it receives its acclaim based on inferences people make about why AA works or intuitively why it should work, or because, as Beutler and Davison argue, it is face valid.

This belief in the efficacy of AA may be based on a number of heuristics. The representativeness heuristic offers one possible explanation for the way in which the public makes sense of psychological treatments. As noted earlier, most persons have a priori explanations of the causes for disturbances in behavior, and these assumptions are generally related to what is viewed as a valid treatment recommendation. For example, the disease model of alcoholism is widely held by the both the professional and lay communities. This explanatory model generally would be assumed to indicate abstinence as a necessary component of treatment, making other forms of therapy such as controlled or managed drinking seem unacceptable.

One additional heuristic which guides what information people attend to is how easily the information comes to mind, or how available it is. There are several factors that influence availability, including familiarity and salience or vividness of the information. Availability is relevant to this discussion in that there is a proliferation of information about psychological matters in the popular media and this media exposure results in public familiarity with such topics. Moreover, the more shocking or vivid the presentation, the more likely it is that the public will attend to it. The recent trial of the Menendez brothers, who were accused of killing both of their parents, provided a striking example of this. The defense in that case justified the brothers' behavior as a sequelae of the trauma they endured as children, including physical, emotional and sexual abuse. Based on this example, the public would be more likely to attribute extremely serious adult problems to a childhood trauma and thus be more likely to seek services to address those issues. However, somewhat paradoxically, some individuals have responded to the same stimuli by questioning the validity of childhood trauma as a causal explanation for psychological difficulties. Yet another facet of this phenomena is the suggestion that the current emphasis on childhood trauma is a function of misguided therapists who have over attended to, or even constructed, abuse memories. This issue, labeled False Memory Syndrome, has also been the focus of a great deal of media attention. Not only is this information widely reported in the print media, it is also a common theme in television programming. The proliferation of talk shows, in which people openly discuss matters that were considered taboo until quite recently, has dramatically increased the public's awareness of these and other psychological issues.

Public Education

We would argue that scientist-practitioners have been very remiss in their efforts to educate the public about the current state of psychological knowledge. This lack of available information, makes the public more vulnerable to the errors in judgment described earlier. While scientific or data oriented psychology has largely remained confined within the walls of the academy, others are reaching out to the public. Go to any bookstore and one will be confronted by shelves of books on all kinds of behavioral or relationship problems. Unfortunately, most of these writings are not based on psychological science, but rather some faddish theory that often amounts to little more than arm chair psychologizing. There are certainly some notable exceptions to this statement, such as Gary Burns' *Feeling Good: The New Mood Therapy* (1980). Psychologists have a responsibility to offer an alternative to "pop-psychology" and to disseminate information that would allow the public to make more informed treatment choices.

Beutler and Davison propose that arbitrated panels should examine psycho-therapies and make recommendations regarding the relative utility of different approaches. We would argue that the state of psychological science is not yet sufficiently advanced to allow many clear cut recommendations. Therefore, in the interim, as science proceeds in an attempt to answer these questions, we can at least convey to the public what information is known. Currently, the available information tends to be presented by advocates of a particular position, and is thus one-sided. Consistent with the Beutler and Davison recommendation, we suggest that a variety of positions be expressed, each by its strongest advocates, in one brief text. For example, there has been a great deal of writing and discussion regarding child sexual abuse and the phenomena of repressed and false memory. Yet we know of no one text that clearly and fairly explicates the state of our scientific knowledge with regard to these issues. Despite the polarization of this debate, even the strongest proponents of "False Memory Syndrome" do not deny the tragic consequences of child sexual abuse. Similarly, reasonable scientist-practitioners in the area of child sexual abuse acknowledge the finding that memory is in fact imperfect and can be affected in a variety of ways. A book that explains what is currently known regarding this problem would be of great public benefit. The text would include matters such as what we know about rates of abuse and what we know about the hypothesized sequelae of that abuse, including data suggesting that some persons do not appear to show significant symptomatology in relation to this event. Current theories of memory would be discussed and a description of the potential for false memories would be presented. Psychological theories of the effects of the abuse and their respective treatment approaches should be explicated, as well as data that either supports or refutes the theory. Suggestions about what to look for in a therapist would be provided, as well as warnings about practices that at this point are considered questionable. Appropriate references should be provided for those individuals who wish to do additional reading. One challenge here is to present all of this information in a straight forward, non jargon laden manner. While this may seem to be a tall order, we believe that the public is eager for this type of information. There is evidence that the general public is capable of reading books that explore very complex phenomena, provided that the material is presented in an accessible manner. As an example, witness the popularity of books such as *A Brief History of Time* (Hawking, 1988) which examines issues such as the nature of time and the universe, or *The Man Who Mistook His Wife for a Hat*, a best selling book on neurological disorders (Sacks, 1985).

Although the truth remains an elusive concept, particularly as it relates to the evaluation of psychological procedures, we need not refrain from action while waiting for the data. Rather, we may work within a dialectic borrowed from another context. Psychologists can accept the limitations of our current state of knowledge and move forward. In this case, moving forward involves continuing to work to advance science about psychological procedures and working much harder to provide information to the public about our area of study. Informed consent need not be limited to the individual interactions between the therapist and client that occur in the privacy of the therapist's office. Instead, it can be distributed via the many sources of information delivery to all interested parties- "professional" and "lay" psychologists alike.

References

Burns, D. (1980). *Feeling good: The new mood therapy*. New York: Signet Books.

Hawking, S. W. (1988). *A brief history of time: From the big bang to black holes*. New York: Bantam Books.

Hayes, L. J. (1993). Reality and truth. In S. C. Hayes, L. J. Hayes, H. W. Reese, & T. R. Sarbin (Eds.), *Varieties of scientific contextualism* (pp. 35-44). Reno, NV: Context Press.

Hayes, S. C. (1993). Analytic goals and the varieties of scientific contextualism. In S. C. Hayes, L. J. Hayes, H. W. Reese, & T. R. Sarbin (Eds.), *Varieties of scientific contextualism* (pp. 11-27). Reno, NV: Context Press.

Kazdin, A. E. (1982). *Single-case research designs: Methods for clinical and applied settings*. New York: Oxford University Press.

Kelly, G. A. (1963). *A theory of personality: The psychology of personal constructs*. New York: W. W. Norton and Company.

Nisbett, R., & Ross, L. (1980). *Human inference: Strategies and shortcomings of social judgment*. New Jersey: Prentice-Hall.

Paul, G. L. (1967). Outcome research in psychotherapy. *Journal of Consulting Psychology, 31*, 109-118.

Sacks, O. (1985). *The man who mistook his wife for a hat*. New York: Summit Books.

Swain, M. A. (1993). Science has no business in the truth business. In S. C. Hayes, L. J. Hayes, H. W. Reese, & T. R. Sarbin (Eds.), *Varieties of scientific contextualism* (pp. 45-49). Reno, NV: Context Press.

Tversky, A., & Kahneman, D. (1982). Judgment under uncertainty: Heuristics and biases. In D. Kahneman, P. Slovik, & A. Tversky (Eds.), *Judgment under uncertainty: Heuristics and biases* (pp. 3-22). New York: Cambridge University Press.

Chapter 2

Standards of Practice

Robyn M. Dawes
Carnegie Mellon University

Standards of practice must guide how people actually practice–not how they are trained, not how they think about practice, not how they discuss practice, but what they actually do. Standards provide bounds for practice. If we accept the prevailing philosophy of AAAPP, what we seek are bounds that are consistent with our best current scientific knowledge.

Behaving Inconsistently with our Best Knowledge

Those of us who believe in such bounds hear a common complaint that our "science" does not provide sufficient information for practice. "I took all those courses. I learned all those psychological principles, but they do not tell me exactly what to do in this here circumstance." Yes. It is true that standards do not yield knowledge of exactly what to do–any more than principles of physics and aerodynamics yield knowledge of exactly how to construct airplanes for specific purposes. But aeronautical engineers do not construct airplanes following the common intuition that their wings should flap; they don't construct airplanes in ways that are inconsistent with principles of physics and aerodynamics. If they did, these airplanes would surely crash, and we could predict that prior to testing them in flight. Similarly–I trust (in part as a potential consumer)–practitioners in psychology would not wish to engage in psychotherapy, or present themselves as experts in forensic and other critical settings, and then practice in ways inconsistent with our best knowledge of psychological principles.

An example of such inconsistency is using hypnosis to help people recall events from early childhood and encouraging them to believe that such hypnotically "aided recall" is historically accurate–or worse yet, that such hypnotic exploration could overcome "repression" of unpleasant events that have occurred, such as being a victim of incestuous sexual abuse. Consistent use of hypnosis, in contrast, takes into account scientific knowledge concerning false-positives in hypnotic recall and concerning the very imperfect relationship between the accuracy of recall and its vividness, which is enhanced under hypnosis. (For discussion of hypnosis and recall see two recent National Research Council reports: Druckman and Bjork, 1991; Druckman and Bjork, 1995.) Another example is the use of the TAT to determine whether a woman is a fit mother during a custody dispute, as happened to a graduate student at Carnegie Mellon. In Allegheny County, Pennsylvania (in which Pittsburgh is located) a judge cannot rule on a custody dispute until both parents are evaluated by an "expert" psychologist, who is free to use whatever method he or she pleases—hence the TAT. A similar law exists in San Francisco, where a brother of a close colleague in a disputed custody case walked into a psychologist's office to be presented with a Rorschach inkblot. Some of us believe it is unconscionable for the fate of children to be determined by their parents' responses to the TAT or to the Rorschach, rather than by a careful and serious assessment of their past behavior.[1] Using the TAT or Rorschach as such an assessment is not consistent with what we know about these tests. It is not consistent with what we know about predicting future behavior, any more than hypnotizing people to discover what happened in their very early childhood, sometimes as early as six months, is consistent with what we know about hypnosis.

Those of us who believe in standards as a basis for socially responsible practice are upset with a lot of things that go on. (I'm going to end this paper by providing evidence that such activity is not just that of a "lunatic fringe.") We may well be losing the battle. Moreover, the battle, sadly, is not to have standards maintained, but to put them back, to reverse the trend—to reverse the trend that once a license is granted, anything goes, with few exceptions. I would like to be able to write: "We shall overcome. We shall win." Instead, my message is: "We should overcome," not that we necessarily will.

Hortatory versus Minatory Standards

What has happened?

First, what do we mean exactly by standards? Standards can be described in two ways, and we often discuss them in both these ways when we talk about them. We can talk about prescriptive standards that are *hortatory*: "Thou shalt." Such standards are positive. Thou shalt practice consistent with scientific principles. Thou shalt be excellent. Thou shalt be outstanding. For years, the *Ethics Code of the American Psychological Association* (APA) begins with a rather dubious grammatical construction that psychologists should always maintain the "highest standards" in the profession. (APA, 1987) That's a hortatory standard *par excellence*.

In contrast minatory standards proscribe. "Thou shalt not..." Thou shalt not, for example, engage in practices that are apt to result in bias and improper recall. Thou shalt not engage in practices that are apt to hurt a client. Thou shalt not perform transorbital lobotomies. Thou shalt not recover memories with guided imagery and hypnosis.

A contrast between hortatory and *minatory* standards can be found in Adam Smith's book, *The Theory of Mortal Sentiments*, published in 1776, sixteen years before he published *The Wealth of Nations*. He pointed out in this earlier book that even though someone could always follow the laws of society—not cheat, lie, steal, purger, etc., etc.—such a person would not be considered desirable unless he or she also possessed positive qualities. In other words, following the Ten Commandments, which are basically minatory (Thou shalt not...) until the last one, is not enough without also possessing what Smith called "sympathy" (which in the famous Psalm is called "charity")–that is, without being concerned about other people, taking joy in other people's joy and sorrow in their sorrow. Simply following the rules by not breaking them is not really a very satisfactory way to live for an ethical person. Smith's book points out this problem with minatory standards. They are unsatisfactory. They are "not enough."

In contrast, the problem with hortatory standards is that there is the hortatory standard itself and then there is "not exactly." Thou should do thus and so, i.e. thou should follow the highest standards of the profession. For example, people who prescribe drugs should take courses A, B, C, D, and perhaps, E, F, G as well. But then how do we judge people who do not exactly follow our prescriptions–for example, not take all of the courses? How do we judge them when the hortatory standard is not exactly met? In such cases, unlike rental cars, not exactly can win out over exactly. The clinical pressures of functioning in an uncertain and imperfect world will lead people to say: "Well I can't really insist that people really understand our principles completely, really behave maximally, really live up to the highest standards of the profession." We must make compromises in judging people by hortatory standards. It is inevitable.

If we are really serious about standards, we're discussing minatory ones. We don't just say: "be excellent." We don't just say: "apply." We say: "whatever you do, it has to be consistent with what we think we know. In this particular case, for these particular purposes we might not be able to tell you exactly what to do, such as following an exact computer printout for a behavioral type of treatment–a printout that indicates a desirable response to each contingency. We don't have such exact guidelines. But we do want your behavior to be consistent with what we believe we know. We would like you to be excellent, but what we *require* is that you *do not* go beyond the bounds." That's basically minatory.

We generally don't like either to proclaim or to enforce minatory standards. (Most of us don't anyway–although the U.S. 1994 election returns may indicate a change in the frequency of such hesitations.) Most of us don't enjoy being "judgmental," or are at least ambivalent about being so, and minatory judgments are intrinsically judgmental.[2] When we observe others derogate "the sin but not the sinner" whom they claim to "love," we are apt to detect hypocrisy–because it is often there. We worry that we will become judgmental and punishing rather than supportive and rewarding. We can't, however, get around the basic problem that if we are to require behavior be within bounds, we must make minatory judgments that people must not violate these bounds–and more importantly, be willing to take action to stop out-of-bounds behavior, even to the point of punishing those who engage in it.

Let me give an example. What do we mean if we say that we have high academic standards for an undergraduate program? Do we simply mean that we tell our students: "be excellent?" Do we mean that we end there, with expectations to work hard as well, and as evidence of our success give only A's, no matter what the students do? Unfortunately, such programs exist. But what we really mean when we say that we have high academic standards for an undergraduate program is that we do not give an A- to semi-coherent English essays that might–to the best of our ability to dig out and project our own ideas on these essays–just might contain some ideas of interest imbedded in the gobble. Instead, we decide that such an essay does not "deserve" an A- (even if we have philosophical difficulties with the concept of "deservingness"). We do not give C's to people simply for showing up 51% of the time and writing something on exams.

I went through an undergraduate program that actually gave B's for doing that. I learned very early on, because I am left-handed and my handwriting is terrible anyway, exactly when to make my handwriting illegible–absolutely illegible. I was very fortunate that I got interested in psychology during my senior year at college, but prior to that I received B's and sometimes A-'s for being illegible. Those are not academic standards. What we really have to face is the fact that an academic standard means willingness to say: "this work does not meet our standards." Such statements are minatory statements, and only when we are willing to endorse them do we have true academic standards. All the urging in the world that says "be good, be excellent, be outstanding," combined with "no matter what you do, I'll reinforce you for doing it" (and perhaps try to "shape" your behavior by reinforcing changes so gradual that you don't notice them) is not going to work. I suggest it's not going to work if we want to have standards of practice as well. That is, simply saying "be good," or simply training people well is not enough.

We have to have a willingness to say: "This is not acceptable. I could be wrong, but I'm in a position where I have to use my judgment, and I believe that this is not acceptable." If we're not willing to say that, we're not going to have any standards at all.

When I served on the Ethics Committee of APA, there were two behaviors that were not acceptable. One was sex with clients and the other was creating a phony resume. Occasionally people who are admitted to good graduate programs but who are asked to leave, then go on to a diploma mill, and then claim to have a Ph.D. from the original program. That's a no-no. Sex with clients is a no-no, but whatever else was done, if the person doing it was trained to do it, that was okay. If, for example, people were trained in how to diagnose child sexual abuse from children's' play with anatomically detailed dolls, or trained in how to use the Rorschach in a completely subjective and intuitive and projective (for the interpreter) way, that was okay. How did such practice get to be okay?

In the early fifties, there were committees of people like E. Lowell Kelly who maintained that standards would naturally evolve if future practitioners were trained in scientific psychology. (For an example, going back to 1947, see Dawes, 1994, page 18.) The "Boulder Model" was to train "scientist-practitioners" who would naturally be interested in practicing in ways consistent with psychological principles. Such people were not to be trained as junior psychiatrists. At the time, many psychiatrists were psychoanalytically oriented. Psychologists were not to be trained to be junior psychoanalysts—except when I entered the graduate program in clinical psychology at the University of Michigan, that's exactly what I was trained to be. If we allow such training to continue, we're going to lose. If whatever training exists, we allow such *practice* to continue, we're going to lose.

The Uncommon Sense of Science

Practitioners should first understand science and secondly be bound by it. Here, we might note that science is not intuitively obvious. We tend to think by association; we believe intuitively that we learn on the basis of experience that does not yield systematic feedback involving comparison with a principle determined by "outside" knowledge. We tend not to think of checking hypotheses by asking tough questions of them, or by looking at their implications that might be inconsistent with common sense. To quote Allan Cromer (1994): "Scientific thinking, which is analytic and objective, goes against the grain of traditional human thinking, which is associative and subjective." Thus, scientific thinking is not a simple extension of our intuitive ways of thinking. It involves testing hypotheses; it involves being your own defense attorney when pursuing the ideas that you wish to prosecute. I have a letter from a very famous psychiatrist that states that in her own article the "standard of evidence was not designed to meet forensic challenge" because there is "a difference between a scientific approach...and the approach taken by defense attorneys." I disagree. Science requires being your own skeptic, checking out alternative possibilities—not just in research but in evaluating a particular course of action or treatment. We are obligated to think about why our pet ideas might not be true. Whether we are practicing scientists or a practitioner using science, this challenging way of thinking really does involve training—but it also importantly includes commitment. Our intuitions may be fine, but they must be checked out.

A basic problem is, as Cromer points out, that intuition is often associative. For example, intuition dictates that if an individual has a symptom that is common among people who have condition X, then this person probably has condition X. Such an inference involves ignoring base rates, which as Meehl pointed out way back in 1955 (Meehl and Rosen, 1955) is a logical fallacy. Such considerations were repeatedly ignored in the psychoanalytic program I was in for a couple of years in Michigan, as was Meehl himself. In fact, when I wrote something myself about base rates, I was almost accused by a professor outside the program of plagiarizing Meehl, but I had never heard of him. When I asked my mentors: "What about this? This is very important," the answer was: "Meehl is a brilliant man, but what he does has nothing to do with what we do." But it does! If we wish to think rationally and coherently, we cannot say: "Gee, in my experience, the symptom is associated with this condition. It happens to be a high rate symptom and a low base rate condition; moreover, my experience happens to be biased in predictable ways, but that's okay. It's an association I've formed and it's reinforced in staff meetings, and therefore I can make this diagnosis." That's a natural way of thinking, it's normatively invalid, and we have to be trained to be aware of both it and its fallacious nature. That doesn't happen automatically.

How we think automatically is captured in an interesting study concerning "intuitive physics." What happens when a ball is placed in a spiral and it comes out the end of the spiral? In a survey of undergraduates at Johns Hopkins University, which is fairly selective, McCloskey (1983) found that about 51% of his student subjects maintained that the ball keeps on spiraling. The ball has momentum; it's going around in a spiral; it comes out at the end of the spiral and it keeps on spiraling. The intuition is that of sportscasters at football games. When one team is doing really well, that team has momentum, but what happens when the other team does well is that the momentum has shifted. We believe in momentum. So the momentum of the ball continues; or some of the students say something very interesting, which is that the momentum continues for a while and later the ball goes in a straight line. There is, however, a very strong relationship between getting the answer right and having studied physics. Knowledge does matter—a lot in this example. Interesting, however, even those who get the answer right often get it right for the wrong reasons. Momentum is still thought to exist *in* the ball. Inertia—which states that an object simply continues in its path without some force acting upon it—is not sighted as an explanation, except by a minority of subjects. Most explain Newtonian Physics in terms of the momentum of the ball and its eventual opposition by the forces of friction. I believe that momentum is the intuitive way of thinking about psychological problems as well.

This belief in momentum may partially explain our obsession with the past (see Dawes, 1993). It may also help explain our belief in training pure and simple; specifically, if we train people to work within the bounds of science, that's how they will work. Unfortunately, people—just like balls exiting enclosures—are affected by forces after they leave confining areas. It is possible to have reasonable training trajectories but not have standards.

I Fish on My Side; You Fish on Your Side

At the same time the Boulder Model was proposed, the APA's membership started mushrooming; many of its members and leaders maintained a certain modesty about psychology, specifically that "we don't know that much yet" (but will soon—somehow). This modesty had the positive effect of inhibiting people from the type of self-confident excesses in the office, in the media, and in the courts that we learn about now on an almost daily basis. It also had the negative effect of inhibiting minatory standards.

A deemphasis on minatory standards may also have been, in part, a reaction to the authoritarianism of medicine at that time. For example, as I myself discovered, if a patient with an ear infection in the late 1950's was told to take pills in a college clinic, asking what was in the pills was considered evidence of mental illness—even after hearing the doctor tell the nurse to "keep up the penicillin" when the patient knew he was allergic to penicillin. Asking was bad. Refusing to take the pills when the nurse refused to answer the question was worse. What was worse yet–considered very unusual and awful behavior–was walking out of the clinic after being "required" to take the pills, at that point you trusting one's own immune system more than the doctor. Such aberrant behavior required a report to the dean combined with a threat that he might veto graduation. Many of us who identified ourselves as "psychologists" believe that "we're not going to be that way." We were going to follow our own understanding, because with good scientific training, we do the right thing–without all that authoritarian intolerance of ambiguity and obedience to higher authorities that characterized medicine. So the basic model APA adopted can be summarized in one word. It is the Native American name for what is now called Lake Webster, in Massachusetts near the Connecticut border. That name is Lake Chargoggaggoggmanchargagoggcharbunagungamaug, which is translated as "Lake I-fish-on-my-side, you-fish-on-your-side, and no-one-fishes-in-the-middle." It was named, apparently, to end a tribal dispute about who gets to fish where. Everybody is allowed to fish in their own private place. Similarly, the APA has a Practice Directorate, a Science Directorate, a Public Affairs Directorate, etc., etc., etc.–in short, anything any member desires. APA is just like Lake Chargoggaggoggmancharga-goggcharbunagungamaug, except that people are fishing in the middle and the fish population may be decreasing .

The Chargoggaggoggmanchargagoggcharbunagungamaug structure is reflected in the Ethics Code. It rarely states that certain things shouldn't be done; in fact, what it says is that anything can be done provided the member is trained to do it. (Training *defines* "competence!") The idea initially was, of course, that people would be trained by providing them with scientific knowledge and skills in scientific thinking so that they would automatically practice within scientific bounds–simply because they would practice in accord with their training. But it didn't work out that way. What happens to practitioners is that social consensus has a great deal of influence: for example what happens in APA-accredited internships, what happens in staff meetings, what happens in casual conversations in the hallway.

Training Trajectories versus the Social Context of Practice

Consider, for example, APA-accredited internships. I was chair of a department for five years that had an APA-accredited clinical psychology program, and all our graduating students of course went to APA-accredited internships. When they left, they had never administered a Rorschach test. They were taught to do so on their internships (often after calls back to our department from their supervisors who were deeply distressed that these students had never administered a Rorschach and confused that a program accredited by APA would fail to train them in such administration). Then the students would come back after a year. Many would say: "I know what all the research shows, and I've been trained to think skeptically, and I look at alternative hypotheses, but you know after administering twenty-five Rorschachs last year, I'm pretty convinced that the Rorschach helps me understand people. Maybe I shouldn't be convinced, but I am." I was also convinced, during my first year at graduate school. For example, when I was working on a in-patient unit, I once tested a very large, extremely depressed man, who looked at the first Rorschach inkblot and said that: "this is a bat that has been crushed on the pavement under the heel of a giant's boot." Wow ! This response was really one-down, and I knew the Rorschach works because this guy was so depressed. My point now is that I knew he was depressed before he gave that response. Alternatively, if he had been extremely hostile, I would have looked at the hostility in the response–the giant crushing the bat. Alternatively, if he had been psychotic, I would have noted that much of the response referred to something that wasn't on the card. Nevertheless, at the time, I concluded that Rorschach really worked.

I now, however, have some understanding about cognition, not just on an intuitive basis but on a research one as well. I understand how people make judgments consistent with their prior beliefs, but nevertheless, do not integrate these beliefs in an optimal manner. Instead–now here's a really technical idea–we often make diagnoses consistent only with the numerator in the likelihood ratio form of Bayes' theorem–thereby making what is technically termed a *pseudo-diagnostic* judgment as a result of evaluating only the degree to which evidence supports a particular hypothesis, rather than comparing that support to the degree to which the evidence supports alternative hypotheses as well. An understanding of pseudo-diagnosticity would leave us unimpressed by the squashed bat.

The students that come back from internship have not spent a year discussing Bayes' theorem; they have spent a year discussing Rorschach results. We know something about social influence, for example, from the work of Asch (1955). Or at least we should know something about social influence from this work. One elaboration on it particularly relevant for our current concerns is that if the lines are removed, the effects of social consensus are increased (Deutsch and Gerard, 1955). And were the clients in staff meeting or in conversations with colleagues? (For a particularly devastating critique of staff meeting–complete with examples of representative thinking and generalizations based on biased availability, long before these biased had been carefully specified and systematically studied- -see Meehl, 1977.) Or–of relevance to the recent epidemic of recovered memory "therapy"– where are the parents in groups of "survivors" who have been urged by their therapists to cut off all contact with these "perps?" Social pressure works, especially in influencing the evaluation of something that isn't there.

To summarize, while training should, of course, provide a reasonable trajectory (including information about such classic findings as the Asch experiments and the mathematical abilities of Clever Hans), actual practice should involve continual monitoring. It doesn't. Consider, again, Rorschach testing. When I was first involved in that, we hoped that research might show that intuitive interpretations of Rorschach responses were valid, just as research might support psychoanalytic hypotheses in general. Research did, in fact, show the Rorschach worked. For example, on various samples, the number of responses tended to correlate roughly .50 with standardized IQ tests. Moreover, various types of "poor form" responses as assessed by the Exner System may have—there is some dispute about the evidence—some statistically valid relationship to various types of pathology. So the idea is that having been taught to attend to the scientific evidence, those who are also taught to administer Rorschach would use it to assess intelligence or to relate poor form responses to various forms of pathology through the Exner System. Surveys indicate that it's generally not used in either of these ways. (See, for example, Shontz &Green, 1992.)

Continuing Education

Why is not "continuing education" solving the problem? Shouldn't the requirement to get continuing education credits to remained licensed guarantee that training is a life-long (or at least career-long) activity? The reason that continuing education does not lead to practice within the bounds of science is that it itself is not limited to conveying methods and approaches that have some scientific support. In fact, even some people with a natural affinity to AAAPP claim[3] that we should not limit continuing education to education in methods and approaches that have been empirically demonstrated to work—because, after all and as usual, "we don't know that much *yet*." (I'm adding the italics to indicate that the "yet" is continually with us, like death and taxes; for example, I first heard this argument around 1958.) The basic problem is that continuing education courses exist on the basis of their ability to attract entrants, and hence when the professional associations are unwilling to restrict their content to convey knowledge that could be termed "scientific," the courses given can in fact encourage people to practice beyond the bounds that our knowledge should impose. Once again, the unwillingness to make a minatory judgment is the culprit. For example, Paul Meehl recently sent me a Minnesota Continuing Education brochure. Licensed psychologists there can receive sixty-four continuing education credits by taking various Rorschach work-shops. Moreover, the humanist society there can provide continuing education for almost any spiritual growth.

And then there is the problem that continuing education can be lucrative for the sponsoring organization, and even organizations of psychologists are not blind to the color of money. Let me give you a personal example. In 1976, the Oregon Psychological Association, of which I became president eight years later—much to my surprise—was facing bankruptcy. Members of the previous Board of Directors "had went and done a silly thing" (in the opinion of some of us) and had voted that the Association should pick up their legal bills, defending against a lawsuit that they lost. In Oregon, a board of directors can vote itself a Rolls Royce if it wishes; that's perfectly legal, because Oregon law is set up on the premise that there are stockholders in every organization, who—of course—would have the power to get rid of any board of directors who behaved in a manner that might be harmful to the organization. The legal fees the previous board had collected were over $20,000; in addition there was a slight payout to the plaintiff. One possibility the organization considered was to declare bankruptcy, but there was another possibility. The Oregon coast is beautiful. People might like to come to the Oregon coast to take courses for continuing education credits. It was at least worth a try. It turned out that APA approval for continuing education workshops on the Oregon coast was not difficult to obtain (in fact "a piece of cake") and that our projection of the number of people who would come to spend time at our Oregon resorts as a business expense or at the least tax free was if anything an underestimate. We charged a certain amount of money per participant, we gave the person running the workshop $500, and then once the workshop had broken even, we gave that person 50% of the excess profits. By the time I was president of the Oregon Psychological Association, over half our income came from such workshops. For example, I arranged one workshop on nursing home care in 1983 run by Ellen Langer that attracted about 50 or so participants, but I don't know about other more recent workshops. As near as I can tell, however, everything's approved; everybody's happy; everybody's getting money. The swimming is fine in Lake Chargoggaggoggmanchargagoggcharbun- agungamaug, and there is nothing more reinforcing than getting paid handsomely for doing what you think is socially good, without being skeptical about whether it really is good.

Professional Schools and the Explosion of Professional Psychology

How did all this happen? For starters, we have professional schools. I have a letter from Donald Peterson (1/20/95) from the Professional School at Rutgers in which he points out that in my recent (1994) book I ignore all the thinking that went into the formation and development of the professional schools. I did, because I'm concerned that "by their fruits shall ye know them." For example, Rorschach interpretation is taught at Rutgers. Peterson (in press) writes: "I would like to see the less useful parts of our programs reduced and the more useful parts expanded, but I see that as a long term developmental process. The education of professional psychologists, like most other professional activities in psychology, takes place in a complex cultural context. Our accountabilities are mixed. Cultural change takes time." I don't think that the parent who realizes that the fate of her children will be dependent on her Rorschach responses will be reassured by knowing that the person testing her was trained to do so as the result to the slowness of cultural change and the "mixed accountability" of the profession of psychology. I suspect that this woman will believe that the profession is accountable to her and her children—rather than to others in a profession who believe in a myth that dies all too slowly.

Let me present some statistics. In 1975 there were two hundred and fifty psychology programs in this country. By 1990 there were three hundred and fifty, most of the increase being in professional schools. In 1970, nobody had received a Psy.D. degree in a professional school. In 1990, 40% of degrees (Ph.D.'s or Psy.D.'s) were given in professional schools, some of whom had recently been granted permission to give a Ph.D. rather than a Psy.D. Nineteen seventy-two was the first year in which there were more clinical and applied than non-clinical degrees given in psychology (all, of course, Ph.D.'s at that time). By 1990, the ratio was three-to-one in the clinical/applied direction. In 1973, 37 1/2% of the Ph.D.s given in clinical psychology came from the top two hundred departments as rated by a conglomeration of committees formed by the National Research Council, the Social Science Research Council, The National Science Foundation, and other interested institutions. By 1990, if a linear decreasing curve is extrapolated, the figure is 13%. Georgine Pion (personal communication 7/21/91) estimates that figure to be 18%; there are no hard data, but it is clear that the percentage had been at least halved in the twenty years since 1973.

Am I exaggerating the resulting problems? No. For example, Yapko conducted a survey of hypnotists who are trained in his own workshops. He was appalled at the number of people in these workshops who believe in the power of hypnosis to reconstruct memory accurately because the reconstruction is vivid and engenders confidence (Yapko, 1994). Debra Poole and colleagues conducted a more systematic survey of the 1600 psychologists in the National Register (Poole, Lindsay, Memon, and Bull, in press). These authors contacted 3.75 % of psychologists in the Register in two waves of questionnaires; the psychologists were chosen randomly in order to obtain a representative sample. They were asked about their beliefs in recovered memory and the techniques they use to recover memories. Only about 40% of those contacted responded, but of those, about 20% said that they were sure or fairly sure within the first session or two that some clients who never mentioned childhood incest abuse had in fact been victims of it. The respondents were also asked what techniques they used to determine whether memories were accurate. Twenty-five percent said they used two or more of the following techniques to uncover memory: hypnosis, age-regression, dream interpretation, guided imagery related to abuse situations, instructions to give free rein to the imagination (in the first wave of questionnaires instructions to "let your imagination run wild"), use of family photographs as memory cues, and interpreting physical symptoms–which are generally high base rate ones such as eating disorders, feeling a lack of energy, and sexual non-responsiveness. A regression analysis indicated that the symptoms were what led to the diagnosis of a repressed memory. The other techniques were used to confirm the diagnosis. Again, we observe only the numerator in the likelihood ratio of the odds form of Bayes Theorem.

Interestingly about the same percentage of respondents disapproved using each of the techniques as used it. Now that's chaotic. Imagine considering going to your medical doctor and believing the probability is about .3 that he or she will use a particular technique and that the probability is also .3 that he or she will believe that the technique would be harmful.

Poole and colleagues also asked the respondents how many women they had seen in the previous two years. The respondents (recall that only 40% answered the questionnaire) saw, on the average, eighty-one women in the last two years. If we extrapolate from the percentage answering assuming that nobody who didn't respond to the questionnaire uses two or more of the techniques, we discover that over 100,000 women in the United States had seen people who had used two or more of these techniques in the previous two years–from the National Register alone.

There are approximately 250,000 people who are therapists of some sort in the United States. Assuming again that nobody in the 60% contacted who didn't respond uses two or more of the techniques listed and extrapolating to the number of therapists in the United States, we obtain a figure of some one million, three hundred thousand women who have been seen in the previous two years by someone who uses two or more of these techniques. That's hard to believe. Worse yet, assuming the 40% that responded are representative of all therapists—or if anything are less apt to use these techniques than the non-responders—we obtain a figure of over 3 million. That sounds fantastic, but recall that 6% of the American public is in therapy each year.

I rest my case. It's time to be—unpleasant as that is—judgmental.

References

American Psychological Association. (1987). *Casebook on ethical principles of psychology*. Washington, DC: American Psychological Association.

Asch, S. E. (1955). Opinions and social pressure. *Scientific American, 193*(5), 31-35.

Cromer, A. (1994). Uncommon sense: The heretical nature of science. *Science, 265*, 688.

Dawes, R. M. (1993). The prediction of the future versus an understanding of the past: A basic asymmetry. *American Journal of Psychology, 106*, 1-24.

Dawes, R. M. (1994). *House of cards: Psychology and psychotherapy built on myth*. New York: The Free Press.

Deutsch, M., & Gerard, H. B. (1955). A study of normative and informational social influences upon individual judgment. *Journal of Abnormal and Social Psychology, 51*, 629-636.

Druckman, D., & Bjork, R. A. (Eds.). (1991). *In the mind's eye: Enhancing human performance*. Washington, DC: National Academy Press.

Druckman, D., & Bjork, R. A. (Eds.). (1994). *Learning, remembering, believing: Enhancing human performance*. Washington, DC: National Academy Press.

McCloskey, M. (1983). *Naive theories of motion*. In D. Gentner & A. S. Stephens (Eds.), *Mental models* (pp. 299-324). Hillsdale, NJ: Erlbaum.

Meehl, P. E. (1977). Why I do not attend case conferences. In P. E. Meehl (Ed.), *Psychodiagnosis: Selected papers* (pp. 225-302). New York: W. W. Norton and Company, Inc.

Meehl, P. E., & Rosen, A. (1955). Antecedent probability and the efficacy of psychometric signs, patterns, or cutting scores. *Psychological Bulletin, 52*, 194-201.

Peterson, D. R. (in press) The reflective education. *American Psychologist*.

Poole, D. A., Lindsay, D. S., Memon, A., & Bull, R. (in press). Psychotherapy and the recovery of memories of childhood sexual abuse: US and British practitioners' opinions, practices, and experiences. *Journal of Consulting and Clinical Psychology*.

Shontz, F. C., & Green, P. (1992). Trends in research on the Rorschach: Review and recommendations. *Applied and Preventive Psychology, 1*, 149-156.

Smith, A. (1969). *The theory of mortal sentiments*. Indianapolis: Liberty Classics.
Smith, A. (1976). *The wealth of nations*. Chicago: The University of Chicago Press.
Yapko, M. (1994). *Suggestions of abuse: True and false memories of childhood sexual trauma*. New York: Simon and Schuster.

Footnotes

1. The best predictor of future behavior is past behavior. This prediction is far from perfect. People change, but we have yet to devise valid psychological techniques to predict who will change, how and when.
2. Psychotherapists must be judgmental to some degree, or they would not consider some behaviors more desirable than others. I am skeptical of a psychotherapist who claims that desirable behavior is simply whatever the clients wishes to achieve and should be defined purely in terms of the client's ideas and wishes— e.g. Adolph Hitler's.
3. For example, on something called SSCPNET, an e-mail group to which I subscribe.
4. In addition to scanning advertisements for continuing education workshops sent to me by Paul Meehl and by the False Memory Foundation, I receive many unsolicited ones—urging me to attend, even though I am not a licensed Psychologist. My two favorites were one to help people overcome codependency on sex and one informing me I often had an ethical obligation to "restructure" my clients' personalities—whether they wished such restructuring or not. Not all workshops are unreasonable, of course; for example, my colleague Ed Zuckerman and I gave one a few years ago on clinical judgment and diagnosis at the Pennsylvania Psychological Association meetings in Pittsburgh. And I admit to having an "availability bias" in memory for the loonier ones. The question is, however, whether such more than questionable "continuing education" courses and workshops should be there *at all*—not what proportion of accredited ones they should constitute.

Discussion of Dawes

Establishing and Implementing Scientific Standards of Psychological Practice

Robert D. Zettle
Wichita State University

Space limitations preclude a comprehensive consideration of the entire domain of issues impacting the establishment and implementation of scientific standards of psychological practice. It is the purpose of this paper to offer a few general considerations that may help facilitate this overall endeavor. Specifically, I will consider, from a behavior analytic perspective, selective issues germane to the establishment of practice standards, the domain of practices to be governed by such standards, and the implementation of practice standards.

Establishing Standards of Practice

The behavior of establishing scientific standards of psychological practice, like most actions, undoubtedly is (and will be) multidetermined. It would seem useful to consider not only a wide range of potential variables exerting functional control over the establishment of practice standards, but also to weigh the relative contributions that specific variables ought to assume in such control. Stated somewhat differently, the essential issue concerns what factors will (should?) determine the establishment of practice standards.

A number of potential controlling variables have been suggested by Dawes and by other conferees. These variables include, but are not necessarily limited to, scientific principles, empirical evidence for the efficacy and efficiency of various psychological practices, and ethical standards. What is unclear is the relative weights these various variables should receive in determining practice standards and how to resolve instances in which one factor is in apparent, if not actual, opposition to another. For instance, the most effective intervention for a particular problem may not be the most efficient, suggesting the need to consider cost-benefit analyses. Such considerations especially may be relevant if practice standards are to include interventions applied to units of analysis beyond the level of individuals. Interventions, such as certain prevention programs, that may be only moderately effective with specific individuals may exert a significant cumulative effect when aggregated across entire communities (Kazdin, 1980).

The paper by Dawes appropriately underscores the role of ethical standards in determining practice standards. In particular, he suggests that both hortatory standards (what should be done) and minatory standards (what should not be done) be considered in formulating practice guidelines. The current ethical code of the APA (American Psychological Association, 1992) may represent a set of standards to, in part, control the behavior of AAAPP, or other organizations for the matter, in establishing practice standards. Additional sources of ethical control, however, may prove useful in this process. For one, the APA ethical principles do not appear to give equal consideration to both hortatory and minatory standards of conduct. More importantly, it would seem useful to go beyond a code of ethics to consider the core of values from which any set of ethical standards is derived.

An ethical code can be viewed as a list of rules to guide the behavior of mental health professionals under conditions in which alternative contingencies control competing responses. From a behavior analytic perspective, rules, such as an ethical code, are themselves specifications of contingencies of arbitrary reinforcement and such contingencies of reinforcement imply a set of values. The set of values from which any derived ethical standards may be used in establishing practice standards, however, has not been made explicit. One set of values that might be useful to consider in this regard has been suggested by Jeger and Slotnick (1982). These values include promoting individual competence, enhancing a psychological sense of community, and supporting cultural diversity. It should be noted that these three general values were proposed to guide behavioral-ecological interventions in community mental health and may not be fully appropriate to the task at hand, depending upon the range of practices for which standards are to be established. Moreover, the set of values proposed by Jeger and Slotnick are being cited not to champion them in particular, but to offer them as an illustration of one attempt to clearly articulate values whereby ethics and practice may be merged. It is suggested that a similar process may be useful to undertake in the development of practice standards by this conference.

The Domain of Practices

Integral to the establishment of practice standards is the issue of what behaviors are to be controlled by any standards that are developed. In this regard, practice standards may be viewed as a set of rules designed to control a repertoire of practitioner behaviors. The breadth of practices that are to be placed under the control of standards remains unclear. At the very least, as suggested by Dawes, it seems appropriate to consider both assessment and intervention practices.

Traditionally, psychometric standards of reliability and validity have been used to evaluate the quality of psychological assessment procedures (Standards for Educational and Psychological Testing, 1985). However, an otherwise psychometrically sound assessment procedure may not necessarily contribute to intervention outcome, suggesting the need to consider alternative standards in evaluating the quality of assessment. One such alternative standard, treatment utility, has been proposed by Hayes, Nelson, and Jarrett (1987). An assessment procedure can be said to possess treatment utility to the extent that it can be shown to contribute to beneficial intervention outcome. If the documented efficacy of a treatment approach is to be used in establishing standards of practice for interventions, it would seem reasonable to include treatment utility as a standard in determining the quality of assessment procedures. That very few assessment procedures and practices have been shown to possess treatment utility underscores the need for continued research that investigates the interrelationship between psychological assessment and effective interventions.

Throughout the conference, the term "treatment" has been used almost exclusively to refer to clinical and counseling practices. Increased linkage between managed mental health care policies and the delivery of clinical and counseling services provides some justification for doing so. However, there would appear to be some disadvantages associated with confining practice standards to clinical and counseling activities. For one, AAAPP is an association that represents both applied *and preventive* psychology and, at this writing, already has formed or is in the process of forming 19 assemblies representing the breadth of scientifically-based practices. An emphasis on clinical and counseling interventions may have the effect of certain membership subgroups feeling excluded from the process of establishing practice standards.

Clinical and counseling psychology typically have been most concerned with delivering tertiary interventions to single individuals or small groups of individuals (e.g., family and marital therapy). The term "intervention," rather than "treatment," is deliberately being used here in a generic way to suggest that scientific standards ought to be considered for a wider range of practices. One way of conceptualizing the domain of practices for which standards eventually might be developed has been suggested by Jason and Glenwick (1980). Specifically, interventions can be viewed as being deliverable across three temporal dimensions: (a) primary prevention, (b) secondary prevention, and (c) tertiary intervention. All three interventions, moreover, can be targeted towards individuals, groups, organizations, communities, and society. Associated with the matrix of interventions and targets are corresponding assessment practices (e.g., needs assessment for community-based interventions). Defining the domain of assessment and intervention activities broadly ensures that few constituencies of AAAPP will feel left out of the process of establishing and implementing practice standards. Providing individual therapies of high quality is not viewed as inherently more valued than developing and implementing primary prevention programs of demonstrated effectiveness, although there may be justifiable reasons for emphasizing the former over the latter at the present time.

Implementation of Practice Standards

From a behavior analytic perspective, practice standards are most likely to result in behavioral change if they establish contingencies that shape-up and maintain such practices. As already suggested, prevailing and developing financial contingencies involving managed mental health care are behind the push to first develop and implement standards of clinical and counseling practices. Such contingencies can be strengthened further by dissemination of practice standards to managed care organizations. Increasingly, the livelihoods of practitioners may be dependent upon their ability to efficiently and effectively deliver services consistent with established practice standards.

Another type of dissemination may prove useful in establishing a second set of contingencies to support the implementation of practice standards. It would seem desirable to inform all possible consumers of psychological services (i.e., individuals, groups, organizations, communities, and society) of emerging practice standards. Doing so should increase the likelihood that consumers will demand that they receive services consistent with practice standards.

Conclusion

The successful establishment and implementation of scientific standards of psychological practice would appear to be dependent upon the effective utilization of several different sets of contingencies. A powerful existing and emerging set of contingencies is, and increasingly will be, controlled by managed mental health care organizations. Another set of contingencies may be established by AAAPP through dissemination to consumers of psychological services. It is hoped that some of the comments offered here will be of some use in establishing and managing these contingencies.

References

American Psychological Association. (1992). Ethical principles of psychologists and code of conduct. *American Psychologist, 47*, 1597-1611.

American Psychological Association, American Education Research Association, and National Council on Measurements in Education. (1985). *Standards for educational and psychological testing.* Washington, DC: American Psychological Association.

Hayes, S. C., Nelson, R. O., & Jarrett, R. B. (1987). The treatment utility of assessment: A functional approach to evaluating assessment quality. *American Psychologist, 42*, 963-974.

Jason, L. A., & Glenwick, D. S. (1980). An overview of behavioral community psychology. In D. Glenwick & L. Jason (Eds.), *Behavioral community psychology: Progress and prospects* (pp. 4-37). New York: Praeger.

Jeger, A. M., & Slotnick, R. S. (1982). Guiding values of behavioral-ecological interventions: The merging of ethics and practice. In A. M. Jeger & R. S. Slotnick (Eds.), *Community mental health and behavioral-ecology: A handbook of theory, research, and practice* (pp. 27-42). New York: Plenum.

Kazdin, A. E. (1980). Afterword. In D. Glenwick & L. Jason (Eds.), *Behavioral community psychology: Progress and prospects* (pp. 465-470). New York: Praeger.

Chapter 3

What Do We Want from Scientific Standards of Psychological Practice?

Steven C. Hayes
University of Nevada

This conference and this book has a revolutionary purpose. The intention in calling everyone together was to support a process that has a chance to change the world of applied psychology. I am not being grandiose here–obviously, this conference or this book by itself is not going to do that–but the movement it is part of *has* the potential to do that, if applied scientists play it right. This chapter is about how we might play it right.

Licensing as a Standard

We are now several decades into an experiment in which the public interest is to be protected in the area of psychological services by licensing, accreditation, and ethical guidelines. In my opinion that experiment has failed miserably.

The word "license" comes from a word that means "law," and you would think, therefore, that it would really have something to do with following the rules, but its main original use was "to give lawful permission." Thus, the dominant meaning of license has been lawful liberty. You get a marriage license, for example, so that you have lawful liberty to wed.

It is very instructive that if you look just a couple meanings down in the Oxford English Dictionary, you see the dark side of liberty. Hundreds of years ago the word "license" had already come *also* to mean "excessive liberty and disregard of law." This bit of etymology and dictionary wisdom says something about human nature, and about the inevitability of what we are now seeing with licensing as a standard of psychological practice. On one hand, most licensed psychologists probably have some sense of pride in their license. I do. On the other hand, licensed psychologists have, in a sense, "taken license" with their clients by providing empirically unproven technologies–as if licensing itself insures the quality of the services that are delivered.

These two meaning of "license" exist for a profound psychological reason: licensing *people* means that some kind of lawful permission is attributed to a *quality of personhood*. We literally say "I *am* licensed" as if that is a property of our being. When you do that some of the restraints that keep people from abusing liberty are taken off. Anything that you do must, *ipso facto*, be orderly, reasonable and lawful, because it comes from a special personal status of lawful permission. But that can be *exactly* the condition in which "excessive liberty and disregard of rules" is most likely. The two go together. As a profession we must do something else to protect the clients we serve.

Science-Based Standards of Care

Science-based standards of psychological practice involve a shift from the idea that lawful permission ("license") should be given to people for something they *have*–something they possess it as a kind of permanent status–to a view that lawful permission should be primarily linked to what a person *does*. The standards of care movement turns the field around and says that what should be certified, licensed, accredited, or approved are *specific forms of professional behavior*. These forms of behavior, in turn, may take some particular kinds of training, but even then what is being certified is not the general form, or location of a training process (as in the current accreditation and licensure procedures) but the training needed to be engage in specified and sanctioned forms of professional behavior. Thus, the standards of care movement has fundamental implications for how we do training, and how we protect the public good.

Why We Do Not Have Such Standards Already

Why do we not already have scientifically-based standards of psychological practice? You might be tempted to say that it has not already been done because the state of the science has not been such that is has been possible. It is true that the state of applied psychological science thirty years ago was nothing like what it is today. But there is more to it than that.

The whole *idea* of scientifically-oriented professional disciplines is not very old. Professions have succeeded for centuries in hiding what they do from public view. Special languages were developed, special training barriers were erected. A fair look at the history of guilds shows that these special qualities and processes were developed in part *precisely because they mystified the public*. The rise of psychology as a profession has been marked by the rise of psychology as a guild. Standards of practice that are science-based are *deeply* foreign to the structure and functioning of professional guilds. This is a transition that will not come easily.

What we are witnessing in the standards of care movement is the development of a new view about what professionals should be, not just in psychology but also in society at large. The people and their representatives (government, industry, the media, the courts) no longer genuflect in front of the centuries old mumbo jumbo of guilds. They are refusing to be put off by undocumented claims to special knowledge. As a result we are beginning to see the vague outlines of a day in which practicing psychologists will actually know and will actually follow the scientific literature. At least at first they will do it *not* because they value science but because they will be held accountable–by insurance companies, by the government, by agencies, by funding sources, by consumers, and by the profession.

This change is not just happening in psychology. It is happening in medicine, engineering, industry–in all areas of human functioning. But we have to face facts:

if we go down this road, the old ways of certifying professionals and of protecting the profession will be threatened. And that is the biggest reason that it has not already happened–intuitively the guild realizes that scinetifically-based standards of care will be a very real threat to the well understood and successful means they have always used to create a sense of value and specialness about the profession.

A Seeming Contradiction: Ethical Standards

An astute observer might disagree. After all, we already impose *many* rules on professionals, and some are very actively promoted by the guild. Professional ethical guidelines are an example. There are all kinds of professional ethical standards, and they greatly limit the kinds of things that psychologists can do. Why isn't there resistance from the guild in this case, as there is with scientific standards of care?

Ethical standards, paradoxically, strengthen my argument. Some rules of behavior actually *enhance* the sense of specialness and value without requiring the more difficult task of actually developing the field substantively and scientifically. Ethical standards can implicitly support psychology as a guild activity. If you can actually credibly argue, for example, that a psychotherapeutic relationship is so *special* and so *powerful* that you must have a lifelong prohibition against ever having a social relationship between a therapist and a former client–well that must be quite a special relationship indeed! This relationship is apparently *totally unlike* any other relationship in all of human affairs since no such prohibitions exist elsewhere. Something so special and powerful surely is precious and worth the high price it commands. Some of what we call "ethics" is just self-engrandizement.

In addition, these standards help make sure that psychologists stay out of the newspapers. Bad publicity hurts guilds and invited scrutiny by those outside of the profession. The fact that tens of thousands of therapists every day supply unproven technologies for high fees will not be page 1 news. If a therapist has an affair with a former client, not only could it be page 1 news, but someone might buy the movie rights. Some of what we call "ethics" is just public relations.

I am not arguing against any of our ethical principles. I am pointing to the fact that most of our ethical codes have the remarkable property of both controlling psychologists behavior and (surprise, surprise) promoting psychology as a guild. Never in the history of APA has an individual psychologist been removed as a member by its Ethics Committee for providing popular interventions that are not supported by the best available scientific evidence.

Science-based rules of conduct are quite different. They immediately bring a profession down to earth–they have a way of providing a heaping helping of humility. They are open for all to see. They entail some significant loss of control on the part of the profession since scientific standards of psychological care will quickly lead to the following question: can *others* with lesser training follow these rules of behavior just as well, at least in some circumstances? That is a *very* threatening idea–few other ideas could be as threatening from a guild perspective. And standards lead directly and unavoidably to the question. It is only when you have a very clear idea about what you are doing and the conditions under which you should do it, that it is obvious to ask "what kind of training does it require to do it?" Often the answer surely will be "a lot less than a doctorate." If it is accurate, this answer can serve the public good but it is hardly an answer that the guild will countenance, whether or not it is accurate.

Does Science-Based Practice Mean Paint-by-Numbers Practice?

Science is a human endeavor that has as its purpose the development of increasingly integrated systems of verbal rules that allow us to accomplish analytic goals with precision, scope, and depth, based on verifiable experience (see Biglan & Hayes, in press, for a discussion of this definition). Science is a special kind of word-producing, rule-making enterprise. The move toward scientific standards of psychological service builds upon that characteristic of science.

Science-based practice is thus, in part, rule-based practice. Some applied psychologists will accept the vision of scientifically-based standards of care without hesitation, but many others will look with fear at the prospect. What is the role, they may ask, of the artistic side of psychological work? Can healing relationships be turned into so many verbal formulae?

It is easy for the most scientifically-oriented to dismiss this concern altogether. They may question whether we know that any of the "art" in applied psychology is actually necessary or even helpful. Dismissing this issue out of hand would be a serious error. I plan to give this point a more extended discussion than might be deserved in the context of the larger scope of this paper, primarily because I am afraid that if I do not address it adequately that no one else will. The art versus science debate cannot and should not be avoided.

Art versus Science

To see why it is an error simply to rule out this conflict in favor of the science side, we can reformulate the issue slightly. In behavioral psychology there is great deal of evidence (Hayes, 1989) showing that behavior that is verbally-regulated (or "rule-governed behavior") differs from behavior that is controlled by direct experience (or "contingency-shaped behavior"). Rule-governed behavior tends to be somewhat more rigid, less modifiable by its direct consequences, more precise it its initial forms, and more subject to arbitrary social contingencies. Contingency-shaped behavior is generally more moldable and modifiable, but it is also more variable, and subject to chance contingencies (see Hayes, Zettle, & Rosenfarb, 1989, for a review of the data in support of all these generalizations).

Developmentally, humans start out with all their behavior being contingency-shaped. As their verbal abilities are established behavior becomes increasingly rule-governed. While science is the best rule-generating institution ever invented, it is wrong to think that all behavior can be *directly* rule-governed. No matter how verbal we become, some of our behavior is shaped. Hitting a baseball, quieting a mind, going to sleep, becoming sexually aroused, or playing the "Flight of the Bumblebee" are all examples of areas in which excessive rule-governance will actually be *detrimental.*

Any instance of rule-governed behavior stands ultimately on contingency-shaped behavior, at least to a degree. There is another way to say this: it is impossible to have a *pure* instance of rule-governed behavior. We can say the same thing in a more controversial way: all science stands on art. Let me explain.

Suppose I stand before you and say "tell me how to walk." Competent walkers will quickly formulate effective rules for this kind of thing: bend one knee, move the leg forward while balancing on the other, place the foot down and shift the weight to it, and so on. If these rules are given to verbally competent walkers, walking will occur. But there is an illusion buried in this simple example. Suppose the person who is told to "bend one knee" is not a competent walker and has not acquired the component behaviors being described? When the persons says "how do I do that?" answers may come initially (e.g., "tense the thigh muscles") but if the person again says "how do I do that?" the problem will be evident. *We can only verbally regulate component behaviors we already have* and ultimately some of these have been learned directly, experientially, or, we may say, artfully. Rule-governed behavior in the area of walking stands on the ground of directly shaped components of walking. You can see this clearly in stroke victims learning to walk once again. They often literally shout at their body (e.g., telling their legs to "move damn you") but walking was not originally learned verbally and words have no power over arms and legs until the components have once again been painstakingly shaped.

All areas of the application of science and of science itself are based upon and depend upon artful, experiential behavior. This is as true of the physicist in the lab as it is of the engineer in the field, as it is of the clinical psychologist talking to another human being. As this issue applies to standards of care it raises this question: since rule-governed behavior depends upon contingency-shaped behavior are standards of psychological practice only half the picture, to be supplemented by a large dollop of unanalyzed artistic experience untouched and unaddressed by these standards? To some degree the answer is "yes," but in its most important aspect I believe the answer is dominantly "no."

Two Kinds of Standards

We should distinguish between two kinds of standards. Many applied psychological procedures lend themselves to topographical description. Standards of practice in these areas can be straightforward. "Thou shalt" do one of several things when dealing with a person with problem "x" and "thou shalt not" do other things. It is quite possible to imagine the formal certification of procedures such as Barlow's MAP protocol (Barlow & Craske, 1989; Barlow, Craske, Cerny, & Klosko, 1989) or Foa's response prevention regime (Foa, Steketee, Grayson, Turner, & Latimer, 1984). I will term these *content standards* to denote the description of effective and ineffective behavioral topographies in given applied situations.

The alternative type of standards apply when rules cannot directly guide effective behavioral topographies. In these instances what will be at issue are the conditions under which effective behavior can be learned by experience. I term these *process standards*.

It is entirely possible to do a *science of art* even though *science is not art*. We can specify the conditions under which artful behavior will be most effectively acquired. If I want to learn how to hit a baseball, the last thing I want to do is to go and talk to some physicist who could tell me something about the parabolic function that describes the path a baseball follows. I want to go and talk to a baseball coach. And I can do a scientific analysis of good coaching, and specify the process a good coach uses to teach people how to hit a baseball.

The biggest part of the variance controlled by scientific standards of psychological practice, at least initially, will be content standards. It would be a big help to get clear on the procedures—the topographies—that people should most rely on to deliver effective services. We all dutifully write treatment manuals that describe such topographies. But we must no go overboard. The recent Division 12 standards of psychological intervention even state that *only* manualized treatment will be eligible for certification. For content standards this is correct, but it is a mistake if is meant generally.

We must not confuse the need for scientific standards with the exclusive relevance of one specific kind of standard: content standards. There may be many process standards that are equally important. Let me give two examples: a simple one, and a more complex one.

When we say we are learning by experience, we mean that we are learning by behaving in a context and by directly contacting the effects of efforts to behave effectively in that context. More technically, contingency-shaped behavior has to be in effective contact with its antecedents and consequences.

An easy example of a process rule might be a rule that specifies how to maximize such contact in an applied situation. We can easily imagine standards that specify that certain kinds of information will be gathered about clients or that the impact of interventions will be continuously evaluated. This is not a *content* standards since doing these things does not itself constitute effective psychological practice. Rather, doing these things makes it more likely that effective behavior will be shaped—a process standard.

Here is a more complex example. It is very hard to train social skills topographically, and yet surely much of what an effective practicing psychologist must do is to behavior in a socially effective manner. Social behaviors are too subtle, and the antecedents and consequences are too complex to place most of them into literal rules. After nearly 30 years of trying we still do not know the "component behaviors" involved in successful social performances, and we have good reason to believe that we never will (Hayes, 1993). And if we *did* know, we probably could not teach them or their effective application via rules. Several minutes at a calculator can quickly confirm that even a few dozen response forms and a few dozen contextual factors can quickly lead to billions of specific combinations and sequences. It is impossible to learn all of this by direct verbal rules. Finally, even if we could know all the components and how they are to be used, the basic literature on rule governance (Hayes et al., 1989) suggests that rule-governed social behavior might be less sensitive to its actual consequences—hardly a desirable end for a practitioner.

There is an alternative, however: shape the behavior directly by presenting and amplifying its consequences. An early study of ours (Azrin & Hayes, 1984) focused on cues of social interest displayed in social interactions, reasoning that these cues may be one of the major modulating events in social interaction. Subjects were asked to view a video tape (no audio) of a person conversing with an unseen other, and each minute to rate how interested they thought the person was in the unseen other. In the original taping, each interactant had actually given such ratings each minute and by using these as a criterion, the subjects' ratings could be assessed for accuracy. Treatment consisted simply of giving subjects feedback on the accuracy of their guesses. This intervention improved subjects social sensitivity considerably, and even lead to direct social kills improvements in role-play situations. Importantly, we could both assess and train social sensitivity, without knowing which specific cues were in fact indicative of social interest. This same basic idea had been replicated with programs designed to teach other forms of social skills by experiential feedback (Rosenfarb, Hayes, & Linehan, 1989; Follette, Dougher, Dykstra, & Compton, 1992), and my colleague Bill Follette has recently applied this approach to the shaping of therapeutic skills (Follette & Callaghan, in press). Observers watch the performance of a junior therapist and give continuous feedback regarding there therapeutic skill.

We might someday be able to shape social sensitivity in therapists to a criterion, and know for sure that the criterion had been reached. The target behavior is still artful, not rule-governed, but the process of establishing that artful behavior is itself scientifically understood. A process standard might result: teach effective therapeutic relationship skills via methods x or y, and make sure that these skills meet criterion z. Because there is no reason in principle why we cannot develop a "science of art," there is no reason to rule art out of psychological standards in the name of the greater glory of science.

We must avoid falling into a kind of scientism in the name of scientific standards. Not all therapy needs to be done from a cookbook. There almost certainly are experiential and artful components of good clinical practice. Our job in these cases is to arrange the kinds of experiences that are known scientifically to create the clinical result desired.

Establishing a Means to Develop Standards

At the conference, AAAPP established a *Board of Scientific Practice Standards and Social Policy Guidelines*. It is being charged with the development of at least two kinds of products: 1. forming panels to write scholarly "state of the science" papers in specific areas and to develop short 4-5 pages practice guidelines drawn from these., and 2. forming similar panels to write guidelines directly, passing along the scientific information to the Board to insure their empirical quality. These guidelines will be written without references and in an easily readable form. It is the job of the Board to satisfy itself that the guidelines are based on sound scientific thinking.

The reason the Board is to deal with both practice standards and social policy guidelines is that it recognizes that in several areas of applied psychology that social policy guidelines *are* practice guidelines. For example, if we can specify how best to prevent juvenile delinquency, this is a social policy guideline but it is also a practice standard for psychologists dealing with that issue.

What Do We Want to Know?

What do we want to know from practice standards? What would we ask such a board to do? Table 1 (on the facing page) shows a list of questions that I think is relatively comprehensive.

1. How are these problems best assessed?

We need to deal with all the various purposes of assessment: prediction, monitoring, and most especially selecting interventions. It is terribly important not merely to recreate the psychometric standards. When we are dealing with practice standards we are dealing with all of the practical uses to which assessment is put. Quality should be measured against those practical goals, and psychometric quality is *not* a synonym for utility (Hayes, Nelson, & Jarrett, 1987).

2. Are there popular assessment methods that are known to be unreliable or inefficient?

Popular assessment methods that are known to be unreliable and inefficient should be put aside with "Thou Shalt Not" standards. Unpopular methods that are useless do not seem worth the effort unless the flaws are egregious.

3. Is this set of problems best approached as a clear syndrome, or is it a loose collection of behaviors, a specific target behavior, or a specific set of discrete behaviors?

We need to get as rapidly as possible to what is going on functionally at the psychological level of analysis. We need to organize our discipline that way. If syndromes are an aid to doing that, fine, but let's be open to other ways (Hayes & Follette, 1992). There is a big danger that standards will needless strengthen syndromal classification schemes, just because they provide convenient categories (Follette, Houts, & Hayes, 1992). Many of the needed standards (e.g., what to do with suicidal behavior) are not about syndromes—they are about behavior.

4. Do you know the functional processes that are characteristic of these problems, and do they overlap with those of others?

There is no substitute for understanding the functional processes involved in a given problem. When we do, these processes make sense of why treatments work. That is a great prize because we can go beyond mere technology. We must be careful

---

Table 1

What We Want to Know from Practice Standards

Questions to Ask of Scientific Practice Standards

1. How are these problems best assessed?

2. Are there popular assessment methods that are known to be unreliable or inefficient?

3. Is this problem or set of problems best approached as a clear syndrome?

4. Do we know the functional processes that are characteristic of these problems and do they overlap with those of others?

5. Is the problem associated with other areas of poorer functioning and if so which general outcomes should be measured to assess the effectiveness of intervention?

6. What are the more and the most effective interventions or means of prevention for these problems as measured by question 1 and by question 5? Are there particular ways these interventions should or should not be delivered (e.g., settings, therapists)?

7. Are any of these interventions or means of prevention known to be slow-acting, costly, more variable in outcome, difficult to train, or dangerous? Do these characteristics suggests a re-ranking of those in question 6?

8. Are there interventions or means of prevention that are known not to work and should be prohibited, or long-standing or popular interventions that have little or no supportive data and should be used only under extraordinary circumstances with in the context of question 6?

9. Can we predict which interventions or means of prevention are most likely to work: a. with certain clients (e.g., are there clear sub-types of this problem, especially with treatment implications? Do things like client personality matter? If the problem co-occurs with other problems, does that change which treatments should be used?) b. with certain therapists (e.g., personality types, level of training, orientation, etc) c. in certain settings (e.g., in outpatient settings, in community based or home based settings)

Table 1 continued on following page

Table 1 continued

10. What is known about how best to train professionals to use the interventions listed in response to questions 6 and 7? How can these interventions be best disseminated?

11. Why are professionals most likely to use interventions listed in response to question 8? How can these views or conditions be changed so that these interventions are put aside?

12. What is the usual course and outcome of the interventions listed in response to question 6 and 7? Can the existing data be used as a guide by third party payers or as a means of informing clients of likely outcomes?

13. Are there innovative assessment or intervention approaches in this area that, while not yet proven, seem promising? Under what conditions might they be used first?

Additional Questions to Ask of Scholarly Papers that Back up Standards

14. Based on the best available evidence, which theory or set of theories seems currently best able to explain the current data, while at the same time being precise and clear in its predictions, clear about its boundary conditions, board in scope, coherent, useful, and consistent with what is known about these problems at other levels of analysis (e.g., biologically, sociologically, etc.)?

15. What kinds of research projects are most needed to advance the state of knowledge about these problems, as reflected by the ability to answer these fourteen questions?

A Final Question about Process to the Panels

16. In answering each of these thirteen (or for full panels, fifteen) questions, what recommendations can you give to the field, including to other panels, about how best to go about answering such questions in general? In other words, regardless of the specific content (e.g., the specific applied problem), are there certain research methods, sources of information, organizational schemes, and the like that could be used to guide the effort to answer such questions in other areas? Are there other questions that should be included in future lists?

in our standards to encourage this, or we could actually harm the development of applied psychology in the effort to help it.

5. Is the problem associated with other areas of poor functioning, and if so, which general outcomes should be measured as effectiveness of treatment?

It is very frustrating to go in the literature with an interest in general functional outcomes. Our measures are usually closely tied to our common-sense theories of psychopathology, and we sometimes never get beyond them. We have hundreds of measures of anxiety and only handfuls of measures of work performance. Yet we say we are interested in anxiety, depression, and so on because of the implications of these psychological events for life functioning. This item says "keep your eye on the big picture." Sometimes the most effective treatment may have more of an effect on general well-being than on a specific target.

6. What are the more and the most effective interventions or means of prevention for these problems as measured by question 1 and by question 5? Are there particular ways these interventions should or should not be delivered (e.g., settings, therapists)?

Ideally, we want to see changes both in 1 (the target problem) and 5 (general functioning). We want to see changes in what the person came in complaining of and in their general life functioning, if that is impacted by the problem. Other measures, it seems to me, are not very relevant to standards of care. If someone for theoretical reasons wants to argue that, say, self-esteem is a key issue, but it is neither a complaint nor an objective measure of life functioning, then it is at best relevant to the underlying theory, but not the direct assessment of the value of the procedure. Standards should specify what are the more and the most effective treatments or means of prevention, using these measures. The Board should decide how to proceed to do this. There may need to be graded steps—approval at different levels.

7. Are any of these interventions or means of prevention known to be slow-acting, costly, more variable in outcome, difficult to train, or dangerous? Do these characteristics suggests a re-ranking of those in question 6?

We have to keep track of the contextual circumstances and not think of this just in terms of a list of approved-procedures in a vacuum. It matters if procedures are known to be particularly slow or fast acting, costly or cheap, more variable or more consistent in outcome. Just because there is a treatment that has a better overall mean effect, doesn't mean that it should be used. The mean impact might be based on some who are helped greatly and others who are really hurt. The treatment might be too risky compared to another treatment, that does not have as high an overall average improvement but in which almost everybody gets at least a little better.

Similarly, if an intervention is very difficult to train, it had better be pretty good, because it costs a lot to do that. We need to know if it dangerous, or if there are there side-effects that we have to keep track of that impact on clients or their families. Finally, given all of these contextual features, do they suggest a re-ranking of all these that we have pointed to in item 6?

8. Are there interventions or means of prevention that are known not to work and should be prohibited, or long-standing or popular interventions that have little or no supportive data and should be used only under extraordinary circumstances within the context of question 6?

This is a "thou shalt not" or minatory standard (see Dawes, this volume). If procedures have been repeatedly tried and failed then at some point you have to say enough is enough. That does not mean the researcher cannot still try to change them to get a good effect. Until then, however, they should be prohibited for general use.

More often there are few data relevant to the question. That is a more complicated situation. If there are well-developed, powerful procedures, as measured against the gold standards of questions 1 and 5, then it is only under extraordinary circumstances (e.g., in which proven technologies are impractical for some reason) that you would even be looking at these alternatives. If there is not much available, then you do the best you can, but with the added burden of more careful evaluation and very clear informed consent. We are no where near a situation in which only proven procedures can be used, because there are so many conditions with no proven procedures exist and even where they do exist they may be refused, or they may not fit the circumstance (e.g., a couples intervention in which the spouse will not participate), or people may not respond.

9. Can we predict which interventions or means of prevention are most likely to work: a. with certain clients (e.g., are there clear sub-types of this problem, especially with treatment implications? Do things like client personality matter? If the problem co-occurs with other problems, does that change which treatments should be used?) b. with certain therapists (e.g., personality types, level of training, orientation, etc) c. in certain settings (e.g., in outpatient settings, in community based or home based settings)

These kinds of complexities have to be considered because they may modify considerably the conditions under which actions are taken. For example, if a person has multiple problems and a package has been shown to work with both types, it might be preferred over two incompatible packages that are the best in their specific areas. The same might be said for specific settings or therapists.

10. What is known about how best to train professionals to use the interventions listed in response to questions 6 and 7? How can these interventions be best disseminated?

This is where the professional implications really begin to be felt. I just don't think we can ethically go in and assume that doctoral level therapists are qualified to use proven procedures—more training may be required—and (to make a different point in the other direction) we cannot assume that MA level people can't be trained to do this work. We have to specify the training needed based on research. Doctoral level psychologists may not *like* the idea that lesser trained therapists can do these things, but if that is what the data suggest then on ethical grounds, on values grounds, on costs to the society grounds, and on human grounds: too bad. Psychology should serve the public good, even if that creates problems for psychology.

11. Why are professional most likely to use interventions listed in response to question 8? How can these views or conditions be changed so that these interventions are put aside?

Item 8 asked "are there treatments that are known not to work and should be prohibited, or long-standing or popular treatments that have little or no supportive data." We should explicitly note the conditions that give rise to the use of such procedures. Often the use of these procedures may be based on the myths of applied work, or outdated laws or regulations. Our standards of care should address these myths and regulations directly so that they can be debunked or changed. For example, very rarely should people be hospitalized for suicidal behavior: the false positive rate is enormous, the base rate is tiny, there is a known cost and stigmatization of hospitalization, and hospitalization does not have a positive impact on the actual likelihood of suicide (Chiles & Strosahl, in press). But, some states have laws that say that you must hospitalize people if they say "I'm going to kill myself." This should be changed, and standards that address these factors explicitly will help create the change.

12. What is the usual course and outcome of the interventions listed in response to question 6 and 7? Can the existing data be used as a guide by third party payers or as a means of informing clients of likely outcomes?

Clients should be informed of such data. This is an ethical issue. And this information should be shared with third party payers. Applied science should work with the health care delivery system to encourage the best available practice.

13. Are there innovative assessment or intervention approaches in this area that, while not yet proven, seem promising? Under what conditions might they be used first?

We should clearly distinguish conditions that bring procedures in under item 13, from those that are brought in under item 6. But sometimes innovative approaches should be tried first. For example, if no proven technologies exist, or they do but they are refused by the client, then less well-developed approaches might be worth trying. Item 13 envisions a kind of lower degree of approval for developing approaches.

Additional Questions

If a full white paper is being developed, the following would be relevant:

14. **Based on the best available evidence, which theory or set of theories seems currently best able to explain the current data, while at the same time being precise and clear in its predictions, clear about its boundary conditions, broad in scope, coherent, useful, and consistent with what is known about these problems at other levels of analysis (e.g., biologically, sociologically, etc.)?**

15. **What kinds of research projects are most needed to advance the state of knowledge about these problems, as reflected by the ability to answer these fourteen questions?**

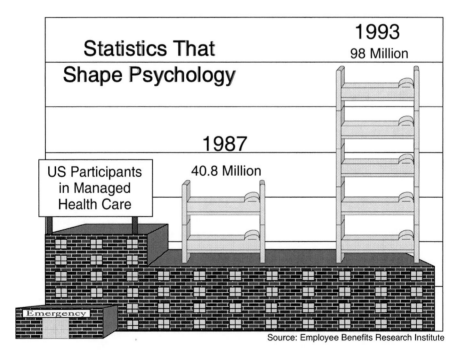

Source: Employee Benefits Research Institute

These are questions for the white paper directed toward the science side—they are not something I think we should be putting in practice standards. But we need to foster the intellectual development of the field, not just freeze a set of standards into place. Finally, all of the panels should be asked this:

16. In answering each of these thirteen (or for full panels, fifteen) questions, what recommendations can you give to the field, including to other panels, about how best to go about answering such questions in general? In other words, regardless of the specific content (e.g., the specific applied problem), are there certain research methods, sources of information, organizational schemes, and the like that could be used to guide the effort to answer such questions in other areas? Are there other questions that should be included in future lists?

We should view the development of standards as itself a kind of grand experiment. We have a lot to learn. The panels should begin to tell us how best to go about answering such questions.

Who Will Listen?

The key to the development of scientifically-based practice standards are the changes that are occurring in the health care delivery system in this country. The figure on the facing page shows the astounding growth occurring in managed care in the country. Especially in fully capitated systems—managed care firms paid on a per member per month basis in which costs cannot be saved by denying service—the only way to succeed is to have both good consumer satisfaction (both the employer and the end consumer) and to avoid unnecessary visits. If you chase people away with bad care or premature termination, you lose on consumer satisfaction. If you see everybody 30 sessions, you lose money. Many of these systems are being forced by consumer demand (especially by the employers paying for the policies) to lift arbitrary session limits. The only way to win under these circumstances is with quality. High utilizers can have many sessions, but it has to work. Easy problems have to be remediated quickly.

HMOs are the lever point right now. Applied scientists have some real power here, because we have something to offer that is a direct economic value to those institutions. And every HMO in the country is developing practice standards as a way of improving quality. But they don't have ready access to the real players: the applied scientists. They know they need standards, and they have the money to buy them, but they don't know exactly what they need, and they don't know exactly how to buy it. I suggest we, as a field, give it to them for free.

We should develop the standards, print thousands of little booklets, and literally give them away to HMOs, treatment facilities, and insurance providers. We should sell them to the individual therapists who will need them to be competitive.

I can envision a circumstance in which a therapist gets on a panel because she or he declares that they follow these guidelines in their work. What is wrong with that? It would be a better guide to quality care than the alphabet soup of degrees and associations that we now allow to be promulgated so as to claim special areas of expertise.

Consumers should have access to this information as well, and I don't see why a book like this wouldn't be widely available in libraries. Yes, it has to be updated periodically—every three or four years. But if we make a good start over the next year or two we could fairly quickly have a well developed, fairly comprehensive, dynamic set of criteria that will change the face of psychology as a profession.

The Implications of Standards for Applied Psychologists

It would be inappropriate for Ph.D. psychologists to be trained about all standardized treatments. By that I don't mean that they should be trained in all kinds of other treatments, but it's just not practical to take a Ph.D. and spend course after course after course, going through Beck's cognitive therapy, Barlow's MAP protocol, and so on. We can't turn our Ph.D.s into technicians. They need to know how to develop, evaluate, train, and supervise psychological work. Psy.D.s could be trained exclusively in these kinds of standardized methods—maybe we need technicians at the doctoral level. But maybe we do not.

In fully capitated HMOs, Ph.D. psychologists are getting pushed upstairs. It doesn't make sense to spend eight years in graduate school and then sit down an treat garden variety phobics. And most cases are not that complicated. A very large of those seeking service in fully capitated HMOs for mental health services are diagnosable only with V codes—adjustment disorders (Strosahl, 1994). When the system is fully capitated there is no reason to "diagnose up" for insurance coverage purposes and suddenly most of what people want help with is fairly normal material—marriages breaking up, children creating problems, or work creating stress. It seems likely that master's level therapists are the future primary mental health care service provider. Ph.D.s are needed to develop programs, evaluate programs, train, supervise, and to treat complicated cases that fail to be helped by standardized treatment protocols delivered by Master's level therapists.

Outside of private services delivered to the well-off, the future service role of doctoral people is important but more limited than in the current system. When the manual does not work, and we don't know what to do, doctoral level people will be brought in. In complex, treatment resistant cases you have to adopt a kind of problem solving strategy—and training in this kind of thinking is what we are doing with science-based training. So, there is a service role for science-oriented Ph.D.s. But it will be primarily behind the front lines, supporting, training, supervising, and only secondarily delivering services, as a kind of net, catching people as they fall out of these well-developed empirically-validated systems.

In this service delivery role I would like those people to know how to use intensive, time-series designs (Hayes, Barlow, & Nelson-Grey, in press). I would like them to know how to demonstrate empirically—one at a time if need be—how to help these complex cases. When that knowledge is acquired, even *that* complicated case can be given to someone else.

Does all this mean that a lot of psychologists are going to have lower incomes? Perhaps, but the incomes will be adequate. Does it mean we need fewer applied doctoral psychologists? Probably—especially those coming out of programs with limited science training. But when you are in a situation in which you have developed technologies that you can give away and that have a big impact, then you must downsize. Dentistry faced this situation as its technology improved and, yes, dentists got hurt. But, to their credit, they adjusted and they did not back up from the technical improvements that had created their problem.

Psychology may not be as sensible. The free-standing professional schools cannot slow down and still survive. And we have many private practitioners now in a full-blown panic as they see the handwriting on the wall. Some want to save psychology by destroying it: they want to become junior psychiatrists, prescription pad in hand, and thus save one form of private practice. But managed care and the new role of psychology is coming, like it or not.

What scientific standards of psychological intervention suggest is this: we can have a profession that is more honorable, more dignified, and more consistent with its disciplinary values. We can have a professional that protects consumers the honest way: by delivering the best available services. Yes, it will mean lowering the barriers the guild has built and facing directly questions about the need for doctoral level psychologists. But if we make this transition we will have a great prize: a profession that is fully integrated with the science of psychology. We will have a profession we can be proud of.

References

Azrin, R. D., & Hayes, S. C. (1984). The discrimination of interest within a heterosexual interaction: Training, generalization, and effects on social skills. *Behavior Therapy, 15,* 173-184.

Barlow, D. H., & Craske, M.G. (1989). *Mastery of your anxiety and panic.* New York: Graywind Publishing.

Barlow, D. H., Craske, M. G., Cerny, J. A., & Klosko, J. S. (1989). Behavioral treatment of panic disorder. *Behavior Therapy, 20,* 261-282.

Biglan, A., & Hayes, S. C. (in press). Should the behavioral sciences become more pragmatic? The case for functional contextualism in research on human behavior. *Applied and Preventive Psychology: Current Scientific Perspectives.*

Chiles, J. A., & Strosahl, K. D. (in press). *The suicidal patient: Principles of assessment, treatment, and case management.* Washington, DC: American Psychiatric Press.

Foa, E. B., Steketee, G., Grayson, J. B., Turner, R. M., & Latimer, P. R. (1984). Deliberate exposure and blocking of obsessive-compulsive rituals: Immediate and long-term effects. *Behavior Therapy, 15,* 450-472.

Follette, W. C., & Callaghan, G. M. (in press). Do as I do not as I say: A behavior analytic approach to supervision. *Professional Psychology: Research and Practice.*

Follette, W. C., Dougher, M. K., Dykstra, T. A., & Compton, S. N. (November 1992). *Teaching complex social behaviors to subjects with schizophrenia using contingent feedback.* Paper presented at the meeting of the Association for Advancement of Behavior Therapy, Boston.

Follette, W. C., Houts, A. C., & Hayes, S. C. (1992). Behavior therapy and the new medical model. *Behavioral Assessment, 14,* 323-343.

Hayes, S. C. (Ed.). (1989). *Rule-governed behavior: Cognition, contingencies, and instructional control.* New York: Plenum.

Hayes, S. C. (1993). Rule-governance: Basic behavioral research and applied implications. *Current Directions in Psychological Science, 2,* 193-197.

Hayes, S. C., Barlow, D. H., & Nelson-Grey, R. O. (in press). *The scientist-practitioner: Research and accountability in clinical and educational settings* (2nd edition). New York: Allyn & Bacon.

Hayes, S. C. & Follette, W. C. (1992). Can functional analysis provide a substitute for syndromal classification? *Behavioral Assessment, 14,* 345-365.

Hayes, S. C., Nelson, R. O., & Jarrett, R. (1987). Treatment utility of assessment: A functional approach to evaluating the quality of assessment. *American Psychologist, 42,* 963-974.

Hayes, S. C., Zettle, R. D., & Rosenfarb, I. (1989). Rule following. In S. C. Hayes (Ed.), *Rule-governed behavior: Cognition, contingencies, and instructional control.* (pp. 191-220). New York: Plenum.

Rosenfarb, I. S., Hayes, S. C., & Linehan, M. M. (1989). Instructions and experiential feedback in the treatment of social skills deficits in adults. *Psychotherapy: Theory, Research, and Practice, 26,* 242-251.

Strosahl, K. D. (1994). Entering the new frontier of managed mental health care: Gold mines and land mines. *Cognitive and Behavioral Practice, 1,* 5-23.

Discussion of Hayes

On the Relation Between Clinical Practice and Psychological Science

Sam Leigland
Gonzaga University

Science has contributed to the treatment of psychological disorders on several fronts. Perhaps the most conspicuous contribution has come from biological, medical, and pharmacological research, but many other fields have direct interests in the traditional domain of psychological disorders, and the treatments advocated in these areas are nonpharmacological. Of these fields, a case could be made that the distinguishing characteristic of clinical psychology is its focus upon the application of scientifically-based methods to the assessment of treatment strategies for psychological disorders. The case would be complicated somewhat by the complexity of clinical psychology as a professional field, with its diversity of views regarding the relation between science and practice, the diversity within the field as to what constitutes "scientific" evidence and methods, and so on. Nevertheless, the scientific orientation which can be seen in a significant segment of professional clinical psychology is part of the broader tradition of scientific psychology more generally.

The purpose of this brief commentary is to raise the issue of what role science plays in that part of clinical psychology that is committed to a scientific orientation. If clinical psychology is to be viewed as an example of applied science, is the role of science the same as that seen in other scientific fields with associated areas of application? If the role is different, how might we account for the difference? If additional or improved connections between scientific and clinical psychology appear to be needed given the goals of the professional/applied area, what might be recommended toward the development of such connections?

As space is limited for this commentary I will not be able to present extensive arguments, examples, and references for each of the two summary statements that will be presented next, but I don't believe that the statements will be viewed as excessively controversial in any case. The first statement is this: the *primary* role of science in clinical practice is in the *evaluation* of the effectiveness of therapeutic interventions. Second, it would seem that this role is unlike that of other science-application interactions (such as that found in the biological sciences and medicine, or the physical sciences and engineering), since in other fields the basic-science areas provide important and *useful information* regarding the *formulation* of applied principles, methods, techniques, or strategic interventions.

Where is the psychological science that would "feed" the development of therapeutic strategies for clinical psychology? The disunity of psychology as a science is an issue of long-standing concern within the discipline (e.g., Hergenhahn, 1992), but it will be argued here that it is more than a simple diversity of views that is responsible for the scientific isolation of clinical practice. The scientific disunity of psychology may be see both within as well as between some of the systems of science that characterize contemporary psychology. While it is certainly true that some useful science-based information may be seen to contribute to the development of therapeutic intervention strategies, it is the fundamental theoretical disunity that makes the basic-to-applied transition particularly difficult in the case of psychological science.

The Problem of Psychological Theory

Issues having to do with basic knowledge in psychology nearly always appeal to "theory." With respect to science-based clinical practice, the problem of theory in psychology may be summarized by examining the dominant scientific perspective in contemporary psychology. This systematic position may be seen as a kind of orthodoxy in what may be regarded as mainstream scientific psychology. A close examination of theoretical practices since the 1930s shows a fundamental continuity between the mediational neobehaviorists (e.g., Hull, 1943), today's "animal learning theorists" (e.g., Staddon, 1993a, b; Timberlake, 1993), and most of the varieties of cognitive psychology (e.g., Anderson, 1980; Gardner, 1986).

While these areas differ along a number of important dimensions, they may be seen as sharing the same general systematic approach; namely, the approach that has been termed "methodological behaviorism" (e.g., Day, 1980/1992, 1983/1992; Hergenhahn, 1992; it should be noted that the philosophical positions commonly associated with cognitive science, such as metaphysical functionalism or eliminative materialism, do not describe scientific systems per se, but rather describe philosophical positions concerning issues of "mind-body" relations; e.g., Block, 1980; Flanagan, 1991). This is the general scientific view that is presented in virtually every general/introductory psychology text available today, and the continuity of general perspective from the mediational neobehaviorists to today's cognitive psychologists is increasingly acknowledged (e.g., Hergenhahn, 1992, p. 392; McBurney, 1994; Simon, 1992).

The general characteristics of methodological behaviorism may be summarized in the following way: (1) the empirical subject matter of the science is publicly-observable, overt behavior (such activities assure intersubjective verifiability and are thus "objective"); (2) the principal methodological emphasis is the experimental method, in which environment-behavior interactions are controlled and analyzed in the laboratory; (3) the general goal is to explain the observed environment-behavior relations at an abstract theoretical "level" by way of "inferring" hypothetical, causal mechanisms, processes, or constructs, which might ultimately comprise an adequate theory; (4) all theoretical or abstract terms (normally taken from folk psychology) must be operationally defined (in the sense of the familiar Boring-Stevens interpretation of operationism; e.g., Day, 1980/1992; Moore, 1975); (5) the theory is evaluated via experimental test, where implications or predictions derived from the theory are matched against experimental outcome (although the nature of the test is somewhat controversial; that is, many philosophers of science now agree that the goal of the experimental evaluation should be falsification rather than confirmation, although this is rarely if ever the case in psychological science; for an excellent overview, see Bechtel, 1988).

There are certain advantages to such a systematic view. For example, natural-language terms (such as "memory," or "attention") may be employed in such a way that complex questions of language and meaning do not interfere with the design of experiments and the collection of data (the legacy of the Boring-Stevens interpretation of operationism). In looking at possible disadvantages to method-ological behaviorism, it is also unfortunately the case that there is no provision in the systematic approach to theory and science that the models and theories produced will have anything in common with other models and theories. A survey of Howard Gardner's (1986) interesting book, *The Mind's New Science: A History of the Cognitive Revolution*, for example, seems to show that the various theories to be found in "cognitive science" have virtually nothing of substance in common with one another, except (1) an affinity for the term "cognition" (with its rich variety of non-technical usages), and (2) an antipathy for "behaviorism" (usually presented and dismissed in terms of a unitary and simple-minded caricature; compare also the remarkably diverse theoretical issues found in Anderson, 1980, Seidenberg, 1993, and Simon, 1992).

Another problem with the traditional theoretical practices associated with methodological behaviorism is a notorious lack of practical usefulness, application, and derived technology. Certainly it is possible to find examples from both cognitive psychology and animal learning theory in which something useful was derived and applied to human affairs in some fashion, but it is equally clear that such examples constitute a vanishingly small proportion of the overwhelmingly vast amount of theory and supporting data which fill the psychological/behavioral research journals each year.

Summary and Conclusions

Clinical psychology faces the problem of attachment to a scientific field that provides very little in the way of basic scientific knowledge regarding clinical phenomena. While part of the problem may involve systematic diversity within scientific psychology, it is proposed that the larger problem is that the mainstream tradition of theory construction in psychological science produces neither coherent nor useful knowledge.

For those scientist-clinicians interested in systematic issues, there may be a value in looking at examples of alternative systematic approaches to science. For example, radical behaviorism is a comprehensive scientific system that provides for a dynamic interplay between basic and applied areas. A systematic position that emphasizes psychological phenomena over psychological theory is what has enabled behavior-analytic science to move readily between basic science (e.g., Catania, 1992), applied science (e.g., Johnson & Layng, 1992; Martin & Pear, 1992), clinical practice (e.g., Hayes, 1987; Hayes & Wilson, 1994; Kohlenberg & Tsai, 1991), and philosophical/conceptual issues (e.g., Leigland, 1992).

It is possible that some gains might be made for clinical science as clinical psychologists, through the professional organizations, explicitly challenge their colleagues in the varieties of psychological science on the issue of useful basic-science knowledge. With respect to specific issues and problems, for example, what can cognitive science contribute to clinical practice in terms of workable, practical information? Such challenges might serve to uncover the usefulness of research areas of current interest in the basic areas, or possibly extend basic research interests into new areas. In any case, the progress of clinical psychology as an effective area of applied science will depend upon more than a set of useful techniques for the evaluation of therapeutic interventions; it will depend upon nothing less than a coherent and useful psychological science.

References

Anderson, J. R. (1980). *Cognitive psychology and its implications*. New York: Freeman.

Bechtel, W. (1988). *Philosophy of science: An overview for cognitive science*. Hillsdale, NJ: Erlbaum.

Block, N. (Ed.) (1980). *Readings in philosophy of psychology: Vol. 1*. Cambridge, MA: Harvard University Press.

Catania, A. C. (1992). *Learning* (3rd Ed.). Englewood Cliffs, NJ: Prentice-Hall.

Day, W. F. (1980). The historical antecedents of contemporary behaviorism. In R. W. Rieber & K. Salzinger (Eds.), *Psychology: Theoretical-historical perspectives* (pp. 203-262). New York: Academic Press. (Reprinted in Leigland, S. (Ed.) (1992). *Radical behaviorism: Willard Day on psychology and philosophy*. Reno, NV: Context Press.)

Day, W. F. (1983). On the difference between radical and methodological behaviorism. *Behaviorism, 11*, 89-102. (Reprinted in Leigland, S. (Ed.) (1992). *Radical behaviorism: Willard Day on psychology and philosophy*. Reno, NV: Context Press.)

Flanagan, O. (1991). *The science of mind* (2nd Ed.). Cambridge, MA: MIT Press/ Bradford.

Gardner, H. (1985). *The mind's new science: A history of the cognitive revolution*. New York: Basic Books.

Hayes, S. C. (1987). A contextual approach to therapeutic change. In N. S. Jacobson (Ed.), *Psychotherapists in clinical practice: Cognitive and behavioral perspectives* (pp. 327-387). New York: Guilford.

Hayes, S. C., & Wilson, K. G. (1994). Acceptance and commitment therapy: Altering the verbal support for experiential avoidance. *The Behavior Analyst, 17*, 289-303.

Hergenhahn, B. R. (1992). *An introduction to the history of psychology* (2nd Ed.). Belmont, CA: Wadsworth.

Hull, C. L. (1943). *Principles of behavior.* New York: Appleton-Century-Crofts.

Johnson, K. R., & Layng, T. V. J. (1992). Breaking the structuralist barrier: Literacy and numeracy with fluency. *American Psychologist, 47*, 1475-1490.

Kohlenberg, R. J., & Tsai, M. (1991). *Functional analytic psychotherapy: Creating intense and curative therapeutic relationships.* New York: Plenum.

Leigland, S. (Ed.) (1992). *Radical behaviorism: Willard Day on psychology and philosophy.* Reno, NV: Context Press.

Martin, G., & Pear, J. (1992). *Behavior modification: What it is and how to do it (4th Ed).* Englewood Cliffs, NJ: Prentice-Hall.

McBurney, D. H. (1994). *Research methods* (3rd Ed.). Pacific Grove, CA: Brooks/Cole.

Moore, J. (1975). On the principle of operationism in a science of behavior. *Behaviorism, 3*, 120-138.

Seidenberg, M. S. (1993). Connectionist models and cognitive theory. *Psychological Science, 4*, 228-235.

Simon, H. A. (1992). What is an "explanation" of behavior? *Psychological Science, 3*, 150-161.

Staddon, J. E. R. (1993a). The conventional wisdom of behavior analysis. *Journal of the Experimental Analysis of Behavior, 60*, 439-447.

Staddon, J. E. R. (1993b). The conventional wisdom of behavior analysis: Response to comments. *Journal of the Experimental Analysis of Behavior, 60*, 489-494.

Timberlake, W. (1993). Behavior systems and reinforcement: An integrative approach. *Journal of the Experimental Analysis of Behavior, 60*, 105-128.

Chapter 4

Managed Care and Outcomes-Based Standards in the Health Care Revolution

Michael S. Pallak
Foundation for Behavioral Health

While Federal health care reform is once again stalled for the foreseeable future, a revolution in health care organization and service delivery has already taken place–and continues to evolve rapidly. That revolution is the shift away from traditional fee-for-service (FFS) financing to managed care with major implications for providers, patients, and payers. The shift offers major opportunities for data collection about clinical issues and treatment effectiveness in terms of patient outcomes. This presentation is not designed as a justification for managed care efforts (a topic of concern among provider communities), but rather as a brief overview of the potential for data collection efforts by which to assess combinations of variables that enhance patient outcome. These empirical efforts enable the management of clinical systems and care based on outcome results that help to delineate clinically effective and efficient treatment. In parallel, however, there are several barriers and sources of inertia in the development of empirically delineated clinical standards and guidelines.

Managed care, implies an additional third entity in the treatment planning and treatment providing process other than the provider and patient. The "entity" serves as a check and balance on the unfettered clinical discretion of the provider. Several excellent reviews provide a description of elements of managed care (Curtiss, 1989; Tischler, 1990a, 1990b) that shape treatment provision and treatment utilization.

Quality Assurance and Service Delivery Data

All managed care organizations (MCOs) operate with criteria by which to guide and make clinical treatment decisions: for admission to treatment and treatment planning, level of treatment intensity (inpatient hospitalization, partial hospitalization, day treatment, outpatient treatment, etc.), change in treatment intensity (moving from a more intense to a less intense treatment level or the reverse), as well as discharge planning and follow-up. These criteria evolved largely through a combination of the available empirical clinical literature and the distillation and codification of clinical experience. A record of the clinical treatment decision in terms of meeting criteria remains part of the patient's chart and may be reviewed to justify or evaluate the clinical decision. Often these may not necessarily be quantifiable as a number but often include at least a record of the evaluator's estimate of the global assessment of functioning (a GAF score).

From one perspective these kinds of data represent a rich mine of empirical evidence about service delivery and clinical decisions in the everyday world of service delivery. These data can be tapped with varying degrees of difficulty depending on the sophistication of the MIS and software systems and the willingness of the MCO to devote resources for the provision of data. The potential, although descriptive, provides a basis for examining, retrospectively, variations in service delivery as a function of provider characteristics, system characteristics, patient characteristics, and clinical characteristics. Descriptive analyses, often under the umbrella of a Quality Assurance (QA) or Quality Improvement function, enable clinical benchmarking so that one can say, for example, that "in general, marital or couples therapy may take 4-8 outpatient sessions, unless there are other complicating factors, e.g., substance abuse." In turn this descriptive summary serves as an empirical "guideline" or "standard" by which to define and then evaluate variations in treatment. Coupled with ongoing "adverse incident" and mortality/morbidity audits (retrospective reviews of what went "wrong"), these strategies represent a tool for altering practices and the service delivery process.

Outcome Data

The question that is implicit and empirically unanswered in the descriptive, QA, orientation above is whether or not the treatment provided resulted in improvement for the patient along dimensions that matter to patients. Traditionally, we assume that patients aren't discharged from treatment until they have improved to a point that further treatment is not indicated—and traditionally we have relied on the service provider's judgment. Only recently have we moved to asking for some form of empirical, quantifiable, objective evidence about the effect of treatment on the patient. There is a mix of currents that have moved the field in the direction of outcome measurement in the everyday world of service delivery (cf. Pallak & Cummings, 1994). In effect empirical outcome results may close the loop in understanding what combinations of variables (above) are most effective in producing positive outcomes for patient and under what conditions those combinations may be effective.

Ideally, MCOs collect outcome data at each point that involves a change in treatment intensity, thereby providing an empirical basis for the decision in addition to the more traditional clinical process controls noted above. In general, MCOs operate in a "continuum of care" environment with patients moving through declining (or increasing) levels of care intensity determined by more quantifiable empirical results. Decisions to move patients from one level to another can then be empirically justified by professionals with the MCO and positive patient outcomes form the basis for treatment guidelines and standards. In general, and perhaps too idealistic, this approach may be viewed as an outcomes based treatment management system driven mainly by empirical data that permit continuing refinement of the system.

There are a variety of outcomes measures that may be adapted for use in service delivery systems. Unlike a research environment, there is little time available in an MCO setting for elaborate measures of patient functioning (cf. Pallak & Cummings, 1994). However there are a variety of simple measures of functioning and well-being available that work well in service delivery settings. Many of these have sophisticated psychometric bases as well as non-patient norms based on thousands of individuals. Thus in ten minutes pretreatment one can obtain a reliable and fairly accurate of patient functioning in relation to normed non-patients equated for age, gender, etc. variables.

For example, in one recent study that we conducted, patients presenting for outpatient treatment filled out the SF-36 (Short Form-36 items) developed by John Ware and his colleagues from the Rand Health Insurance Study. The SF-36 measures eight dimensions of physical and mental-emotional functioning and patients ranked at the eighth percentile of the national normed distribution of non-patients. At the end of treatment patients ranked at the 28th percentile of the same distribution—an improvement that was reliably different from zero change. Further, we collected responses to the instrument three months after treatment completion and found no reliable change from end of treatment to the follow-up—patients neither improved nor deteriorated after treatment.

We did not have a baseline to assess whether a change from the eighth to the 28th percentile may have simply been due to the passing of time (rather than to treatment) or to hypothetical unreliability of the instrument. However, the results from the end of treatment to follow-up provided an estimate of change due to unreliability and a baseline for evaluating the reliability of change during treatment. The change obtained during treatment (8%-ile to 28%-ile) was reliably greater than from the change from end of treatment to follow-up.

This simple one-shot case study illustrates some of the problems generally inherent in data collection in an ongoing service delivery system. In addition to constraints on the patient's time (although patients may volunteer more time if responding to questionnaires is presented as part of the treatment process), it is usually impossible to develop an "untreated" condition ethically, it is virtually impossible to randomly assign patients to condition (except perhaps for very small scale studies), and mailed out surveys may have low return rates. However, there are strategies to deal with at least some of these (these situations may be viewed as challenges to creativity).

By far the single challenge is inertia within the MCO to provide the resources for large scale administration of questionnaires beyond those designed to measure patient satisfaction. On the other hand, the sophistication of optical scanning systems and the supporting software coupled with paper-less charting systems should make it easier to conduct outcomes studies on a more routine basis.

Further Impetus for Outcomes Research: An Evolving System

The move to comprehensive care management based on outcome results is also fostered by shifts to capitated payment systems. In these, the MCO contracts to provide clinical services to a defined population for a negotiated fee. As a result, successful MCOs will need to refine and track estimates of morbidity, resource utilization, and clinical effectiveness of alternative treatment procedures. Without these outcomes based efforts an MCO cannot easily assure financial viability under a specified contract. In addition, echoing concerns from the past about capitation arrangements and incentives to profit by truncating treatment, clients and payers are increasing their requests for evidence that services are safe, clinically appropriate and clinically effective in producing positive outcomes for their defined population.

The twin motives of financial and clinical efficacy are motivating MCOs and their providers toward more comprehensive outcomes management systems. These motives will foster an emphasis on clinical strategies for prevention, maintaining wellness, early intervention and for illness management.

In essence a new from of service delivery has evolved and continues to evolve with implications for practice standards and treatment guidelines for service delivery and clinical training in psychology. The potential size of a national data base within managed care frees the field in part from reliance on randomized controlled experiments as the "gold standard" for understanding treatment effectiveness. Although descriptive, the inclusion of outcomes measurement enables a close look at empirically defined variables related to treatment outcome. The theoretical interpretation of the meaning of those variables and the relationship to outcomes may then be rigorously investigated in standard experimental designs. Each kind of data (descriptive-correlational, experimental) provide an anchor by which to interpret the other in the context of service delivery and treatment effectiveness.

As MCOs continue to evolve and as capitation strategies become the modal system for financing care and service delivery, psychologists have major roles to play. The need to define and evaluate treatment standards and guidelines can be met through a process of examining data bases (as above) from the perspective of both what is clinically relevant and what outcomes obtain under what conditions. The concept of defining and refining "best practices" in terms of outcomes for patients means collaborating in the collection and interpretation of outcome data. It also means collaboration in the interpretations of variations in patient, therapist and treatment process variables related to patient outcome. While few of these issues may be encountered or confronted by those who remain in a solo practice setting, these issues are evolving rapidly and are being shaped by other players in the field of service delivery. Psychology as a field and psychologists within the field have always had an appreciation for the necessity of empirical clinical data as a grounding for service delivery. In this sense psychologists do not have to discard their empirical roots in the process of developing approaches to standards and guidelines. Managed care represents an opportunity to document the clinical effectiveness of what we do in terms of outcomes for patients and outcomes research strategies. Regardless of one's orientation it is still possible at least to administer questionnaires in one's own service delivery setting as part of larger overall efforts to evaluate what is best for patients. Investigations of the cause and effect for variations in patient outcome relate to our traditional theoretical and conceptual issues in the field and to the evolution of empirically based and documented treatment strategies.

References

Curtiss, F. R. (1989). Managed health Care. *American Journal of Hospital Pharmacy, 46,* 742-63.

Pallak, M. S., & Cummings, N. A. (1994). Outcomes research in managed behavioral health care: Issues, strategies and trends. In S. A. Shueman, W. C. Troy, & S. L. Mayhugh (Eds.), *Managed behavioral healthcare: An industry perspective.* Springfield, IL: Charles C. Thomas, 1994.

Tischler, G. L. (1990a). Utilization management of mental health services by private third parties. *American Journal of Psychiatry, 147,* 967-973.

Tischler, G. L. (1990b). Utilization management and the quality of care. *Hospital and Community Psychiatry, 41,* 1099-1102.

Discussion of Pallack

Managed Care: Some Implications for Practice and Training

Stephen R. Reisman
ServiceNet, Inc.

The movement toward managed health services, which gathered momentum in the mid-1980s, was a clear response to ever rising health costs (Goran, 1991). For at least one hundred million Americans, it is no longer possible to obtain mental health services without first passing through some form of managed care approval (Oss, 1994). The pressure to be efficient and regularly justify one's work has been manifested in increased oversight and demands for accountability that have caused discomfort for many mental health providers. One need only glance at the newsletters of any state or national organization of psychologists, psychiatrists or social workers to appreciate the extent of concern and emotion among professional groups.

The first of two challenges which emerge in the current changing situation is to find practical and valid ways to measure the effects of psychotherapeutic interventions. The second is to be creative in devising and empirically validating more effective methods for treating specific disorders. Under managed care systems, providers will find a requirement to demonstrate that there is a positive result attributable to treatment. The social context for such expectations in the business community is enhanced by the growth of the Total Quality Management movement (Deming, 1986) which emphasizes the responsibility to satisfy the customer and to quantify all aspects of performance. Clearly, the burden on clinical psychology is to find ways to be responsive to the practical needs of the client population, effective and efficient in the delivery of services that meet the goals of the payer, and accountable to all for cost effective results.

In order to measure the success of therapeutic interventions it will be necessary to agree on some definitions of progress. Those measures finally chosen will constitute *de facto* operational definitions of mental health in the United States. Treatments and practitioners with the greatest success in producing positive scores on these measures will be favored in this Darwinian struggle for survival. It is not clear who will have the opportunity to set those standards. Those groups that do not actively participate in these decisions, or are excluded, are likely to feel imposed upon.

The choice and number of standardized measures selected has important practical and financial ramifications. How many different instruments would be needed to provided useful outcomes measures for all client populations across all diagnoses in the DSM IV? It is unlikely that the same measurement instrument would be appropriate for autistic children, substance abusing adults, long-term psychotic clients and functioning adults with adjustment disorders. Imagine a provider organization with a wide range of client populations, therapeutic services and payers. If each payer required a different measurement tool in all or some populations, the total number of instruments used in a given organization could be substantial. If payers further required different methods for reporting the data gathered, then the number of clerical procedures and the costs involved in completing them would rapidly increase beyond reasonable limits.

We may take the example of a group practice or community mental health agency that serves four distinct populations: children, adults, elders and mentally retarded adults. Assume that these people fall into only five diagnostic groups. Finally, let there be only five major payers. If each payer required a different measurement instrument for each population and diagnostic group, the provider organization would need to sort out one hundred different assessment possibilities. The example ignores the likelihood that payers will choose among a few relatively broad instruments, but it is conservative in estimating the number of possible client and diagnostic categories. The example also does not take into account the probability that some payers will require electronic reporting of raw data, some will want summary data in quarterly reports and others will set different requirements. Given the demands and cost of managing such complex situations, it is not surprising to hear predictions of the extinction of individual private practice. Such costs would be an unnecessary burden added to the overhead of providing behavioral health care services. Payers in at least one state, Massachusetts, have recognized the problem and joined together in an effort to make their requests for information compatible (Perlman, 1994).

Perhaps the most unsettling aspect of scrutiny from outside the profession is the probability that long accepted techniques will be questioned, resulting in the need for creativity and change. The focus of attempts at containing costs is not so much on the control of individual psychotherapy as on the reduction of inpatient days. One day in the hospital may well cost more than an entire course of short-term therapy. Alternatives to hospitalization proliferate and offer opportunities for research and creative treatment. These alternatives often provide treatment at a daily rate of one quarter to one half of the per diem hospital cost and complete their work in far fewer days. Clients served return to normal life settings earlier with less disruption of their day-to-day routines. The design and evaluation of treatment alternatives is an area in which the scientist practitioner may make useful contributions. Consideration of future needs suggests avenues for graduate training. We may look at some currently used treatment alternatives:

Mobile Evaluation Teams: One or more workers is available to respond to crises in order to provide triage service. Evaluations may be performed by individuals with varying levels of training, including paraprofessionals who remain in touch with centralized supervisors. Services may be provided on site, at an individual's home, or in community settings such as hospital emergency rooms or police stations.

In Home Crisis Stabilization: Workers are provided to come into a home to help manage a crisis. Individual or family therapists may also provide services in non-traditional settings.

Short-Term Respite: Respite may be provided for several hours, days or weeks. This service is usually provided in a community residential setting. Respite clients may be able to resume work or school before returning home and often can continue seeing their usual care providers.

Supportive Housing and Employment: Clients remain in their own homes and jobs. They receive supportive assistance from para-professional workers in order to maintain those functions. The amount of support varies according to needs of the client.

Case Management: Professional and para-professional workers provide support, education, and therapeutic services to individuals and their families as it is needed. The goal is to keep the client functioning as successfully as possible in the community. The case manager works with the client on the full range of daily activities needed for independent living.

Total Care: The treating organization provides all required clinical services for a predetermined rate. This may include any of the alternatives listed above as well as more traditional therapy and medication. The effect is to coordinate treatment, limit cost and transfer responsibilities for decision making from the managed care organization to the treating organization. This service is often sought out by managers for cases that have frequent crises and use more than their share of management time.

These treatments sound very little like the techniques of individual or group psychotherapy which form a substantial part of graduate education in clinical psychology. They more closely resemble what many students experience while on internships in hospital settings. However, as the number of hospital admissions and lengths of stay continue to decrease, the pressures to change traditional treatments will increase. Therapeutic intervention will need to be evaluated on its efficacy in achieving functional change. Although many clients may continue to desire basic change in personality, they will have to pay for it themselves. Empirically minded practitioners will be able to work toward finding interventions that are useful in reaching well defined goals. The challenge is to produce clinical psychologists with a thorough understanding of pathological conditions and an enthusiasm for flexibility and creativity.

References

Deming, W. E. (1986). *Out of the Crisis.* Cambridge, MA: MIT Press.

Goran, M. J. (1991). Managed mental health and group health insurance. In S. Feldman (Ed.), *Managed mental health services* (pp. 27-44). Springfield, IL: Charles Thomas.

Oss, M. (1994). Industry statistics: Managed behavioral health programs widespread among insured Americans. *Open Minds, 8,* 3.

Perlman, S. (1994). *Measuring outcomes of mental health services: A statement of principles by Mental Health Corporations of Massachusetts.* A paper prepared for Mental Health Corporations of Massachusetts, Boston, MA.

Footnote

Send correspondence to Stephen Reisman, ServiceNet, Inc., 129 King Street, Northampton MA 01060-3258.

Chapter 5

Compliance with Standards of Care: Evidence from Medical Research

Kathleen E. Grady
Massachusetts Institute of Behavioral Medicine, Inc.

If there were standards of care, if they magically already existed, what would happen? Would they be followed? Would some parts be followed and others ignored? Or would some clinicians follow the standards and others completely ignore them? How would standards of care be enforced? How would they even be monitored? These difficult questions deserve much more attention than can be given here. However, it is important to begin.

The question has been raised in several contexts as to whether a "psychological Food and Drug Administration (FDA)" is needed to review and approve psychological treatments the way the FDA reviews drugs and devices. Recently I have become involved in auditing clinical drug trials to determine, prior to an FDA final application for approval, whether the trial meets scientific standards of good clinical practice (GCP). I shall discuss my experiences auditing these trials, providing some background on how clinical trials and the FDA work. The mistakes, misjudgments and misconduct in clinical trials and the reasons for them provide one example of the kinds of problems that arise when relatively rigorous standards are imposed on a clinical practice. Enforcement of standards of care in medicine is then briefly considered. Finally, some data about physician adoption of a single, simple standard of care will be drawn from a current research study. Despite the many differences between psychological and medical practices, these various kinds of evidence may shed some light on what life would be like if there were standards of psychological care.

Background of the FDA and Clinical Drug Trials

The Food and Drug Administration was created after the sensational "muckraking" at the turn of the century with books like Upton Sinclair's expose of the meat-packing industry, *The Jungle*. The 1906 original law was amended in 1938 to add that drugs had to be safe after 100 people died because of a single drug, sulfanilamide (diethylene glycol) manufactured by Massengill/Tenn. The thalidomide tragedy in 1962 led to another major change in the law. At the time of the initial reports from Europe of thalidomide's teratogenic effects, the FDA believed that only 40-50 physicians in the United States were working with the drug. However, as the tragedy unfolded, they found that 1,250 physicians had dispensed 2.5 million tablets to more than 20,000 patients. The law was then changed to require submission to the FDA of protocols for the testing of new drugs *before* testing is begun, close monitoring of the studies by the sponsor (i.e., the drug company), and immediate reports of any alarming findings. Throughout the 1960's and 1970's, the FDA developed and refined standards and inspected manufacturing and laboratory practices (Pharmaceutical Manufacturer's Association, 1994).

It was not until 1977 that the Bioresearch Monitoring Program was begun with the understanding that the FDA would ensure the quality and integrity of data submitted to the agency in support of the safety and efficacy of products. Over the next few years, regulations were proposed for the conduct of the research, its monitoring, and the necessary qualifications of clinical investigators. In general, the gold standard for a research method that has evolved is the placebo-controlled clinical trial. In 1980, the Institutional Review Board (IRB) regulations for the protection of human subjects were finalized.

The FDA's ability to review thoroughly data about the safety and efficacy of a drug is therefore relatively recent. The compliance program has the responsibility of determining the scientific validity of the studies submitted in support of products pending approval. It is not a small task to assure that a drug or device works, that it is both safe and effective. After successful completion of initial studies, including animal studies, the drug sponsor must perform a series of studies in humans, i.e., clinical trials. The process is lengthy and expensive.

Clinical trials occur in three phases. Phase I studies are basically safety studies, involving what is called "the first trial in man [*sic*]," that is, the first time this drug is ingested by a human being. A few healthy subjects take the drug under closely monitored circumstances, usually for a few days, sometimes for as long as two weeks. What the investigator is watching for are "adverse events." "Serious adverse events (SAE's)" include death. More commonly, adverse events can include a generalized toxic reaction, such as nausea, vomiting, dizziness, etc., and specific reactions to this drug that might be predicted based on the preceding animal studies or the nature of the drug. For example, a topical treatment may lead to burning, itching, rashes or another localized reaction. Adverse events are to be reported immediately to the sponsor and the FDA.

Phase II studies involve a clinical trial of perhaps 30-60 subjects for a somewhat longer period. These subjects are usually patients of the type to be treated with the drug. The trial therefore more closely approximates intended use. Again, this is basically a safety study and may include tests of different doses. At the same time, measures of efficacy may be developed and tested to see if there is any evidence that the drug is doing what it is supposed to do, including having predicted effects on intervening variables. Serious adverse events may be different for patients who have the condition or who are taking concomitantly other medications which may interact with the new drug being investigated.

Phase III studies are the efficacy studies, the large clinical trials that may involve a hundred sites and principal investigators in Europe as well as the United States.

The subjects are patients, and the principal investigators are practicing physicians who are sometimes, but not always, affiliated with a major research institution. Some of the investigators are primarily community physicians of the type who will be prescribing the drug should it ultimately be marketed. These trials often last a year. They provide the primary data concerning the effectiveness of the drug, as well as confirming its safety in the less structured environment of clinical practice. These are the trials where physician compliance can become a problem.

Mistakes, Misjudgments, and Misconduct in Clinical Trials

The job of the auditor is not to examine each datum collected but to recreate the clinical trial as it occurred at a particular site, to follow the flow of events for the study as a whole and for a sample of subjects, and to compare what happened with what was supposed to happen given the protocol and guidelines for good clinical practice. The goal is to determine whether the trial supports the conclusions (Mackintosh, 1993). Applying logic, common sense, and a few rules of thumb (e.g., were any subjects enrolled on a Sunday?) inevitably uncovers gaps, omissions, discrepancies and questions. Determining whether these constitute a mistake, a misjudgment or misconduct is not straightforward. Gross misconduct, such as inventing subjects and fabricating data, is relatively rare but somewhat easier to identify than more subtle errors and problems.

Errors in clinical trials tend to occur in just a few areas. Many errors occur in the inclusion/exclusion criteria for subject participation in the trial. There may be no documentation that they have the condition which is supposed to respond to treatment. They may have comorbidity which is excluded because its signs or symptoms may confuse the interpretation of clinical outcomes. They may be taking proscribed concomitant medications that can interfere with or mask the effects of the drug being tested. Or they may violate some other criterion such as age. Whichever criterion is violated, the result is that subjects are in the study who should not be and from whom appropriate generalizations cannot be made.

Another common error is a failure to adequately protect subjects' rights. The Informed Consent reading level may be too high. There may be no procedures for illiterate or non-English-speaking subjects. The Informed Consent may not be signed prior to receiving the drug. State-mandated specific procedures for HIV testing may not have been followed. In the worst case, the subject's signature may be forged, and there is no informed consent at all. Although these are ethical violations, they can have scientific consequences. They may affect who is involved in the study and their ability to participate fully and according to protocol.

Errors of omission are evidenced in a failure to collect completely all the data required for the trial. There may be no before *and* after laboratory work when a baseline measure is crucial for evaluating post-treatment levels. There may no follow-up for out-of-range laboratory values although a serious side-effect may be indicated. Weight and blood pressure may be recorded on sticky notes with no patient name, no date, and no way to use the data for the trial. Data recorded on the case report form for the study may not be verifiable by data in the patient chart.

The most serious errors occur in the identification and reporting of adverse events. Distinguishing what is a serious adverse event, an adverse event, or merely a side effect can be a murky judgment, which is left up to the investigators and the drug company. Protocols cannot always cover every case, and often the differences between a side-effect and an adverse event are a matter of degree.

Any of these errors can compromise the conclusions of the study. All of them can affect the scientific basis for concluding that a drug is safe and effective. Although some errors are to be expected, ideally they would be random and would not skew the results. However, there appear to be biases at work that are inherent in clinical practice, in the selection of people who agree to be clinical investigators, and in the incentive structure of clinical trials. These are biases of compassion, expertise, and greed.

Compassion is necessary for clinical practice but can be an impediment to scientific objectivity. When the clinician has very sick patients for whom he/she can do no more, when other treatments are unsuccessful, when other drugs do not work or have unacceptable side effects, the clinical trial offers the patient (and the clinician) some hope. The patient may therefore be enrolled in the study although ineligible for treatment according to the protocol. However, simple enrollment does not guarantee treatment with the experimental drug. The patient might be randomized to the placebo arm of the study. To ensure that the patient is given the drug, the clinician must "break the blind" of a double-blind study and assign the patient to the treatment condition.

A recent, well-publicized example of breaking the eligibility rules occurred in the National Surgical Adjuvant Breast Cancer Project (NSABP). This project was not a single trial but a series of trials over many years that involved a group of investigators coordinated by Dr. Bernard Fisher at the University of Pittsburgh. Dr. Poisson of St. Luc's hospital in Montreal enrolled ineligible patients whose breast cancer was diagnosed too long ago or in other ways violated the inclusion/exclusion criteria for the trial. Dr. Poisson explained his reasoning in a letter to the editor of the *New England Journal of Medicine* (Poisson, 1994):

> I believed I understood the reasons behind the study rules, and I felt that the rules were meant to be understood as guidelines and not necessarily followed blindly. My sole concern at all times was the health of my patients. I firmly believed that a patient who was able to enter into an NSABP trial received the best therapy and follow-up treatment. For me, it was difficult to tell a woman with breast cancer that she was ineligible to receive the best available treatment because she did not meet 1 criterion out of 22, when I knew that this criterion had little or no intrinsic oncologic importance (p. 1460).

Dr. Poisson reveals another common reason for deviation from a protocol when he judges a criterion as unimportant. Clinicians who serve as principal investigators are usually specialists or experts in the field or condition under study. They may therefore disagree with the inclusion/exclusion criteria. They may say or think things like "I would give this type of drug if the enzyme level were only ____." "My years

of clinical experience tell me that this drug could work just as well on recurrent
_____." "I don't think that having diabetes would matter." "What difference
could Tylenol or Mylanta make?" These experts may violate the protocol based on
their own clinical judgment. This is an honest disagreement. Not listing the
concomitant medications or in other ways falsifying the data sent to the sponsor and
then to the FDA, however, is fraud (Kracov, 1995).

Another kind of expert bias is based on what the clinician thinks he/she knows.
Clinicians, like other members of society, may stereotype certain people. These
stereotypes can influence who is enrolled in the study. For example, they may think
older women are chronic complainers, therefore not really sick, and therefore not
eligible to be in the study. They may think minorities will not follow instructions,
not be compliant, and are therefore not eligible to be in the study. The under
representation of women and ethnic minorities in studies of all types is a serious
problem for generalizing study findings to the population at large. The federal
government now has regulations about the inclusion of women and ethnic
minorities in clinical studies. After submission, the FDA may require additional
studies to ensure adequate inclusion of women and minorities. Clinicians who,
because of their own stereotypes, do not sample women or ethnic minorities in the
same way as white males can seriously compromise study findings.

Greed is an obvious but often overlooked motive that should always be
considered when money is involved. Principal Investigators are paid for participation in the trial. If they can be paid for participation and actually have nurses do all
the work, they save money. If they get a bonus for minority patients, they will get
more minority patients but more protocol violations as well, especially with regard
to eligibility. The scandal in the breast cancer trials unearthed the fact that
participating institutions and clinicians were paid based on the number of patients
enrolled. Perhaps Dr. Poisson was just being compassionate toward his patients by
enrolling them in the trial when they were ineligible, or perhaps he wanted to be the
largest contributor of patients (which he was) earning him not only the most money
but coveted co-authorship on several papers with his name immediately following
those of the principal investigator and the epidemiologist (e.g., Fisher et al., 1989).

Although greed may operate as a significant negative bias at the investigator
level, it can be a positive force at the sponsor level. Better clinical trials save drug
companies money, because they are more likely to be approved by the FDA, and the
new drug can be brought to market earlier. In this case, time is definitely money. It
is therefore in the drug sponsor's interest to monitor and audit clinical trials carefully
and to impose standards strictly.

Enforcing Standards of Care

The experience of attempting to enforce standards of care in medicine may
prove instructive for psychology's efforts. A recent series on medical malpractice in
The Boston Globe (O'Neill et al., 1994) highlights the mechanisms and results of
enforcement attempts. Although this was not a scientific study, the method was
impressive. The investigators hand-pulled from court records every case of medical

malpractice in the last 10 years, over 1,000 cases. They also obtained data from the licensing board and the largest malpractice insurer in Massachusetts, a quasi-public entity.

They found a surprising and heartening result. The insurance data showed that a small number of doctors are responsible for almost all of the malpractice claims. Since 1988, about 7% of the physicians have accounted for all of the payout to damaged clients and 10% of the physicians have accounted for all of the claims. Most of the cases did not involve high-risk or esoteric medicine, as doctors frequently argue, but rather stem from basic errors in routine procedures, misdiagnosis or delayed treatment. Frequently sued physicians were more likely to have attended foreign medical schools and were less likely to be board certified in their specialties, usually obstetrics or surgery.

However, all of the malpractice cases filed only represent a small sample of possible malpractice cases because most instances never make it into the court system. A landmark study in New York by the Harvard School of Public Health found that less than 2% of patients injured by negligence file a malpractice claim and only about half of these receive any compensation (Localio et al., 1991). In the *The Globe* study, the rate of compensation for suits filed was even lower. Insurers paid no money in 62% of all malpractice claims filed and settled 37%, paying usually modest amounts with the terms nearly all cloaked in secrecy. Only 1% of the suits went to trial, and of these, 91% were won by doctors.

The Harvard study concludes that malpractice litigation is of limited usefulness in promoting high quality medical care. In fact, they imply, its only value is in comparison to other poor alternatives.

> The results demonstrate that the civil-justice system only infrequently compensates injured patients and rarely identifies and holds health care providers accountable for substandard medical care. Although malpractice litigation may fulfill its social objectives crudely, support for its preservation persists in part because of the perception that other methods of ensuring a high quality of care and redressing patients' grievances have proved to be inadequate. The abandonment of malpractice litigation is unlikely unless credible systems and procedures, supported by the public, are instituted to guarantee professional accountability to patients (p. 250).

In Massachusetts, the chief alternative to the court system is the Board of Registration in Medicine. It licenses and monitors physicians. The *Boston Globe* study found that the regulatory system is in a shambles (O'Neill et al., 1994). The Board of Registration is ranked 45th out of 50 states in disciplining physicians. Deficient doctors rarely lose their licenses, never lose their malpractice insurance, and are passed from one hospital to another. The Board does not even know who the repeatedly sued physicians are. Four out of ten malpractice suits are not even reported to the Board as required by law. The insurers know which physicians are being sued, but they shroud everything in secrecy. The quasi-public Massachusetts Professional Insurers Association, which insures two-thirds of the physicians, is dominated by physicians and hospital executives, and as they told *The Globe*, they just pay bills and process paper. They do not get involved in discipline.

Interestingly, discipline for complaints other than malpractice is much more common than discipline for malpractice. Although malpractice is the most frequent kind of consumer complaint filed, only 5% of 230 license restrictions in the period studied were for malpractice while 61% were for narcotics, impairment, or sex abuse. One notorious obstetrician-gynecologist, who was sued eight times since 1985 and settled five of the cases, never had his license threatened until he was accused of improper sexual conduct with patients, touching the breast of one and asking improper sexual questions of another. For those violations, he was temporarily suspended from practice by the Board of Registration.

Indeed, the Board of Registration has sanctioned 26 of 39 psychiatrists accused of sexual abuse in the last decade, an astonishingly high proportion compared to other physicians and other complaints. However, and here's the catch, even without a license, psychiatrists continue to see patients simply billing themselves as "therapists." And neither the medical board nor any other state board has any authority over "therapists." Since the punishment is so toothless, many victims go directly to civil court where they are very successful: patients walked away with money in 38 of 40 cases with an average payment of $417,000 per claim. *The Globe* claims that this difference in success rate is because sexual contact is clear and, once proved, is clearly a breach of standards.

A Field Examination of a Standard of Care

This project concerns a simple, well-publicized standard of care for women over 50 years of age: annual mammography[1]. Despite some disagreement about frequency for younger women, this standard is endorsed by every major health organization. Nonetheless, most women over 50 years of age do not receive annual mammograms. In surveys of women, they say that a major reason is that their physicians do not refer them. In surveys of physicians, they say that their patients do not follow through on the referrals and obtain mammograms. This study was designed to track both physician referral and patient follow-through to determine where the slippage is occurring. At the same time, some simple behavioral methods are being tested to attempt to increase referral rates: chart reminders and feedback are being tested in a randomized experimental design.

To conduct this study, more than 100 community-based, primary care physicians were recruited in Springfield, MA and Dayton, OH by myself and my colleague, Dr. Jeanne Lemkau at Wright State University. Excluded from the study were university- and hospital-based practices, HMO's, and practices with more than six physicians. The goal was to reach physicians in solo or in small group practices, who may be more likely to serve older women and less likely to receive continuing medical education. Following the model of drug company representatives, physicians were brought lunch and, while eating, were told about the study and given information to use in persuading their reluctant patients to have mammograms. The response of physicians to the project was surprisingly positive. About two-thirds of eligible physicians met with us to discuss the project, and three-quarters of them became participants.

Responses to an initial questionnaire indicated that these physicians knew the recommendation, and, for the most part, they agreed with it. Only a minority disagreed, but the direction of the disagreement was always toward more screening for younger women and less screening for older women. Their self-reported referral rates reflected these disagreements: referral rates consistently declined over age groups. Examining these referral rates by physician characteristics showed that the only significant main effects were related to being foreign medical graduates and to not being board certified in a specialty, both of which were associated with lower referral rates.

These results are positive in at least two ways. First, they suggest that the standard is operating appropriately. A standard ought to over-ride differences in practice that could be related to practitioner sex, age, length of time in practice, etc. A standard should result in some uniformity of practice. Second, the variables that are related to differences in practice are differences in training. These differences in training could potentially be changed either at the source or through remedial education, i.e., continuing medical education.

Conclusions

Several conclusions emerge from these disparate data sources. The evidence suggests that most clinicians will comply voluntarily with standards to a reasonable extent. The success of large, even huge, clinical trials which involve practicing physicians support this conclusion. Clinical trials impose a very rigid set of standards on a clinical practice, and yet, to a very great extent, these standards are met. The malpractice findings that a small proportion of physicians account for most of the malpractice suits also support the idea that standards will generally be followed.

When clinicians do not comply, there are some identifiable factors accounting for that non-compliance:

- There are some clinicians who are incompetent or impaired. The profession has to figure out how to deal with them and/or support appropriate regulatory bodies.
- There are some deficiencies in training which perhaps can be remedied through continuing education. Being a graduate of a foreign medical school and not being board certified in a specialty are both factors which appear to be related to substandard practice.
- There are biases and errors of compassion where clinicians honestly believe that whatever is being done or not being done will benefit the patient. The perceived needs of the individual patient are placed above more general requirements of science or practice.
- There are conflicts of expertise in which clinicians honestly and thoughtfully disagree with the standard-setters. These disagreements can lead to dialogue and perhaps even a change in standards.

♦ If the incentives are structured so that outcomes like volume of patients are rewarded, then greed will work against the even-handed application of standards. However, just as there is a strong financial press for good clinical trials, there could be a strong financial press for psychological treatments of proven safety and efficacy.

The generalizability from the clinical practice of medicine to the clinical practice of psychology is clearly limited. Nonetheless, because models are so badly needed as we begin down this road, other professions must be examined. Medicine is far ahead of psychology in the establishment of its profession. Yet, an accepted method for the promulgation of standards of care has not been developed, and novel approaches are still being tested. Enforcement of standards of care is uneven and, in many cases, ineffective. However, broad-based voluntary compliance and individual commitments to professional standards support the need for continuing efforts. Setting and enforcing standards of care is a daunting but worthwhile professional responsibility.

References

Fisher, B., Redmond, C., Poisson, R., Margolese, R., Wolmark, N., Wickerham, L., Fisher, E., Deutsch, M., Caplan, R., Pilch, Y., et al. (1989). Eight-year results of a randomized clinical trial comparing total mastectomy and lumpectomy with or without irradiation in the treatment of breast cancer. *New England Journal of Medicine, 320*(13), 822-828.

Kracov, D. A. (1995). United States v. Garfinkel: Expanding criminal liability for clinical investigators. *Applied Clinical Trials, 4*(2), 34-38.

Localio, A. R., Lawthers, A. G., Brennan, T. A., Laird, N. M., Hebert, L. E., Peterson, L. M., Newhouse, J. P., Weiler, P. C., & Hiatt, H. H. (1991). Relation between malpractice claims and adverse events due to negligence. *New England Journal of Medicine, 325*(4), 245-251.

Mackintosh, D. R. (1993). Building quality assurance into clinical trials. *Applied Clinical Trials, 2*(4), 42-49.

O'Neill, G., Lehr, D., Mooney, B., Butterfield, B., Kong, D., & Douglass, K. (1994). Medical malpractice in Massachusetts. *The Boston Globe*, October 2-5, 1994.

Pharmaceutical Manufacturer's Association. (May, 1994). *History of the FDA*. Paper presented at Training Course on Good Clinical Practices, Princeton, New Jersey.

Poisson, R. (1994). Letter to the editor. *New England Journal of Medicine, 330*(20), 1460.

Footnote

1. "Mammography Referral in Primary Care," K. E. Grady, Principal Investigator, grant from the National Cancer Institute, R01 CA528243.

Discussion of Grady

Lessons from Medicine

Gregory J. Hayes
University of Nevada

Eighty-five years ago, Abraham Flexner published a report which, coupled with the increasingly stringent requirements of state licensing bodies, changed the face of medicine. The experience offers useful insights to those who now struggle to bring scientific standards to psychological practice.

At the turn of the century the American Medical Association (AMA) was in the process of reorganization. As part of that reorganization, it established the Council on Medical Education and set about the task of fulfilling its top priority: reforming medical schools. The first step was a survey, completed in 1906, which revealed an ugly truth: only half the medical schools in the United States (82 out of 160) merited an acceptable rating; 20% were deemed unsalvagable (Starr, 1982).

The next step was a more detailed analysis of medical education as it then existed, including recommendations for corrective action. As is true in many professions, physicians within the AMA were loath to take up arms, as it were, against their peers. In fact, the AMA ethics code expressly forbade it. Instead, the Council on Medical Education turned to the Carnegie Foundation for the Advancement of Teaching to conduct an independent investigation. The Carnegie Foundation in turn appointed Flexner, a young, independent thinking educator and researcher who, as it turned out, was to devote his distinguished career to educational reform (Starr, 1982).

The details of Flexner's investigation make interesting reading. The bottom line, however, is simply stated. Flexner recommended that only the best schools survive. Though the number of medical school closures he advocated was more extreme than was politically possible (he felt only 31 should remain, which would have left more than 20 states without a medical school), more than half did close. His report was an effective catalyst for change in part because his findings met with broad approval on the AMA Council on Medical Education. The Council in turn, with the financial assistance of the Rockefeller Foundation, aggressively sought nationwide acceptance by lobbying the licensing boards in each state. So effective was this effort that states voluntarily formed the Federation of State Medical Boards and "accepted the AMA's rating of medical schools as authoritative" (Starr, 1982, p. 121). Without federal involvement, a national system evolved in which the unacceptable medical schools—the most notorious of which were for-profit diploma mills—simply had no place to hide. Within little more than a decade no state could be found which would sanction their presence or license their graduates. Those schools that did survive in the years following the Flexner Report were either already part of a university or quickly affiliated with one. Each school offered a curriculum steeped in the scientific knowledge of the day. Each acknowledged the importance of research and sought to incorporate research into its mission, although at the time only the very best schools, with substantial and continued funding from the Rockefeller Foundation, could mount significant research agendas.

What Flexner recommended was harsh medicine. But he felt strongly that society was being denied the fruits of current scientific knowledge, that America was overrun with poorly trained physicians, and that fewer but better practitioners was the key to bringing the true benefits of medicine to the public (Flexner, 1910). As is true of psychology today, America at that time had some of the world's best medical schools and some of its worst. Flexner's success in closing the diploma mills and compelling mediocre, often underfunded schools to link with universities was on the whole a matter of timing. Scientific knowledge in medicine was mushrooming, building on the contributions of Lister, Pasteur, Koch, and others, as well as the availability of effective anesthesia, x-rays, the electrocardiogram, and other new manifestations of technology. Medicine, properly done, suddenly had much to offer. Yet most medical practitioners were too poorly trained to understand or make use of these advances. Something dramatic had to be done. The best trained of the profession attacked the issue through the vehicle of the AMA. Once they convinced state licensing boards of the value of higher standards in medical education, together they were able to squeeze the unacceptable medical schools out of existence.

Improved standards of medical education were a major step forward, but as Kathleen Grady's presentation has revealed, many problems still remain. In part the problems she cataloged—insufficient safety studies and violations of research protocols for reasons of expediency, compassion, or greed, for example—are a function of a remaining defect in medical education. In spite of Flexner's call for a strong scientific base for medical education—something that did indeed occur—most medical students are not actually trained as scientists. While they are exposed to a great deal of hard science and while a significant minority may involve itself in medical research, relatively few physicians can truthfully be called scientists. The number who have even taken a statistics class, for example, is surprising small (statistics is not a requirement for medical school admission and not part of most medical school curricula). Even fewer have a intimate, working knowledge of research methods or an appreciation of the sometimes subtle forms of bias which can distort research outcomes or cloud clinical decision-making.

As with most psychologists, physicians by and large are not interested in validating what they do. Rather they function primarily at an anecdotal level: "You don't have to tell me what to do, I've seen a thousand cases just like it." The pattern is hard to break. In spite of medical education standards, physicians have functioned autonomously—generally in solo practice until recent years—and without much in the way of standards for clinical practice. The bounds of acceptability governing how a particular medical problem might be evaluated and treated remain very broad.

While Flexner advocated sufficient flexibility to avoid stifling creativity, he would have been saddened to find that his efforts to improve medical education were not sufficient to assure adequate standards of clinical care. Times, however, are changing. Whether or not the federal government ever enacts a health reform measure, the current demand for greater efficiency and cost containment is spawning a huge managed care marketplace—fully 60% of Americans will be covered by some form of managed care by the turn of the century. This shift to managed care is reigning in the once nearly free-wheeling autonomy of the medical professional. While physicians may chafe under the bit of treatment protocols, outcome evaluations, and required justifications for atypical diagnostic or treatment regimens, the need to use the health care dollar wisely requires it. Health organizations and physicians alike are finding that they must indeed begin to validate what they do. This in turn is leading to the need to establish scientific standards of practice, at least in the managed care setting. In short, physicians are being asked for the first time to begin to function as both scientists and practitioners.

The creation of a scientific base for psychology has lagged behind that of medicine. But it has nonetheless made great strides in the past several decades—the work of many of AAAPP's members makes this point quite clearly. Psychology has reached a level in its development where it can offer effective diagnosis and treatment in many circumstances. But as was true of medicine 85 years ago, not all psychologists are competent to utilize this knowledge. Many lack the training and the skills. It is thus clear that the need for a Flexner-like report on psychological education in the United States (and perhaps Canada—Flexner studied both countries) is fast approaching. The growing pressures for maximizing quality and minimizing cost in the health and mental health arenas demand that we pursue practical, workable, yet scientific standards of clinical practice in both medicine and psychology without delay. With sufficient energy on the part of AAAPP and like-minded groups, the burgeoning managed care industry offers an immediate vehicle for this needed reform.

References

Flexner, A. (1910). *Medical education in the United States and Canada, bulletin no. 4*. New York: Carnegie Foundation for the Advancement of Teaching.

Starr, P. (1982). *The Social transformation of American medicine*. New York: Basic Books.

Chapter 6

The Dialectics of Science and Practice

Gerald C. Davison
University of Southern California

Arnold A. Lazarus
Rutgers University

Statement of the Issue

In this article we will underscore the continuing importance of clinical practice and the creative hunches derived therefrom. We will also address the limits of existing conceptual frameworks; the need for some kind of psychotherapy integration; the inevitable gaps between data and application; the inherent art that resides in any effort to apply general principles (a goal of science) to individual cases/situations; the personal and societal biases that color what we choose to study or treat; and the ways we choose to conceptualize our efforts and the problems to which they are directed (with the treatment of homosexuality used as a kind of case study).

The desirability of teaching and practicing only methods (and presumably also their underlying theoretical frameworks) that enjoy strong (how strong?) empirical support must, we would argue, be balanced off with the desirability and inevitability of testing new approaches and theories in applied contexts. Said another way, our current beliefs about empirically validated assessments and interventions are a long distance from what we should know if we are to restrict application and training to what is "empirically validated." This dialectical tension, we would argue, is healthy because it keeps advocates at both extremes working hard to prove the utility of their respective positions and, for some, it facilitates the creation of a maximally effective/efficient synthesis. This synthesis comes in the form of assessments and interventions that rely, whenever possible, on scientific data, but that also recognize the inherent limits of such knowledge, and appreciate the importance of constantly generating clinical hypotheses about how to address particular practical challenges.

We hope that this paper can serve as a useful counterpoint to those who would have us rely only on controlled laboratory-based (often analogue) research. We adopt the role of the scientifically-minded *clinician* who does not think that art or nondata-based innovations are bad. Indeed, we will argue that such innovations are central to effective empirically-based practice as well as to a relevant science of practice.

What Is Worth a Controlled Look?

It is our view that innovations by clinicians are the lifeblood of advances in the development of new therapeutic interventions. Whether or not attention is paid to a discovery–especially if that discovery borders on the unbelievable–depends in large measure on a prior *pro hominem* judgment we have made about the integrity and standing of the person making the claims. In our view, the major clinical discoveries are usually made by clinicians and then investigated by more experimentally-minded workers whose subsequent findings may persuade others that the previously unbelievable technique is worth a closer look.

The Limits of Controlled Looking

Many regard the laboratory and the clinic as opposite ends of a continuum. Research is said to be precise, controlled, and uncontaminated. The ideas that flow from applied settings are often regarded as woolly, riddled with bias, purely anecdotal, and even useless. Our abiding belief is that the path between the laboratory and the clinic is a two-way street (Woolfolk & Lazarus, 1979). As just stated, we aver that most new methods have come from the work of creative clinicians.

Scientists and practicing clinicians can each offer unique contributions in their own right and can conceivably open hitherto new and unsuspected clinical-experimental dimensions for research and practice. Certainly this is inherent to the scientist-professional model that we all purport to adhere to. *Ideas tested in the laboratory may be applied by the practitioner who, in turn, may discover important individual nuances that remain hidden from the laboratory scientist simply because the tight environment of the experimental testing ground makes it impossible for certain behaviors to occur or for certain observations to be made.* Conversely, ideas formulated in the clinic, provided that they are amenable to disproof, can send scientists scurrying off into laboratories and other research settings to subject the claims of efficacy to controlled tests. Cases in point will be cited further on.

While it is proper to guard against ex cathedra statements based upon flimsy and subjective evidence, it is a serious mistake to discount the importance of clinical experience per se. *There is nothing mysterious about the fact that repeated exposure to any given set of conditions makes the recipient aware of subtle cues and contingencies in that setting that elude the scrutiny of those less familiar with the situation. Clinical experience enables a therapist to recognize problems and identify trends that are usually beyond the perceptions of novices, regardless of their general expertise.* It is at this level that new ideas can come to the practitioner and often constitute breakthroughs that could not be derived from animal analogues or tightly controlled investigations. It is when we try new things that true innovators have the capacity to appreciate relationships that may go unnoticed by less resourceful and less observant workers. Different kinds of data and differing levels of information are obtained in the laboratory and the clinic. Each is necessary, useful, and desirable.

Clinical Innovation—What Do I Do Now?

Clinical innovation demands some form of experimentation, not in the sense of controlled inquiry but in the sense of trying out something that the clinician may never have done before and/or that lacks empirical validation (that the clinician is aware of). The actual experimental operations will usually be determined in part by the therapist's own theoretical orientation. Those with a proclivity for organic notions will obviously be more inclined to search for an effective combination of drugs or some other biological mode of intervention. The psychologically-oriented therapist will search for more effective psychosocial procedures. For instance, the cognitive therapist might look for newer and deeper mediating belief systems rather than for novel means of psychomotor expressiveness which those who espouse various experiential theories might be inclined to develop. Occasionally, a sense of desperation may lead a clinician to make a response that fits neither his/her theoretical preconceptions nor his/her more usual empirical resources. Many clinical advances are preceded by what we might term a *frustration-observation* sequence.

Let us consider the practitioner who has expended energy, time and effort to alleviate the suffering of a somewhat depressed but extremely demanding individual. The therapist has exhausted his or her fund of methods and techniques to no avail. Despite attempts to intervene at the level of family relationships, to tap the underlying guilts and hostilities, to assess for and alter biased thinking and dysfunctional beliefs, and to ply the patient with appropriate medication and inspiration, the net result is a demanding and threateningly dependent person whose desperation evokes anxiety, even annoyance, in the therapist. At this stage, the harassed and perplexed practitioner may advocate a course of action dictated solely by pragmatic convenience rather than by theoretical confidence. Out of keeping with her usual practices, she may confine the patient to bed for ten days and forbid any patient-therapist communication during this period. In all candor, the therapist's principal motive might simply be to "get the patient off my back" for a while. Ten days later, the patient is seen again and quite remarkably, reports feeling much better.

Unplanned or unexpected clinical improvements are often dismissed as "fortuitous events" or "spontaneous remissions," but the clinical innovator is the one who carefully notes a variety of possible cause-effect sequences and thus discovers therapeutic levers that less inquisitive colleagues are apt to overlook. A propitious clinical outcome might stimulate innumerable questions. In the hypothetical case already mentioned, one might simply pose the obvious question: "Of what value might enforced bed rest be for certain cases of depression?" The clinician might then look for an additional case presenting with similar problems and try the bed-rest intervention, this time not out of frustration but in an increasingly systematic effort to evaluate its potential effectiveness. If favorable changes are again observed, discussion at professional meetings and publication of case reports can set the stage for comparing experiences with other practitioners and conceivably stimulate experimentally minded clinical researchers to conduct clinical trials, where experimental design, in its most rigorous sense, becomes essential.

Borrowing Techniques—Benefits and Costs

Another important kind of innovation occurs when one borrows a technique from another orientation and incorporates it into one's own (different) conceptual framework and mode of practice. The complex epistemological issues surrounding this practice were the subject of a lively debate several years ago (Lazarus & Messer, 1991) and will not be repeated here. What is relevant to us is Messer's contention that, for example, when a non-Gestalt therapist like Lazarus uses the empty chair technique, the importation of that procedure into a different framework necessarily changes it enough so that it becomes something else. The technique may well effect improvement unanticipated by the founder and also lend itself to beneficial modifications and extensions. Such an eclectic maneuver represents an important source of clinical innovation.

The down side of this creative step is that any evidentiary justification of the original technique is probably not applicable to the new conceptual and applied setting. Simply stated, Perls' empty chair is not Lazarus's empty chair. But the advantage of this eclectic strategy is that one is necessarily creating a new technique both by virtue of how one *thinks* about it and by virtue of operational changes that are almost certainly going to be introduced (and we assume that the latter follow from the former or are at least correlated with it). (Some interesting complexities of this argument are contained in our later section on Eclecticism and Integration).

Some Relationships Between Theory and Practice

Many difficulties arise when different theorists endeavor to reconcile identical empirical facts within divergent theoretical models. The efficacy of the aforementioned "bed-rest hypothesis," if empirically established, will be explained organically by organicists, psychoanalytically by psychoanalysts, behaviorally by behaviorists, and so forth. All too often, a useful method will be employed by practitioners of different theoretical persuasions only if it can be "explained" according to their own favorite theories.

A common avenue of clinical experimentation consists of the development of techniques arising out of the therapist's predilections. This was the route followed by most of the psychoanalytic offshoots. Very often, although departing from his teachings and generating independent hypotheses of their own, Freud's former pupils did not deviate very widely in matters of technique—free association, dream interpretation, and analysis of transference retained their preeminence. The differences revolved around points of emphasis, timing, and content of interpretations. The respective deviations in technique were usually dictated by the different theoretical views that the Freudian revisionists espoused (although none of them systematically evaluated the effects of their innovations).

It stands to reason that a theorist who believes that emotional disturbances arise out of feelings of inferiority might develop and use different methods and techniques than a therapist who holds to a theory of unconscious sexual repression. The grave error is then to assume that if a technique proves successful in achieving its desired results, the process that gave rise to it is thereby necessarily strengthened or confirmed. For example, a Rankian might have reasoned that a depressed individual is actively reliving his birth trauma and craving for an intrauterine respite. Employing enforced bed rest as a symbolic return to the womb, and then discovering a clinical improvement in X number of patients, the committed Rankian is most likely to resist the notion that the clinical outcome might be unrelated to Rankian theories about the basic therapeutic process. *Techniques may, in fact, prove effective for reasons that do not remotely relate to the theoretical ideas that gave birth to them.*

There is another side to the theory-practice issue, however, that we feel is sometimes dismissed. When selecting therapeutic techniques it matters very much which theoretical notions a clinician espouses during the conduct of all clinical activities. For example, if one assumes that a given phobic reaction is best conceptualized as an anxiety-avoidance gradient, and furthermore is not secondary to a basic underlying condition which is the proper focus for treatment, one is more likely to employ, with confidence, a technique like desensitization or other exposure-based interventions (Wolpe, 1958). Conversely, if one holds to a view that all phobias are adaptive to the extent that they protect the individual from libidinal impulses that would be devastating were they allowed expression, it would seem likely that the clinician will choose to dwell upon the presumed unconscious conflicts and ignore the manifest phobia. This is not to say that only one particular theoretical stance will lead to a particular intervention; rather, it is to say that the "set" with which a clinician approaches a problem determines his/her own clinical behavior and his/her view of what occurs. This is one reason why we would advocate caution, tentativeness, and empirical testing when adopting any theoretical position. Often such positions harden commitments rather than facilitate discovery, which is the real purpose of theories.

Once one has assimilated certain theoretical constructs, it is necessary to apply these nomothetic principles to an idiographic case (Levine, Sandeen, & Murphy, 1992). Gordon Allport (1937) was identified with the so-called "nomothetic-idiographic controversy," but almost thirty years ago, Brendan Maher (1966) made a convincing argument against a necessary incompatibility between these two approaches. The application of a general principle in a particular case depends not only on a familiarity with the principle but also on an accurate assessment of the given case. Maher uses an engineering example to make his point: "In order to build a bridge over a certain river, we must know the details of the soil mechanics, water flow, prevailing winds, topography, traffic usage, availability of labor and materials, and so on. When we consider all these, the total picture might not be like any other bridge that has ever been built. Nevertheless, none of the principles or assumptions that go into the final decisions could be made in contradiction to the laws of physics, economics, and the like (p. 112)."

Some Characteristics of Case Studies as Related to Controlled Research

An awareness of what information can and cannot be derived from clinical work is critical in forging a synthesis between science and practice. As we articulated in a chapter in the first edition of the Bergin-Garfield handbook (Lazarus & Davison, 1971), there seem to us to be several characteristics unique to case studies that earn for them a firm place in psychological research.

1. A case study may cast doubt upon a general theory.
2. A case study may provide a valuable heuristic to subsequent and better-controlled research.
3. A case study may permit the investigation, although poorly controlled, of rare but important phenomena.
4. A case study can provide the opportunity to apply principles and notions in entirely new ways.
5. A case study can, under certain circumstances, provide enough experimenter control over a phenomenon to furnish "scientifically acceptable" information.
6. A case study can assist in placing "meat" on the "theoretical skeleton."

1. A Case Study May Cast Doubt Upon a General Theory

The successful handling of a particular case may underscore an important exception to a theory. For example, a given theory may hold that a certain kind of problem is untreatable. If a therapist succeeded in making an impact upon the recalcitrant problem, this would cast doubt upon the tenets of the theoretical viewpoint under consideration.

A particular theory may also predict that certain methods will prove antitherapeutic. Thus, when presenting (what we considered) successful case histories to two different audiences—one made up mainly of psychodynamic practitioners, the other comprising clinicians who espoused a family systems perspective—both groups predicted rapid relapse for different reasons. On one occasion, a senior clinician made the dire prediction that because certain essential psychodynamic underpinnings had not been addressed, the client would decompensate and end up in a mental hospital within three to five years. The fact that a 7-year follow-up revealed that the client in question had maintained and further extended his therapeutic gains brings some of these theoretical notions into serious question. Let it be remembered that only one clearly negative instance is sufficient to cast doubt on any general hypothesis.

2. A Case Study May Provide a Valuable Heuristic to Subsequent and Better-Controlled Research

Case studies are probably best known for suggesting new directions that can be pursued systematically by laboratory investigators. Examples are legion. The research in systematic desensitization that virtually exploded in the late 1960s into the 1970s would probably not have been undertaken without the clinical successes that were reported by Joseph Wolpe in the 1950s (e.g., Wolpe, 1958). The cognitive behavior therapy movement of the later 1970s that extends into the present is derived largely from the clinical reports and theoretical propositions first propounded by Ellis (1962) and Beck (1967). The more recent interest we see in making connections between experimental–and nonclinical–cognitive research and clinical research in psychopathology and intervention would, we suggest, never have become manifest without the clinical insights, hunches, and, yes, speculative clinical reports of practitioners like Ellis and Beck. Davison's own program of research in Articulated Thoughts in Simulated Situations (ATSS) (Davison, Robins, & Johnson, 1983) is another example of the way in which case studies can provide a valuable heuristic to subsequent and better-controlled research. For a review of findings of ATSS research, see Davison, Navarre, and Vogel (1995) and Davison and Neale (1994, p. 98). This research would never have been undertaken–for better or for worse!–had Davison not been working clinically for many years in a cognitive-behavioral framework.

3. A Case Study May Permit the Investigation, Although Poorly Controlled, of Rare but Important Phenomena

Human beings are capable of harming themselves and others in the most unusual ways. It is the practicing clinician who is most likely to encounter the vagaries and extremes of human conduct. It is doubtful if research in PTSD, for example, would be as vigorous and promising as it has been in recent years if not for scores of practitioners who, after two world wars and other major conflicts, had been commissioned by military authorities to do something about "shell shock," and "battle fatigue," which taught us a good deal about posttraumatic stress disorder.

4. A Case Study Can Provide the Opportunity to Apply Principles and Notions in Entirely New Ways

The clinical setting affords the opportunity and challenge to develop new procedures based on techniques and principles already in use. It is a truism that one will look in vain for the "textbook case." Clinicians are often faced with problems for which existing procedures seem unsuitable or insufficient. At the same time, certain aspects of a particular clinical problem may call for a new way of relating old principles and procedures to the resolution of the problem. This issue is not unrelated to Point 6 below, but it seems worthy of separate illustration here.

In one of our early case reports (Davison, 1966), some "tried and true" procedures were employed in a novel context. The use of deep-muscle relaxation has an extensive history in medicine, clinical psychology and psychiatry. The many and varied applications of relaxation probably share the implicit or explicit purpose of reducing subjective feelings of anxiety. In the case described below, it was possible to use relaxation in a different way to handle a problem that was hitherto considered unapproachable by relaxation training. Clinical innovation implies the discovery that "old" methods can be applied to new problems, as well as the discovery of new methods for overcoming common but seemingly intractable syndromes.

A middle-aged male hospital patient had been diagnosed as paranoid schizo-phrenic, primarily on the basis of his complaints about "pressure points" on his forehead and in other parts of his body that were believed by him to be signals from outside forces impelling him towards certain decisions. The man had received treatment for two months without any change in these "pressure points." In fact, he had even managed to have the medical staff approve the removal of a cyst over his right eye in the hope that this might eliminate the "pressure points." Unfortunately, this had no effect upon his paranoid delusions. Because of their theoretical orientation, the psychiatrists and residents had been restricting their clinical investigations to his past history, and, not surprisingly, were finding events in his past to which they assigned considerable etiological significance. Nonetheless, the "pressure points" remained unabated.

Davison met this man in a Grand Ward Round in a psychiatric hospital, during which he inquired of the patient whether he would describe himself as a "tense" or "anxious" individual. This aspect of the clinical picture had been largely ignored by the presenting physician. When the patient reported that he was indeed very anxious, the therapist agreed to attempt therapy with him as a demonstration case.

During the first session, the therapist concentrated on clearly delineating those situations in which the man became particularly aware of his "pressure points." The patient was able to identify several such situations which were, at the same time, clearly anxiety-provoking. Having established a close relationship between anxiety and the "pressure points," the patient was taught specific tension-relaxation contrasts. When the patient stated that specific muscle tension felt very much like a "pressure point," he was offered an alternative interpretation. Perhaps the "pressure points" were simply a consequence of his becoming tense and anxious in particular kinds of situations. It was suggested to the man that, in the absence of a naturalistic scientific explanation, he, like other people, tended to explain strange occurrences in somewhat supernatural or mystical terms. The patient agreed that the merit of the therapist's hypothesis was that it seemed amenable to an empirical test. The means would be to train him in deep muscle relaxation and then to determine whether the relaxation could control the occurrence of the "pressure points." The man consented to this, and relaxation training was conducted over several weeks. Outside of therapy, the man was instructed to pay careful attention to the occurrence of the "pressure points" and to confirm or weaken the assumed connection between anxiety and the emergence of troublesome "pressure points." The man cited enough occurrences to confirm the hypothesis, and as he was becoming more and more proficient in relaxation, he also reported some degree of control over the intensity and even the persistence of the "pressure points" by means of differential relaxation. After eight additional sessions over a nine-week period, the man was beginning to refer to the "pressure points" as "sensations," and his conversation was generally losing its "paranoid flavor."

What we have here is the application of differential relaxation as a means of testing a nonparanoid hypothesis about bodily sensations. Clearly, there is much more to the case than can be explained by relaxation principles alone. For instance, it is likely that new cognitions were induced simply via persuasion. Nevertheless, a functional analysis of the man's clinical picture led to the hypothesis that the "pressure points" were part of a general anxiety reaction to specific kinds of situations. While it is possible that they had complex symbolic meanings for the patient, relaxation was effective in controlling the sensations. This helped the patient to account for the sensations in terms of a tension reaction rather than as a product of external forces. That the man became less paranoid as therapy proceeded does suggest that the use of differential relaxation in conjunction with what was called "cognitive restructuring" was indeed an important element in the therapy. Furthermore, having the patient create his own "pressure points" and then applying learned relaxation skills to reduce them as a way to alter their meaning presaged an important component of Barlow's empirically validated therapy for panic disorder. By spinning in a chair or repeatedly climbing up and down a step, the patient learns that sensations hitherto interpreted as an impending panic attack are actually controllable by relaxation or other coping skills and therefore nothing to fear. There is a growing body of research attesting to the clinical efficacy of Barlow's treatment (e.g., Craske & Barlow, 1993).

5. A Case Study Can, Under Certain Circumstances, Provide Enough Experimenter Control Over a Phenomenon to Furnish "Scientifically Acceptable" Information

We have a least implicitly accepted thus far the commonly held view that case reports are intrinsically uncontrolled. However, one can look to the work of the Skinnerians in both laboratories and clinical settings for disproofs of this point of view. As has been documented in many places, one can establish a reliable baseline for the occurrence of a given behavior in an individual case and then demonstrate changes that follow the alteration of a particular contingency. Then we may return the behavior to its original level by changing the contingency once again. This is the familiar A-B-A design; numerous and ingenious variations on the basic reversal design have been described elsewhere (e.g., Barlow & Hersen, 1984; Hayes & Leonhard, 1991; Kazdin, 1982).

6. A Case Study Can Assist in Placing "Meat" on the "Theoretical Skeleton"

Recall our earlier suggestion that the theoretical notions to which clinicians subscribe bear importantly on the specific decisions made in a particular case. Clinicians in fact approach their work with a given set, a framework for ordering the complex data that are their domain. But frameworks are insufficient. The clinician, like any other applied scientist, must fill out the theoretical skeleton. Individual cases present problems that always call for knowledge beyond basic psychological principles.

Illustration of this point can be underscored by referring to desensitization procedures. The general technique of desensitization has been detailed quite specifically (e.g., Wolpe, 1990). In the management of less simple and straightforward cases, however, the mechanistic sequences may not hold up. In these instances, the "meaty" issues involve decisions about precisely what idiosyncratic variations to place on the hierarchy, whether desensitization is even appropriate to the case, and if so, whether crucial dimensions of anxiety have been properly spelled out.

Limitations of Group Designs

Clinicians and other applied workers are usually concerned with particular cases. Since group designs, such as in the usual comparative outcome studies, provide information on averages, therapy researchers have long appreciated their limitations in informing the practitioner about how to proceed with an individual case. As alluded to earlier, this dialectical tension between the nomothetic and the idiographic has been a theme in psychology at least since Gordon Allport's classic writings on personality (e.g., Allport, 1937).

There is, however, an important limitation of group research that is seldom if ever discussed. Consider the simplest of all therapy studies, involving an experimental group and a placebo-control group. We have become accustomed over the years to expect some degree of improvement in placebo groups, sometimes even to the degree that within-condition changes are significant. The researcher, of course, hopes that any such improvement will be exceeded by positive changes in the experimental condition. But consider the following situation, which is probably not infrequent. Subject A in the experimental group improves significantly, and Subject B in the placebo control group improves to the same degree. Can we attribute the improvement of Subject A to a particular feature of the experimental condition? Another way to put the question is as follows: given that Subject A improved in the experimental condition, can we say he would *not* have improved to the same degree if he had been assigned to the control condition (for Subject B showed the same improvement, and it is common to find some degree of improvement even in placebo conditions)? Furthermore, since placebo elements are admittedly a part of the experimental condition—hence the inclusion of a placebo control group—can we say with confidence that Subject A's improvement was not due to the placebo elements inherent in the experimental condition? We suggest that the answers to these questions is No.

Reports of comparative outcome research imply, if not assert outright, that improvements in experimental subjects are due to something particular about that condition vis-a-vis a control group, even though there is always variance in change scores in both groups. But consider this. As Bergin long ago alerted us (1966; 1970), there is usually some *deterioration* among some subjects in experimental conditions, even when the group on average improves significantly with respect to pre-treatment status and more than control conditions. How frequently do authors attribute this worsening to something special about the experimental condition? Our answer: Never.

Studying the Individual Case

Individual patients may be studied in two ways. First, they may be used as "their own control." In this connection, individual patients are studied more carefully than is usual when group comparisons are under investigation, but the findings can be added to hypotheses that still center around *group* norms. Second, in the truly intensive individual clinical design, the subject becomes his or her own laboratory, and hypotheses that arise are tested solely with reference to that particular individual. In the latter instance, the patient's variability and reaction patterns may be studied minute-to-minute, hour-to-hour, day-to-day, session-to-session, and so on. Statistical probabilities can be computed, and experimental design in its most rigorous sense can be applied. The patient's behavior can be described in terms of a multidimensional or multivariate probability distribution, and therapeutic progress can then be assessed in relation to these probability distributions. Symptom frequency and symptom intensity can be woven into the measures obtained and form part of the overall evaluation of treatment effects. Much greater precision in these studies has followed the use of recordings, films, and videotapes. Advances in telemetry and other electronic recording devices have added further impetus to objectivity and quantitative accuracy.

The general trend in clinical research is in the direction of greater specificity. Broad questions such as "Is psychotherapy effective?" are now considered meaningless and have been replaced by the standard scientific question: *What specific treatment is most effective for this individual with that particular problem working with this therapist of that orientation, and under which set of circumstances?* (cf. Paul, 1967; Strupp & Bergin, 1969). Yet, when aiming for specificity, the major drawback of extensive statistical designs is, as just mentioned, the fact that they yield only group norms and probabilities, and do not tell us very much about a given individual in the group. Only fine-grained study of individual cases permits one to relate therapeutic effect to specific patient-characteristics.

Eclecticism and Integration

Without doubt, one of the liveliest and most controversial themes in contemporary psychotherapy involves eclecticism and integration, developments that we advocated in our earlier effort (Lazarus & Davison, 1971). It is appropriate to consider these trends again, for they represent vivid articulations of the nature and importance of clinical innovation.

There are different types of eclecticism. One variant refers to "a largely pragmatic approach in which the therapist uses whatever techniques he or she believes are likely to be effective, with little or no underlying theory to guide these choices" (Arkowitz, 1992, p. 262). This strategy is not well regarded by many mental health professionals, including the present authors, for it lacks a rationale for deciding which techniques to use and under what circumstances. Without theoretical guidelines to help the therapist conceptualize the client's problem and the processes of therapeutic change, eclecticism is equivalent to chaos, in which choices are made on whim, on the basis of "what feels right," or for any number of other reasons that make neither for good science nor sound practice.

On the other hand, *systematic, prescriptive* or *technical eclecticism* (Beutler & Hodgson, 1993; Lazarus, 1967, 1992; Lazarus & Beutler, 1993) conceives of the therapist working within a particular theoretical framework, for example, cognitive-behavioral, but sometimes using techniques from other orientations deemed effective *without subscribing to the theories that spawned them.*

Under the general rubric of integration, Arkowitz (1989) delineated three approaches: technical eclecticism, common factorism, and theoretical integration. As just mentioned, "use whatever works" is the operating principle of the technical eclectic, but it is deemed crucial to conceptualize the use of a technique from within the framework of one's own working theory.

A common factors approach (e.g., Frank, 1961, 1982; Frank & Frank, 1991; Garfield, 1980, 1991; Goldfried, 1980, 1991; Schofield, 1964) seeks elements that all therapy schools might share, for example, the importance of a working alliance in the therapist-patient relationship, or of feedback to the patient about how he or she affects others. These factors are probably employed by many different kinds of therapists and are believed by some (e.g., Brady et al., 1980) to be important components of effective psychotherapy.

The third approach, theoretical integration, tries to synthesize not only techniques but theories. As we understand the term, concepts from Therapy A are imported into the practice of Therapy B and slowly become incorporated into the *theory* underlying Therapy B. As this happens, Theory-Therapy B becomes something different–call it Theory-Therapy AB–as procedural and conceptual integration takes place. As in technical eclecticism, a technique is imported into a new framework, but in so doing, that conceptual context begins to change as theoretical elements from the technique's framework are inevitably incorporated. In this way, one's original theory evolves, becoming something different–presumably more comprehensive and useful. Wachtel's (1977) well-known efforts to justify and make sense of the use of systematic desensitization and assertion training within a revised psychoanalytic framework is a prime example of an effort toward theoretical integration.

There are vast differences between a haphazard, subjective, smorgasbord conception of eclecticism (known as *syncretism*), and one that attempts to apply the findings of psychological science (Norcross & Goldfried, 1992). As already mentioned, technical (or systematic) eclecticism borrows or imports techniques from diverse sources without subscribing to the theories that spawned them. Nevertheless, technical eclecticism is neither antitheoretical nor atheoretical. As a technical eclectic, Lazarus subscribes mainly to a social and cognitive learning theory (Bandura, 1986) because its tenets are open to verification or disproof. The efficacy of any technique from free association to behavioral shaping will be accounted for in social learning theory terms. The active ingredients of techniques as diverse as the empty-chair, projected imagery, cognitive restructuring, relaxation, assertiveness training, abreaction, biofeedback, flooding, structured daydreams, and so forth, are explainable by social and cognitive learning principles (Lazarus, 1989, 1992). Thus, a rhythmic breathing technique to offset certain anxiety-inducing cues may be adopted from yoga practice, but its efficacy, Lazarus suggests, does not require one to subscribe to yoga principles. In this fashion, one can operate within a coherent theoretical framework while being open to possibly effective techniques that have developed within different conceptual frameworks.

Technical eclectics may draw ideas, strategies, and observations from Adlerian, Rogerian, and Ericksonian schools, or from any other approach–e.g., Psychodrama, Gestalt, Reality, Transactional–without embracing any of the diverse *theoretical* positions. Blending bits and pieces of different theories is likely to obfuscate matters, technical eclectics believe. Remaining theoretically consistent but technically eclectic (see Dryden, 1987) enables therapists to spell out precisely what procedures they use with various clients, and the means by which they select those particular methods.

Those who favor a *theoretically integrative* over an *eclectic* viewpoint are also apt to employ techniques from various sources, but in addition they seek to harness greater power by combining different theories or aspects of particular schools of thought. Some theoretical positions can readily be amalgamated with others. For example, general systems theory (Von Bertalanffy, 1974) seems to be compatible with social learning theory. Indeed, Franks (1982), a vociferous opponent of the eclectic or integrative movement, concedes that to combine systems theory with the precepts of behavior therapy "offers considerable promise" (p. 5). Kwee and Lazarus (1986) addressed some clinical avenues that may be enriched by a systems/social learning theory merger. But for the most part, one must be cautious about the dangers of combining elements from two or more theories because many theoretical positions that appear to be compatible one with the other are actually irreconcilable if not antithetical (Arkowitz & Messer, 1984). Furthermore, premature efforts at integration can impede both procedural and conceptual progress (Haaga & Davison, 1991). Let us address one of the most prevalent errors in this connection.

Many clinicians have contended that when treating phobias, they employ desensitization to get rid of the symptoms, while drawing on psychodynamic concepts to achieve insight (e.g., Fensterheim & Glazer, 1983; Wachtel, 1987). On the face of it, this psychodynamic-behavioral hybrid combines the best of two worlds, but if one understands that phobias, from a psychodynamic perspective, entail conflicting urges, symbolic processes, and often serve hidden (unconscious) purposes, desensitization would violate the very essence of the "real" problem and its attendant functions. So-called "symptomatic treatment" is at odds with psychoanalytic drive theory, ego psychology, object relations theory, and self-psychology.[1]

Conversely, from a social learning perspective, most psychodynamic insights draw on putative processes that are not verifiable or capable of disproof, and are therefore outside the scientific paradigm in which learning theorists operate. A cognitive-behavioral conception of phobias rests on entirely different assumptions from those embraced by psychodynamic thinkers, both from the viewpoint of the origin of the disturbance and from the point of view of their appropriate method of treatment (Bandura, 1986; Lazarus & Messer, 1988; O'Leary & Wilson, 1987).

Nevertheless, a thorough assessment may reveal that a given phobia patient is riddled with conflict, is struggling with triangulated and enmeshed familial relationships, and is deriving secondary gains from his or her avoidant behaviors. A salubrious treatment outcome calls for attention to, and remediation of, each of these aspects of the problem. Similarly, as emphasized elsewhere (Lazarus, 1991), if a person is claustrophobic and he or she feels trapped in an untenable marriage, it is unlikely that treatments addressed only to the external stimuli will be adequate. But when enabling patients to resolve their conflicts or undo unfortunate familial collusions, we try to avoid psychodynamic theorizing as well as the theoretical assumptions of family therapists, first put forth by Bowen (1978), Haley (1976), Minuchin (1974) and Whitaker and Napier (1978) since these views are often untestable and directly opposed to one another.

Instead of drawing on potentially incompatible theories, many of which, over time, may prove inaccurate, a technical eclectic may draw quite freely on *observations* from many and diverse sources. For example, we believe that psychodynamic thinking enables one to appreciate that people are capable of denying, projecting, disowning, displacing, splitting, and repressing their emotions, and that unconscious motivation is often important for the full understanding of behavior—which should not be confused with reified versions of "the unconscious mind" and "defense mechanisms" (Lazarus, 1989).

But do theories differ from observations? And can one talk of observations in a theory-neutral way? Theories are essentially speculations that attempt to account for or explain various phenomena. A theory endeavors to answer *how* and *why* certain processes arise, are maintained, can be modified, or be eliminated. Observations, in contrast, are much closer to empirical data without offering explanations. Given that observations do not occur in a vacuum but are influenced by our viewpoints (we bring our theoretical ideas to what we observe—see our discussion below of constructionism), is it in fact possible to separate observations from theories? According to extreme views of social constructionism (Gergen, 1982), we create what we observe to the extent that we cannot discover what is inherent in nature. We invent our theories and categories, and view the world through them. From this perspective, it is impossible to separate observation from theory. A less extreme view would concede that, while psychologists probably have no "hard" facts, "brute" data, or "pure" observations, the distinction between observations and theories is nevertheless worth upholding—despite the fact that observations cannot be entirely separated from theory (Lazarus, 1993).

"Observations" refer to notions that call for minimal speculation. Compare the following two statements: "People overheard him arguing with his boss, and when he came home he kicked the dog." "His kicking the dog was a manifestation of displaced conflictual impulses towards his boss, a father figure who exacerbated his castration anxiety based on ego-dystonic homosexual fantasies." While the first statement (the observation) contains some low level inferences and is not 100% theory-neutral, the range of assumptions conveyed in the second statement makes it quantitatively and qualitatively different from the first. The point at issue is that observations do not have to constitute pure facts in order to be separable from theories. If it were deemed impossible ever to separate the two, how would we ever test our theories?

The technical eclectic holds that it is futile to garner bits of information and blend theoretical elements from the hundreds of different psychotherapeutic schools in the hopes of constructing a superordinate umbrella under which disparate ideas can be reconciled. This type of theoretical integration only breeds confusion. But the effective practice of psychotherapy requires a basis from which we can draw to account for the complexities, vagaries, and idiosyncrasies of human temperament, personality, and behavior. What concepts and observations (not theories) from any source are necessary to provide a basis for understanding human psychology and creating a comprehensive and scientific approach to psychotherapy? Wielding Occam's razor, technical eclectics would want only those concepts that are absolutely necessary.

Whichever viewpoint one embraces—technical eclecticism, common factors, or theoretical integration—there is one theme that has captured the imagination of many psychotherapists in recent years, namely, that existing theoretical frameworks and their associated techniques are insufficient to account for complex clinical phenomena and to enable the clinician to formulate the most efficient, effective, and humane interventions. Nevertheless, although it seems sensible to cross theoretical and therapeutic boundaries, to venture beyond one's own borders in search of nuggets that may be deposited among the hills and dales of other camps, there are numerous booby traps that lie in wait for the unsuspecting. Lazarus (1995) has recently spelled out many of the dangers of combining treatments and theories in psychotherapy and put forward five challenging observations:

(1) There appear to be no data to support the notion that a combination of different theories has resulted in a more robust therapeutic technique.

(2) It is techniques, not theories, that are actually used on people (cf. London, 1964).

(3) The effectiveness of techniques may have no bearing on the theories that begot them.

(4) Different treatment combinations should be tried only when well-documented methods do not exist for a particular condition, or when proven techniques are not achieving the desired results.

(5) It is an egregious error to assert that the use of certain techniques implies that one is practicing the doctrine that generated them.

Treatment Manuals, Assessment, and Controlling Variables

As discussed recently in Goldfried and Davison (1994), a major contribution of behavior therapy is the widespread use of treatment manuals both in comparative therapy research and in training. Indeed, one cannot obtain federal funding for an outcome study without the use of a manual. Without question the status of comparative therapy outcome research has been enhanced by the use of manuals, but their increasing use is a double-edged sword. To our minds, an unintended consequence of the use of manuals is that they obfuscate clinical artistry and create the illusion of seemingly homogenized clinical entities, a mistaken notion that is reinforced by increasing acceptance of each new revision of the DSM. In many instances, it is important for cases to receive idiographic formulations before interventions are selected. However, when a therapist follows a treatment manual— designed primarily for use in controlled outcome studies— he or she may overlook important personalistic factors. And beginning therapists may incorrectly assume that prepackaged interventions can be used with any patient having a particular DSM diagnosis. It is important to guard against anything that undermines the central role of assessment and case formulation.

Let us cite depression as a case in point. A DSM diagnosis of depression will not inform us as to whether a given client is depressed as a consequence of unfortunate life circumstances, or because of having set unrealistically high standards, or whether interpersonal deficits that elicit opprobrium from significant others are responsible, or if a passive style has compromised the individual's personal effectiveness. Furthermore, a meaningful assessment will determine if a client entertains *misperceptions* of his or her capacity to exert a positive influence, if there is indeed a *lack of ability* to do so, and/or if an *unyielding environment* is basically responsible. A therapy manual that predetermines the crucial variables associated with a DSM disorder is limiting and conceivably irrelevant.

The significance of fully understanding controlling variables is also crucial. Consider the widespread use of a treatment manual designed to overcome anxiety reactions via relaxation and desensitization. A novice therapist might proceed to apply these stepwise methods to an anxious subject or client, without realizing that the basis of the individual's anxiety rested on significant interpersonal deficits. We envision the novice exclaiming: "Oops! I plugged in the wrong manual. I should have used the Social Skills Training Manual!" Similarly, a depressed individual who receives desensitization or cognitive inoculation to real or perceived rejection may be worse off in the end if the reason for others' disapproval stemmed from the client's consistently obnoxious behavior towards them. In short, while DSM diagnoses and the use of treatment manuals have a definite place, they perform a disservice when taking us away from the necessary search for controlling variables in an idiographic assessment and tailored treatment of the individual patient.

Constructionism, Clinical Innovation, and the Politics and Ethics of Scientifically Based Assessment and Intervention

In a refinement of an argument we made twenty years ago about ethical issues in sexual orientation change for homosexuals (Davison, 1974, 1976), we have proposed a constructionist epistemology as a useful way to conceptualize clinical assessment and, by implication, clinical intervention (Davison, 1991). It is suggested that clients seldom come to mental health clinicians with problems as clearly delineated and independently verifiable as those a patient brings to a physician. The latter practitioner/scientist has better data on which to make a diagnosis (and yet even here reliability is far from perfect). In contrast, a client usually goes to a psychologist or psychiatrist in the way described by Halleck (1971):

"The patient usually has considerable difficulty in finding the way in which he would wish to change his behavior, but as he talks to the psychiatrist [or other mental health worker] his wants and needs become clearer. In the very process of defining his needs in the presence of a figure who is viewed as wise and authoritarian, the patient is profoundly influenced. He ends up wanting some of the things the psychiatrist thinks he should want (p. 19)."

When patients come to see a therapist, they are unhappy and often uncertain of what they need or want, other than relief from their emotional pain. Life is going badly; nothing seems to be meaningful or effective; sadness is deeper than life circumstances would seem to warrant; the mind wanders when trying to concentrate; unwanted images intrude on consciousness and into dreams. The clinician *transforms* such often vague and complex complaints into a diagnosis or assessment, a set of ideas about what is wrong and, usually, what might be done to alleviate what is wrong. The argument, then, is that psychological problems are for the most part *constructions* of the clinician: our clients come to us in pain, and they leave with more clearly defined problems that we assign to them. If a therapeutic intervention is also attempted, the assessment naturally influences both its goals and character.

This epistemological perspective was taken in an analysis of the processes of assessment and treatment for homosexual patients (Davison, 1974, 1976, 1991). When homosexuals go to a therapist, whatever psychological or physical woe they may have has all too often been construed as being caused entirely or primarily by their sexual orientation. Further, this happens because, arguably, (a) their sexual orientation is usually the most salient part of their personhood, and because (b) it is regarded as abnormal—regardless of whatever "liberal" stance the clinician takes overtly. This is not to say that a homosexual orientation may not sometimes cause people distress! Rather, it is to say that this salient feature of their personality—because it is negatively sanctioned, still, even with the advances made in DSM-IV and elsewhere in the professional literature—colors the clinician's perceptions and guides his or her data-gathering activities in a direction that implicates homosexuality and implies the desirability of a change in sexual orientation.

This is of course a very difficult proposition to verify, and it causes an empiricist not a little discomfort, but there exists a body of data on clinician bias that presumptively supports this general contention. For example, in an analogue study conducted some years ago, Davison and Friedman (1981) found that descriptions of a hypothetical anxious client elicited judgments of more serious psychopathology when it was mentioned (in passing) that the client was homosexual than when he was described as heterosexual. Related findings come from the research of Lopez (Lopez, 1989; Lopez & Hernandez, 1986; Lopez & Nunez, 1987), showing that the stereotypes clinicians have about Hispanics affect their understanding of clinical complaints.

More generally, the role of subjective factors in perception, problem-solving, theory construction, and research design has been acknowledged and demonstrated in experimental psychology since the work of Wundt more than one hundred years ago and confirmed time and again in cognitive psychology, from the "new look" in perception of the 1940s and 1950s (e.g., Bruner & Goodman, 1947) to the schema-oriented work of today in cognitive science (e.g., Neisser, 1976). Moreover, in epistemological writings such as Kuhn (1962) as well as in some experimental studies (Davison, 1964), paradigms in science are explicitly compared to perceptual biases that affect profoundly the way data are collected and even defined. A generation of thoughtful scientists and philosophers has been sensitized to the nontrivial influences that our often unspoken assumptions have on our organization of the world.

Implications for Education and Training

Much of what we have discussed thus far relates to education and training. Publications, after all, are intended not only to communicate one's ideas and findings but also to have an impact on training models and curricula and ultimately to influence future generations.

The meteoric rise of "professional" or practitioner programs in the 1970s was both cause and effect of the Vail Conference on clinical training in psychology (Korman, 1976). Like the earlier Boulder conference (Raimy, 1950), it set the tone for future directions in clinical psychology education at the same time as it justified already existing trends. In particular, Vail made a case for the development of a training model that relied less on research than on the training of applied workers to employ techniques and pursue approaches deemed to be properly evaluated and verified. To our minds the core of the issue has been clear and simple: does the state of clinical psychology as an empirically based discipline justify the training of independent practitioners in currently existing procedures, or is the evidentiary base of our field too weak to make such guild-like training possible or justifiable, both empirically and morally?

Debate on this question continues, and the National Conference on Scientist-Practitioner Education and Training for the Professional Practice of Psychology, held in Gainesville, Florida, in January 1990, made the case for the continuing vigor and viability of the scientist-practitioner (s-p) model. In a sense, the Conference paraphrased W. C. Fields that the reports of the demise of the Boulder Model are greatly exaggerated. Given the present vitality of s-p programs and of associated professional organizations such as the Association for Advancement of Behavior Therapy, the Society for a Science of Clinical Psychology (Section III of Division 12 of the American Psychological Association), the American Psychological Society, and the Association for Applied and Preventive Psychology, it may be difficult for younger colleagues to appreciate the challenge, even threat, that was felt by "ivory tower" clinical training in the 1970s. During that time there were ardent (sometimes shrill) cries for "relevance", and there was impatience with the alleged triviality of most psychological research and with the emphasis placed in s-p clinical programs on basic science as the foundation of clinical training, indeed, as an inextricable part of it. Other pressures against the science core in clinical training came from revisions in the APA Accreditation Criteria in the 1970s, which began to emphasize practice at the expense of research; and from the clinical training grant program of the NIMH, which encouraged focus on certain applied problems rather than general education and training in the science of psychology.

One of us (GCD) was a working chair of one of the study groups at the Gainesville Conference and as such contributed to the statement issued by that group (Belar & Perry, 1992). It is useful to quote from the statement, which speaks to the complex relationships between clinical work and scientific inquiry:

"The scientist-practitioner model of education and training in psychology is an integrative approach to science and practice wherein each must continually inform the other. This model represents more than a summation of both parts. Scientist-practitioner psychologists embody a research orientation in their practice and a practice relevance in their research. Thus, a scientist-practitioner is not defined by a job title or a role, but rather by an integrated approach to both science and practice. The model entails development of interlocking skills to foster a career-long process of psychological investigation, assessment and intervention.... The model extends beyond current domains to newly emerging areas that embody science and practice, and is not restricted to specific content areas. It represents an overall theoretical, empirical, and experiential approach to science and professional practice in psychology.... Both the knowledge base in psychology and the practice problems addressed by the scientist-practitioner are constantly evolving and changing. Therefore, the scientist-practitioner is able to extend simultaneously the boundaries and applications of scientific knowledge, and to adapt to the changing needs of professional practice. Training in research prepares the scientist-practitioner for distinguishing fact from opinion in applications of the science of behavior and for innovation in existing theory and techniques.... [T]he scientist-practitioner is, by definition... committed to bridging the gap between scientific foundations and professional practice.... The intent of [teaching how to apply scientific thinking to applied problems] is to foster a unique process of case/problem conceptualization that entails operational delineation of problems useful for the planning of intervention. These constructions and the interventions that flow from them are continuously refined through scientific validation.... One of the particular characteristics of the scientist-practitioner model is that it facilitates the emergence of ideas in the field (it is generative rather than static) (Belar & Perry, 1992, pp. 72-74)."

The foregoing are not "mere administrative" matters, cloaked in dull and uninteresting greys and of concern only to bureaucrats. Rather, they lie at the very core of the nature of applied psychology and its future. Two interrelated sets of questions inhere in our considerations, and these are as central to science in general as they are to that part of psychological science that we call clinical/applied psychology: (1) How do we know what to study, and where do new ideas and creative hunches come from? (2) What is the role of verification/evaluation in justifying current application and in nurturing future conceptual formulations and effective and humane applications?

Most of this paper thus far has addressed the first question. We turn now to the second question, verification and evaluation, an aspect of clinical endeavor that, regrettably, has not been as high a priority in our field as the more artistic pursuits just mentioned. While research in psychotherapy has, since Carl Rogers, been a flourishing and vigorous enterprise, supported heavily by NIMH, it is debatable to what extent research affects the actual clinical activities of practitioners. Most readers are no doubt aware of respected s-p (and APA-approved) clinical programs that, nonetheless, teach and encourage the use of well-established assessments and interventions that do not enjoy much in the way of empirical support. Indeed, these same programs spend time on such weakly supported procedures at the expense of research-based techniques. When one asks faculty and training directors why such procedures are still taught and employed, the answers come in such forms as, "Well, the internships our students compete for require X hours of experience with assessment technique A and Y hours of experience with intervention approach B;" or "Well, I know that the supportive literature isn't so great, but folks have been using these things for so many years that we can't allow our students to enter the professional world in ignorance of them."

Between us, the authors of this chapter have over 60 years of experience in all aspects of clinical endeavor, so we are not unsympathetic to the guild and other practical pressures that can influence decision-making about curriculum and practicum training. Graduate students, after all, need clinical internships, and even when funding was more plentiful than it has been the past twenty-plus years, respected internships have always had their pick of applicants during those frenetic two days in the first week of February when internship directors, clinical training directors, and applicants nervously negotiate to put together the best possible cohort of interns and to make the wisest decisions about where to spend another year of one's already extended educational career. *But* we regard it as a serious problem in the continuing development of clinical psychology that training and educational decisions do not rely more heavily than they do on efforts to analyze dispassionately the considerable evaluation efforts in clinical research.

At the same time, we do not, because we cannot, endorse the radical view that nothing a clinician does when dealing with a patient should lack clear empirical-experimental support. As we have written elsewhere (Lazarus, 1989; Lazarus & Davison, 1971; Davison & Neale, 1994; Goldfried & Davison, 1976), there is much that clinicians do that lacks empirical support at a given place and time (e.g., that empathy is critical in assessment for and conduct of cognitive behavior therapy); and there is inevitably a research/practice gap that must be bridged by creative, idiographic leaps (cf. our earlier discussion about meat on the theoretical skeleton). Our argument is broader in scope as well as more subtle than these reservations. Plainly put: is it responsible for us as scientists, practitioners, trainers, and therapists to allow bureaucratic pressures and professional inertia to determine how we educate the next generation of clinicians/clinical researchers?

Conclusions

We have explored the complex interplay of clinical discovery and controlled evaluation, demonstrating how experience in the applied arena provides invaluable insights and ideas about the complexity of the human condition and of ways to intervene effectively. Case studies have features that earn them a firm place in psychological research, and to ignore their potential contributions is to limit severely the kind of knowledge that can be generated by more systematic modes of inquiry. Some limitations of group designs in comparative therapy research were also reviewed, again highlighting the importance of idiographic analyses of single cases. Our position is that innovation and creative advancement are most readily nurtured via immersion in clinical/applied work, but at the same time the nature of that work is inevitably shaped by theories and hypotheses that clinicians bring into the applied setting. These abstractions are themselves influenced by the clinician's interpretations of data, which interpretations are molded by theoretical and metatheoretical preconceptions. In this complex and interactive fashion, clinical innovation is part of a nonlinear network of forces that includes personal biases, professional allegiances, epistemological assumptions, theoretical preferences, and familiarity with and use of certain bodies of data. In our efforts at establishing science-based standards of psychological care, we should not overlook the unique importance of clinical innovation and discovery. We believe that the kinds of continuing interactions detailed in this paper between innovations in the applied arena and controlled inquiry in research settings represent promising strategies for enhancing conceptual and procedural knowledge in what might properly one day become the clinical sciences.

References

Allport, G. W. (1937). *Personality: A psychological interpretation.* New York: Holt, Rinehart, & Winston.

Arkowitz, H. (1989). The role of theory in psychotherapy integration. *Journal of Integrative and Eclectic Psychotherapy, 8,* 8-16.

Arkowitz, H. (1992). Integrative theories of therapy. In D. Freedheim (Ed.) *The history of psychotherapy: A century of change* (pp. 261-303). Washington, DC: American Psychological Association.

Arkowitz, H., & Messer, S. B. (Eds.). (1984). *Psychoanalytic therapy and behavior therapy: Is integration possible?* New York: Plenum.

Bandura, A. (1986). *Social foundations of thought and action.* Englewood Cliffs, NJ: Prentice-Hall.

Barlow, D. H., & Hersen, M. (1984). *Single-case experimental designs: Strategies for studying behavior change* (2nd ed.). New York: Pergamon.

Beck, A. T. (1967). *Depression: Clinical, experimental, and theoretical aspects.* New York: Harper & Rowe.

Belar, C. D., & Perry, N. W. (1992). National conference on scientist-practitioner education and training for the professional practice of psychology. *American Psychologist, 47,* 71-75.

Bergin, A. E. (1966). Some implications of psychotherapy research for therapeutic practice. *Journal of Abnormal Psychology, 71,* 235-246.

Bergin, A. E. (1970). The deterioration effect: A reply to Braucht. *Journal of Abnormal Psychology, 75,* 300-302.

Beutler, L. E., & Hodgson, A. B. (1993). Prescriptive psychotherapy. In G. Stricker & J. R. Gold (Eds.), *Comprehensive handbook of psychotherapy integration* (pp. 151-163). New York: Plenum.

Bowen, M. (1978). *Family therapy in clinical practice.* New York: Jason Aronson.

Brady, J. P., Davison, G. C., DeWald, P. A., Egan, G., Fadiman, J., Frank, J. D., Gill, M. M., Hoffman, I., Kempler, W., Lazarus, A. A., Raimy, V., Rotter, J. B., & Strupp, H. H. (1980). Some views on effective principles of psychotherapy. *Cognitive Therapy and Research, 4,* 269-306.

Bruner, J. S., & Goodman, C. C. (1947). Value and need as organizing factors in perception. *Journal of Abnormal and Social Psychology, 42,* 33-44.

Craske, M. G., & Barlow, D. H. (1993). Panic disorder and agoraphobia. In D. H. Barlow (Ed.), *Clinical handbook of psychological disorders* (2nd ed., pp. 1-47). New York: Guilford Press.

Davison, G. C. (1964). The negative effects of early exposure to suboptimal visual stimuli. *Journal of Personality, 32,* 278-295.

Davison, G. C. (1966). Differential relaxation and cognitive restructuring in therapy with a "paranoid schizophrenic" or "paranoid state." *Proceedings of the 74th Annual Convention of the American Psychological Association.* Washington, DC: American Psychological Association.

Davison, G. C. (1974). *Homosexuality: The ethical challenge.* Presidential address to the Annual Convention of the Association for Advancement of Behavior Therapy, Chicago.

Davison, G. C. (1976). Homosexuality: The ethical challenge. *Journal of Consulting and Clinical Psychology, 44*, 157-162.

Davison, G. C. (1991). Constructionism and therapy for homosexuality. In J. Gonsiorek & J. Weinrich (Eds.), *Homosexuality: Research Implications for Public Policy* (pp. 137-148). Newbury Park, CA: Sage.

Davison, G. C., & Friedman, S. (1981). Sexual orientation stereotypy in the distortion of clinical judgment. *Journal of Homosexuality, 6*, 37-44.

Davison, G. C., & Neale, J. M. (1994). *Abnormal psychology* (6th ed.). New York: Wiley.

Davison, G. C., Navarre, S. L., & Vogel, R. S. (1995). The articulated thoughts in simulated situations paradigm: A think-aloud approach to cognitive assessment. *Current Directions in Psychological Science, 4*, 29-33.

Davison, G. C., Robins, C., & Johnson, M. (1983). Articulated thoughts during simulated situations: A paradigm for studying cognition in emotion and behavior. *Cognitive Therapy and Research, 7*, 17-40.

Dryden, W. (1987). Theoretically consistent eclecticism: Humanizing a computer "addict." In J. C. Norcross (Ed.), *Casebook of eclectic psychotherapy* (pp. 221-237). New York: Brunner/Mazel.

Ellis, A. (1962). *Reason and emotion in psychotherapy*. New York: Lyle Stuart.

Feather, B. W., & Rhodes, J. M. (1972). Psychodynamic behavior therapy II: Clinical aspects. *Archives of General Psychiatry, 26*, 503-511.

Fensterheim, H., & Glazer, H. I. (1983). *Behavioral psychotherapy: Basic principles and case studies*. New York: Brunner/Mazel.

Frank, J. D. (1961). *Persuasion and healing*. Baltimore: Johns Hopkins Press.

Frank, J. D. (1982). Therapeutic components shared by all psychotherapies. In J. H. Harvey & M. M. Parks (Eds.), *The Master Lecture Series: Vol. 1. Psychotherapy research and behavior change*. Washington, DC: American Psychological Association.

Frank, J. D., & Frank, J. B. (1991). *Persuasion and healing* (3rd ed.). Baltimore, MD: Johns Hopkins University Press.

Franks, C. M. (1982). Behavior therapy: An overview. In C. M. Franks, G. T. Wilson, P. C. Kendall, & K. D. Brownell (Eds.), *Annual review of behavior therapy: Theory and practice*. (Vol. 8, pp. 1-38). New York: Guilford.

Garfield, S. L. (1980). *Psychotherapy: An eclectic approach*. New York: Wiley.

Garfield, S. L. (1991). Common and specific factors in psychotherapy. *Journal of Integrative and Eclectic Psychotherapy, 10*, 5-13.

Gergen, K. J. (1982). *Toward transformation in social knowledge*. New York: Springer-Verlag.

Goldfried, M. R. (1980). Toward the delineation of therapeutic change principles. *American Psychologist, 35*, 991-999.

Goldfried, M. R. (1991). Research issues in psychotherapy integration. *Journal of Psychotherapy Integration, 1*, 5-25.

Goldfried, M. R., & Davison, G. C. (1976). *Clinical behavior therapy*. New York: Holt, Rinehart & Winston.

Goldfried, M. R., & Davison, G. C. (1994). *Clinical behavior therapy*. Expanded edition. New York: Wiley-Interscience.

Haaga, D. A. F., & Davison, G. C. (1991). Disappearing differences do not always reflect healthy integration: An analysis of cognitive therapy and rational-emotive therapy. *Journal of Psychotherapy Integration, 1*, 287-303.

Haley, J. (1976). *Problem solving therapy*. San Francisco: Josey Bass.

Halleck, S. L. (1971). *The politics of therapy*. New York: Science House.

Hayes, S. C., & Leonhard, C. (1991). The role of the individual case in clinical science and practice. In M. Hersen, A. E. Kazdin, & A. S. Bellack (Eds.), *The clinical psychology handbook* (2nd ed., pp. 223-238). New York: Pergamon.

Kazdin, A. E. (1982). *Single-case research designs: Methods for clinical and applied settings*. New York: Oxford University Press.

Korman, M. (Ed.). (1976). *Levels and patterns of professional training in psychology* (Vail conference). Washington, DC: American Psychological Association.

Kuhn, T. S. (1962). *The structure of scientific revolutions*. Chicago: University of Chicago Press.

Kwee, M. G. T., & Lazarus, A. A. (1986). Multimodal therapy: The cognitive-behavioural tradition and beyond. In W. Dryden & W. Golden (Eds.), *Cognitive-behavioural approaches to psychotherapy* (pp. 320-355). London: Harper & Row.

Lazarus, A. A. (1967). In support of technical eclecticism. *Psychological Reports, 21*, 415-416.

Lazarus, A. A. (1989). *The practice of multimodal therapy*. Baltimore, MD: Johns Hopkins University Press.

Lazarus, A. A. (1991). A plague on Little Hans and Little Albert. *Psychotherapy, 28*, 444-447.

Lazarus, A. A. (1992). Multimodal therapy: Technical eclecticism with minimal integration. In J. C. Norcross & M. R. Goldfried (Eds.), *Handbook of psychotherapy integration* (pp. 231-263). New York: Basic Books.

Lazarus, A. A. (1993). Theory, subjectivity and bias: Can there be a future? *Psychotherapy, 30*, 674-677.

Lazarus, A. A. (1995). Different types of eclecticism and integration: Let's be aware of the dangers. *Journal of Psychotherapy Integration, 5*, 27-39.

Lazarus, A. A., & Beutler, L. E. (1993). On technical eclecticism. *Journal of Counseling and Development, 71*, 381-385.

Lazarus, A. A., & Davison, G. C. (1971). Clinical innovation in research and practice. In A. E. Bergin & S. L. Garfield (Eds.), *Handbook of psychotherapy and behavior change* (pp. 196-213). New York: Wiley.

Lazarus, A. A., & Messer, S. B. (1988). Clinical choice points: Behavioral versus psychoanalytic interventions. *Psychotherapy, 25*, 59-70.

Lazarus, A. A., & Messer, S B. (1991). Does chaos prevail? An exchange on technical eclecticism and assimilative integration. *Journal of Psychotherapy Integration, 1*, 143-158.

Levine, F. M., Sandeen, E., & Murphy, C. M. (1992). The therapist's dilemma: Using nomothetic information to answer idiographic questions. *Psychotherapy, 29*, 410-415.

Lopez, S. (1989). Patient variable biases in clinical judgment: Conceptual overview and methodological considerations. *Psychological Bulletin, 106*, 184-203.

Lopez, S., & Hernandez, P. (1986). How culture is considered in evaluations of psychopathology. *Journal of Nervous and Mental Disease, 176*, 598-606.

Lopez S., & Nunez, J. A. (1987). Cultural factors considered in selected diagnostic criteria and interview schedules. *Journal of Abnormal Psychology, 96*, 270-272.

Maher, B. A. (1966). *Principles of psychopathology: An experimental approach.* New York: McGraw-Hill.

Minuchin, S. (1974). *Families and family therapy.* Cambridge, MA: Harvard University Press.

Neisser, U. (1976). *Cognition and reality.* San Francisco: Freeman.

O'Leary, K. D., & Wilson, G. T. (1987). *Behavior therapy: Application and outcome* (2nd ed.). Englewood Cliffs, NJ: Prentice-Hall.

Norcross, J. C., & Goldfried, M. R. (Eds.). (1992). *Handbook of psychotherapy integration.* New York: Basic Books.

Paul, G. L. (1967). Strategy of outcome research in psychotherapy. *Journal of Consulting Psychology, 31*, 109-118.

Raimy, V. (1950). *Training in clinical psychology* (Boulder conference). New York: Prentice-Hall.

Schofield, W. (1964). *Psychotherapy: The purchase of friendship.* Englewood Cliffs, NJ: Prentice-Hall.

Stampfl, T. G., & Levis, D. J. (1967). Essentials of implosive therapy: A learning-theory-based psychodynamic behavioral therapy. *Journal of Abnormal Psychology, 92*, 496-503.

Strupp, H. H., & Bergin, A. E. (1969). Some empirical and conceptual bases for coordinated research in psychotherapy. *International Journal of Psychiatry, 7*, 18-90.

Von Bertalanffy, L. (1974). General systems theory and psychiatry. In S. Arieti (Ed.), *American handbook of psychiatry* (Vol. 1, pp. 1095-1117). New York: Basic Books.

Wachtel, P. L. (1977). *Psychoanalysis and behavior therapy: Toward an integration.* New York: Basic Books.

Wachtel, P. L. (1987). *Action and insight.* New York: Guilford.

Whitaker, C., & Napier, A. (1978). *The family crucible.* New York: Harper & Row.

Wolpe, J. (1958). *Psychotherapy by reciprocal inhibition.* Stanford, CA: Stanford University Press.

Wolpe, J. (1990). *The practice of behavior therapy.* New York: Pergamon.

Woolfolk, R. L., & Lazarus, A. A. (1979). Between laboratory and clinic: Paving the two-way street. *Cognitive Therapy and Research, 3*, 239-244.

Acknowledgments

Portions of this chapter are based on "Clinical Innovation and Evaluation: Integrating Practice with Inquiry," by Gerald C. Davison and Arnold A. Lazarus, published in *Clinical Psychology: Science and Practice*, 1994, *1*, 157-168, by permission of Oxford University Press.

Footnote

1. Wachtel (1977) attempts to deal with this conceptual incompatibility in two ways. First, as already mentioned, he offers a reformulated psychoanalytic theory, which he calls "cyclical psychodynamics," and which emphasizes more than most (ego) analytic theories the importance of present-day interactions with putatively repressed conflicts. And second, he proposes that behavioral treatments like Wolpe's desensitization are effective because they expose fearful patients to anxiety-laden unconscious cues. In this latter respect he is influenced by the theoretically integrative work of Feather and Rhoades (1972) and Stampfl (Stampfl & Levis, 1967). Debate continues on how successful this proposed theoretical integration is, even between the co-authors of this paper.

Discussion of Davison and Lazarus

Achieving Synthesis

Linda J. Hayes
University of Nevada

Empirical findings as to how the average client, presenting symptoms characteristic of a particular diagnostic category, responds to a necessarily idiosyncratic iteration of a specific therapeutic procedure surely provides *some* guidance to a clinician faced with a particular client exhibiting some of the same symptoms. Admittedly, there may not be *much* guidance here, and this may have something to do with many therapists' lack of interest in clinical research. Indeed, relating knowledge formulated at the level of a group to the actions of an individual is not without problem, and presumably it is this problem that accounts for Davison and Lazarus's title: *The dialectics of science and practice.*

A dialectic, at least in the Hegelian sense, is not merely the juxtaposition of two domains having different characteristics and variant purposes, however. A dialectic suggests a tension of opposites and a promise of synthesis. It does not seem to this reader, at least, that "opposition" captures the relationship between research and the practice of therapy, though. And whatever the authors might have conceptualized as a synthesis of these two domains is obscured by a tangential argument supporting technical eclecticism. I am intrigued by Davison and Lazarus' idea of a dialectic nonetheless, and hope to suggest a sense in which this idea might be elaborated. Let me begin by addressing the practice of therapy.

Therapy involves changes in the interactions of a client with his or her life circumstances, facilitated by the practices of a therapist. From the client's perspective, therapy is a process through which the events of one's life, brought to bear in the immediate situation by way of language, come to have different functions in the sense that one's reactions to them are different. This is not to say that one's history is somehow erased. How one interacts with particular events in any given present may be understood as reflecting the current point in the evolution of such interactions (Hayes, 1992), differentiated from time to time by virtue of circumstances or settings and having the character of being more or less inclusive of other historical reactions.

The therapy setting constitutes a critical variable in this process. The therapy setting is both a familiar one, in which one person converses with another; and a novel one, in which the conversation is quite unlike any other and occurs between people with a relationship quite unlike any other. Without the familiarity of this situation, the client's historical interactions with particular events could not be expected to occur; and without the novelty, they could not be expected to change. These are not so much empirical arguments as philosophical ones.

It is not only the setting and its characteristics than account for changes in the clients' interactions with his or her life events, though. It is also the actions or practices of the therapist. At least in part, these practices are designed to rearrange the usual organization of experiences so as to lay bare, explicate, or even construct relationships among events not ordinarily seen or appreciated. (That is to say, the therapist is not mere conversing). The artistry, intuition or skill of the therapist as to how experiences might be structured or sequenced so as to reveal these relationships come from an awareness of commonalities in interactions of many people with particular sorts of life experiences.

This awareness has more than one source. It comes from clinicians' direct experience of their own successes, to be sure; though it is unlikely that any one clinician sees enough clients in a lifetime to operate effectively on the basis of this experience alone. Functional relations in the complicated and convoluted circumstances of even one client are difficult to identify. Clearly, the artistry of the clinician is owing to the work of others as well, among which may be included those who have supervised their clinical training, those who have generated diagnostic categories, conducted research, and those who have articulated broader frames of understanding through which to interpret particular happenings. In other words, what a therapist does in therapy is act upon his or her history, and all therapists have historical circumstances of these kinds in common, more or less. (At least if they don't, therapy is, in fact, mere conversation).

So what does this say about the tension of opposites? The tension of research and practice, the promise of their synthesis? The purpose of research, at least for the most part, is to characterize events in terms their causes. To do this, events must be grouped into classes as it is not possible to predict nor control unique events. Further, classification is necessarily achieved on the basis of only *some* of the attributes of individual events, the implication being that no individual event is characterized fully by the class construction. This does not mean that the individual event is overlooked in the research domain, however. Neither does it mean that the individual event stands in *opposition* to the group. On the contrary, the individual event is *included* in the group. There does not appear to be any tension between research and practice from this perspective.

There is a tension to be reckoned with, however. But it is not a tension between research and therapy. It exists instead between research and *philosophy*, or more specifically, how unique events such as the individual client are understood from the standpoints of research and philosophy. There are, of course, many different philosophies, and I am speaking about a particular class of philosophies, namely one in which observers' histories are assumed to participate in their observations and contribute to their descriptions of those observations. From a non-realistic perspective of this sort, an individual event is not viewed an effect of some cause, as the research tradition would have it. The unique event is instead constructed as an ongoing field of interaction. From this perspective, whatever factors are invoked as causes by researchers are taken rather to be *aspects* of the event under study, participants in the interactive field—not causes of it. In short, to fulfil the descriptive purpose of philosophy, events are held to evolve without agents; while to fulfill the applied research agenda, unique events are regarded as substance for the identification of causal forces.

A synthesis of these opposites, to be true to the idea of a dialectic, would require changes in the conceptualizations of the individual event in both domains. A synthesis would require a state of affairs in which the unique event—the individual client's action—can be neither predicted nor controlled in the sense in which these terms are employed in science. And it would require a state of affairs in which the individual client's action undergoes directed change. It would seem that therapy may constitute such a state—that the synthesis is therapy.

Reference

Hayes, L. J. (1992) The psychological present. *The Behavior Analyst, 15,* 139-145.

Chapter 7

Models of Training and Standards of Care

Richard M. McFall
Indiana University–Bloomington

In his classic paper, "The functional autonomy of psychotherapy," Astin (1961) suggested that psychotherapeutic practices tend to become autonomous from their origins and foundations. Over time, treatments develop such a life of their own that they are able to survive without any apparent theoretical justification or empirical support. Unfortunately, this same indictment can be applied to much of what goes on today in clinical psychology—in psychotherapy, assessment, theory, and training. The present chapter looks critically at the justification for current patterns of practice in clinical psychology. Then it discusses the implications of this analysis for standards of training. A fitting subtitle for this chapter might be, "The functional autonomy of clinical psychology."

Clinical Psychology, as a field, seems to be committed to the perpetuation of horse-and-buggy models of mental health care delivery and professional training when, in fact, the one thing that now seems certain is that the future of mental health care delivery requires new and better models. The new models of delivery, in turn, will require very different models of training. Thus, if clinical psychology is to survive in the future, it must rethink its mission, justify its existence, and undergo the difficult process of self-examination, reengineering, and renewal (Hammer & Champy, 1993). This chapter is aimed at fostering this process, especially with regard to models of training.

The chapter is organized into three sections. The first attempts to clarify the meanings of concepts fundamental to the discussion of clinical psychology. The second illuminates the assumptions underlying the traditional roles of clinical psychology in the mental health system. These assumptions then are examined in the light of current evidence, asking the question, "Which roles are warranted; which seem to be functionally autonomous?" Finally, the third section discusses the implications of this analysis for the future training of clinical psychologists.[1]

Conceptual Issues

Definitions of Clinical Psychology

What is "clinical psychology?" Unfortunately, this term has at least three different meanings:

Psychology as a profession. Here, clinical psychology refers to a professional guild. The guild is a limited-access collection of members with common interests; the purpose of the guild is to advance the common interests of its members; and membership in the guild is governed by a set of criteria primarily related to professional credentials. Thus, clinical psychologists are card-carrying members in the professional guild of clinical psychology. The guild is dependent on the support of allied organizations—accreditation agencies and state licensing boards—for its status and influence. Accreditation agencies recognize certain training programs as qualified to certify that their graduates have the credentials needed for membership in the guild. State licensing boards, in turn, decide which of the individuals claiming to have such credentials actually will be permitted by law to call themselves psychologists and to engage in those psychological activities that have been proscribed by the licensing laws.[2]

Psychology as a set of activities. Here, clinical psychology is defined by "what clinical psychologists do"—for example, administering tests, assessing, diagnosing, administering psychotherapy, testifying in court, conducting research, publishing books and papers, etc. This is the definition typically favored by textbooks for undergraduate courses in clinical psychology. This also is the public view of clinical psychology: Bob Newhart—playing the psychotherapist—is the prototype of what clinical psychology *is*. This conception of clinical psychology seems to attract the majority of applicants to doctoral training programs in clinical psychology; these applicants want to *practice* clinical psychology.

The first problem with this definition is that it tends to be circular (i.e., clinical psychology is what clinical psychologists do —> clinical psychologists are individuals who practice clinical psychology —> etc.). The second problem is that there is no activity that uniquely identifies either clinical psychology or clinical psychologists.[2]

The circularity problem is not trivial. Licensed clinical psychologists engage in a wide range of activities. For example, some have reported engaging in "model train therapy," "landscape therapy," and "Primal Scream Therapy." Others have conducted assessments aimed at uncovering repressed memories of childhood sexual abuse; have testify as expert witnesses in court cases concerning child custody decisions; have written advice columns in newspapers; have hosted phone-in talk shows on radio; or have engaged in sexual intercourse with patients. Which of these varied activities should be included in the definition? Does anything go, or are certain activities by clinical psychologists legitimate, while others are not? If there are limits, what defines the borders between the legitimate and illegitimate?

The circularity problem can be deferred by making a list of the legitimate activities of clinical psychologists; however, any such list introduces yet another two-part problem. First, a finite list of approved activities in clinical psychology either tends to promote stagnation, if rigid, or to be doomed to early obsolescence, if flexible. That is, on the one hand, such a list may discourage the development of new activities and make it difficult to eliminate old activities that have outlived their original justification. On the other hand, each time the list changes, the list-based definition must be discarded and replaced, making such a definition unstable and unreliable.

Second, the existence of any list of approved activities still requires that the list makers specify the standards or criteria by which their selections are made. Thus, the definitional problem cannot be finessed entirely by a list of activities. Such a list merely begs the criterion question. Unless everyone is willing to accept a decision process that is arbitrary, authoritarian, or secretive, the decision criteria governing the list must be made explicit and defended.

Psychology as a scientific discipline. Here, clinical psychology is defined by its problem focus, theoretical perspective, and epistemological approach to solving the target problems. Clinical psychology is defined as a psychological science directed at the promotion of adaptive functioning; at the assessment, theoretical understanding, amelioration, and prevention of human problems in behavior, affect, cognition or health; at the accumulation of empirically based knowledge concerning these areas of human functioning; and at the application of this knowledge in ways consistent with the best scientific evidence.

While this definition identifies a set of problems and objectives, it does not specify who is pursuing these problems and objectives, what set of activities or techniques is required to achieve the objectives, or what training or credentials are required of participants. In addition to its problem focus, clinical psychology is defined by the conceptual perspective from which it views problems. Finally, it is defined by its fundamental commitment to a scientific epistemology.

This emphasis on science requires that knowledge be advanced by using empirical and quantitative methods to evaluate the validity and utility of testable hypotheses. It also requires that any application of knowledge be guided by the same scientific epistemology.

A critical feature of this definition is that anyone who either advances or applies knowledge in this way is engaging in clinical psychology—i.e., is acting as a clinical psychologist—regardless of whether this person is a card-carrying member of the guild, engages in traditional activities such as testing and psychotherapy, has received training in an accredited doctoral program in clinical psychology, or holds a state license to practice as a psychologist.

Furthermore, according to this definition, even though an individual may have guild membership, a doctoral degree from an accredited clinical training program, and a license to practice, when this person fails to employ a scientific epistemology or to be guided by the empirical evidence when investigating or treating a psychological problem, this person is not engaging in legitimate clinical psychology and, hence, is not at that moment acting as a clinical psychologist.

Thus, this third definition of clinical psychology centers on a general epistemological approach—science as a "way of knowing"—that has proven successful in numerous other problem areas. It applies this "way of knowing" as part of a *commercial* enterprise aimed at solving the interpersonal and intrapersonal problems of human beings. The fact that this problem-solving enterprise is commercial (i.e., psychologists are paid for what they do) has significant legal and ethical implications: clinical psychology must be honest about any services being offered, must deliver on promises, and must avoid doing harm.

Manifesto for a Science of Clinical Psychology

The implications of construing clinical psychology as a science, in this way, have been set forth at length in a "Manifesto for a Clinical Science" (McFall, 1991). For the sake of clarity, the Manifesto summarized the implications in a set of formal propositions, consisting of a Cardinal Principle and two Corollaries, each accompanied by a rationale and extended discussion. These propositions, recapped here, are consistent with the definition of clinical psychology as a science, as presented above:

Cardinal Principle: Scientific Clinical Psychology is the Only Legitimate and Acceptable Form of Clinical Psychology.

First Corollary: All psychological services offered to the public (except under controlled experimental conditions) must meet these minimal criteria:

1. The exact nature of the service must be described clearly.

2. The claimed benefits of the service must be stated explicitly.

3. These claimed benefits must be validated scientifically.

4. The possible negative side effects that might outweigh any benefits must be considered and ruled out empirically.

Second Corollary: The primary and overriding objective of doctoral training programs in clinical psychology must be to produce the most competent clinical scientists possible.

In writing the Manifesto, I made a number of assumptions about the backgrounds and values of most readers. I also tried to anticipate and to address preemptively the readers' most likely questions and concerns. Subsequent reactions to the Manifesto have shown, however, that I had taken too much for granted. To avoid some of the common misconceptions and objections, I needed to spell out in more detail my underlying assumptions.

Donald Peterson's (in press) critique of the Manifesto has been helpful in highlighting many of the points that require clarification and amplification. In response to that critique (McFall, in preparation), I have proposed adding two corollaries to the Manifesto, both aimed at making explicit some of the assumptions that had been implicit previously. The first of these new corollaries explicates some of the ground rules and implications of a scientific epistemology in clinical psychology:

Third Corollary: A scientific epistemology distinguishes science from pseudoscience. According to this epistemology:

1. Skepticism is the appropriate and legitimate stance toward any claims about psychological services.

2. The burden of proof regarding the validity of any psychological service rests squarely with the proponents of that service.

3. Skeptics are not required to prove the negative case. The absence of negative evidence is not equivalent to positive support for the validity of a service.

4. Untested services do not deserve special status; the world is full of untested notions. Skeptics should treat untested services as "invalid" until convinced otherwise by the empirical evidence.

5. Beware of the logical fallacy, "Affirming the Consequent." Claims about outcomes and theoretical explanations for those outcomes must be tested separately. For example, although evidence may show that a treatment is beneficial, this does not mean that the theoretical explanation offered for this effect also is correct.

6. Results are specific. Be conservative about generalizing positive results to untested problems, stimuli, methods, therapists, patients, measures, conditions, etc. Small changes sometimes produce dramatically different results.

7. In the absence of specific evidence, it is better to make decisions cautiously on the basis of the best empirical evidence available than to ignore such evidence and proceed to make decisions idiographically on the basis of clinical intuition and judgment.

The second addition to the Manifesto's corollaries is a direct response to charges that a scientific epistemology is anti-practice and insensitive to the suffering of patients.

Fourth Corollary: The most caring and human psychological services are those that have been shown empirically to be the most effective, efficient, and safe. Genuine caring requires the highest level of scientific rigor. Anything less, no matter how well intentioned, is likely to yield less beneficial results for the individuals being served.

1. Scientific rigor requires that assessment and treatment protocols should be specified in as much detail as possible, validated as specified in the protocol, followed faithfully in clinical applications, and monitored objectively—both in administration and results—in individual cases.

2. The most compassionate procedure for choosing a protocol is one that promotes a fully informed choice, based primarily on a careful review of the scientific evidence and secondarily on a conservative appraisal of the local circumstances.

3. The overriding concern of service providers must be to avoid doing harm or making matters worse. Withholding untested and unproven services often is the most caring and responsible choice.

Clinical Psychology in the Mental Health System

Against this conceptual background, we turn now to a critical analysis of the current and future roles of clinical psychology in the mental health system. As a first step, we will examine the assumptions upon which the current mental health system is built. Because these assumptions seldom are stated explicitly, they seldom receive the scrutiny they deserve. The following list is not exhaustive, but it identifies some of the key assumptions. The importance of each assumption should be self-evident; without each assumption, certain critical components of the current system would be indefensible. After presenting the entire list, we will examine critically the justification for each.

Assumptions Behind the Mental Health System

- Mental health services are beneficial to the recipients.
- These benefits outweigh any potential negative side-effects.
- The benefits are a good return on the consumers' and public's investment in such services.
- Mental health specialists have unique knowledge and skills that make their services more beneficial and cost-effective than those of nonspecialists.
- The cost of training mental health specialists is justified by the increased benefits derived from their services.
- Guild accreditation of mental health training programs protects the public by ensuring that program graduates have the essential knowledge and skills of mental health specialists.
- Governmental licensing and regulation of mental health specialists protects the public by ensuring that licensed individuals are legitimate mental health specialists.

Are the Services Beneficial?

This is a deceptively complex question for which there is no single answer. As Kiesler (1966) and Paul (1969) have warned us, it is a mistake to assume that all services are equivalent; the answer depends on which services are being evaluated (testing, diagnosis, psychotherapy, prediction and evaluation). We need to ask a much more complex and sensitive question: What is the effect of this specific service, delivered by whom, to what client, with what problem, in what context, compared to what alternative, as evaluated by what method and criteria?

The answer also depends on how "beneficial" is defined. Who decides what is counted as a positive outcome, by what criteria, as measured in what way? Furthermore, the benefits of a service cannot be assessed in isolation, but always must be considered in comparison to the effects of something else–e.g., base rates, alternative services. Treatment outcome studies, for example, typically compare experimental treatments with no-treatment control conditions, placebo controls, or minimal-treatment controls. Less common are comparisons with full-fledged competitive treatments. Even less common—but equally appropriate—are outcome comparisons with interventions from outside the mental health system, such as interactions with friends, clergy, or support groups; or spending an equivalent amount of money to join a health club, take a vacation, or make other significant life changes. Obviously, the choice of comparisons alters the likely answer to the "benefit" question.

Only recently have clinical scientists begun to ask detailed questions about the benefits of specific psychological interventions for specific problems. The "Chambless Report" (1993) and reports stimulated by the Agency for Health Care Policy and Research (e.g., Clinton, McCormick & Besteman, 1994; Munoz, Hollon, McGrath, Rehm, & VandenBos, 1994; Schulberg & Rush, 1994) provide selected summaries of the resulting answers. In general, the answers are encouraging: some specific services seem to offer specific benefits.

At the same time, other research reports cast serious doubt on the benefits of other psychological services, such as treatments for obesity (Garner & Wooley, 1991), marital conflict (Jacobson & Addis, 1993), and sexual offenses (Furby, Weinrott & Blackshaw, 1989). Similarly, there is good reason to doubt the value of some common assessment and prediction practices, such as the prediction of violence (Monahan, 1981), the assessment of childhood memories (Dawes, 1994), the assessments of expert witnesses (Faust & Ziskin, 1988), the judgments of clinicians (Dawes, Faust, & Meehl, 1989), and the use of "improved" projective assessments (Wood, Nezworski, & Stejskal, in press).

In short, the available evidence concerning the benefits of psychological services is mixed, at best, suggesting that the benefits of each service must be assessed and evaluated independently. Thus, it is dangerous to assume, in the absence of specific proof, that any psychological service is beneficial.

Do the Benefits Outweigh Potential Negative Side-Effects?

This question has been ignored, so there is little or no research evidence. We can imagine, however, that negative side-effects might take several forms. They might be a direct consequence of some service, such as when psychotherapy actually makes the target problem worse or creates entirely new problems. Negative side-effects also might occur as an indirect consequence of some service; included here might be the financial costs of the service, lost opportunities to obtain alternative services, costs in time and energy, and emotional costs and possible social stigma associated with receiving psychological services. Finally, negative side-effects might be exerted on the larger social system. For example, when incest perpetrators receive psychotherapy, family members are led to believe that this should decreases the likelihood of recidivism. Actually, there is little empirical support for such a reassuring prediction. However, family members who feel reassured are likely to be more trusting of the perpetrator than they should be and, as a result, are likely to be at increased risk of being victimized again.

Clearly, far more research is needed before clinical psychologists can begin to make informed decisions about the relative risks vs. benefits of specific psychological services. In the meantime, skeptics will question the assumption that the benefits of mental health services outweigh their risks. The potential for doing harm must not be minimized.

Are the Services a Good Investment?

The current mental health care system is "breaking the bank." It simply is becoming too expensive to be sustained. The current move toward health-care reform, especially mental health care reform, is being driven by economic realities more than by political ideologies. Governmental agencies and health-insurance companies are looking for ways to reduce the costs of such services while increasing their efficacy. In short, consumers and public officials no longer seem convinced that psychological services are a good investment.

The traditional mental health system was based on a "fee-for-services" model of funding. Unfortunately, this model offers providers few intrinsic incentives for delivering cost-effective services; in fact, the model's incentives actually work against efficient and effective service. Providers make money by delivering as many services as possible to as many customers as possible for as long as possible.

Proposed alternatives to the traditional model are designed to change the incentives. For example, under a "capitation" model, providers agree to assume responsibility for the future mental health care of a specified population within a geographical area for a single up-front fee. Thus, the incentives in this system have been reversed, making the provider bear most of the financial risk associated with the delivery of services. The provider now makes money by delivering the most efficient and economical services to the fewest number of customers.

We still do not know how the mental health care system of the future will be structured and funded. It does seem clear, however, that the new system will be shaped by evidence from cost-benefit analyses, consumer satisfaction data, and market analyses. It will not take for granted that psychological services represent a good investment; instead, it will require that the value of any such services be documented before they are included in the reformed system.

Are Specialists More Effective than Nonspecialists?

It is a widely held assumption that clinical psychologists, by virtue of their specialized training and experience, have unique knowledge and skills that make their services more beneficial than those of nonspecialists (Matarazzo, 1990). Unfortunately, research bearing on this assumption is unlikely to convince a skeptic. For example, recent reviews (Berman & Norton, 1985; Christensen & Jacobson, 1994) of relevant psychotherapy research found few differences in treatment outcome associated with amount of training or experience. Furthermore, other research (Chapman & Chapman, 1969; Dawes, 1986; Dawes, Faust, & Meehl, 1989;

Faust & Ziskin, 1988; Garb, 1989) has shown that the accuracy of psychological assessments based on clinical intuition and judgment does not increase as a function of clinical experience and training.

To some extent, the failure to find research support for the assumed value of professional training and experience may reflect limitations in the way the research question was asked. Specifically, what unique knowledge and skill did investigators think was acquired through training and experience? And by what process would an increase in this knowledge and skill lead to increased benefits from psychological services?

On the one hand, training and experience do not seem to increase a clinical psychologist's warmth and sensitivity, clinical judgment, insight, ability to generate valid explanations, or skill in test interpretation? On the other hand, there is abundant evidence from examination data and measures of on-the-job performance that training and experience can increase a clinical psychologist's knowledge and skills in measurement and prediction, in quantitative methods and research design, in the evaluation and integration of research evidence, in theory building and testing, and in the use of scientific epistemology to study specific problem areas. Thus, there may be more justification for some kinds of training and experience than for others. This has implications for the design of training programs and for the allocation of scarce training resources.

Is Doctoral Training in Clinical Psychology Justified?

The sobering evidence summarized thus far suggests that it is difficult to justify the costs of training doctoral-level clinical psychologists whose primary career goal is to become service providers. If there are few significant differences between doctoral-level clinical psychologists and Masters-level social workers, for example, in terms of the relative effectiveness of their psychotherapeutic services, then what is the added value of the expensive doctoral-level training? Furthermore, if the services of the doctoral-level clinical psychologist cost two to three times as much as the services of the Master's-level social worker, and if there are no discernible differences in the relative effectiveness of their services, then what is the justification for paying extra for the psychologist's services. Faced with such questions, market forces are likely to reduce the number of mental health service-provider jobs for doctoral-level clinical psychologists. In turn, this will undermine further the justification for continued training of doctoral-level service providers.

In contrast, doctoral training in clinical psychology may be justified if the primary goal is to train clinical scientists. Scientific training should prepare graduates for a variety of valuable and specialized career roles: program development and evaluation; supervision and training of service providers; program administration; specialized diagnosis, triage, and system planning; and basic research production, integration, and interpretation. Doctoral-level training with this goal is consistent with the scientific model of clinical psychology that has been developed throughout this chapter.

Does Guild Accreditation Ensure Quality Training?

Does Government Licensing Ensure Professional Competence?

By now, readers should be able to anticipate the answers to these two questions. To the extent that current accreditation and licensing procedures are designed to maintain the status quo in clinical psychology, they provide no assurance whatsoever that training will be high-quality or that practitioners will be competent. There need to be changes in accreditation and licensing aimed at promoting clinical psychology as a science.

Implications for Training in Clinical Science

Although this third and final section is the focal point of the chapter, it also can be succinct. The presentation thus far leads logically to the following conclusions concerning the future of clinical training:

1. **Train fewer doctoral-level students overall**. There will be a decreased demand for clinical psychologists to fill roles as service providers. Therefore, doctoral programs with this orientation should scale back their number of students.

2. **Train more research-oriented students**. As the mental health system changes, there will be an increased number of legitimate roles for clinical scientists. Therefore, more resources should be devoted to this kind of training.

3. **Decrease the number of doctoral training programs overall**. With a shift in emphasis toward science training and away from training for traditional roles, there also will be a significant shift in the overall resources required to meet the demand for such training in clinical psychology. The number of graduate training programs will decrease as a result.

4. **More and better science-training programs are needed**. There are two ways to satisfy an increased demand for clinical scientists: (a) the current number of science-training programs must train more students, or (b) there must be more science-training programs. Science training is labor-intensive, setting a limit on the number of students that can be trained adequately by a faculty of a given size; therefore, the solution is either to expand the number of faculty within a program or to increase the number of programs committed to science training.

5. **Reengineer training programs**. Every aspect of a training program's design should be laid on the drawing board for reconsideration, including program goals, selection procedures, curriculum, organization, duration, financial support systems, allocation of resources, evaluation and feedback systems, and outcome criteria. In particular, it is important to assess the value of traditional practicum training, internship training, and other applied-experiential training in light of research evidence that challenges the incremental validity of such experiences.

6. **Reengineer professional accreditation standards and procedures.** As the models of training undergo change, the systems charged with the responsibility of ensuring quality control in training also must be reexamined and redesigned accordingly. Here again, it may be best to start with a fresh sheet of paper in

rethinking and redesigning the purposes, standards, and procedures of any accreditation enterprise.

7. **Reengineer professional licensing laws.** If there still is some need for professional licensing laws in the revised system—and this is not yet clear—then they, too, must be redesigned with an eye toward ensuring that they actually protect the public, rather than the profession.

8. **Reengineer the mental health care system.** The ultimate and ideal system should provide consumers with the most efficient, effective, and reliable services at the lowest possible cost and with the highest level of safety. The system should be consumer-oriented, not provider-oriented. This suggests that the legitimate roles for clinical psychologists in the future will be those that capitalize on their special scientific training and knowledge.

9. **Reeducate and empower the consumer and public.** The mysticism and magic that have shrouded clinical psychology must be removed. The public must be told honestly what mental health specialists can and cannot do. Consumers must be empowered to make informed choices.

10. **Integrate clinical psychology with the rest of psychological science.** We have made significant progress in recent years toward improving the scientific foundations of clinical psychology and toward integrating it with the rest of scientific psychology. However, we still have a way to go. The remaining gaps are evident in clinical psychology's failure to attend to, incorporate, and build on the most advanced research, theory, and technique from other areas of psychology. For example, cognitive-behavioral theories and methods in clinical psychology bear little relation to the latest advances in cognitive science. Clinical psychologists specializing in neuropsychology seem strangely disconnected from advances in basic neuroscience. And behavior therapists purporting to employ reinforcement techniques too often seem unfamiliar with important developments in reinforcement theory and research over the past several decades (Viken & McFall, 1994).

Summary

In this chapter, I have argued that the only acceptable model of clinical training in the future will be one aimed at training clinical scientists. The only acceptable standards of care in the future will be those grounded in a scientific epistemology. The only legitimate professional roles for clinical scientists in the future will be those that exploit the specialized research training that is the hallmark of doctoral training in psychology. For clinical psychology to justify its existence as an applied science, it must end the functional autonomy that has characterized much of its professional practice and training over the last half-century. This will require a thorough reengineering of training programs, professional organizations, governmental regulations, and health care systems. It also will require a new level of honest, informative communication with the public. Finally, for clinical science to fulfill its promise, it must become fully integrated, at long last, with the rest of psychological science.

References

Astin, A. W. (1961). The functional autonomy of psychotherapy. *American Psychologist*, *16*, 75-78.

Berman, J. S., & Norton, N. C. (1985). Does professional training make a therapist more effective? *Psychological Bulletin*, *98*, 401-407.

Chambless, D. (Chair). (October 1993). Task Force on Promotion and Dissemination of Psychological Procedures. Report to the Board of Division 12, American Psychological Association.

Christensen, A., & Jacobson, N. S. (1994). Who (or what) can do psychotherapy: The status and challenge of nonprofessional therapies. *Psychological Science*, *5*, 8-14.

Chapman, L. J., & Chapman, J. P. (1969). Illusory correlation as an obstacle to the use of valid psychodiagnostic signs. *Journal of Abnormal Psychology*, *74*, 271-287.

Clinton, J. J., McCormick, K., & Besteman, J. (1994). Enhancing clinical practice: The role of practice guidelines. *American Psychologist*, *49*, 30-33.

Dawes, R. M. (1986). Representative thinking in clinical judgment. *Clinical Psychology Review*, *6*, 425-441.

Dawes, R. M. (1994). *House of cards: The collapse of modern psychotherapy*. New York: The Free Press.

Dawes, R. M., Faust, D., & Meehl, P. E. (1989). Clinical versus actuarial judgment. *Science*, *243*, 1668-1674.

Faust, D., & Ziskin, J. (1988). The expert witness in psychology and psychiatry. *Science*, *241*, 31-35.

Furby, L., Weinrott, M. R., & Blackshaw, L. (1989). Sex offender recidivism: A review. *Psychological Bulletin*, *105*, 3-30.

Garb, H. N. (1989). Clinical judgment, clinical training, and professional experience. *Psychological Bulletin*, *105*, 387-396.

Garner, D. M., & Wooley, S. C. (1991). Confronting the failure of behavioral and dietary treatments for obesity. *Clinical Psychology Review*, *11*, 729-780.

Hammer, M., & Champy, J. (1993). *Reengineering the corporation: A manifesto for business revolution*. New York: Harper Collins.

Jacobson, N. S., & Addis, M. E. (1993). Research on couples and couple therapy: What do we know? Where are we going? *Journal of Consulting and Clinical Psychology*, *61*, 85-93.

Kiesler, D. J. (1966). Some myths of psychotherapy research and the search for a paradigm. *Psychological Bulletin*, *65*, 110-136.

Matarazzo, J. D. (1990). Psychological assessment versus psychological testing: Validation from Binet to the school, clinic, and courtroom. *American Psychologist*, *45*, 999-1017.

McFall, R. M. (1991). Manifesto for a science of clinical psychology. *The Clinical Psychologist*, *44*, 75-88.

McFall, R. M. (in preparation). Making psychology incorruptible.

Meehl, P. E. (1973). *Psychodiagnostics: Selected papers*. Minneapolis: University of Minnesota Press.

Monahan, J. (1981). *Predicting violent behavior: An assessment of clinical techniques.* Beverly Hills: Sage.

Munoz, R. F., Hollon, S. D., McGrath, E., Rehm, L. P., & VandenBos, G. R. (1994). On the AHCPR Depression in Primary Care Guidelines: Further considerations for practitioners. *American Psychologist, 49,* 42-61.

Paul, G. L. (1969). Behavior modification research: Design and tactics. In C. M. Franks (Ed.), *Behavior therapy: Appraisal and status* (pp. 29-62). New York: McGraw-Hill.

Peterson, D. R. (in press). Making psychology indispensable. *Applied & Preventive Psychology.*

Rotter, J. B. (1971). On the evaluation of methods of intervening in other people's lives. *The Clinical Psychologist, 24,* 1-2.

Schulberg, H. C., & Rush, A. J. (1994). Clinical practice guidelines for managing major depression in primary care practice. *American Psychologist, 49,* 34-41.

Sechrest, L. (1992). The past future of clinical psychology: A reflection on Woodworth (1937). *Journal of Consulting and Clinical Psychology, 44,* 75-88.

Viken, R. J., & McFall, R. M. (1994). Paradox lost: Implications of contemporary reinforcement theory for behavior therapy. *Current Directions in Psychological Science, 3,* 121-125.

Wood, J. M., Nezworski, M. T., & Stejskal, W. J. (in press). The Comprehensive System for the Rorschach: A critical examination. *Psychological Science.*

Footnotes

1. This chapter focuses on clinical psychology, the author's specialty. This narrow focus is not intended as a slight to other applied specialties. Undoubtedly, many of the issues raised here may apply to other areas of psychology, but the author prefers to allow specialists from these other areas to decide for themselves which parts of the presentation may be most relevant to them. The arguments offered here are not novel. I am indebted to the influences of earlier authors (Meehl, 1973; Rotter, 1971; Sechrest, 1992), although these authors are not responsible for the present paper.

2. This regulation does not imply exclusivity. No activity is reserved exclusively for psychologists; only the use of the professional label is exclusive. Other guilds are allowed by law to engage in similar activities under other professional labels. Thus, psychiatrists, social workers, marital therapists, clergy, lawyers, spiritualists, palm readers, etc. engage in activities that compete directly with activities of clinical psychologists.

Discussion of McFall

Is There a Skeptic in the House?

Ursula Delworth
The University of Iowa

Dick McFall urges us to adopt the role of "Amazing Randy", the "Skeptical Inquirer", as we view clinical practice and training. We need, he believes, to be much more skeptical regarding our assumptions, what we do, and how we educate. He laid our a strong case for clinical psychology as a scientific discipline, and discussed what such a definition and stance means for our work.

While McFall specified that he was talking only about clinical psychology, his points would seem to apply equally well to other psychology specialties, i.e., counseling and school, that define themselves as science-based. In fact, later in his talk, he spoke more in terms of "mental health specialists" and appeared to broaden his message beyond clinical psychology.

As scientific clinicians, McFall stated, we are responsible for being able to make four key statements regarding our practice. First, we need to specify what our service is, then what it can do. We need to back this up with evidence, and we have to be able to discuss any negative side effects. He later looked at negative side effects in more detail, noting that they can be direct or indirect, and range from making the problem worse to societal/system impacts. Placing sex offenders back in their original situations is one example of the latter effect. As McFall noted, there are almost no studies of the negative effect of our work and it's a subject we rarely discuss. This looks like a fertile ground for important work! Outside of a number of program evaluation reports, I can't remember a systematic study of negative effects either.

Genuine caring, states McFall, requires the highest level of scientific rigor. Given the idea that science and caring are not antithetical, but rather partners in the work of an effective practitioner, why do so many clinicians persist in offering unproved or even untested services? "They like what they do," responds McFall. "Systematic desensitization is boring." Indeed, I remember visiting counseling centers in the 70's where staff had developed, implemented, and evaluated effective treatments for a number of the concerns of college students, i.e., study skills, test anxiety. Yet the manuals sat on the shelves and staff noted, "We're not doing that anymore." Some of us began successful programs to train and supervise paraprofessionals in offering these treatments, which provided staff members with a new role as trainers/supervisors, and allowed students to receive appropriate services.

A key point made by McFall is that there is a difference between demonstrating that a specific intervention is effective and proving the validity of the underlying theoretical explanation. These two must be examined separately. In applying an effective intervention to new populations, he cautions us to move carefully from what we know, but not to go back and begin at "ground zero." His advice seems particularly relevant as we move toward applying treatments to individuals and groups that vary in terms of gender, age, ethnicity, or culture form the population with which the intervention was validated.

Do mental health specialists really "do it better"? McFall notes that studies are difficult to find. In fact, in studies done as long as a quarter century ago (my own dissertation included) trained paraprofessionals and professionals (vs. untrained volunteers) were shown to be fairly equally effective in providing specific services. Both the evidence, and lack of evidence, over that time period is fairly sobering. If we are going to continue to train doctoral level professional psychologists, what is the basis for doing this, and how should they be trained? McFall's position is that doctoral training can be justified only if the majority of resources go toward education in a scientific epistemology, toward helping students to understand principles and becoming quantitatively competent. They should know philosophy of science, and be prepared to "sort out" theories. In McFall's program students are introduced to these ideas right at the beginning of the program, rather than three years later in a History & Systems course, which is the norm for many of us.

What then, should doctoral students learn in terms of specific competencies? What should they be able to say they can do? McFall argues for education in program development, supervision and training, program evaluation, diagnosis/system planning, and research production and integration. He also sees program administration as potentially useful. Effective, empirically validated treatments would of course be taught, but McFall emphasized that not every treatment needs to be learned in a graduate program. Doctoral-level professionals need to be able to think through the clinical issues and examine effectiveness of treatments as they are developed. Certainly, the mental health structures that are currently in place and emerging, i.e., managed care, place doctoral-level professionals in roles that require the competencies articulated by McFall. How close are our programs coming to this type of education? At our best, my hunch (with some evidence in the literature) is that we're doing more in supervision and perhaps program evaluation. To get from "here" to "there", McFall stresses the necessity to focus on competence rather than "clock hours" or a set number of years of preparation. He foresees fewer doctoral students, more scientifically trained; fewer programs, but better ones.

McFall calls for the integration of clinical training with psychology as a larger science, and thus circles back to his earlier statement that "scientific clinical psychology as the only form of clinical psychology." And perhaps counseling and school psychology as well? The revolution in roles for doctoral professionals in practice is well underway. The question is whether we will heed McFall's call for education based on a scientific epistemology and including the scientifically based competencies called for in effective practice. For once, what is being increasingly called for in practice is also the kind of education many of us believe is the appropriate type to offer. The opportunity provides a unique "window" for change. McFall offers us a challenge and a clear direction.

Chapter 8

Why Practicing Psychologists are Slow to Adopt Empirically-Validated Treatments

Jacqueline B. Persons
Center for Cognitive Therapy, Oakland, CA

"Peter," an accountant, sought treatment for anxiety and checking rituals that occupied, on average, more than an hour a day and were interfering with his work and his time with his wife and children. After several months of therapy, his symptoms were unchanged. When he asked his therapist for suggestions, the following dialogue ensued:

Therapist: "It looks like you're expecting me to tell you what to do to solve your problem."

Peter: "Yes, I am."

Therapist: "Well, I can't do that. That's something you'll have to figure out on your own."

Fortunately, Peter accepted this intervention. He went to the library and read until he learned that his problem had a name (obsessive-compulsive disorder; OCD) and that it was treatable. Through a self-help group, the Obsessive Compulsive Foundation, he sought out a behavior therapist because he had learned through his reading that behavior therapy had been shown in outcome studies to be the most effective available treatment for the disorder. His therapist referred him to a psychiatrist who prescribed one of the drugs shown to be effective in treating OCD. After about 35 sessions of combined behavior therapy and pharmacotherapy, Peter had learned a battery of useful coping strategies and his symptoms were much improved; he was spending less than 15 minutes a day on rituals.

Peter's case exemplifies the problem that is the focus of this paper: therapists are slow to adopt methods that have been demonstrated effective in the empirical literature (cf. Boudewyns, Fry, & Nightingale, 1986; Glynn, 1990). Lags in adopting innovations occur in other fields as well, including medicine, dentistry, nursing, carpentry, plumbing, and others (Sackett, 1989; Beutler, 1994).

I discuss six hypothesized causes of psychologists' slowness in adopting treatments of demonstrated efficacy and I offer recommendations for alleviating the problem based on those causes. Others have discussed (and studied) these and other obstacles to dissemination of new psychosocial treatments (see Backer, Liberman, & Kuehnel, 1986). The six causes I discuss are: (1) psychologists receive little training in methods that are supported by empirical evidence of efficacy; (2)

psychologists often receive extensive training in methods that are not supported by empirical evidence of efficacy; (3) many clinicians do not read the outcome literature; (4) research findings are difficult for clinicians to utilize; (5) many clinicians believe that all psychotherapies are equally effective; and (6) consumers are uninformed.

Cause 1: Psychologists Receive Little Training in Methods that are Supported by Empirical Evidence of Efficacy

Many graduate students receiving training in psychology today do not learn to conduct the treatments that have been shown in the outcome literature to be effective. The Task Force on Promotion and Dissemination of Psychological Procedures of the Division of Clinical Psychology of the American Psychological Association (APA), chaired by Diane Chambless, recently surveyed predoctoral training programs and internship programs and asked whether they provided training in 25 treatments that met the Task Force's definition of well-validated treatments (American Psychological Association, 1993). The Task Force labelled 18 treatments as *well established* treatments; these were supported by efficacy evidence from two controlled outcome studies conducted by different investigators or by a large series of single case studies; an additional 7 treatments were supported by somewhat weaker evidence, and these were labelled *probably efficacious treatments*; the total comprised a list of 25 validated treatments. The Task Force surveyed all 167 Directors of Clinical Psychology Ph.D. and Psy.D. programs in the US and Canada that are accredited by the APA. Responses indicated that the average program provided didactic instruction in 46% of the validated treatments. This figure is difficult to interpret, as it may not be possible for all programs to teach all 25 efficacious treatments. However, if "minimal coverage" is defined as teaching a minimum of 25% of these treatments, then 22% of programs did not meet this criteria; this number is disturbingly high.

Another aspect of the training problem is that psychologists who were trained many years ago did not receive *any* training in validated treatments because they are new and had not yet been developed when these psychologists were trained. Although most states require that psychologists participate in continuing education to retain their license, continuing education need not involve the study of empirically-validated procedures. As the Chambless Report points out, the APA pays little attention to whether empirical support is available for the material taught in the continuing education courses they endorse.

The fact that part of the training problem is due to the innovation of new treatments suggests that, in part, the problem may solve itself over time. As a new generation of faculty, trained in the newer empirically-supported methods, is appointed, and the old generation retires, training may become more empirically-driven. However, this is certainly not a complete solution. What else can be done?

■   My general recommendation is that psychology training programs place more emphasis on empirically-supported methods. The Chambless report also made this recommendation, and offered suggestions to the APA that will help accomplish this, including the suggestion that those conducting APA site visits of training programs make training in empirically-validated treatments a high priority issue, and that the APA pay more attention to its guideline that continuing education programs it endorses ought to have validation evidence supporting them. However, the APA must be responsive to many constituencies (including many therapists who use methods that do not have empirical support) and therefore other professional associations may have more power to bring about change. What else, and more specifically, can be done?

■ I recommend that professional associations like the Association for Advancement of Behavior Therapy (AABT), the Society for Behavioral Medicine (SBM), and the American Association for Applied and Preventive Psychology (AAAPP) expand the training opportunities they offer. This recommendation is consistent with evidence (Cohen, Sargent, & Sechrest, 1986) indicating that psychologists prefer workshops and supervision to literature when they are receiving training in a new method and by evidence (Backer et al., 1986) that personal contact is a well-validated principle in the research studying dissemination and adoption of innovative methods.

The AABT provides clinical training at its annual convention in the latest cognitive-behavioral methods (not all of which have firm empirical support but many of which do). There is need for more training of this sort, including extended supervision contacts, perhaps by videotape or audiotape. I recommend that the AABT and other professional organizations whose members are expert in validated treatments consider establishing clinical training programs to provide travelling training workshops to clinicians all over the country.

■ I recommend that scientist-practitioners in the community establish training programs for psychologists, including graduate students, interns, and practicing clinicians. For example, several free-standing training programs in providing excellent training in empirically validated methods of cognitive-behavior therapy have sprung up in several cities across the country (e.g., New York, Philadelphia, Cleveland, Atlanta, and Newport Beach). A similar institute could be established to provide training in interpersonal therapy, a well-validated method in which it is particularly difficult to obtain training (APA, 1993). These institutes can meet the needs of clinicians who need training in the latest validated methods. Because they are smaller, more flexible institutions, these centers may be able to adopt innovations more quickly than large universities and they can provide the sort of hands-on clinical training that universities may not wish to support directly, but would like their students to receive.

■ I recommend that graduate students in programs that are weak in training in empirically-supported treatments speak up about this. Students are consumers and their voices count; this is particularly true of free-standing professional schools, who are heavily dependent on tuition. I recommend that AAAPP and other organizations direct dissemination efforts toward the consumers of psychology training.

Cause 2: Psychologists Often Receive Extensive Training in Methods that are Not Supported by Empirical Evidence of Efficacy

Psychologists often receive extensive training in methods that are not supported by empirical evidence of efficacy, as shown in the Chambless Task Force's survey of APA-accredited internship programs. For programs providing training in treating adults, the intervention most often required for completion (20% of programs) and for which supervision was most likely to be available (74% of programs) was "other short-term dynamic therapy," a therapy that does not have any efficacy data meeting the Task Force's criteria. Similarly, for programs providing training in treating children, the two interventions most likely to be required for completion are strategic family therapy (required by 50% of programs) and structural family therapy (required by 50% of programs), neither of which are supported by strong efficacy data!

Psychologists who receive training in methods that are not supported by evidence of efficacy are learning, implicitly, that efficacy evidence is not important. If the teachers and models that students respect are conducting and teaching a model of treatment that is not supported by empirical evidence of efficacy, this must mean that empirical evidence of efficacy is not an important consideration when choosing a psychotherapy.

■ I recommend that we decrease training in methods that are not supported by empirical evidence of efficacy. Decreasing training in methods that are not supported by efficacy evidence will prevent many of the problems that arise when therapists adopt models that do not value outcome evidence.

Psychologists who receive training in methods that do not have empirical support of efficacy often learn a model that itself holds the value that efficacy evidence from controlled clinical trials is not relevant to the practice of psychotherapy. This value is, I would argue, characteristic of psychodynamic models which, until recently, have dominated psychology training. The low value placed on empirical evidence of outcome efficacy by psychodynamic therapists is evidenced by the dearth of controlled outcome studies of psychodynamic psychotherapies (for exceptions, see Crits-Christoph, 1992; Elkin et al., 1989). The belief that therapies supported by outcome data are superior to therapies not supported by outcome data is a value, and therefore not subject to empirical test.

■ I recommend that we increase training in methods that have empirical support of efficacy. This, of course, repeats a recommendation given above. I repeat this recommendation here because it addresses the issue of values. Levenson and Bolter (1988) showed that long-term therapists who received training in brief therapy showed value changes in the direction of the values underlying brief therapy.

Because many graduate students receive training in models that are not supported by controlled outcome studies showing they are efficacious, and because these models often devalue the empirical method and data, many graduate students, in effect, are trained to reject the scientific method as a method for evaluating psychotherapy! This problem arises to a surprising degree (my observation) even in doctoral training programs where the research training is rigorously empirical. Students receive research training that emphasizes the empirical method and clinical training that ignores the scientific method. Sometimes this problem arises because students receive clinical training off campus, where clinicians are not trained to think empirically. However, sometimes the split between "scientific thinking" and "clinical thinking" can be seen even within an academic department of psychology or even within an individual psychologist who adopts the scientific method for his/her research but not for his/her clinical work.

■ I recommend that Directors of Clinical Training and others responsible for training consider adopting the model of Beutler (this volume). Beutler notes that he requires efficacy evidence for all training he authorizes in his department, particularly by outside supervisors.

■ I recommend that we teach and discuss the value that psychotherapies supported by empirical outcome evidence are superior to psychotherapies that are not.

■ I recommend that we offer assistance (stress inoculation, coping skills, assertiveness training) to graduate students trained in empirically-driven research programs who receive training from and interact with clinicians who are not empirically-minded.

The value that empirical evidence of efficacy is not important is embedded not just in the therapist's theoretical model of change, to which s/he may have a great deal of allegiance, but is likely to be part of a large neural network of meanings, including the therapist's professional identity, his/her place in the professional community, his/her relationship to important teachers and mentors, views of processes of change in his/her own psychotherapy, and so on (see Figure 1). Thus, when these clinicians are asked to conform their practice to the outcome evidence, they are not simply being asked to develop a new billing system or to reduce their rates (although they are being asked to do that too!). They are being asked to restructure an elaborated and interconnected set of beliefs, values, and attitudes. As psychotherapists know, this is not easy to accomplish!

The reader can get a feel for the challenge confronting these clinicians by doing the following thought experiment: Imagine that you, a clinician, who depends on your clinical practice for your livelihood, are told that, beginning tomorrow, insurance companies will reimburse your work only if you base your treatment on the theory that all patients with psychological difficulties require one month of intensive thumb-sucking treatment. The rationale for this directive is that the CEO of the ABC Insurance Company recovered from severe depression after receiving this therapy. That is, beginning tomorrow, to earn your living you must use a novel approach to treatment that does not make sense to you and that is supported by evidence that you do not view as relevant. This thought experiment may give the

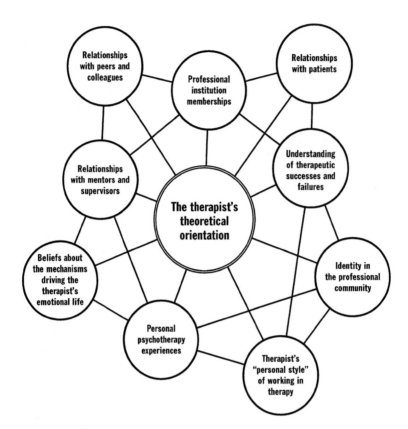

Figure 1. Hypothesized network of meanings linked to therapists' theoretical orientations

reader some ideas about the types of interventions that are likely to be needed if therapists are to adopt new treatments that violate many of the values and assumptions they hold dear.

■   I recommend that AAAPP members or others design interventions, perhaps in workshop format, to help clinicians shift from outdated to new models. These might be modelled on the types of interventions we have developed to assist others who need to make major changes, as when a person who decides to stop drinking needs to make changes in her daily routine, her leisure activities, her circle of friends, her relationships with family members, and even her identity.

Certainly, as I outline in section (4) below, utilizing findings from the research literature in one's clinical work is not easy. However, the problem we are discussing now arises very early in the chain of behaviors that leads to the clinician's utilizing the research literature. The clinicians I'm discussing now do not turn to the empirical literature and find it difficult to use; they do not turn to the empirical literature at all because they do not view it as relevant to their clinical work. The "stages of change" model developed by Prochaska and DiClemente (1986) is useful here.

Prochaska and DiClemente specified that change involves four stages: precontemplation, contemplation, action, and maintenance. The therapists we are discussing here are in the "precontemplation" stage; these therapists do not view the empirical literature as relevant to what they do and therefore do not take any steps to read it or to change their behavior in response to reading it.

Prochaska and DiClemente (1986) describe three processes that help people move from precontemplation to contemplation: "consciousness raising," "dramatic relief," and "environmental reevaluation." *Consciousness raising* involves "observations, confrontations, and interpretations ... that help clients become more aware of the causes, consequences, and cures of their problems ... *dramatic relief* provides clients with helpful affective experiences (e.g., psychodrama or the Gestalt intervention using the empty chair) which can raise emotions related to problem behaviors. Life events such as the disease or death of a friend or lover can also move precontemplators emotionally, especially if such events are problem related." (p. 304).

■ I recommend that we use the methods suggested by Prochaska and DiClemente to help clinicians move from precontemplation to contemplation of using empirical findings in their work. *Consciousness raising* might involve empirically-minded therapists becoming more assertive when interacting with therapists who use ineffective methods. *Dramatic relief* might involve using affectively-charged case reports or videos to convey to clinicians the power of effective new methods. The advent of managed care may serve as a life event that prods clinicians to attend to efficacy data.

Cause 3: Many Clinicians Do Not Read the Outcome Literature

Information about effective new treatments is presented in the empirical literature. However, many clinicians do not read the outcome literature (Cohen et al., 1986; Morrow-Bradley & Elliott, 1986; O'Donohue, Curtis, & Fisher, 1985), probably for many of the reasons discussed in the previous section. Psychologists have not devoted efforts to disseminating information about new treatments. As Barlow (1994) points out: "A drug company spends hundreds of millions of dollars in promotion when a new drug is developed, when we develop a new approach it just sits there." (p. 7). Linda Sobell devoted her presidential address to the AABT membership in November, 1994 to this topic, arguing that behavior therapists have developed effective treatments but that these treatments are not being widely used because not resources have been devoted to disseminating them.

■ I recommend that psychologists present information about effective new treatments outside the empirical literature (see also Beutler, Williams, and Wakefield, 1993). I recommend several types of dissemination efforts, including:

■ **Journals for the clinician.** We need journals that present information about effective new treatments in a readable, compelling way. We need, for example, case reports of patients with panic disorder successfully treated with cognitive-behavior therapy and moving writeups of depressed patients who show positive responses to interpersonal therapy.

Successful therapists often do not write these types of reports, for several reasons. Case reports have been undervalued (Davison & Lazarus, 1994). Clinical writing has also been undervalued. Behavior therapists, for example, may have been so heavily indoctrinated into the experimental method that they are reluctant to write up a case unless it advances knowledge in some way.

In addition, until recently, there were no publication outlets for writing of this sort. Moreover, therapists are not trained to do professional, clinical writing; thus, good clinicians often do not have the needed writing skills, whereas those with good writing skills do not always have the needed clinical savvy.

Recently, several outlets for good clinical writing have emerged. One is *Cognitive and Behavioral Practice*, published by the AABT and developed during Jerry Davison's tenure as chair of the AABT Publications Committee. The first issue of CBP appeared in the summer of 1994, edited by Denise Davison with the assistance of Lizette Peterson, editor of *Behavior Therapy*. CBP is intended as an outlet for "empirically informed methods of clinical practice." (Davis & Peterson, 1994, p. 1).

Another is *In Session: Psychotherapy in Practice*, published by Wiley and edited by Marvin Goldfried. Goldfried's journal will emphasize theoretical diversity, in contrast to the AABT journal, which publishes material about cognitive and behavioral therapies. Wiley also recently began publishing another journal for clinicians, titled *Clinical Psychology and Psychotherapy: An International Journal of Theory & Practice*, edited by Paul Emmelkamp and Mick Power; the first volume appeared in 1994. Already-existing outlets include *Psychiatric Annals: The Journal of Continuing Psychiatric Education*. It provides readable pieces for clinicians to keep them abreast of the latest findings, and includes quizzes that clinicians can complete for CE credits.

Certainly the dissemination to practicing clinicians of the treatments supported by the latest outcome data helps solve the problem addressed in this paper (why clinicians are slow to adopt empirically-validated treatments). However, when clinicians are invited to write about their work, many present ideas and interventions that are not supported by outcome data. Beutler et al. (1993) pointed to this difficulty, and it deserves serious attention. Journal editors and reviewers can play a key role here, encouraging authors to present interventions supported by outcome data, and asking authors whose interventions are not supported by outcome data to say so.

■ **Treatment protocols and practitioner-oriented guidebooks.** The availability of the session-by-session treatment protocols used in the controlled outcome studies is certainly a boon to the practicing clinician. Cohen et al. (1986) reported that practicing psychologists stated that availability of the details of a positively evaluated treatment would increase their use of the treatment. The first book of this sort to be published was probably Beck, Rush, Shaw, & Emery (1979) *Cognitive*

Therapy for Depression, which presents the protocol used in the NIMH Treatment of Depression Collaborative Research Program. Others include Klerman, Weissman, Rounsaville and Chevron's (1984) manual for interpersonal therapy, and Linehan's (1993) treatment for women with borderline personality disorder.

Videotapes, such as those recently published by the American Psychological Association, can also be useful in providing clinicians with the details of new treatments (APA, 1994). The APA videotapes display psychologists demonstrating therapies that have some supportive empirical outcome data as well as some with little or no outcome data.

Dissemination efforts to consumers can also reach clinicians; I discuss those in a section below. I turn now to a discussion of one reason clinicians may ignore the empirical literature.

Cause 4: Research Findings are Difficult for Clinicians to Use

Clinicians who attempt to utilize the findings of the empirical outcome literature encounter several difficulties. I discuss two here.

First, research samples do not match clinical samples. That is, the patients seen in clinicians' offices and the patients treated in research protocols are not the same patients. Second, standardized protocols are not easily adapted to clinicians' usual modes of working, which emphasizes the use of individualized treatment plans based on a case conceptualization. A third difficulty (not discussed here) is that research studies often do not address issues of clinical significance; this issue has been extensively discussed by Neil Jacobson and colleagues (cf. Jacobson, Follette, & Revenstorf, 1984), among others.

Research samples do not match clinical samples. This fact can be seen from the extensive screening criteria and resulting low acceptance rates of patients who seek treatment in the controlled outcome studies. Thus, in the NIMH Treatment of Depression Collaborative Research Program (TDCRP), many patients who sought to participate were screened out, including those with serious medical problems, those with significant substance abuse problems, significant anxiety disorders, or suicidality severe enough that hospitalization was necessary. In the TDCRP, only 250 of 560 (45%) of patients who passed an initial prescreen met the selection criteria and were admitted into the study. Selection rates for other outcome studies are similar; for the outcome study conducted by Murphy, Simons, Wetzel, and Lustman (1984) it was 33%, and for the one conducted by Rush, Beck, Kovacs, & Hollon (1977) it was 37%.

The high exclusion rates of the controlled clinical trials is in part a function of the fact that the clinical outcomes field in psychiatry is a relatively young one. Investigators, very reasonably, began with studies of homogeneous patient populations, and are now beginning to study more heterogeneous samples that are more representative of the patients seen by clinicians in routine practice. However, the strategy of developing standardized protocol treatments for single disorders seems to break down when patients with multiple comorbidities are involved. For example, although standardized protocol treatments are now available for patients with major depression, social phobia, substance abuse, and marital problems, no protocol is currently available—or likely ever to be available—for treating a depressed social phobic who is abusing alcohol and has marital problems and diabetes. Thus, the practicing clinician is faced with the difficulty of deciding when to use and how to adapt the protocols developed for homogeneous patient populations to the patients s/he treats in his office.

Standardized protocols are not easily adapted to clinicians' usual modes of working, which emphasizes the use of individualized treatment plans based on a case conceptualization. Most models of psychotherapy teach clinicians to use an individualized, formulation-driven (not standardized) approach to treatment. A formulation-driven strategy is even central to behavior therapy, despite the fact that behavior therapists have been responsible for most of the standardized protocol treatments that are now available. Behavior therapists have been trained to view each case as an $N = 1$ experiment in which the role of the therapist is to conduct an assessment, develop a hypothesis (formulation) about the nature of the mechanisms controlling the target problems, use the formulation to make a treatment plan, and then monitor the outcome of the treatment as a way of "testing" the formulation (Barlow, Hayes, & Nelson, 1984). This hypothesis-driven, theory-driven approach to assessment and treatment is very different from the standardized protocol approach to treatment utilized in the controlled outcome studies. This discrepancy makes it difficult for the clinician to utilize the findings of controlled outcome studies in which patients were treated with standardized protocols.

To address these difficulties, I offer the following recommendations. These are recommendations for teachers and researchers, not clinicians.

■   I recommend that psychologists teach an empirical approach to clinical work. I suggest we teach clinicians—of all orientations—to use an empirical, hypothesis-testing approach to their clinical work. Barlow, Hayes, and Nelson (1984) have written an outstanding textbook of this sort for behavior therapists; similar texts are needed for therapists using other models. The recent practice guideline for treatment of depression in primary care published by the Agency for Health Care Policy and Research (1994) also provides an elegant model of an empirical approach to the management of clinical depression.

■   I recommend that psychologists write standardized protocols for conducting individualized, hypothesis-testing therapies (Persons, 1991). This recommendation is "orientation-neutral," as I believe this sort of protocol could be written for any theoretical orientation. The efficacy of these treatment protocols must then be subjected to empirical study, of course. These types of protocols would be particularly useful for treating patients with multiple comorbidities and for evaluating clinically significant change.

Cause 5: Many Clinicians Believe That all Psychotherapies are Equally Effective

The view that all therapies are equally effective contributes to the slow pace of adoption of effective new treatments by discouraging therapists and teachers from reviewing the literature to choose the most effective treatments for their patients and students. The view that all psychotherapies are equally effective is a widely-held one with several underpinnings. One is the outcome literature. Beginning perhaps most prominently with the Luborsky, Singer, and Luborsky (1975) paper titled "Comparative studies of psychotherapies: Is it true that everyone has won and all must have prizes?", comparative outcome studies and reviews of comparative outcome studies have repeatedly concluded that no efficacy difference can be found between psychotherapies. The failure to find differences in the very important NIMH Treatment of Depression Collaborative Research Program (Elkin et al., 1989) has also contributed to the view that all psychotherapies are equally effective.

The conclusion that all psychotherapies are equally effective also gains strength because it is reinforcing to clinicians from different orientations who interact professionally, including in professional associations like the American Psychological Association. The "all therapies are equally effective" myth eases tensions and facilitates collegiality. In professional settings the clinician quickly learns that it is extremely poor manners to assert that one's method of treatment is superior to the method used by others.

However, like others (Giles et al., 1993; Lazarus, Beutler, & Norcross, 1992) I believe that the outcome data do not support the view that all therapies are equally effective. Two types of data do not support this view.

First, recent studies have begun to show differential effects of psychotherapies more than earlier studies did. For example, Steketee and Lam (1993) recently argued, as have others, that the empirical data show that exposure and response prevention is the treatment of choice for obsessive-compulsive disorder. Linehan and her colleagues (1991) showed that dialectical behavior therapy for women with borderline personality disorder was more effective than treatment as usual in reducing parasuicidality and the need for inpatient hospitalization. Giles, Neims, and Prial (1993) recently argued that the outcome literature shows superiority of "prescriptive forms of care, especially those of a behavioral of cognitive-behavioral nature," over traditional treatments for a wide variety of disorders of children and adults.

The second type of outcome evidence that does not support the view that all therapies are equally effective does not rely on comparative outcome studies at all. It relies on the fact that some psychotherapies are supported by efficacy data from controlled clinical trials, whereas others are not, or are supported by much less data. Like Klerman (1990), I would argue that interventions supported by outcome data from controlled clinical trials are superior to interventions not supported by such data. This line of reasoning was adopted by the Agency for Health Care Policy and Research (AHCPR, 1993) in its practice guideline for treatment of depression in primary care. The AHCPR recommended that only treatments supported by efficacy evidence be used as first-line treatments.

Thus, for example, in the instance of major depression, no controlled clinical trial has compared the efficacy of cognitive-behavior therapy (CBT) and long-term psychodynamic therapy. Of the many controlled clinical trials comparing the efficacy of CBT and antidepressant medication, the vast majority have found no difference between the treatments. Do these findings mean that these three treatments are equally effective? Do they mean that the clinician ought to recommend any of these treatments, with equal confidence, to his/her patient?

If we use the approach proposed by Klerman (1990) (interventions supported by outcome data from controlled clinical trials are preferred over interventions not supported by such data), then CBT is superior to long-term psychodynamic psychotherapy in the treatment of depression. This argument also leads to the conclusion that pharmacotherapy is superior to CBT in the treatment of major depression, due to the far greater number of controlled clinical trials of antidepressant medication! (As Barlow (1994) recently pointed out, once a "respectable number" of studies have been carried out, we might not wish to compare treatments on the basis of a tally of studies.)

Thus, here again, we have the problem that practicing clinicians hold a belief (all treatments are equal) that is simply not supported by the empirical literature! How can this problem be remedied?

If belief in the myth that all psychotherapies are equally effective is based in part on comparative outcome studies, and if studies of differential efficacy become more common, then this problem may begin to remedy itself, as data continue to emerge and as newer and more powerful treatments are developed. However, if clinicians do not read the outcome literature, as argued earlier, they will not see these new studies.

■ I recommend that well-informed psychologists publish attention-grabbing articles debunking this myth in places likely to be encountered by practicing clinicians, including the clinically-oriented journals described earlier.

To address the interpersonal causes of the problem described above,

■ I recommend that empirically-minded psychologists establish guidelines for interacting with other clinicians and with patients when another psychologist or other mental health professional is conducting treatment that is not guided by empirical considerations. For example, what does the responsible clinician say when interacting with a clinician who is recommending long-term psychodynamic psychotherapy as a first-line treatment for major depression? O'Donohue and Szymanski (1994) suggest that clinicians use a heuristic offered by Paul Meehl: "How would I respond to the clinician's assertions if I knew that these assertions were involved in the treatment of one of my loved ones?"

Cause 6: Consumers are Uninformed

Most consumers are unaware of the outcomes literature in psychotherapy; in addition, they are accustomed to following doctors' orders. As a result, they accept the treatment procedures offered by psychologists even when they are not supported by outcome data. Often these traditional procedures are provided by highly-regarded university clinics and medical centers.

However, as consumers (both patients and insurance companies) are becoming more sophisticated, they are asking clinicians about outcome data, and they are learning about and asking for new treatments of demonstrated efficacy. Consumers are increasingly reluctant to pay a professional to carry out traditional treatments that have not been shown to be effective. As a result of these marketplace pressures, practitioners themselves are learning (often from their patients and insurance companies) more about these treatments and, seeing the need to conduct them in order to stay in business, are becoming increasingly willing to learn about new treatments of demonstrated effectiveness. Because practitioners must meet the needs of their customers in order to stay in business, educated consumers hold quite a lot of power to change practitioners' behavior. Thus, efforts expended to educate consumers about effective new treatments seem likely to lead to behavior change on the part of practitioners. I recommend that psychologists educate consumers. Many types of efforts can be carried out to do this, including:

■ Appear on "Oprah!" and similar TV shows to "show off" an effective new treatment.

■ Write articles about effective, empirically-supported interventions for lay publications. For example, a very excellent article in *The Atlantic Monthly* titled "Therapy for Children" appeared in June 1991; it described psychodynamic, cognitive-behavioral, and family-systems therapies for the sophisticated lay reader.

■ Write a trade book describing an empirically-validated treatment. Books like *Feeling Good* (a presentation of cognitive therapy for depression by David Burns, first published in 1980), *Stop Obsessing* (behavior therapy for obsessive-compulsive disorder by Foa and Wilson, published in 1991), and *Dying of Embarrassment* (cognitive-behavioral strategies for coping with social phobia, by Markway, Carmin, Pollard, & Flynn, 1992) provide excellent up-to-date information to lay readers about new treatments of demonstrated efficacy. These books are quite useful in educating therapists as well; Burns' (1980) book, for example, was used to train the cognitive-behavior therapists in the NIMH Collaborative Study.

■ Write a letter to the editor of your local newspaper or the New York Times on outcome topics of current interest. For example, the recent burst of publicity about sexual abuse by Catholic priests raises important questions about the efficacy data for treatment of pedophiles. Experts in this area can make an important contribution to the education of the lay public by offering their expertise in newspapers and other public forums. I also encourage psychologists to write to "Dear Abby" or "Ann Landers" when these columnists are providing outdated or incomplete information. These items, if published, will have far wider distribution and impact than many articles published in high-powered academic journals.

■ Publish a mental health letter for the lay public. The Harvard Mental Health Letter is an example of this type of publication. I suggest that AAAPP and AABT consider publishing a mental health letter for the lay public. This idea has the potential to make money.

■ Support self-help organizations like the Obsessive Compulsive Foundation, the Anxiety Disorders Association of America, and others who carry out responsible efforts to educate consumers about effective new treatments. Pay your dues, read the newsletter, and encourage your patients, students, and colleagues to do the same.

The efforts described here are pitched to the patient consumer. Insurance companies and managed care companies are also important consumers of psychological services. To educate managed care and insurance companies, the AAAPP plans to issue practice guidelines describing the disorders for which effective treatments are available, and describing the treatments. This will allow insurance companies to encourage practitioners to carry out those treatments.

Another consumer that deserves mention is the graduate student, particularly the Psy.D. student and the student attending a professional school of psychology. These students often pay high tuition but do not receive training in empirically-supported treatments that are increasingly preferred by patients and insurance companies. I recommend these students develop strategies for encouraging their professional schools to provide more training in treatments of demonstrated efficacy. If students reward the schools that provide training in empirically validated treatments, schools will increase their training in these methods.

Concluding remarks

I have outlined six causes of practicing psychologists' reluctance to adopt treatments of demonstrated efficacy and I've made recommendations based on these causes that might address the problem. Of course, whether these interventions are helpful is an empirical question. Let me conclude with several remarks.

Failure to use empirical evidence is not specific to practicing psychologists. It can also be seen in psychiatrists, social workers, alcohol counselors, and other mental health professionals. In fact, it is typical of all of us. None of us are very good at drawing on scientific findings when we make decisions and process information in our day-to-day life (see Paulos, 1988). Instead, as Kahneman and Tversky (1973) and Paulos (1988) have shown, we draw on invalid heuristics and fall prey to fallacies and distortions.

I mention here one additional suggestion for speeding the adoption of treatments of demonstrated efficacy that I do not discuss in detail: legal action. The Chestnut Lodge case and the attention it received in the professional literature (Klerman, 1990; Stone, 1990) illustrate the power of this strategy. The AAAPP and other professional associations might consider legal action.

To generate additional strategies for solving this problem, I recommend research to enhance our understanding of it.

References

Agency for Health Care Policy and Research, U. S. Public Health Service. (1993). *Clinical Practice Guideline Number 5. Depression in Primary Care: Volume 2. Treatment of Major Depression.* Rockville, MD: Author.

American Psychological Association. (1993). *Task Force on Promotion and Dissemination of Psychological Procedures.* A Report adopted by the Division 12 Board, October 1993.

American Psychological Association. (1994). *Psychotherapy videotape series.* Washington, D. C.

Backer, T. E., Liberman, R. P., & Kuehnel, T. G. (1986). Dissemination and adoption of innovative psychosocial interventions. *Journal of Consulting and Clinical Psychology, 54,* 111-118.

Barlow, D. H. (1994). Interview published in *The Scientist Practitioner,* newsletter of the American Association of Applied and Preventive Psychology, October 1994, *4,* 6.

Barlow, D. H. (1994). Psychological interventions in the era of managed competition. *Clinical Psychology: Science and Practice, 1,* 109-122.

Barlow, D. H., Hayes, S. C., & Nelson, R. O. (1984). *The scientist-practitioner: Research and accountability in clinical and educational settings.* New York: Pergamon.

Beck, A. T., Rush, A. J., Shaw, B. F., & Emery, G. (1979). *Cognitive therapy of depression.* New York: Guilford.

Beutler, L. E. (1994). *Bridging the gap from science to practice.* Keynote address, Association for Advancement of Behavior Therapy, San Diego, November 11, 1994.

Beutler, L. E., Williams, R. E., & Wakefield, P. J. (1993). Obstacles to disseminating applied psychological science. *Applied and Preventive Psychology, 2,* 53-58.

Boudewyns, P., Fry, T., & Nightingale, E. (1986). Token economy programs in the V. A. medical centers: Where are they today? *The Behavior Therapist, 6,* 126-127.

Burns, D. D. (1980). *Feeling good: The new mood therapy.* New York: William Morrow.

Cohen, L. H., Sargent, M. M., & Sechrest, L. B. (1985). Use of psychotherapy research by professional psychologists. *American Psychologist, 41,* 198-206.

Crits-Christoph, P. (1992). The efficacy of brief dynamic psychotherapy: A meta-analysis. *The American Journal of Psychiatry, 149,* 151-158.

Davis, D., & Peterson, L. (1994). Cognitive and behavioral practice. *Cognitive and Behavioral Practice, 1,* 1-4.

Davison, G. C., & Lazarus, A. A. (1994). Clinical innovation and evaluation: Integrating practice with inquiry. *Clinical Psychology: Science and Practice, 1,* 157-168.

Elkin, I., Shea, M. T., Watkins, J. T., Imber, S. D., Sotsky, S. M., Collins, J. F., Glass, D. R., Pilkonis, P. A., Leber, W. R., Docherty, J. P., Fiester, S. J., & Parloff, M. B. (1989). NIMH Treatment of Depression Collaborative Research Program: General effectiveness of treatments. *Archives of General Psychiatry, 46,* 971-982.

Foa, E. B., & Wilson, R. (1991). *Stop obsessing! How to overcome your obsessions and compulsions.* New York: Bantam.

Giles, T. R. (Ed.). (1993). *Handbook of effective psychotherapy.* New York: Plenum.

Giles, T. R., Neims, D. M., & Prial, E. M. (1993). The relative efficacy of prescriptive techniques. In T. R. Giles (Ed.), *Handbook of effective psychotherapy* (pp. 21-39). New York: Plenum.

Glynn, S. (1990). The token economy: Progress and pitfalls over 25 years. *Behavior Modification, 14,* 383-407.

Jacobson, N. S., Follette, W. C., & Revenstorf, D. (1984). Psychotherapy outcome research: Methods for reporting variability and evaluating clinical significance. *Behavior Therapy, 15,* 336-352.

Kahneman, D., & Tversky, A. (1973). On the psychology of prediction. *Psychological Review, 80,* 237-251.

Klerman, G. L. (1990). The psychiatric patient's right to effective treatment: Implications of *Osheroff v. Chestnut Lodge. Journal of Psychiatry, 147,* 409-418.

Klerman, G. L., Weissman, M. M., Rounsaville, B. J., & Chevron, E. S. (1984). *Interpersonal psychotherapy for depression.* New York: Basic Books.

Lazarus, A. A., Beutler, L. E., & Norcross, J. C. (1992). The future of technical eclecticism. *Psychotherapy, 29,* 11-20.

Levenson, H., & Bolter, K. (1988, August). Short-term psychotherapy values and attitudes: Changes with training. In H. Levenson (Chair), *The reluctant therapist: Attitudes and resistances toward short-term psychotherapy.* Symposium conducted at the annual meeting of the American Psychological Association, Atlanta.

Linehan, M. M. (1993). *Cognitive-behavioral treatment of borderline personality disorder.* New York: Guilford.

Linehan, M. M., Armstrong, H. E., Suarez, A., Allmon, D., & Heard, H. L. (1991). Cognitive-behavioral treatment of chronically parasuicidal borderline patients. *Archives of General Psychiatry, 48,* 1060-1064.

Luborsky, L., Singer, B., & Luborsky, L. (1975). Comparative studies of psychotherapies: Is it true that "Everyone has won and all must have prizes"? *Archives of General Psychiatry, 32,* 995-1008.

Markway, B. G., Carmin, C. N., Pollard, C. A., & Flynn, T. (1992). *Dying of embarrassment: Help for social anxiety and phobia.* Oakland, CA: New Harbinger Publications.

Morrow-Bradley, C., & Elliot, R. (1986). Utilization of psychotherapy research by practicing psychotherapists. *American Psychologist, 41,* 188-197.

Murphy, G. E., Simons, A. D., Wetzel, R. D., & Lustman, P. J. (1984). Cognitive therapy and pharmacotherapy. *Archives of General Psychiatry, 41,* 33-41.

O'Donohue, W., Curtis, D. D., & Fisher, J. E. (1985). Use of research in the practice of community mental health: A case study. *Professional Psychology: Research and Practice, 16,* 710-718.

O'Donohue, W., & Szymanski, J. (1994). How to win friends and not influence clients: Popular but problematic ideas that impair treatment decisions. *The Behavior Therapist, 17*, 29-33.

Paulos, J. A. (1988). *Innumeracy: Mathematical illiteracy and its consequences.* New York: Vintage Books.

Persons, J. B. (1991). Psychotherapy outcome studies do not accurately represent current models of psychotherapy: a proposed remedy. *American Psychologist, 46*, 99-106.

Prochaska, J. O., & DiClemente, C. C. (1986). The transtheoretical approach. In J. C. Norcross (Ed.), *Handbook of Eclectic Psychotherapy* (pp. 163-200). New York: Brunner/Mazel.

Rush, A. J., Beck, A. T., Kovacs, M., & Hollon, S. (1977). Comparative efficacy of cognitive therapy and pharmacotherapy in the treatment of depressed outpatients. *Cognitive Therapy and Research, 1*, 17-38.

Sackett, D. L. (1989). Inference and decision at the bedside. *Journal of Clinical Epidemiology, 42*, 309-316.

Steketee, G., & Lam, J. (1993). Obsessive-compulsive disorder. In T. R. Giles (Ed.), *Handbook of effective psychotherapy* (pp. 253-278). New York: Plenum.

Stone, A. A. (1990). Law, science, and psychiatric malpractice: A response to Klerman's indictment of psychoanalytic psychiatry. *Journal of Psychiatry, 147*, 419-427.

Author Notes

I thank Joan Davidson and Andrew Bertagnolli for helpful discussions. Andrew Bertagnolli drew the figure.

Discussion of Persons

Dissemination of What, and to Whom?

Barbara S. Kohlenberg
Reno Veterans Administration Medical Center

Jacqueline Persons contends that when clinical science develops a treatment that has demonstrated efficacy, then that treatment should be disseminated broadly to both practitioners and to the lay public. This argument is based on her beliefs that consumers would be provided with increased quality of care if scientists attended more closely to those involved in direct service, and if those who provide direct service would attend more consciously to the findings of science. Educating the lay public about efficacious treatments, in turn, would both encourage practitioners to attend more closely to the findings of science, and would build in protection for the consumer of mental health services. Many practical suggestions are offered in support of developing the two-way information exchange between scientists and practitioners. The spirit of this argument is sensible and compelling on many levels. For the argument to develop and maintain widespread support, the following matters might be considered.

Outcome Measures

Dr. Persons argues that symptom reduction is the dependent measure against which all treatments may be compared. She notes that other approaches in psychology embrace other dependent measures, such as psychoanalysts valuing "increased understanding" as a valuable outcome, and process oriented clinicians in general looking at the overall clinical value of an intervention, rather than symptom reduction per se. She justly observes that these differences in dependent measures across practicing psychologists reflect differences in world views. Dr. Persons' agenda, however, is to assert that her world view (that which embraces symptom reduction as the most critical outcome measure) really is the one that should be the standard.

Dr. Persons' argument is weakened if she remains isolated from other empirically minded psychotherapy researchers who consider and attempt to measure other aspects of gain resulting from psychotherapy (e.g., Greenberg, 1994; Hayes, 1987; Koerner, Jacobson & Christensen, 1994; Weiss & Sampson, 1986). It might be the case that an attempt to be more integrative about outcome measures would open the door to consider the benefits offered by positions other than those that are strictly cognitive behavioral. If left to the consumer, might not a treatment offering symptom reduction, increased understanding, and improved intimate relationships be more compelling than only one of the above, offered alone? Furthermore, if attempts are made to be well positioned politically and within managed care, it would seem that the broader the base of empirical support for what is efficacious would only lend strength to the standards developed.

Problems with Existing Research

While some argue studies comparing cognitive behavioral treatments with other treatments show no difference in outcome (Shapiro, Barkham, Rees, Hardy, Reynolds, & Startup, 1994), and sometimes even show that other treatments are superior to behavior therapy along some dimensions (Snyder, Wills, & Grady-Fletcher, 1991), it is also true that there are many studies which point to the superiority of behavioral treatments. For example, behavioral couples therapy has been shown in over two dozen studies to be superior to control groups (Hahlweg & Markman, 1988).

Whatever position one chooses to embrace does not obviate the difficulties inherent in the data to which one appeals. Dr. Persons' points to several problems in existing clinical research such as stringent exclusion criteria (in order to produce controlled research) and similarly, the lack of co-morbidity in research samples. She also notes that an abundance of data exists supporting cognitive behavioral techniques, perhaps in part because research activities are more valued by cognitive behaviorists than those affiliated with other process oriented orientations. The empirical base for the superiority of cognitive behavioral/behavioral treatments must also be tempered by the possible generalizability of the finding that in the area of behavioral couples therapy, in no published study has the experimental condition (behavioral or otherwise) failed to prove more efficacious than the control groups (Jacobson & Addis, 1993). These are not small problems, and they underscore the notion that the persuasiveness of data are determined largely by the audience viewing the data (Cordova & Koerner, 1993).

Dissemination of What, to Whom?

The dissemination of information produced by clinical science is a very important value on several levels. Clinicians who are not involved in producing or consuming clinical research would be stronger, both politically and practically, by establishing a closer relationship to the research literature. Similarly, researchers could produce more pervasive effects if they broadened their intended audience from strictly other clinical researchers to clinicians. In addition, the lay public could only benefit by being better informed about the mental health services that they seek. We would hope as well that managed care would also base decisions made on research findings that point to quality rather than on strictly efficiency or monetary concerns.

However, in the service of supporting the end goal of providing the most valuable services the most efficiently to the consumer, the idea of using empirical data as the driving force for decision making must be done intelligently, not blindly. Empirical data are not entirely objective, as is learned when one observes different audiences reactions to the same data set. What is convincing to one group of empirically-based scientific psychologists, may or may not be embraced by the next group of empirically-based scientific psychologists (Koerner, et al., 1993). And it appears that those willing to live by the sword are not always willing to die by the sword. This is not simple-minded arrogance at work, it is a reflection of sophisticated, thoughtful researchers who may be trying to conduct a drag race comparing two treatments but who in actuality are racing different directions.

While racing toward "symptom reduction" is a goal probably shared at some level by most therapists (alleviation of suffering is probably embraced by all schools of therapy), this goal is weighted differently by process-oriented therapists. Process oriented treatments base their techniques on the notion that clinical change occurs indirectly, and that directly attacking clinical symptoms and dysfunctions can actually be damaging in the long run (Gold, 1995). It is of interest that this approach coincides with findings in the experimental human operant laboratory looking at rule-governed verses contingency shaped behavior. Essentially, what data from basic laboratories in this area suggest is that while rule-governed behavior might produce the most rapid results, contingency shaped behavior tends to produce behavior that takes longer to emerge but when it does it is more flexible and adaptable than what is produced by rule governed behavior (e.g. Hayes, 1989).

While protecting the consumer, dissemination of efficacious techniques, and encouraging scientist practitioner dialogue are goals scientific psychology should absolutely stand behind, we must not be narrow or chauvinistic about the particular theoretical orientation or brand of empiricism we happen to embrace. There are those who would argue that behavior therapy does not have the corner on efficacious techniques, nor are our target behaviors embraced by all. These perspectives must be carefully considered when attempting to arrive at standards that will be palatable to a broad base of empirically minded psychologists. After all, strength is in numbers and if our goal is to work toward the alleviation of suffering, we must attempt to unify, not divide in our pursuit of this end.

References

Cordova, J. V., & Koerner, K. (1993). Persuasion criteria in research and practice: Gathering more meaningful psychotherapy data. *The Behavior Analyst, 16*, 317-330.

Gold, J. R. (1995). The place of process-oriented psychotherapies in an outcome-oriented psychology and society. *Applied & Preventive Psychology, 4*, 61-74.

Greenberg, L. (1994). Acceptance in experiential therapy. In S. Hayes, N. Jacobson, V. Follette, & M. Dougher (Eds.), *Acceptance and change: Content and context in psychotherapy* (pp. 53-67). Reno, NV: Context Press.

Hahlweg, K., & Markman, H. J. (1988). The effectiveness of behavioral marital therapy: Empirical status of behavioral techniques in preventing and alleviating marital distress. *Journal of Consulting and Clinical Psychology, 56*, 440-447.

Hayes, S. C. (1987). A contextual approach to therapeutic change. In N. S. Jacobson (Ed.), *Psychotherapists in clinical practice: Cognitive and behavioral perspectives* (327-387). New York: Guilford.

Hayes, S. C. (Ed.). (1989). *Rule-governed behavior: Cognition, contingencies and instructional control.* New York: Plenum.

Jacobson, N., & Addis, M. (1993). Research on couples and couple therapy: What do we know? Where are we going? *Journal of Consulting and Clinical Psychology, 61,* 85-93.

Koerner, K., Jacobson, N., & Christensen, A. (1994). Emotional acceptance in integrative behavioral couple therapy. In S. Hayes, N. Jacobson, V. Follette, & M. Dougher (Eds.), *Acceptance and change: Content and context in psychotherapy* (pp. 109-118). Reno, NV: Context Press.

Shapiro, D., Barkham, M., Rees, A., Hardy, G., Reynolds, S., & Startup, M. (1994). Effects of treatment duration and severity of depression n the effectiveness of cognitive-behavioral and psychodynamic-interpersonal psychotherapy. *Journal of Consulting and Clinical Psychology, 62,* 522-534.

Snyder, D, Wills, R., & Grady Fletcher, A. (1991). Long-term effectiveness of behavioral versus insight-oriented marital therapy. *Journal of Consulting and Clinical Psychology, 59,* 138-141.

Weiss, J., & Sampson, H. (1986). *The psychoanalytic process: Theory, clinical observation, and empirical research.* New York: Guilford Press.

Chapter 9

Empirically Validated Treatments as a Basis for Clinical Practice: Problems and Prospects

G. Terence Wilson
Rutgers University

The promise of behavior therapy has always been its commitment, at least in principle, to the scientific approach to assessment and treatment of clinical disorders (O'Leary & Wilson, 1987). In recent years, adherents to other theoretical orientations to psychotherapy have similarly espoused the importance of developing scientifically based standards of care (e.g., Klerman & Weissman, 1994). Adding particular force to these developments is the changing health care policy in this country, which is increasingly emphasizing accountability and cost-effectiveness in the provision of clinical services. Moving aggressively in the direction of developing and implementing empirically validated treatment methods would seem imperative in securing the place of psychological therapy in future health care policy and planning. It goes without saying–although it is too often left unsaid–that it is also in the best interests of our patients.

My purpose here is to give an example of progress in developing and implementing an empirically validated treatment, the sort of research that this requires, how this type of clinical research translates into clinical practice, and what problems can be anticipated. The example is from the treatment of eating disorders, specifically bulimia nervosa. Although this is a relatively specific problem, the treatment issues I raise have much broader relevance to clinical practice.

But before moving to this discussion, it is important to underscore some of the problems that still impede the movement towards the use of empirically validated treatments in clinical practice.

Opposition to the Use of Empirically-Validated Treatments

The development and implementation of empirically-validated treatments is seen by many mental health professionals as not only desirable but ethically imperative. It has been commonplace for some time now to emphasize patients' right to treatment and their right to refuse treatment. But patients should have a right to safe and effective treatment. In his incisive analysis of the legal and public health implications of the *Osheroff vs. Chestnut Lodge* case, Klerman (1990) recommended that "the patient has the right to be informed as to the alternative treatments available, their relative efficacy and safety, and the likely outcomes of these treatments" (pp. 416-417). This emphasis on discriminating among different treatment methods for different disorders on the basis of evidence from controlled clinical trials remains a minority view within the field. It is not the position that is emphasized by organized clinical psychology in the United States. Sechrest (1992) recently lamented that "Clinical psychology today cannot agree on its scientific base because it cannot even agree on what is scientific. Across the full range of the field, apparently about anything goes. Maybe even worse, across the range of the field, clinical psychologists do not even agree that clinical psychology should be scientific, many practitioners seeming to believe that art, intuition, literature, philosophy, and so on are the more dependable bases for practice" (p. 20).

A particularly disturbing example of the lack of commitment to the use of empirically-validated treatments in clinical practice comes from a recent Task Force report to Division 12 of the American Psychological Association (Chambless,

---

Table 1. Criteria for Empirically Validated Treatments: Well-Established Treatments

---

I.   At least two good groups design studies, conducted by different investigators, demonstrating efficacy in one or more of the following ways.

   A.   Superior to pill or psychological placebo or to another treatment.

   B.   Equivalent to an already established treatment in studies with adequate statistical power (about 30 per group; cf. Kazdin & Bass, 1989).

OR

II. A large series of single case design studies demonstrating efficacy. These studies must have:

   A.   Used good experimental designs, and

   B.   Compared the intervention to other treatment as in I.A.

FURTHER CRITERIA FOR BOTH I AND II:

III. Studies must be conducted with treatment manuals.

IV. Characteristics of the client samples must be clearly specified.

1993). The Task Force spelled out criteria for what constituted empirically validated techniques. These rather modest (if not minimalist) criteria are listed in Table 1. They then identified 18 treatment methods that, in their opinion, met these criteria.

Examples included Beck's cognitive therapy for depression, cognitive behavioral therapy (CBT) for panic disorder with and without agoraphobia, exposure treatment for phobic disorders, Klerman and Weissman's interpersonal psychotherapy for depression, and behavior modification for developmentally disabled people. The Task Force then sent a listing of these empirically validated treatments to all 167 Directors of Clinical Psychology Ph.D. and Psy.D programs in the United States and Canada. They were asked to indicate whether their doctoral training programs provided either didactic course instruction or supervised clinical training in each of the different treatment methods. The response rate was an impressive 83%.

The data indicated that those programs that provided course instruction in the treatment methods also tended to offer supervised clinical training (a correlation of 0.44). For treatments covered in course instruction, the typical treatment was taught 47% of the programs. But it is the variability that is eye-catching. The range was 0% to 96%. The pattern was similar for clinical supervision. In short, some APA accredited clinical training programs provide no course instruction or clinical supervision in any of the empirically validated methods. Underscoring the lack of attention to empirically validated treatments, the report revealed that more than one fifth of the programs did not teach anything about 75% or more of the treatment methods listed by the Task Force. These numbers take on added significance when it is realized that the report probably overstated the extent to which the empirically validated methods are meaningfully taught in graduate programs. For example, respondents were not asked to specify what "course instruction" or "supervised clinical work" actually involved.

The Task Force also sent the list of treatments to the program directors of the 428 APA-approved clinical internship directors. The response rate was a dismal 55%. As the Task Force noted in their report, the finding that nearly half of the APA-approved internship programs apparently found the question of empirically validated treatments to be unimportant is dismaying. Bad news turns to worse in the analysis of the findings from those internships that did respond. In general, they did not require competency in the empirically validated treatments, especially in programs focusing on adult patients. Roughly half did report providing supervision in cognitive-behavioral treatments for mood and anxiety disorders. But the treatments that were most likely to be required for completion, and for which clinical supervision was most available (74%), were short-term dynamic psychotherapies for which the Task Force had been unable to identify any evidence of effectiveness. The situation appeared less unsatisfactory in the internships devoted to children's problems, mainly because they offered supervision in some behavioral methods.

The third prong of the Task Force's investigation was an analysis of continuing education workshops that carried the official sponsorship of the American Psychological Association. They found little evidence to show that continuing education workshops are required to provide empirical support for what is offered.

Conclusion

Of course there are problems with the report of the Task Force. You can argue with the methodological criteria they used as a standard for identifying empirically validated treatments. You can question the bases on which they determined which treatments met these criteria. But it would be churlish to focus on such concerns at this point. In taking an important first step towards revealing what has long been suspected about the failure to take seriously the findings of clinically relevant research, and for pointing the way to improving standards of care, Division 12 and the Task Force have served the profession well.

It is undeniable that in effect, as Sechrest (1992) and others have observed, essentially "anything goes" when it comes to what treatment methods are taught in doctoral training programs in the United States. The accreditation criteria for doctoral programs in clinical psychology are conspicuously silent on the need for instruction in the use of empirically validated treatment methods. In the recent past some clinical training programs have voiced concern about what are perceived to be intrusive requirements that are foisted upon them by APA. Given the wide range of requirements imposed upon doctoral training programs, it is ironic that a commitment to training students in empirically validated treatments is not part of the accreditation criteria. If professional psychology is interested in promoting the use of empirically validated treatments, it would seem imperative to include such a requirement in the accreditation standards, as the Task Force recommended.

Psychotherapy Integration

The ideal of an integrated, unified approach to psychological treatment that would embrace demonstrably effective therapeutic strategies from diverse theoretical orientations has obvious appeal. Few therapists would dissent from the view that proponents of different psychological approaches might make greater efforts to understand and perhaps incorporate each other's principles or techniques. The question is how to go about it. Some approaches have the potential to advance the field, but others may only serve to perpetuate the status quo of the "anything goes" practice of psychotherapy and reduce the likelihood of developing and implementing empirically validated treatments.

As someone identified with the cognitive-behavioral approach to treatment, I would recommend integrating or combining CBT with any other psychological or pharmacological treatment that significantly improves patient outcome beyond that achieved by CBT alone. The point I wish to emphasize in the present context is that in moving towards a more integrative or combined approach it is imperative to heed a fundamental point made by Kazdin (1984), among others (e.g., Agras, 1987; Wilson, 1982). Kazdin noted that "Integrationism as a general movement represents a highly significant development in psychotherapy. However, it may be the general movement that is worth promoting rather than the specific attempt to integrate psychodynamic and behavioral views. At this point, individual positions suffer from loose concepts and weak empirical bases, problems that are not resolved and perhaps may even be exacerbated by their combination. The overall goal is establishing an empirically based and theoretically viable account of therapy. *Premature integration of specific positions that are not well supported on their own may greatly impede progress*" (1984, pp. 141-142, emphasis added).

Preserving the Status Quo

In arguing against the dangers of premature integration I am advocating the demonstration of effectiveness based on research such as randomized controlled studies—or at least the standards adopted by the Division 12 Task Force report. I am also reaffirming the claim that differential effects of alternative treatments have been established in some disorders (Barlow, 1994; Lazarus, 1989).

The mainstream position among professional psychologists is quite different. The lore here is that the effectiveness of different forms of psychotherapy has been established. Moreover, no single treatment is more effective than any other. The various forms of psychotherapy are equally effective.[1] They typically cite the influential meta-analysis by Smith, Glass and Miller (1980) (e.g., Beitman et al., 1989; Stricker, 1994). In so doing, they ignore the well-documented inadequacies in this particular meta-analysis, ranging from fundamental conceptual shortcomings to simple failure to include a large number of highly relevant studies (Paul, 1985; Wilson & Rachman, 1983). In addition, they exclude other meta-analyses that consistently show differences among treatments (see Wilson, 1985). But leaving aside such objections, it is revealing to focus on one of the findings that does not get mentioned by those who commonly cite Smith et al. (1980) in support of the conclusion that all forms of psychotherapy are equally effective.

Recall that Smith et al. (1980) found that there was no relation between the effect size of treatment and duration of therapy, experience of the therapist, diagnosis of the patient, or the form of therapy (group vs. individual). Other evidence has shown that the credentials and experience of therapists are unrelated to treatment outcome, however counterintuitive it may seem (Christensen & Jacobson, 1993; Dawes, 1994). Commenting on this extraordinary finding, Wilson and Rachman (1983) noted that "psychotherapy can afford few such victories" (p. 60).

If Smith et al. (1980) are correct, why bother to integrate? Why not choose therapies based on practical considerations such as cost and ease of administration? Why not simply find the least expensive (but equally effective, of course) method? Shoham-Salomon (1991) made the same point in observing that "If common factors were the core of all therapies while specific techniques only served as 'fillers,' why would anybody bother to incorporate fillers used by another orientation?" (p. 36).

Identifying common factors among different psychological therapies might be a useful first step. The assumption would be that the identification of common elements could result in the development of better theory and therapy. But the record indicates that this position, which has been promoted over the past 15 years

(Goldfried, 1980), has yet to deliver on its promise. Arkowitz (1992), an unabashed advocate of psychotherapy integration, has put it as follows: "I believe that we are not yet sure what integrative therapies look like. They are probably not fixed hybrids. They may grow out of general strategies of frameworks, but they remain elusive. Several promising starts have been made in clinical proposals for integrative therapies, but it is clear that much more work needs to be done in the area of integrative therapies, as well as in integrative theory and research" (p. 292).

The common factors approach is likely to be a conceptual dead-end. At a sufficiently general level it is clear that there are commonalities among different psychological therapies (Goldfried, 1980). For example, all therapies emphasize the importance of a good therapist-patient relationship. But this commonality is shown to be superficial when the precise role of the therapeutic relationship across different therapies is analyzed more closely (Sloane et al., 1975; Wilson, 1982). The same holds true for other common factors such as corrective learning experiences and feedback about the patient's behavior (see Wilson [1982] for detailed analyses of the fundamental differences between cognitive-behavioral conceptualizations of these factors).

Assimilative integration and clinical expertise. A mainstream clinical view is that not only are different treatment methods equally effective, but they also have only a modest role in producing change. Relying once more on the Smith et al. (1980) meta-analysis, many psychotherapists attribute little outcome variance to technique variables. Preexisting patient factors are said to account for most of the variance, followed by therapist factors. In this sort of analysis, importance attaches to the clinical judgment and expertise of the therapist rather than specific techniques—empirically validated or not. A problem with this position is finding that the experience of the therapist is unrelated to treatment outcome (Christensen & Jacobson, 1994; Dawes, 1994, Smith et al., 1980).

Assimilative integration is an approach to integration in which a commitment to one theoretical position is expanded by the incorporation of selected techniques from other orientations (Stricker, 1994). The contention is that in the emergent process of incorporating techniques from other conceptual frameworks, operational changes are made in the technique. It becomes something else, to the extent that its original empirical validation no longer applies to the new theoretical application (Lazarus & Messer, 1991).

This approach to integration sanctions whatever theoretical position the therapist wishes to adopt. Again, anything goes. The choice of techniques is neither constrained nor demanded by empirical validation. At best, such research data would compete with the therapist's personal experience, theoretical orientation, and idiosyncratic judgment of the individual case in determining how the patient is to be treated. The prospect of therapists choosing freely from a dizzying array of competing and often contradictory techniques from different theoretical approaches in order to complement their subjective impressions is a daunting one. As discussed below, psychological research has consistently shown that clinicians do not fare well in making such complex judgments.

Evidence for Combined (Integrative) Treatment Methods

So what would be constructive approaches to integrating or combining different treatment methods? One example would be combining CBT (or any other empirically validated psychological method) with pharmacotherapy. The advantage here is that unlike so many of the psychodynamic, humanistic and systemic methods which are promoted as ways to overcome the limitations of CBT (Castonguay & Goldfried, 1994), specific drugs have been shown to be effective in controlled clinical trials. Consider an example of what Schacht (1984) has called complementary integration. CBT is the preferred treatment of bulimia nervosa, as I shall argue shortly. It can be usefully complemented with antidepressant medication in the treatment of cases with comorbid mood disorder. The latter is an effective treatment for depression and can be administered concurrently with the CBT. This combination may be more effective in reducing comorbid depression in bulimia nervosa than psychological therapy plus pill placebo (Mitchell et al., 1990).

In the synergistic model of integration "two therapies may be applied to the same problem and are expected to interact in the patient to produce clinical results superior to what might be obtained by either therapy alone. The techniques of each therapy remain unchanged, but the locus of their integration lies in their effects on the patient" (Arkowitz, 1992, p. 271). For example, several studies have shown that a combination of exposure and imipramine is more effective in treating panic disorder with agoraphobia than either exposure treatment or drug treatment alone (Telch & Lucas, 1994). Both psychological and biological mechanisms likely explain this synergistic effect (Barlow, 1988). In contrast, combining exposure treatment with benzodiazepines may undermine the effects of exposure treatment alone (Marks et al., 1993). Knowing whether a particular combination of specific psychological and pharmacological treatments will prove synergistic or otherwise requires understanding the psychopathological processes of the disorder, and the mechanisms whereby treatments whereby have their effects. For the most part, both with respect to psychological and pharmacological treatments, we are far from such an understanding. Research on the mechanisms whereby empirically validated treatments produce their effects should be a priority.

One of the best studied applications of combined therapies has been the use of CBT with antidepressant medication in the treatment of depression. These applications may be seen as either complementary or synergistic. To quote Munoz et al. (1994), " there is every indication that combining drugs and psychotherapy retains the specific advantages inherent in either single modality and enhances the patient's overall breadth of response. Even if combined treatment were not to produce greater change with respect to acute symptom reduction (and it would be premature to say that it does not), it might still be worth instituting if it retains the unique benefits associated with each of the specific modalities. Moreover, although a few predictors of differential response have yet been identified, different people are likely to respond to different modalities; to the extent that this is true, combined treatment clearly increases the likelihood that any given patient will receive some treatment to which he or she will respond. Finally, combining drugs and psycho-therapy also increases the likelihood that at least one of the treatment modalities will be adequately implemented" (p. 10).

Finally, it is desirable to integrate clinical practice with the principles and procedures of experimental psychology wherever possible. The transformation of behavior therapy from its narrow 1950s version to contemporary practice is a case in point. For example, in the 1970s it "went cognitive" for two reasons. One was what was happening to scientific psychology as a whole. The other was pragmatic good sense to incorporate the clinical methods of practitioners such as Beck which were shown to be effective in empirical outcome research (Hawton et al., 1989; Wilson, 1982).

An Illustrative Case: Treatment of Bulimia Nervosa

Some of the promise and problems of developing empirically validated treatments and applying them in clinical practice can be illustrated with reference to the treatment of bulimia nervosa.

The DSM-IV criteria for bulimia nervosa are summarized in Table 2. What has now emerged as the standard CBT treatment for this eating disorder is a manual-based, individual therapy originally developed by Fairburn (1985) at Oxford University. In brief, the treatment exemplifies the time-limited, problem-oriented, and directive nature of cognitive-behavior therapy in general. It consists of cognitive and behavioral procedures for promoting regular meals which incorporate previ-ously avoided foods, for developing more constructive skills for coping with high risk situations for binge eating and purging, for modifying abnormal attitudes, and for preventing relapse at the conclusion of formal treatment (Fairburn, Marcus, & Wilson, 1993).

Effectiveness of CBT

Craighead and Agras's (1991) summary of 10 studies yielded a mean reduction in purging of 79%, with a 57% remission figure. The results for binge eating were similar. Findings of the most recent and best controlled studies show a mean percentage reduction in binge eating ranging from 93% to 73%; the comparable figures for purging range from 94% to 77%. Mean remission rates for binge eating range from 51% to 71%, and for purging from 56% to 36% (Agras, Schneider, Arnow, Raeburn, & Telch, 1989; Agras et al., 1992; Fairburn et al., 1991; Garner et al., 1993). Aside from clinically significant reductions in binge eating and purging, studies have consistently shown that dietary restraint is reduced (Fairburn et al., 1991; Garner et al., 1993; Wilson, Eldredge, Smith, & Niles, 1991), with an increase in the amount of food eaten between bulimic episodes (Rossiter, Agras, Losch, & Telch, 1988). Attitudes to shape and weight, a key psychopathological feature and one

---

Table 2. DSM-IV Criteria for Bulimia Nervosa

A. Recurrent episodes of binge eating. An episode of binge eating is characterized by both of the following:

> (1) eating, in a discrete period of time (e.g., within any 2-hour period), an amount of food that is definitely larger than most people would eat during a similar period of time and under similar circumstances
> (2) a sense of lack of control over eating during the episode (e.g., a feeling that one cannot stop eating or control what or how much one is eating)

B. Recurrent inappropriate compensatory behavior in order to prevent weight gain, such as self-induced vomiting; misuse of laxatives, diuretics, enemas, or other medications; fasting; or excessive exercise.

C. The binge eating and inappropriate compensatory behaviors both occur, on average, at least twice a week for 3 months.

D. Self-evaluation is unduly influenced by body shape and weight.

E. The disturbance does not occur exclusively during episodes of Anorexia Nervosa.

---

which is central to the cognitive-behavioral view on the disorder, also improve (Fairburn et al., 1991; Garner et al., 1993; Wilson et al., 1991).

CBT versus pharmacotherapy. Aside from CBT, the most intensively researched treatment for bulimia nervosa has been antidepressant medication. Both tricyclics and fluoxetine have been shown to be significantly more effective than pill placebo (Fluoxetine Bulimia Nervosa Collaborative Study Group, 1992; Mitchell & de Zwaan, 1993). Consequently, antidepressant medication provides a stringent standard of comparison for the effects of CBT or any other psychological treatment.

Four studies have evaluated the relative and combined effectiveness of CBT and antidepressant drug treatment in controlled studies. In the first, Agras and his colleagues at Stanford compared three treatments: CBT alone; medication (desipramine) alone; and CBT combined with medication (Agras et al., 1992). Medication (desipramine) was administered for either 16 or 24 weeks. CBT alone and combined treatment were equally effective in reducing the frequency of binge eating and purging. The combined treatment with medication for 24 weeks was superior to CBT alone on a self-report measure of hunger. This combined group, but not CBT alone, showed significantly greater reduction in binge eating and purging than the 16-week medication group at the 32-week assessment. Agras et al. (1992)

interpreted these results as indicating that a combined treatment produces the best overall effects. Nonetheless, it is worth noting that CBT alone was administered for only 15 weeks (with three additional "booster" sessions), so it is difficult to compare it with 24 weeks of combined treatment. Moreover, the data failed to show differences between CBT alone and either combined condition except on the secondary measure of hunger.

The second study compared CBT with desipramine and a combined CBT plus desipramine condition (Leitenberg et al., 1994). The study was terminated prematurely after only 7 subjects had been treated in each condition, because of the high dropout rate and poor response of the desipramine-alone patients. Of the 7 subjects receiving the drug only, 4 dropped out early, without showing any improvement, because of negative side effects of the drug. Two subjects in the combined treatment condition dropped out because of side effects from the drug, and a third refused to continue to take medication after the 9th week of the 20-week program. Only 1 CBT subject dropped out. Five of the 6 CBT subjects, and 4 of the 5 subjects in the combined treatment, had ceased purging at posttreatment. These results were maintained at a 6-month follow-up.

A third study evaluated the combined effectiveness of an intensive group psychotherapy condition, which included many of the core components of CBT, with imipramine (Mitchell et al., 1990). This group of researchers found that imipramine alone was superior to placebo, but inferior to intensive group psychological treatment combined with either drug or placebo. The two conditions with psychological treatment showed mean percent reductions in binge eating of 89% and 92%; 51% were in remission during the last two weeks of treatment, and an additional 35% averaged one or fewer binges. Adding imipramine to the psychological treatment had no effect other than to produce greater reductions in symptoms of depression and anxiety.

A fourth study compared intensive inpatient behavioral treatment with the addition of either fluoxetine or pill placebo (Fichter et al., 1991). Both treatments produced significant but comparable reductions in the core psychopathology of bulimia nervosa. Fichter et al. (1991) suggest that the lack of a significant difference could be attributed to a "ceiling effect." Binge eating, however, decreased by only 46%, however, indicating room for further improvement.

Collectively, these studies indicate that, at best, there is only modest incremental benefit to adding antidepressant medication to CBT in the treatment of bulimia nervosa.

CBT versus alternative psychological therapies. CBT has proved to be as effective or significantly more effective than any psychological treatment with which it has been compared in a controlled study.[2] In the first of two studies by Agras and his group at Stanford, group CBT was superior to a form of supportive psychotherapy (with self-monitoring), although this difference was no longer present at four-month follow-up (Kirkley, Schneider, Agras, & Bachman, 1985). In the second study, CBT conducted on an individual basis was found to be more effective than supportive psychotherapy (again with self-monitoring), both at the end of treatment and at six-month follow-up (Agras et al., 1989). Garner and colleagues compared CBT with supportive-expressive psychotherapy (SET) (Garner et al., 1993). Both treatments produced substantial improvements by the end of treatment. The two treatments were equally effective in reducing binge eating, but CBT was significantly superior to SET in decreasing purging, lessening dietary restraint, and modifying dysfunctional attitudes to shape and weight. Significantly, CBT produced greater improvement in depression, self-esteem, and general psychological distress. These differences were maintained over a one year follow-up (Garner, 1989). Laessle et al. (1991) compared what they called a nutritional management (NM) treatment with stress management (SM). The former closely approximated the behavioral components of CBT; the latter included standard cognitive-behavioral strategies such as active coping and problem-solving, but never focused directly on the modification of eating or attitudes about weight and shape. The results showed marginally significant but consistent differences in favor of NM both at posttreatment and one year follow-up.

Other studies have found fewer differences between CBT and comparison psychological treatments on measures of BN. Freeman, Barry, Dunkeld-Turnbull, and Henderson (1988) compared CBT, behavior therapy (BT), group psychotherapy, and a waiting-list control condition. All three treatments were equally effective and superior to a waiting list condition. Group psychotherapy had the highest drop-out rate (37%) and both therapists and patients expressed the most dissatisfaction with it, although it was also the most cost-effective. In the first of two outcome studies, Fairburn et al. (1986) compared CBT with a form of brief focal psychotherapy. Both treatments produced marked and lasting reductions in binge eating and purging. Since the focal psychotherapy included some behavioral techniques (e.g., self-monitoring), the finding is difficult to interpret. Beyond the specific eating disorder psychopathology, CBT was more effective than the psychotherapy in its effects on patients' social adjustment and overall clinical state both at posttreatment and one year follow-up.

The second study from the Oxford group (Fairburn et al., 1991) pitted CBT against two comparison conditions: 1. behavior therapy, comprising the CBT treatment minus cognitive restructuring, and behavioral and cognitive methods for modifying abnormal attitudes about weight and shape; and 2. interpersonal psychotherapy (IPT), which was adapted from Klerman, Weissman, Rounsaville, and Chevron's (1984) interpersonal treatment of depression. At posttreatment, the three therapies were equally effective in reducing binge eating. However, CBT was significantly more effective than IPT in reducing purging, dietary restraint, and attitudes to shape and weight, and superior to BT on the latter two variables despite equivalent ratings of suitability of treatment and expectations of outcome. This pattern of results shows that CBT has specific effects on different measures of outcome consistent with its theoretical rationale.

The closed, one year follow-up of this study revealed a different picture (Fairburn et al., 1993). Fully 48% of the BT group dropped-out or were withdrawn from the study because of lack of improvement. The drop-out rate was 20% for CBT which maintained its improvement throughout follow-up. The contrast between these results and Freeman et al.'s (1988) study is puzzling. The latter found no difference between ostensibly similar BT and CBT treatments on binge-eating and attitudes toward weight and shape. Unfortunately, Freeman et al. (1988) did not report a systematic follow-up evaluation which might have clarified the longer-term effects of BT. In perhaps the most intriguing finding from the follow-up of the Oxford study, IPT showed continuing improvement to the point where it was as successful as CBT on all measures at eight and 12 month evaluations. Forty-four percent of IPT patients had ceased all binge-eating and purging at the one year follow-up. Collectively, these data rebut the argument that all treatments are equally effective. BT was clearly inferior to CBT and IPT. Similarly, the striking differences in the temporal pattern of results between CBT and IPT suggests that each treatment has specific effects, probably via different mechanisms.

Psychotherapists who assert that there are few if any consistent differences between CBT and other psychological therapies usually miss an important point. There are few good comparative outcome studies that reliably show the superiority of CBT or any other approach. But this relative dearth of comparative studies should not be taken to imply that there is no empirical basis for choosing between different treatments. What stands out in the treatment of bulimia nervosa (and in other clinical disorders such as depression and the anxiety disorders [Barlow, 1994]), is the consistency with which CBT has been shown to be effective in different clinical research centers in different countries. The choice between such a well-established treatment and one that lacks empirical documentation, however clinically appealing it might seem, would seem straightforward.

Criteria For Evaluating Overall Effectiveness of CBT

Table 3 lists the criteria for fully evaluating the effectiveness of any psychological or pharmacological treatment of bulimia nervosa.

Acceptability. Although data are sparse, many patients with bulimia nervosa appear reluctant to take antidepressant medication and seem to prefer psychological treatment (Mitchell et al., 1990). Leitenberg et al. (1994) reported that 15% of potential subjects for their study rejected participation in the medication only treatment condition.

Attrition rate. The drop-out rate has been consistently lower in CBT than pharmacological treatments (Fairburn et al., 1992; Wilson, 1993a). In the Mitchell et al. (1990) study, for example, the drop-out rates for imipramine with and with group psychological treatment were 25% and 42.6% respectively. The comparable rates for patients who received the pill placebo with and without psychological treatment were 14.7% and 16.1%. Agras et al. (1992) had only one CBT patient drop-out, a rate of 4.3%, compared with 17% for desipramine.

Table 3. Criteria for Evaluating Clinical Effectiveness of Psychological and Pharmacological Treatments

---

ACCEPTABILITY

ATTRITION RATE

EFFECTIVENESS (CLINICAL SIGNIFICANCE)

SPEED OF ACTION

BREADTH OF EFFECTS

DURABILITY OF EFFECTS

DISSEMINABILITY

COST-EFFECTIVENESS

Fluoxetine is not more effective than tricyclic drugs in reducing binge eating and purging (Walsh, 1991), but would be the preferred medication because of fewer adverse side-effects. Nonetheless, the largest clinical trial of fluoxetine yielded a drop-out rate of over 30% before the eighth week of the double-blind phase of treatment (Fluoxetine Bulimia Nervosa Collaborative Study Group, 1992).

Clinical effectiveness. The statistically significant results of controlled treatment trials are summarized above. Clinical significance can also be judged terms of the importance of the change produced by treatment (Kazdin & Wilson, 1978). One relevant index is the extent to which patients engage in normative levels of behavior after treatment.

Fairburn et al. (in press) reported that at their 5.8 year follow-up, 74% of patients who had received CBT had global scores on the Eating Disorder Examination (EDE) within one standard deviation of the mean for young women in that community. The EDE is a semi-structured interview generally regarded as the "gold standard" of a assessment for eating disorders (Wilson, 1993b). Another study found that EDE scores of patients treated by CBT were lower (namely, less disturbed) than those of a comparison group of restrained eaters who neither binged nor purged (Wilson & Smith, 1989).

Speed of action. CBT is quick-acting. It produces more rapid improvement than supportive-expressive therapy (Garner et al., 1993), stress management therapy (Laessle et al., 1991), and IPT (Fairburn et al., 1991). This quick-acting effect is consistent with data from CBT treatment of panic disorder (Clark et al., 1994) and depression (Ilardi & Craighead, 1994).

Breadth of effects. CBT reliably produces changes across all four of the specific features of bulimia nervosa, namely, binge eating, purging, dietary restraint, and abnormal attitudes about body shape and weight (Fairburn et al., 1992). Only IPT at the one year follow-up has equalled the breath of CBT's effects (Fairburn et al., 1993).

Antidepressant drug treatment has focused primarily on reductions in binge eating and purging. But there is evidence indicating that both desipramine (Walsh et al., 1991) and fluoxetine (Goldbloom & Olmsted, 1993) result in improvement in attitudes about body shape and weight. Unlike CBT, however, antidepressant drugs have not been shown to produce improvement in patients' eating between binge eating/purging episodes. One study found that desipramine actually increased rather than decreased dietary restraint between episodes of binge eating (Rossiter et al., 1988).

Another reliable finding has been the broad effects CBT has had on associated psychopathology. Most studies have shown striking improvements in depression, self-esteem, social functioning, and measures of personality disorder (e.g., Fairburn, Kirk, O'Connor & Cooper, 1986; Fairburn et al., 1992; Garner et al., 1993).

Durability of effects. Keller et al. (1992) have described "extraordinarily high rates of chronicity, relapse, recurrence, and psychosocial morbidity" in patients with bulimia nervosa. None of their sample was treated with CBT. On average, studies of CBT have shown reasonably good maintenance of change at six month and one year follow-ups (Agras et al., 1989; Agras et al., 1994; Fairburn et al., 1993; Garner, 1989). The most impressive findings are those from the most rigorously conducted follow-up evaluations by the Oxford group. At one year both binge-eating and purging had declined by over 90%. Thirty-six percent of patients had ceased all binge-eating and purging. Given that the follow-ups were closed ensured that patients seeking additional or different treatment did not confound evaluation of maintenance of change (Fairburn et al., 1993). A subsequent follow-up (mean = 5.8 years; range = 3 to 11 years) showed that the effects of CBT were maintained (an abstinence rate of 48%) (Fairburn et al., in press). There is some evidence that CBT may have a delayed effect in some patients. Agras et al. (1994) found that half of the patients in their CBT plus desipramine condition who were symptomatic at posttreatment had recovered fully at the one year follow-up.

Long-term effects of pharmacological treatment have, with few exceptions, been ignored. In the Minnesota study, all patients who had responded to treatment (defined as no more than two binge-purge episodes during the final two weeks) were assigned to a four month maintenance program and followed-up at six months (Pyle et al., 1990). Only nine of 54 patients (17%) who received drug treatment could be classified as responders. Of these nine, only two maintained their improvement at six months. The psychological treatment, by contrast, showed good maintenance at follow-up. Walsh et al. (1991) required that patients in their study of desipramine versus placebo show a minimum reduction of 50% in binge-eating in order to be entered into a maintenance phase. But only 41% (29 of 71) met this criterion. Of these patients, eight declined participation in the maintenance phase because of lack of interest, intolerable side-effects, or other problems (e.g., alcohol abuse). Therefore, 21 patients entered the maintenance phase of the protocol. Eleven (52.4%) patients completed the 16-week maintenance phase; six (28.6%) patients relapsed (i.e., binged more than 50% of their baseline binge frequency); two (9.5%) dropped out to seek treatment elsewhere; and two (9.5%) patients were discontinued due to intolerable side-effects. Patients who completed the full 16 weeks of maintenance failed to show statistically significant improvement over this period. These results indicate that over the longer term, patients even relapse or drop out while on active medication.

The only sign of maintenance of the effects of pharmacological therapy comes from the Agras et al. (1994) study. Patients who had recovered after six months of desipramine maintained this improvement at one year follow-up. The four month trial of desipramine, however, was followed by a high relapse rate, but one that was prevented when the drug was combined with CBT. These results should be interpreted with caution given the small sample size involved.

Disseminability. The findings discussed above are the product of studies involving highly trained, closely supervised therapists administering CBT in major research centers. A critically important question is how readily CBT can be disseminated to the broad population of practitioners. What level of training is required? Can CBT be done by non-doctoral level mental health personnel? These questions have yet to be addressed. More is required than the ability to form a positive therapeutic relationship. Technical skill is important, although this can undoubtedly be imparted through appropriate training.

In the absence of data on the treatment of bulimia nervosa, it may be instructive to examine the application of CBT to other disorders. Barlow (1994b) has suggested that it takes skilled, doctoral level therapists to administer manual-based CBT treatment for the anxiety disorders. Thase (1994) has suggested that it requires more extensive training to develop therapists who are competent in using CBT for depression than to develop therapists who are equally competent in IPT. He points out that the much-publicized National Institute of Mental Health Treatment of Depression Collaborative Study (TDCS) reported a treatment type by site interaction (Elkin et al., 1989). The interaction resulted from the variable performance of CBT across the three treatment sites. It is generally believed that CBT did well at the site where the therapists had the most extensive prior training, but fared poorly at the site where therapists had little or no prior experience and training in this approach (Hollon & Beck, 1994). Although the TDCS study group have yet to confirm this view, Thase (1994) concludes that "the most parsimonious explanation for CBT's disappointing showing is that it is less 'exportable' than IPT, at least with respect to settings in which therapists' prior training has emphasized more traditional, psychodynamic methods" (p. 49). Should IPT be shown to be as effective as CBT in the treatment of bulimia nervosa, as seems to be the case (Fairburn et al., in press), then research on their relative exportability would become a priority.

At present the availability of therapists skilled in the use of CBT for eating disorders is very limited. The findings of the Chambless (1993) Task Force described earlier indicate that relatively few clinical psychologists are being exposed to these methods in the course of their training. In contrast, access to physicians who can prescribe antidepressant drugs in a standardized and competent manner is considerably greater. CBT fares poorly in comparison with pharmacological therapy when it comes to disseminability. The same may hold true for other specialized psychological treatments such as IPT.

Cost-effectiveness. There are no data on this issue which will undoubtedly become increasingly important in the wake of health care reform in the U.S. The cost of having highly trained doctoral level clinical psychologists administer CBT will be relatively high. More cost-effective ways delivering the strategies of CBT need to be explored, as discussed below. It is difficult, if not impossible, to compare the cost-effectiveness of CBT with drug treatment. The latter involves fewer sessions and less time, but is off-set by the higher cost of physician training as well as medical monitoring of patients. Moreover, a drug such as fluoxetine (Prozac) is not inexpensive.

Limitations of CBT

CBT is an effective treatment, but this cannot obscure the reality that no more than roughly 50% of patients cease binge eating and purging. Of the remainder, some show partial improvement, whereas a small number derive no benefit at all. Obviously this is not good enough. Clinical research must now focus on these non-responders to CBT. Several treatment options present themselves.

Expand the scope of CBT. Although the CBT package that has been evaluated in controlled trials allows the therapist some flexibility in using a variety of behavioral and cognitive techniques (Fairburn et al., 1993), it remains a truncated version of the unrestricted clinical practice of cognitive behavioral therapy. By carrying out a more idiographic assessment of individual patients' particular problems and by drawing upon the wider range of cognitive and behavioral strategies, practitioners should, in principle, be able to tailor therapy to an individual patient's particular needs.

Expanding CBT for bulimia nervosa could take several forms (Wilson, 1995). An example would be an increased focus on interpersonal issues. The now standardized treatment manual addresses interpersonal issues only insofar as they constitute proximal triggers for specific episodes of binge eating or purging (Fairburn et al., 1993). Imposing this boundary allows researchers to compare CBT with IPT without fear of procedural overlap between the two treatments, a critical requirement for comparative outcome research. However, this has entailed excluding commonly used cognitive-behavioral strategies. From its inception, behavior therapy has focused on interpersonal anxieties, conflicts, and deficits using a number of different treatment techniques (Lazarus, 1971; O'Leary & Wilson, 1987). If IPT were shown to differ from manual-based CBT it would be unclear whether the difference is attributable to the focus on the interpersonal domain of functioning or the structure and style of the therapy (e.g., nondirective vs. directive) itself (see Figure 1).

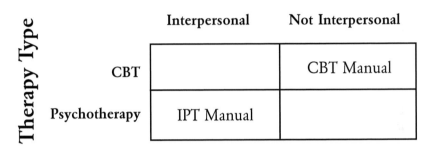

Figure 1. Target domains of functioning of CBT and IPT treatment manuals for bulimia nervosa.

More intensive (inpatient?) CBT. The CBT described here is outpatient treatment. An insufficiently explored option would be a day hospital program, or full hospitalization, for more direct and intensive treatment of the patient's disordered eating habits. Food intake can be better regulated, and binge eating and purging prevented, in such a structured setting. Day hospital treatment is preferred because it is less expensive and does not completely remove the patient from the psychosocial situations that are associated with binge eating and purging. Tuschen and Bent (in press) describe a promising example of intensive inpatient CBT.

Alternative therapies. When CBT fails, instead of modifying it, therapists can switch to a different approach. IPT would be an empirically validated choice. It has been shown to be effective in the treatment of depression (Klerman & Weissman, 1994) and in bulimia nervosa (Fairburn, 1993). Note that this switching of tactics is not assimilative or theoretical integration in which therapists incorporate a treatment into their own conceptual framework and possibly make changes in how it is implemented. By switching to IPT the therapist abandons both the style and content of CBT. IPT is a nondirective albeit focused approach that is procedurally and conceptually incompatible with CBT (Fairburn, 1993). The two treatments can be sequenced but not integrated. The broader strategy behind this sequencing option is pragmatic eclecticism.

The goal would be to identify treatment-specific predictors of outcome that might permit matching different treatments to different patients. Matching treatments to patients is a clinically appealing but still distant notion. What is perhaps not recognized enough is the possibility that some patients will not respond regardless of the type of treatment they receive. Bulimia nervosa patients who do not respond to CBT might prove intractable. For example, Fairburn et al. (in press) report that of those patients who were diagnosed with an eating disorder at the 5.8 year follow-up, two-thirds had received additional psychiatric treatment to no avail.

In contrast to this strategy of sequencing empirically validated treatments, clinical practice more often hinges on pre-existing theoretical commitments. For example, Johnson et al. (1990) suggested that CBT is appropriate for patients with "simple" but not "complex" bulimia nervosa. So-called "complex" cases refer to the complicating presence of borderline personality disorder. For these cases, Johnson et al. (1990) assert, longer-term psychodynamic therapy is recommended.

Some data exist indicating that cluster B personality disorders are a negative prognostic factor for treatment of bulimia nervosa with CBT, although this is not well-established (Rossiter, Agras, Telch, & Schneider, 1993). But there is no evidence to suggest that CBT will fare less well than an alternative psychodynamic approach in treating patients with a comorbid personality disorder. This is what Dawes (1994) has termed the "argument-from-a-vacuum" approach. The focus shifts from research evidence that is available to hypothetical studies. The little evidence there is suggests that behavior therapy is as least as effective as psychodynamic therapy with personality disorders (Sloane et al., 1975). The best empirical evidence to date of an effective psychological treatment for borderline personality disorder is Linehan's "dialectical behavior therapy," which, as the name connotes, consists primarily of CBT combined with other concepts (Linehan et al., 1991).

In the TDCS, CBT was equally effective in the treatment of depressed patients with or without comorbid Axis II psychopathology (Shea et al., 1990). In contrast, both IPT and the antidepressant medication treatment fared less well with patients with Axis II psychopathology (Thase, 1994). Other research has also shown that Axis II comorbidity does not alter the effectiveness of CBT in the treatment of depression (Stuart et al., 1992). It is worth noting that Rossiter et al. (1993) reported data consistent with the foregoing analysis. Cluster B personality disorders predicted a poorer response not only to CBT, but also to pharmacological therapy. There is no evidence across any clinical disorder to suggest that CBT is more likely than alternative psychological therapies to be disadvantaged by the presence of Axis-II psychopathology. If anything, the reverse might hold true.

A Stepped Care Model of Treatment

Thus far I have addressed the need to develop effective interventions for patients who do not respond to CBT. If CBT is not always sufficient to overcome bulimia nervosa, neither is it always necessary. Preliminary studies have begun to evaluate more cost-effective ways of implementing the principles and procedures of manual-based CBT. One promising line of enquiry is the supervised use of a self-help version of the manual. Fairburn (1995) has published such a self-help guide. Cooper, Coker, and Fleming (1994) have treated bulimia nervosa patients with a similar self-help manual accompanied by 6 to 12 brief (20 to 30 minute) sessions with a social worker who focused on implementing the self-help manual. The data suggest that more than half the patients reported marked clinical improvement.

An alternative means of efficiently implementing the principles and procedures of manual-based CBT would be psychoeducational group therapy. Using a series of four 90 minute group session, Davis, Olmsted, and Rockert (1990) have reported encouraging results. There seems little doubt at this point that many bulimia nervosa patients might need no more than either guided self-help or group psychoeducational therapy. Identifying predictors of which patients are appropriate for these interventions is a priority. Figure 2 summarizes an overall stepped-care model of the treatment of bulimia nervosa (Fairburn, Agras, & Wilson, 1992).

A Stepped Care Approach to the Treatment of Eating Disorder

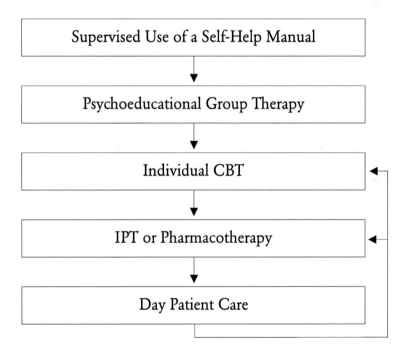

Figure 2. Stepped-care model of the treatment of bulimia nervosa. (Adapted from Fairburn, C. G., Agras, W. S., & Wilson, G. T. (1992). The research on the treatment of bulimia nervosa: Practical and theoretical implications. In G. H. Anderson & S. H. Kennedy (Eds.), The biology of feast and famine: Relevance to eating disorders. New York: Academic Press.

From Research to Clinical Practice

The relevance of the research findings I have summarized above to clinical practice will be predictably contested by many clinicians. There are several dimensions along which research studies might depart from the typical clinical situation. Among these dimensions are the target clinical disorder; the patients and how they are recruited; the characteristics and training of the therapists; and the variation of treatment and its departure from common clinical practice (Kazdin & Wilson, 1978).

The Target Clinical Disorder

The objection here is that bulimia nervosa is a discrete disorder and hence relatively easy to treat. In clinical practice as opposed to controlled research, it is alleged, therapists treat more complex cases in which patients have multiple problems. This more or less reduces to the common observation that the "textbook case" is something of a rarity in "real" clinical practice. The reality is that comorbid psychiatric disorders are common in bulimia nervosa (American Psychiatric Association, 1994). Patients in research studies often have multiple problems. But even if it is assumed that this objection is valid, the point to be made is that the so-called simple and discrete cases of bulimia nervosa are rarely treated with an empirically validated treatment (e.g., Stunkard, 1989). We know from the Chambless (1993) report that current training programs do not do particularly well in preparing therapists to use such methods. Practitioners unskilled in these methods do not typically refer to those who are. Practice is unrelated to what, in this case at least, is an indisputably relevant clinical research base. This failure is part of a larger picture. Barlow (1994a) points out that the majority of patients with phobic and panic disorders, for which there are empirically validated therapies, do not receive effective treatment.

Undoubtedly, some particularly difficult and complicated cases come to the attention of clinical practitioners. These cases may well require interventions that go beyond what is available in the form of empirically validated techniques. It is also possible, however, to overstate the uniqueness of patients in practice. All too often this serves to undercut the potential influence of clinical research findings, and to justify therapists doing what they are accustomed to doing regardless of the research evidence.

Patients and How They are Recruited

A common misconception is that difficult patients are screened out of controlled clinical trials and that the subjects constitute a select group with a better prognosis than their counterparts in "real life" clinical practice. Yet, it can be argued that patients who seek treatment in controlled trials might have a worse than average prognosis. They often have failed in previous forms of treatment, following which they seek therapy from specialized research centers. Moreover, they typically do not have the financial resources to seek preferred private treatment, and are attracted by the offer of free treatment. At least in the U.S., participation in controlled clinical research often reduces to subjects' last resort.

The degree to which findings from controlled research generalize to clinical practice can be determined by an examination of the patient characteristics in individual studies. Some will be more representative of the target clinical practice population than others. Bulimia nervosa is associated with significant psychiatric comorbidity, and the patients who have been subjects in the controlled research trials described here are no exception to this rule. In the Fairburn et al. (1991) study, for example, 34% of subjects had previously been diagnosed with anorexia nervosa. More than three-quarters of the subject sample had previously received treatment for an eating disorder, and 28% had received treatment for other psychiatric problems. In the Agras et al. (1992) study, 43% met DSM-III-R criteria for at least one personality disorder, with at least one in five meeting diagnostic criteria for borderline personality disorder (Rossiter et al., 1993). The authors pointed out that these figures were comparable to other controlled studies in the literature. In two ongoing multisite treatment studies involving CBT, my colleagues and I exclude potential patients only if they have an associated physical or psychiatric disorder requiring hospitalization, current physical dependence on drugs or alcohol, current low bodyweight below a BMI of 17.5 (thereby excluding patients with anorexia nervosa), and current psychiatric treatment of any type. As a result, comorbid anxiety disorders, depression, personality disorders, and marital and family conflict are commonplace.

The Therapists

It needs to be emphasized that effective implementation of manual-based treatment requires well-trained, competent therapists. It takes therapeutic skill to keep patients focused on the treatment. Although the treatment is standardized, therapists still have some flexibility in precisely when and how they introduce different components of the therapy, and which elements they emphasize. Manual-based therapy should not be confused with mechanistic or rote administration of preordained techniques.

The therapists in controlled trials are usually highly trained and closely supervised. They are probably chosen, at least in part, because they are known to be competent. Effectiveness of treatment might well decline when CBT or any other psychological therapy is administered by therapists who are less able or lack the necessary training. Research on the dissemination and exportability of the treatments evaluated in controlled trials will need to examine how effective the treatments prove when administered by therapists with different degrees of training and expertise (Kazdin & Wilson, 1978).

The Therapy

The manual-based CBT used in controlled clinical trials may differ from the more flexible and expansive application of cognitive behavioral therapy in clinical practice, as discussed above. It is certainly more restricted than a technically eclectic approach in which CBT is complemented by the addition of methods from other systems (Lazarus, 1981). Whether or not this difference influences treatment outcome is ultimately an empirical question. Putting the question to a test would require a controlled comparison between unrestricted clinical practice of CBT, replete with idiographic assessment, and the now standard manual-based treatment.

On the face of it, the greater range and flexibility of the textbook idiographic implementation of CBT are clinically appealing. Nonetheless, there are reasons to question whether a more idiographically-based intervention would improve upon the CBT manual. First, the CBT manual has been repeatedly shown to be effective. Second, the highly structured and time-limited nature of this treatment focuses the attention of both therapist and patient in working hard to make well-defined changes. Third, adding additional elements to the treatment requires either replacing some aspects or making it longer. Both options have disadvantages. It is unclear whether extending treatment has any advantages. Patients are being helped to be their own therapists so that they can continue to make progress following the termination of formal treatment.

Clinical judgement vs. actuarial prediction. Beyond these considerations there is a more fundamental issue, namely that of clinical judgment versus actuarial prediction. It is well-established that when it comes to predicting behavior, highly trained clinical experts who assess all available information, and integrate it based on their own understanding of the niceties of the individual case, do no better if not worse than actuarial prediction (Dawes, Faust, & Meehl, 1989). The explanation is well-known. Human judgment is not as effective as systematic research in selecting robust predictors of behavioral outcomes. Is this finding about predicting behavior similar to the therapist's task of idiographically assessing an individual patient with a view to selecting from an array of often competing and incompatible treatment techniques?

Seasoned therapists might decry strict manual-based treatment that precludes the opportunity to freelance, to modify and even disregard the protocol based on their clinical experience and expert assessment of the patient. This is probably true of all psychological therapies. It certainly is the case with CBT. The hallmark of behavioral assessment and therapy has been the functional analysis of the individual case (O'Leary & Wilson, 1987). It goes against the grain to ignore this dictum and fit a standardized treatment to a DSM-IV diagnosis. Clinical psychologists are especially likely to object to this practice on the grounds that it does not provide a psychological analysis of the presenting problem. Bulimia nervosa, as is the case with most clinical disorders, is heterogeneous in nature. The specific variables that maintain the problem probably vary from case to case. Hence the need for the so-called functional analysis of the individual case (Kanfer & Saslow, 1969).

It might be that the time has come to question the uncritical or incautious use of idiographic assessment, and to call attention to its potential downside. In conducting an idiographic clinical assessment, therapists will be guided by their personal experience. Research has shown that cognitive processes such as the availability heuristic and confirmatory bias undermine the utility of personal experience (Garb, 1994). O'Donohue and Szymanski (1994) point out that "Clinicians tend to find relationships between variables based on their prior expectations of what relationships they expect should exist rather than what relationships actually exist" (p. 32). The prospects of assimilative integration become all the more unpromising when what is being urged is examined in the light of evidence of clinical judgment. For example, Stricker (1994) calls for the integrative therapist to select and then mesh together the appropriate treatment techniques from multiple systems of psychotherapy for the individual patient, based in part on personal experience and theoretical preference. This mosaic is then to be "tested in the crucible of the therapeutic experience, and both the therapist and the patient will provide correctives to initial misconceptions. Thus, directionality among the three tiers of experience, technique, and theory is multiple and circular, as each one can influence the others" (p. 7). Such a challenging exercise would seem to be fertile ground in which the well-documented biases of clinical judgment can take root. Weighting the findings of clinical research more heavily in selecting treatment methods would reduce the potential influence of such biases (O'Donohue & Szymanski, 1994).

The fine-grained analysis of the individual case will yield more information, but does this increase effectiveness in selecting and implementing effective techniques? More information often increases judges' confidence in their decisions but not their accuracy (O'Donohue & Szymanski, 1994). The therapist might be better off following the simple empirically derived guideline that the best first line treatment for someone meeting diagnostic criteria for bulimia nervosa is manual-based CBT. If this does not work, move to the next empirically validated method, or the approach that is most consistent with what is known.

A common objection to randomized control designs, as Davison and Lazarus (1994) note, is that they "yield only group norms and probabilities, and they do not tell us very much about a given individual in the group. Only fine-grained study of individual cases permits us to relate therapeutic effect to specific patient characteristics" (p. 166). But with adequate sample sizes, randomized control designs can presumably reveal specific predictor variables that might refine the empirical heuristic described above. Moreover, the problems of individual assessment have to be borne in mind when noting the limitations of group comparison research.

Some Realities of Clinical Practice

It is a truism to repeat that we obviously cannot limit clinical practice to those areas that have been scientifically examined and for which empirically validated techniques are available. Nonetheless, we should insist on their use when they are available. Clinical training programs—professionals schools and too many of the more traditional "scientist-practitioner" programs alike—are doing an inadequate job in this regard as the Chambless (1993) reveals. Thoughtful proponents of the unique contributions and role of the practitioner recognize the value of drawing upon research-based treatments (Peterson, 1995). But I am concerned that this recognition does not go far enough. For example, Peterson (1995) offers the following quote from

Schon's (1983) advocacy of the "reflective practitioner": "The dilemma of 'rigor or relevance' arises more acutely in some areas of practice than in others. In the varied topography of professional practice, there is a high, hard ground where practitioners can make effective use of research-based theory and technique, and there is a swampy lowland where situations are confusing 'messes' incapable of technical solution. The difficulty is that the *problems of the high ground, however great their technical interest, are often relatively unimportant to clients or to the larger society*, while in the swamp are the problems of greatest human concern. Shall the practitioner stay on the high, hard ground where he can practice rigorously, as he understands rigor, but where he is constrained to deal with problems of relatively little social importance? Or shall he descend to the swamp where he can engage the most important and challenging problems if he is willing to forsake technical rigor" (p. 42). emphasis added).

As far as psychological therapy is concerned, this is an overstatement at best. If by "rigor" Schon (1983) means the product of controlled clinical research, then the dichotomy he draws is simply false. The applicability of empirically validated treatments extends well beyond a few simple problems of "technical interest" to a large number of patients with some of the most common disorders. Take the anxiety disorders as an example. Collectively, they may be the most prevalent psychiatric disorders in the U.S (Kessler et al., 1994). If empirically validated therapies did nothing other than provide the most effective means for treating the anxiety disorders it would be socially significant. When depression is added to the list, not to mention the other disorders identified by Barlow (1994a), a wide spectrum of clinical disorders with serious morbidity is included. Then include alcohol use and abuse, one of the most prevalent clinical disorders with personal and societal costs that are enormous. Miller and his colleagues (1994) have shown that there is a negative correlation between scientific evidence of the effectiveness of treatment techniques and their application in routine clinical practice.

If the empirically validated treatments discussed above are the high ground to which Schon refers, it is hardly the place to abandon as we might try to drain the "swamp" of clinical practice. The failure to recognize this point perpetuates the dismissal of empirically validated treatments as appropriate for a few simple problems of minor social importance–and, however inadvertently, encourages the "anything goes" philosophy that has characterized too much of clinical practice.

It is a question of balance–of figure/ground (or at least, swamp/high ground) perception. Following Barlow's (1994a) lead, I would be positive about pointing to the applicability of empirically validated treatments to number of serious problems. This must be accompanied by the clear recognition of the broad areas where no such base informs practice, where practitioners are largely on their own. The alleged failure to be more explicit about what we do not know as clinical practitioners is the essence of what Dawes (1994) takes professional psychology to task for.

The reverse of my framing of the issues is to emphasize the lack of a research base, and exalt the unique contributions of the practitioner. Perhaps practice cannot be reduced to applied science as some would have it (McFall, 1991). Perhaps you do need a different epistemology of practice as Peterson and Peterson (1995) and

Schon (1983) have proposed. In advocating empirically validated techniques, I suspect that I inevitably would be viewed by Schon and adherents to such views as misguidedly trying to apply an inappropriate positivist epistemology of science to professional practice. But problems remain that are not swept away by philosophical revisions.

If practitioners know more than they can say, which is the essence of Schon's (1983) thesis, then practical experience would be of paramount importance. What else could account for this tacit knowledge that defines and distinguishes practitioners from scientists? Yet the available evidence seems consistent. As Peterson (1995) himself concedes, experience has yet to be shown to be related to treatment outcome using traditional psychodynamic therapy. This finding severely undermines the unique contribution of the practitioner, at least insofar as traditional psychotherapy is concerned.

The broad conclusion that clinical experience is unrelated to treatment outcome may well be premature. Is this another "uniformity myth," with which we are more than a little familiar in the field of clinical psychology? What precisely is "clinical experience?" It is not necessarily the same as expertise. It is reasonable to enquire whether this bald statement applies equally to different forms of experience, with different types of treatment methods, and with different patient groups (Beutler, 1994). In a preliminary study, Burns and Nolen-Hoeksema (1992) found that experienced cognitive-behavioral therapists were more effective than novices in treating depressed outpatients. Speaking from a cognitive-behavioral perspective, Davison and Lazarus (1994) assert that "Clinical experience enables a therapist to recognize problems and identify trends that are usually beyond the perceptions of novices, regardless of their general expertise." Those of us who have extensive histories of doing therapy and clinical supervision might find the this statement difficult to dispute. Nonetheless, however counterintuitive it might seem, we must take seriously Dawes's (1994) admonition to be skeptical of such a seemingly correct impression in the absence of hard data.

The foregoing analysis has addressed clinical practice when relevant empirically validated methods are available. The next question is what to do in areas where there is little or no scientific research, no treatment manuals and no empirically validated techniques. Clinicians should apply principles of behavior change that are consistent with (at least not in violation of) what is known. The creative and innovative use of general principles of behavior change is one of the ways in which practitioners make a distinctive contribution. Practice is often a matter of informed trial and error. More prosaically, clinicians should be guided also by the best available standards of clinical care.

Unique Contributions of the Practitioner

A commitment to applied science—the development and use of empirically validated techniques—need not entail the derogation of clinical practice as Schon (1983) and others suggest. Practitioners have an important and unique role to play in what necessarily must be a partnership with clinical researchers if the field is to advance. This collaboration has been described elsewhere (e.g., Davison & Lazarus, 1994), and it suffices here simply to highlight some of its features.

Practitioners are key players in clinical innovation and the process of discovery. Informed by their unique perspective, clinicians can formulate testable hypotheses about behavior change that must subsequently be examined in controlled research. They can generate novel techniques, or improvements in existing methods. Cognitive behavior therapy provides many informative instances of such contributions. For example, CBT for bulimia nervosa was developed by Fairburn (1981) in Oxford based on his knowledge of cognitive behavioral principles in general, and his clinical understanding of eating disorders in particular. He first developed and described the treatment in a series of uncontrolled clinical cases, then set about evaluating it in controlled research (Fairburn et al., 1993). Current CBT for bulimia nervosa has a joint pedigree, one that ineluctably blends research with clinical practice.

The common principle in the several empirically validated behavioral treatments of the different anxiety disorders is exposure to the anxiety eliciting situation (Barlow, 1988). The principle is derived directly from research on avoidance behavior in the animal laboratory (Mowrer, 1960). Its creative application to phobic disorders using imagery was Wolpe's (1958) clinical innovation. Its subsequent elaboration in the treatment of different anxiety disorders was influenced both by experimental research and clinical innovation (Bandura, 1986; Barlow, 1993). Its adaptation to treating obsessive-compulsive rituals in the form of response prevention was a product of Meyer's (1966) clinical savvy which was successively refined by Rachman and Hodgson (1980) and Foa and her colleagues (Riggs & Foa, 1993).

As another revealing example of clinical innovation, one need look no further than cognitive behavior therapy for depression (Beck, Rush, Shaw, & Emery, 1979). Its theoretical formulation was only superficially linked to actual research on cognitive processes. The treatment has been shown to be effective, but has been increasingly criticized as insufficiently based on experimental cognitive psychology (Teasdale, 1993). Of course, even within CBT, some clinical innovations have not stood the test of time or empirical research. Hence the corresponding need for empirical evaluation.

Practitioners need not be "mere users" of the products of controlled clinical research (Schon, 1983). For example, they have an important contribution to make in the process of disseminating research-based CBT to the general ranks of mental health professionals. They can identify problems that have been overlooked, suggest improved strategies for implementation, and record observations about unusual patients or problems. This information can lead to refining and improving the existing treatment. It is inevitable that practitioners will push to depart from standardized, manual-based therapies even if they offer flexible strategies. A healthy tension between controlled research and clinical practice can sharpen the focus of both sets of activities and provide the type of collaboration that will benefit both endeavors.

Concluding Comment

Too few patients with wide range of diagnosable problems receive treatment that has been empirically validated in controlled research. What Barlow (1994a) has documented for anxiety disorders appears true of the eating disorders, at least in the U.S. Too few clinical psychologists are being trained in the use of empirically validated methods (Chambless, 1993). Such training is extremely rare among psychiatrists and other mental health professionals. Clinical research should focus on the development and evaluation of effective psychological treatments. Research is overdue on the dissemination and exportability of available manual-based treatments that have been shown to be effective in research settings.

References

Agras, W. S. (1987). So where do we go from here? *Behavior Therapy*, *18*, 20-217.

Agras, W. S., Schneider, J. A., Arnow, B., Raeburn, S. D., & Telch, C. F. (1989). Cognitive-behavioral treatment with and without exposure plus response prevention in the treatment of bulimia nervosa: A reply to Leitenberg and Rosen. *Journal of Consulting and Clinical Psychology*, *57*, 778-779.

Agras, W. S., Rossiter, E. M., Arnow, B., Schneider, J. A., Telch, C. F., Raeburn, S. D., Bruce, B., Perl, M., & Koran, L. M. (1992). Pharmacologic and cognitive-behavioral treatment for bulimia nervosa: A controlled comparison. *American Journal of Psychiatry*, *149*, 82-87.

Agras, W. S., Rossiter, E. M., Arnow, B., Telch, C. F., Raeburn, S. D., Bruce, B., & Koran, L. (1994). One-year follow-up of psychosocial and pharmacologic treatments for bulimia nervosa. *Journal of Clinical Psychiatry*, *55*, 179-183.

American Psychiatric Association. (1994). *Diagnostic and statistical manual of mental disorders* (4th ed.). Washington, DC: Author.

Arkowitz, H. (1992). Integrative theories of therapy. In D. K. Freedheim (Ed.), *History of psychotherapy: A century of change* (pp. 261-303). Washington, DC: American Psychological Association.

Bandura, A. (1986). *Social cognitive theory*. Englewood Cliffs, NJ: Prentice Hall.

Barlow, D. H. (1988). *Anxiety and its disorders*. New York: Guilford Press.

Barlow, D. H. (1993). *Clinical handbook of psychological disorders* (2nd ed.). Englewood Cliffs, NJ: Prentice Hall.

Barlow, D. H. (1994a). Psychological interventions in the era of managed competition. *Clinical Psychology*, *1*, 109-122.

Barlow, D. H. (1994b). Setting the stage for standards of care. *The Scientist Practitioner*, *4*, 6-8.

Beck, A. T., Rush, A. J., Shaw, B. F., & Emery, G. (1979). *Cognitive therapy of depression*. New York: Guilford Press.

Beitman, B. D., Goldfried, M. R., & Norcross, J. C. (1989). The movement toward integrating the psychotherapies: An overview. *American Journal of Psychiatry*, *146*, 138-147.

Beutler, L. E. (1994). Applications of psychotherapy research to the question of therapist training and experience. *Clinical Science*, Fall, 4-5.

Burns, D. D., & Nolen-Hoeksema, S. (1992). Therapeutic empathy and recovery from depression in cognitive-behavioral therapy: A structural equation model. *Journal of Consulting and Clinical Psychology, 60*, 441-449.

Castonguay, L. G., & Goldfried, M. R. (1994). Psychotherapy integration: An idea whose time has come. *Applied and Preventive Psychology, 3*, 159-172.

Chambless, D. (1993). *Task force on promotion and dissemination of psychological procedures*. Unpublished manuscript, Division 12 American Psychological Association.

Christensen, A., & Jacobson, N. S. (1994). Who (or what) can do psychotherapy: The status and challenge of nonprofessional therapies. *Psychological Science, 5*, 8-14.

Clark, D. M., Salkovskis, P. M., Hackmann, A., Middleton, H., Anastasiades, P., & Gelder, M. (1994). *British Journal of Psychiatry, 164*, 759-769.

Craighead, L. W., & Agras, W. S. (1991). Mechanisms of action in cognitive-behavioral and pharmacological interventions for obesity and bulimia nervosa. *Journal of Consulting and Clinical Psychology, 59*, 115-125.

Cooper, P. J., Coker, S., & Fleming, C. (1994). Self-help for bulimia nervosa: A preliminary report. *International Journal of Eating Disorders, 16*, 401-404.

Davis, R., Olmsted, M. P., & Rockert, W. (1990). Brief group psychoeducation for bulimia nervosa: Assessing the clinical significance of change. *Journal of Consulting and Clinical Psychology, 58*, 882-885.

Davison, G. C., & Lazarus, A. A. (1994). Clinical innovation and evaluation: Integrating practice with inquiry. *Clinical Psychology, 1*, 157-168.

Dawes, R. M. (1994). *House of cards*. New York: Free Press.

Dawes, R. M., Faust, D., & Meehl, P. E. (1989). Clinical versus actuarial judgment. *Science, 243*, 1668-1674.

Elkin, I., Shea, M. T., Watkins, J. T., Imber, S. D., Sotsky, S. M., Collins, J. F., Glass, D. R., Pilkonis, P. A., Leber, W. R., Docherty, J. P., Fiester, S. J., & Parloff, M. B. (1989). National Institute of Mental Health treatment of depression collaborative research program: General effectiveness treatments. *Archives of General Psychiatry, 49*, 802-8809.

Fairburn, C. G. (1981). A cognitive behavioural approach to the management of bulimia. *Psychological Medicine, 11*, 707-711.

Fairburn, C. G. (1985). Cognitive-behavioral treatment for bulimia. In D. M. Garner & P. E. Garfinkel (Eds.), *Handbook of psychotherapy for anorexia nervosa and bulimia* (pp. 160-192). New York: Guilford Press.

Fairburn, C. G. (1993). *Interpersonal psychotherapy for bulimia nervosa*. Washington, DC: American Psychiatric Association.

Fairburn, C. G. (1995). *Overcoming binge eating*. New York: Guilford.

Fairburn, C. G., Agras, W. S., & Wilson, G. T. (1992). The research on the treatment of bulimia nervosa: Practical and theoretical implications. In G. H. Anderson

& S. H. Kennedy (Eds.), *The biology of feast and famine: Relevance to eating disorders.* New York: Academic Press.

Fairburn, C. G., Jones, R., Peveler, R. C., Carr, S. J., Solomon, R. A., O'Connor, M. E., Burton, J., & Hope, R. A. (1991). Three psychological treatments for bulimia nervosa. *Archives of General Psychiatry, 48,* 463-469.

Fairburn, C. G., Kirk, J., O'Connor, M., & Cooper, P. J. (1986). A comparison of two psychological treatments for bulimia nervosa. *Behaviour Research and Therapy, 24,* 629-643.

Fairburn, C. G., Marcus, M. D., & Wilson, G. T. (1993). Cognitive behaviour therapy for binge eating and bulimia nervosa: A comprehensive treatment manual. In C. G. Fairburn & G. T. Wilson (Eds.), *Binge eating: Nature, assessment and treatment.* New York: Guilford Press.

Fairburn, C. G., Norman, P. A., Welch, S. L., O'Connor, M. E., Doll, H. A., & Peveler, R. C. (in press). A prospective study of outcome in bulimia nervosa and the long-term effects of three psychological treatments. *Archives of General Psychiatry.*

Fairburn, C. G., Jones, R., Peveler, R. C., Hope, R. A., & O'Connor, M. (1993). Psychotherapy and bulimia nervosa: The longer-term effects of interpersonal psychotherapy, behaviour therapy and cognitive behavior therapy. *Archives of General Psychiatry, 50.* 419-428.

Fichter, M. M., Leibl, K., Rief, W., Brunner, E., Schmidt-Auberger, S., & Engel, R. R. (1991). Fluoxetine versus placebo: A double-blind study with bulimic inpatients undergoing intensive psychotherapy. *Pharmacopsychiatry, 24,* 1-7.

Fluoxetine Bulimia Nervosa Collaborative Study Group. (1992). Fluoxetine in the treatment of bulimia nervosa. *Archives of General Psychiatry, 49,* 139-147.

Freeman, C. P. L., Barry, F., Dunkeld-Turnbull, J., & Henderson, A. (1988). Controlled trial of psychotherapy for bulimia nervosa. *British Medical Journal, 296,* 521-525.

Garb, H. N. (1994). Judgment research: Implications for clinical practice and testimony in court. *Applied and Preventive Psychology, 3,* 173-184.

Garner, D. M. (1989). A comparison between cognitive-behavioural and psychodynamic psychotherapy for bulimia nervosa. Paper presented at World Congress of Cognitive Therapy, Oxford, June 30.

Garner, D. M., Rockert, W., Davis, R., Garner, M. V., Olmsted, M. P., & Eagle, M. (1993). Comparison between cognitive-behavioral and supportive-expressive therapy for bulimia nervosa. *American Journal of Psychiatry, 150,* 37-46.

Goldbloom, D. S., & Olmsted, M. P. (1993). Pharmacotherapy of bulimia nervosa with fluoxetine: Assessment of clinically significant attitudinal change. *American Journal of Psychiatry, 150,* 770-774.

Goldfried, M. R. (1980). Toward the delineation of therapeutic change principles. *American Psychologist, 35,* 991-999.

Hawton, K., Salkovskis, P., Kirk, J., & Clark, D. (1989). *Cognitive Behavior Therapy.* Oxford: Oxford University Press.

Hollon, S. D., & Beck, A. T. (1994). Cognitive and cognitive-behavioral therapies. In S. L. Garfield & A. E. Bergin (Eds.), *Handbook of psychotherapy and behavior change: An empirical analysis* (4th ed.). New York: Wiley.

Ilardi, S. S., & Craighead, W. E. (1994). The role of nonspecific factors in cognitive-behavior therapy for depression. *Clinical Psychology*, *1*, 138-156.

Johnson, C., Tobin, D. L., & Dennis, A. (1990). Differences in treatment outcome between borderline and nonborderline bulimics at one-year follow-up. *International Journal of Eating Disorders*, *9*, 617-627.

Kanfer, F. H., & Saslow, G. (1969). Behavioral diagnosis. In C. M. Franks (Ed.), *Behavior therapy: Appraisal and status*. New York: McGraw-Hill.

Kazdin, A. E. (1984). Integration of psychodynamic and behavioral psychotherapies: Conceptual versus empirical syntheses. In H. Arkowitz, & S. B. Messer (Eds.), *Psychoanalytic therapy and behavior therapy: Is integration possible?* New York: Plenum Press.

Kazdin, A. E., & Wilson, G. T. (1978). *Evaluation of behavior therapy: Issues, evidence, and research strategies*. Cambridge, MA: Ballinger.

Keller, M. B., Herzog, D. B., Lavori, P. W., Bradburn, I. S., & Mahoney, E. M. (1992). The naturalistic history of bulimia nervosa: Extraordinarily high rates of chronicity, relapse recurrence, and psychosocial morbidity. *International Journal of Eating Disorders*, *12*, 1-10.

Kessler, R. C., McGonagle, K. A., Zhao, S., Nelson, C. B., Hughes, M., Eshleman, S., Wittchen, H. U., & Kendler, K. S. (1994). Lifetime and 12-month prevalence of DSM-III-R psychiatric disorders in the United States. *Archives of General Psychiatry*, *51*, 8-19.

Kirkley, B. G., Schneider, J. A., Agras, W. S., & Bachman, J. A. (1985). Comparison of two group treatments for bulimia. *Journal of Consulting and Clinical Psychology*, *53*, 43-48.

Klerman, G. L. (1990). The psychiatric patient's right to effective treatment: Implications of Osheroff vs. Chestnut Lodge. *American Journal of Psychiatry*, *147*, 409-418.

Klerman, G., & Weissman, M. (Eds.). (1993). *New applications of interpersonal psychotherapy*. Washington: American Psychiatric Association.

Klerman, G. L., Weissman, M. M., Rounsaville, B. J. & Chevron, E. S. (1984). *Interpersonal Psychotherapy of Depression*. New York: Basic Books.

Laessle, R. G., Beumont, P. J. V., Butow, P., Lennerts, W., O'Connor, M., Pirke, K. M., Touyz, S. W., & Waadt, S. (1991). A comparison of nutritional management with stress management in the treatment of bulimia nervosa. *British Journal of Psychiatry*, *159*, 260-261.

Lazarus, A. A. (1971). *Behavior therapy and beyond*. New York: McGraw Hill.

Lazarus, A. A. (1981). *The practice of multimodal therapy*. New York: McGraw Hill.

Lazarus, A. A. (1989). *The practice of multimodal therapy*. Baltimore: Johns Hopkins University Press.

Lazarus, A. A., & Messer, S. B. (1991). Does chaos prevail? An exchange on technical eclecticism and assimilative integration. *Journal of Psychotherapy Integration, 1,* 143-158.

Leitenberg, H., Rosen, J. C., Wolf, J., Vara, L. S., Detzer, M. J., & Srebnik, D. (1994). Comparison of cognitive-behavior therapy and desipramine in the treatment of bulimia nervosa. *Behaviour Research and Therapy, 32,* 37-46.

Linehan, M., Armstrong, H. E., Suarez, A., Allmon, D., & Heard, H. L. (1991), Cognitive-behavioral treatment of chronically parasuicidal borderline patients. *Archives of General Psychiatry, 48,* 1060-1064.

Luborsky, L., Singer, B., & Luborsky, L. (1975). Comparative studies of psychotherapies: Is it true that everyone has won and all must have prizes? *Archives of General Psychiatry, 32,* 995-1008.

Marks, I. M., Swinson, R. P., Basoglu, M., Kuch, K., Noshirvani, H., O'Sullivan, G., Lelliott, P. T., Kirby, M., McNamee, G., Sengun, S., & Wickwire, K. (1993). Alprazolam and exposure alone and combined in panic disorder with agoraphobia: A controlled study in London and Toronto. *British Journal of Psychiatry, 162,* 776-787.

McFall, R. M. (1991). Manifesto for a science of clinical psychology. *The Clinical Psychologist, 44,* 75-88.

Meyer, V. (1966). Modification of expectations in cases with obsessional rituals. *Behaviour Research and Therapy, 4,* 273-280.

Miller, W. R. (1980). *The addictive behaviours.* New York: Pergamon Press.

Miller, W. R., Brown, J. M., Simpson, T. L., Handmaker, N. S., Bien, T. H., Luckie, L. F., Montgomery, H. A., Hester, R. K., & Tonigan J. S. (1994). What works? A methodological analysis of the alcohol treatment outcome literature. In R. K. Hester, & W. R. Miller (Eds.), *Handbook of alcoholism treatment approaches* (2nd ed.). Massachusetts: Allyn & Bacon.

Mitchell, J. E., & de Zwaan, M. (1993). Pharmacological treatments of binge eating. In C. G. Fairburn & G. T. Wilson (Eds.), *Binge eating: Nature, assessment, and treatment* (pp. 250-269). New York: Guilford.

Mitchell, J. E., Pyle, R. L., Eckert, E. D., Hatsukami, D., Pomeroy, C., & Zimmerman, R. (1990). A comparison study of antidepressants and structured intensive group psychotherapy in the treatment of bulimia nervosa. *Archives of General Psychiatry, 47,* 149-157.

Mowrer, O. H. (1960). *Conditioning and learning.* New York: Wiley.

Munoz, R. F., Hollon, S. D., McGrath, E., Rehm, L. P., & VandenBos, G. R. (1994). On the AHCPR depression in primary care guidelines. *American Psychologist, 49,* 1-20.

O'Donohue, W., & Szymanski, J. (1994). How to win friends and not influence clients: Popular but problematic ideas that impair treatment decisions. *The Behavior Therapist, 17,* 30-33.

O'Leary, K. D., & Wilson, G. T. (1987). *Behavior therapy: Application and outcome* (2nd ed.). Englewood Cliffs, NJ: Prentice-Hall.

Paul, G. L. (1985). Can pregnancy be a placebo effect? Terminology, designs, and conclusions in the study of psychosocial and pharmacological treatments of behavioral disorders. In L. White, B. Tursky, & G. E. Schwartz (Eds.), *Placebo: Theory, research, and mechanisms* (pp. 137-163). New York: Guilford Press.

Peterson, D. R. (1995). Preconference paper, Conference on *Standards for Education in Professional Psychology II: Implementation and Dissemination*. National Council of Schools and Programs of Professional Psychology, New Orleans, January 1995.

Peterson, D. R., & Peterson, R. L. (1994, January). *Ways of knowing in a profession: Toward an epistemology for the training of professional psychologists*. Paper presented at the National Council of Schools and Programs of Professional Psychology midwinter conference on "Standard for Education in Professional Psychology: reflection and integration." Cancun, Mexico.

Pyle, R. L., Mitchell, J. E., Eckert, E. D., Hatsukami, D. K., Pomeroy, C., & Zimmerman, R. (1990). Maintenance treatment and 6-month outcome for bulimic patients who respond to initial treatment. *American Journal of Psychiatry*, *147*, 871-875.

Rachman, S., & Hodgson, R. J. (1980). *Obsessions and compulsions*. Englewood Cliffs, NJ: Prentice-Hall.

Riggs, D. S., & Foa, E. B. (1993). Obsessive compulsive disorder. In D. H. Barlow (Ed.), *Clinical handbook of psychological disorders* (2nd ed.) (pp. 189-239). New York: Guilford Press.

Rossiter, E. M., Agras, W. S., Losch, M., & Telch, C. F. (1988). Dietary restraint of bulimic subjects following cognitive-behavioral or pharmacological treatment. *Behaviour Research and Therapy*, *26*, 495-498.

Rossiter, E. M., Agras, W. S., Telch, C. F., & Schneider, J. A. (1993). Cluster B personality disorder characteristics predict outcome in the treatment of bulimia nervosa. *International Journal of Eating Disorders*, *13*, 349-358.

Schacht, T. E. (1984). The varieties of integrative experience. In H. Arkowitz & S. B. Messer (Eds.), *Psychoanalytic therapy and behavior therapy: Is integration possible?* (pp. 107-132). New York: Plenum.

Schon, D. A. (1983). *The reflective practitioner*. Basic Book.

Sechrest, L. (1992). The past future of clinical psychology: A reflection on Woodward. *Journal of Consulting and Clinical Psychology*, *60*, 18-23.

Shea, M. T., Pilkonis, P. A., Beckham, E., Collins, J. F., Elkin, I., Sotsky, S. M., & Docherty, J. P. (1990). Personality disorders and treatment outcome in the NIMH treatment of depression collaborative research program. *American Journal of Psychiatry*, *147*, 711-718.

Sloane, R. B., Staples, F. R., Cristol, A. H., Yorkston, N. J., & Whipple, K. (1975). *Psychotherapy versus behavior therapy*. Boston: Harvard University Press.

Smith, M. L., Glass, G., & Miller, T. (1980). *The benefits of psychotherapy*. Baltimore: Johns Hopkins University Press.

Stricker, G. (1994). Reflections on psychotherapy integration. *Clinical Psychology, 1*, 3-12.

Strupp, H. H. (1989). Psychotherapy: Can the practitioner learn from the researcher? *American Psychologist, 44*, 717-724.

Stuart, S., Simons, A. D., Thase, M. E., & Pilkonis, P. (1992). Are personality assessment valid in acute major depression? *Journal of Affective Disorders, 24*, 281-290.

Stunkard, A. J. (1989). Review of Schwartz, H. J. (Ed.), Bulimia: Psychoanalytic treatment and theory. Madison, CT: International Universities Press, 1988. *Psychiatric Annals, 19*, 279.

Teasdale, J. D. (1993). Emotion and two kinds of meaning: Cognitive therapy and applied cognitive science. *Behaviour Research and Therapy, 31*, 339-354.

Telch, M. J., & Lucas, R. A. (1994). Combined pharmacological and psychological treatment of panic disorder: Current status and future directions. In B. E. Wolfe & J. D. Maser (Eds.), *Treatment of panic disorder*. Washington, DC: American Psychiatric Press.

Thase, M. E. (1994). After the fall: Perspectives on cognitive behavioral treatment of depression in the "post collaborative" era. *The Behavior Therapist, February*, 48-51.

Tuschen, B., & Bent, H. (in press). Intensive brief inpatient treatment of bulimia nervosa. In K. D. Brownell & C. G. Fairburn (Eds.), *Comprehensive textbook of eating disorders and obesity*. New York: Guilford Press.

Walsh, B. T. (1991). Fluoxetine treatment of bulimia nervosa. *Journal of Psychosomatic Research, 35*, 33-40.

Walsh, B. T., Hadigan, C. M., Devlin, M. J., Gladis, M., & Roose, S. P. (1991). Long-term outcome of antidepressant treatment for bulimia nervosa. *American Journal of Psychiatry, 148*, 1206-1212.

Wilson, G. T. (1982). Psychotherapy process and procedure: The behavioral mandate. *Behavior Therapy, 13*, 291-312.

Wilson, G. T. (1985). Limitations of meta-analysis in the evaluation of the effects of psychological therapy. *Clinical Psychology Review, 5*, 35-47.

Wilson, G. T. (1982). Psychotherapy process and procedure: The behavioral mandate. *Behavior Therapy, 13*, 291-312.

Wilson, G. T. (1993a). Psychological and pharmacological treatments of bulimia nervosa: A research update. *Applied & Preventive Psychology, 2*, 35-42.

Wilson, G. T. (1993b). Assessment of binge eating. In C. G. Fairburn & G. T. Wilson (Eds.), *Binge eating: Nature, assessment and treatment*. New York: Guilford Press.

Wilson, G. T. (1995). Pharmacological and psychological treatments for bulimia nervosa. Paper presented at the World Congress on Cognitive and Behavior Therapy, Copenhagen, July.

Wilson, G. T. (1995). *When cognitive behavioral therapy fails*. Paper presented at the World Congress on Cognitive and Behavior Therapy, Copenhagen, July.

Wilson, G. T., Eldredge, K. L., Smith, D., & Niles, B. (1991). Cognitive-behavioral treatment with and without response prevention for bulimia. *Behaviour Research and Therapy*, *29*, 575-583.

Wilson, G. T., & Rachman, S. (1983). Meta-analysis and evaluation of psychotherapy outcome: Limitations and liabilities. *Journal of Consulting and Clinical Psychology*, *51*, 54-64.

Wilson, G. T., & Smith, D. (1989). Assessment of bulimia nervosa and evaluation of the Eating Disorder Examination. *International Journal of Eating Disorders*, *8*, 173-180.

Wolpe, J. (1958). *Psychotherapy by reciprocal inhibition.* Stanford, CA: Stanford University Press.

Footnotes

1. Some proponents of this view except "circumscribed problems such as simple phobias, panic, and obsessive-compulsive disorders" from this general conclusion about the lack of consistent differences among treatments (Castonguay & Goldfried, 1994, p. 161).

2. Ironically, CBT for bulimia nervosa was not included among the list of empirically validated treatments in the Division 12 Task Force Report (Chambless, 1993).

Discussion of Wilson

Making the Case

Ted Packard

University of Utah

Terence Wilson has made the case in a credible and comprehensive fashion for the necessity of the scientist-practitioner model. While the level of detail and sophistication in his argument goes considerably beyond the Boulder proclamation of 1947, the core concept remains unchanged that behavioral science and professional practice are inextricably and necessarily linked. The sorrow is that almost a half century has passed since professional psychology committed itself to this approach. The challenge is to utilize the body of relevant research now accumulated (and continuing to expand at a rapid rate) as a basis for establishing broadly accepted standards of practice for professional psychology. Accomplishing this in a relatively short period of time will likely call for political adroitness equal at least to the scientific skill of clinical researchers like Dr. Wilson. Whether or not as a profession we are up to this task remains to be seen.

An initial step in approaching this daunting task is to recognize that professional psychology is much broader than the "clinical psychology" that is frequently referred to in this and other chapters in this text. While AAAPP can play a pivotal role in initiating the development of practice standards, the ultimate success of the endeavor will depend on (1) acceptance and support from large numbers of professional and academic psychologists , and (2) the endorsement of the standards by managed care and related funding sources. Although a positive response from managed care entities seems reasonable to assume, the diverse and fractionated field of professional psychology will likely be a much greater challenge. Wilson acknowledges this problem in the introductory section of his chapter. A brief perusal of the most recent booklet describing characteristics of licensure candidates who recently completed the Examination for Professional Practice in Psychology is sobering indeed (Professional Examination Service, 1994). Almost half of the several thousand candidates for psychology licensure across North American completing the examination between 1988 and 1993 identified themselves as graduates of programs other than clinical psychology. Large numbers of counseling and school psychology graduates were represented as well as individuals from a great variety of other psychology specialties. Note also that the identified clinical programs represented two dissimilar ends of the professional spectrum: the traditional clinical programs housed in research universities (abundantly represented in AAAPP) and the more recently founded professional schools of psychol-

ogy (with minimal representation in AAAPP). Sensitivity and tact, as well as
scientific rigor and an ecumenical spirit, are qualities that will be sorely needed for
effective promulgation of empirically validated practice standards. Assuming such
standards are achievable, there remains a very large and challenging dissemination
and compliance task.

Another vexing issue concerns the criteria used to identify the empirically
validated treatments that form the basis for defensible practice standards. Wilson
references the criteria developed by the Task Force report to Division 12 of the
American Psychological Association (Chambless, 1993), noting that they are "rather
modest (if not minimalist) criteria." While the Task Force, according to Wilson, has
"served the profession well", it is obvious that broad consensus on the adequacy of
the criteria or their application to various empirically validated treatments is yet to
be achieved. A notable example is the omission from these preliminary listings of
"Well-Established" and "Probably Efficacious" treatments of the protocol for
bulimia nervosa so admirably supported in the chapter by Wilson. A potentially
troubling aspect of the move toward practice standards is the apparent lack at this
point in time of broad consensus on criteria for identifying empirically validated
treatments. Is the cart before the horse in this instance? Might not AAAPP
accomplish more in the long run by first tackling the problem of generating widely
accepted criteria? To illustrate, the Task Force standard for demonstrating "Well-
Established" efficacy includes as a primary criterion "at least two good group design
studies." Is two really enough? Can treatment efficacy across geographic regions,
diverse cultural groups, and multifaceted service settings in fact be based on one
original study and one replication? (Replication is one of a handful of concepts on
which virtually all research methodologists agree, e.g., Cohen, 1994). Over and
above answers to such questions, general acceptance by psychologists of practice
standards will rest squarely on a foundation of widely supported and minimally
controversial inclusion criteria.

The importance of this issue is underscored by Wilson's thoughtful analysis of
the criteria for evaluating the overall effectiveness of CBT where the argument is
advanced that multiple criteria are needed for "...fully evaluating the effectiveness
of any psychological or pharmacological treatment...". Eight criteria are described,
in addition to traditional statistical measures of treatment effects, each of which is
logically related to the utility and value of implementing various psychological
treatments in diverse settings. The eight criteria include acceptability, attrition or
drop-out rate, clinical effectiveness or significance, speed of action, breadth of
effects, durability of effects, disseminability to the broad population of practitioners, and cost-effectiveness. Wilson notes that limited data are available on some
of these dimensions, at least for bulimia nervosa treatments, but little if anything
is available on others (e.g., disseminability and cost-effectiveness). Many intriguing
and important considerations follow. For example, might a moderately effective
treatment characterized by minimal patient attrition be a better choice in some
circumstances than a highly effective treatment with consistently high drop-out

rates? Are faster-acting treatments generally preferable to slower-acting interventions? What if the slower-acting treatment has a greater breadth of effect (e.g., consistently at one year follow-up anxiety and depressive symptoms have decreased and self-esteem has increased) and is also more easily learned and implemented by various mental health professionals? Many additional important questions could be posed, all of which speak to the importance of having comprehensive and well supported criteria in place as a precursor to the effective promulgation of practice standards.

Wilson also discusses the possibility of tailoring a structured and manualized treatment (e.g., his bulimia nervosa intervention) to a unique patient whose special problems have been highlighted through a more idiographic assessment procedure. Although the purpose of manualized approaches is to standardize treatment interventions shown to be effective for specific problems, Wilson tacitly acknowledges that not all potential patients fit the standard. This brings to mind recent speculations by Beutler (1994) that manualized and validated approaches to treatment may prove to be efficacious for the majority of patients, but there will likely remain a substantial minority who do not fit the mold. Based in part on projections from treatment response data, Beutler hypothesized that the 20% or more of patients who do not respond to standardized interventions would likely need individualized treatments devised and administered by highly trained professionals (e.g., doctoral level psychologists). His hope was that this might represent a special niche in the increasingly competitive mental health market place for experienced and skillful psychologists.

In somewhat paradoxical but stimulating fashion, Wilson also explores possible parallels between actuarial prediction and standardized treatment approaches. Meehl (1954) concluded four decades ago that actuarial prediction was in general superior to clinical judgment, and this finding has stood well the test of time (e.g., Dawes, 1994). Wilson proposes that standardized and empirically validated treatments may in fact work best for the majority of patients if they are not "fine tuned" or modified based on the "clinical experience and wisdom" of seasoned practitioners. The data supporting the superiority of actuarial prediction is overwhelming. The accumulating data on use of standardized treatments with specific client populations is suggestive and intriguing. Perhaps we will conclude in the not-to-distant future that many of our patients will be best served if we do not stray far from our validated and manualized procedures. And besides, we may take solace from Beutler (1994), and our accumulated experience, that there will continue to be many opportunities for creative work with the challenging and idiosyncratic minority who do not fit well into contemporary "best practice" approaches.

References

Association of State and Provincial Psychology Boards. (1994). *EPPP performance by designated doctoral program in psychology, 1994.* New York: Professional Examination Service.

Beutler, L. E. (1994, August). *Tailoring treatments to patient needs*. Workshop presented at the meeting of the American Psychological Association, Los Angeles, CA.

Chambless, D. (1993). *Task force report on promotion and dissemination of psychological procedures*. Unpublished manuscript, Division 12, American Psychological Association.

Cohen, J. (1994). The earth is round (p < .05). *American Psychologist, 49*, 997-1003.

Dawes, R. M. (1994). *House of cards*. New York: Free Press.

Meehl, P. E. (1954). *Clinical vs. statistical prediction: A theoretical analysis and a review of the evidence*. Minneapolis: University of Minnesota Press.

Chapter 10

Assessment Practice Standards

John D. Cone
United States International University

"Psychologists work to develop a valid and reliable body of scientific knowledge based on research" (from the Preamble to the Ethical Principles of Psychologists and Code of Conduct [American Psychological Association, 1992]).

The inauguration of new professional organizations of psychologists in recent years has resulted in part from concern for the basic scientific underpinnings of the discipline. Specifically, numerous psychologists are afraid the field has drifted from its scientific roots. They are concerned it has moved from a commitment to the values required by the preamble just quoted, and into an emphasis on service and application that is based more on belief and impression than on generally accepted canons of scientific proof. Partly as a result of these fears, the American Association for Applied and Preventive Psychology (AAAPP) has spearheaded an effort to refocus attention on the science of psychology. A major element of its campaign involved convening a conference at the University of Nevada in January 1995 at which invited speakers presented their suggestions for scientific standards to govern psychological practice. This paper is based on a presentation by the author at that conference. It offers initial suggestions for a set of scientific standards applicable to assessment and measurement practices.

The paper begins with some context setting discussion of the meaning of assessment, measurement, and standards. Attention is called to some of the different purposes served by assessment and the importance of distinguishing different subject matters. Next, existing ethical standards governing assessment practices are discussed. These are followed by a more extensive discussion of existing technical standards. Then, seven recommendations are made that might supplement existing technical standards. Finally, a process is suggested for having these proposals and others considered by the psychological community.

Definitions and Distinctions

Setting standards to govern activities is aided by having a clear understanding of the different meanings standards can have. Haney and Madaus (1991) call attention to four such meanings. One is that standards represent a level of attainment regarded as adequate. A second view is that standards refer to a measure of excellence, as in the "gold standard." They can also mean the practices commonly accepted by a group or profession, as in "standard in the practice of medicine" or moral standards of a community. Finally, a standard can refer to some emblem or symbol of an individual or group, as in the American flag. As Haney and Madaus (1991) note, present standards for assessment and measurement have taken all these meanings at one time or another.

Standards can be discussed meaningfully only in the context of the activities one is trying to govern. It is common in psychology to refer to assessment and measurement as interchangeable terms. There is merit in distinguishing them, however. Haring (1977) described "assessment" as obtaining a snapshot-like view of a person at a moment in time in order to determine the person's status with respect to cumulative skill or knowledge. "Measurement" can be seen as the dynamic act of charting changes in dimensional quantities of all or a portion of that repertoire over time. Assessment provides a static representation of a person at a point in time, whereas measurement provides a dynamic picture of change. These clearly different activities suggest the possibility of different standards. It is likely that an instrument designed to provide a static description of a number of characteristics of a person would have somewhat different qualities than one designed to track changes in these characteristics. This point has been made in the literature contrasting norm-referenced and criterion-referenced forms of assessment, for example (e.g., Messick, 1983). Typically the former are designed to provide consistent measures of stable differences between people. The latter are more often employed to detect differences from a criterion of absolute performance, and change in those differences over the course of some intervention. The types of indicator (Bollen & Lennox, 1991) or item comprising assessment devices on the one hand, and measurement devices on the other are likely to be quite different, given the respective requirements for sensitivity to stable differences and change.

It is also likely that different considerations will apply when assessment/ measurement is used for different purposes. Among the purposes most often mentioned are (a) description/classification/categorization, (b) understanding, (c) predicting, (d) controlling, and (e) monitoring. For example, if individuals are being assessed for diagnosis or classification, it is important that instruments result in accurate assignments. Issues such as sensitivity and specificity become relevant in judging the adequacy of the assessment activity. Similarly, when the assessment purpose is predicting some outcome, clear connections between the assessment device and criteria representing the outcome are relevant. If the major purpose is control, the instrument will need to produce specific enough data on the assessed characteristic that appropriate environmental events can be manipulated to determine their functional relevance. Special qualities of instruments used for monitoring purposes have already been mentioned.

Finally, it is likely that different considerations will apply when assessment/ measurement is applied to different subject matters. If latent traits or other hypothetical constructs are the subject matter of interest, different technical considerations take precedence than if behavior is the focus of the assessment interest. This is so because the definition of constructs is based on variability in measures of them (Johnston & Pennypacker, 1980). Behavior can be defined in terms of physical dimensions, and thus relatively absolutely. One has only to think of the example of thermometers to realize the difference. The temperature assessor's interest is not in the movement of mercury in a glass tube, per se, but in what that movement is thought to represent. The exercise physiologist counting the repetitions of a person doing sit-ups can be interested in how many sit-ups the person does. Sit-ups do not have to be used to represent something unseen.

Existing Ethical Standards

Unlike less well-developed areas of psychological practice, assessment activities have a long history of governance by standards. The discipline has applied both ethical and technical standards in this area for some time. This section takes a brief look at existing ethical standards. Technical standards are examined in the following section.

There are ten standards in the current American Psychological Association (APA) Ethical Principles of Psychologists and Code of Conduct pertinent to assessment (APA, 1992). Paraphrased, these include:

(1) Evaluations and diagnoses occur in a professional context using information and techniques "sufficient to provide appropriate substantiation for their findings" (Standard 2.01).

(2) Psychological assessment techniques are used competently and appropriately (Standard 2.02).

(3) Psychologists who develop and conduct research using tests use current knowledge in design, standardization, validation, bias control, and recommendations for the use of tests and other assessment techniques (Standard 2.03).

(4) Tests are administered, scored, interpreted, and otherwise used with appropriate awareness of reliability, validity, and standardization issues, and the uses appropriate for them (Standard 2.04).

(5) Assessment results are interpreted appropriately (Standard 2.05).

(6) Psychologists do not promote the use of assessment techniques by unqualified persons (Standard 2.06).

(7) Interpretations and recommendations are not based on outmoded, obsolete instruments (Standard 2.07).

(8) Psychologists who use, or offer for others, test scoring and interpreting services do so with appropriate knowledge of the validity of the service and describe its purpose and technical characteristics accurately to others (Standard 2.08).

(9) Assessment results are explained appropriately to the person being assessed (Standard 2.09).

(10) The integrity and security of tests is maintained (Standard 2.10).

A review of these standards reveals their use to represent commonly adhered to examples or criteria of acceptable practice (Haney & Madaus, 1991). As such, their formal promulgation dates to the first code of ethics formally adopted by APA in 1952 (APA, 1953). To be sure, these standards have undergone modification over the 40+ years since their initial appearance. Interested readers are referred to Haney and Madaus (1991) for a discussion of the historical journey taken by the ethical standards during this period. The technical standards have an even longer history as the next section makes clear.

Existing Technical Standards

Joint committees of the American Psychological Association, the American Educational Research Association, and the National Council on Measurement in Education have produced several sets of technical standards or guidelines governing assessment activities in psychology and education over the years (APA, AERA, & NCMUE, 1954; 1974; AERA, APA, & NCME, 1985), and a joint committee is currently revising the standards again (De Angelis, 1994). The intent of the guidelines is to provide a codification of the activities of persons involved with tests and the testing process. The 1985, or present version, consists of 180 guidelines covering 16 categories pertaining to the activities of test developers, test users, and test takers. As Cronbach (1984) has observed, the standards can best be viewed as an educational aid for the professions, not a set of regulations. Moreover, they emphasize the provision of information about the test, its development, and use, rather than the quality of the test. That is, they spell out the kind of information and evidence necessary to assure testing activities are being pursued competently, e.g., types of reliability explored, size and composition of standardization samples. There is no requirement that certain values, e.g. an alpha level of .85, be reached in order for the test to meet a standard viz its reliability.

The technical standards cover tests in general use and are not designed to apply to tests developed by individual teachers, therapists, or companies for local use only. The standards cover structured, formalized, standardized activities of three types: (a) constructed performance tasks, e.g., achievement tests, intelligence tests, and other ability tests interpreted as maximum performance tests; (b) questionnaires and inventories; and (c) structured behavior sample tests, e.g., direct observation in a standardized way of "personal skills and styles relevant to clinical, employment, and educational decision making" (AERA et al., 1985, p. 4). Thus, the standards are meant to apply to both "tests", e.g., assessment situations in which persons are told to try their best, and questionnaires, inventories, and checklists used to identify attitudes, interests, and personality characteristics.

As revealed in Table 1, the existing standards are organized into four parts. The first deals with technical standards for test construction and evaluation. This is the largest of the sections, comprising 40% of the 180 standards. The second part of the guidelines covers the ways tests are used. Approximately a third (34%) of the standards deal with test use.

Table 1. Standards for Educational and Psychological Testing

Part 1: Technical Standards for Test Construction and Evaluation

Validity (n = 25)
Reliability and Errors of Measurement (n = 12)
Test Development and Revision (n = 25)
Scaling, Norming, Score Comparability, and Equating (n = 9)
Test Publication: Technical Manuals and User's Guides (n = 11)

Part 2: Professional Standards for Test Use

General Principles of Test Use (n = 13)
Clinical Testing (n = 6)
Test Use in Counseling (n = 9)
Employment Testing (n = 9)
Educational Testing and Psychological Testing in the Schools (n = 12)
Professional and Occupational Licensure and Certification (n = 5)
Program Evaluation (n = 8)

Part 3: Standards for Particular Applications

Testing Linguistic Minorities (n = 7)
Testing People Who Have Handicapping Conditions (n = 8)

Part 4: Standards for Administrative Procedures

Test Administration, Scoring, and Reporting (n = 11)
Protecting the Rights of Test Takers (n = 10)

The third part of the standards covers particular applications. As can be seen from Table 1, these guidelines treat the special considerations important when testing persons for whom the language of the assessment situation is not native, and those for whom a disability might require accommodations or modification of the standard testing conditions. A relatively small percentage (8.3%) of the standards is devoted to these considerations. Finally, Part 4 of the standards deals with administrative procedures.

As with earlier versions of the standards, the current edition assigns one of three levels of importance to each guideline. Those designated "primary" include conditions that should be met by all tests before their operational use. For example, Standard 7.4 states "test users should determine from the manual or other reported evidence whether the construct being measured corresponds to the nature of the assessment that is intended" (APA, 1985, p. 47). "Secondary" standards are those that are desirable, but likely to be beyond reasonable expectations in many situations. For example, Standard 12.8 states "When tests are used wholly or in part to allocate funds to geographic or political jurisdictions, such as school districts, the positive and negative anticipated consequences of such use should be described to policy makers by those test professionals who are closest to the policy before the policy is implemented" (APA, 1985, p. 69).

Finally, "conditional" standards are those for which the importance varies, depending on the application. They would be considered primary for some applications, secondary for others. For example, "When criterion-related evidence is presented, a rationale for choosing between a predictive and a concurrent design should be available" (APA, 1985, p. 69).

Standards for testing and assessment have a long history in psychology. Haney and Madaus (1991) trace them at least as far back as 1895 when a committee was formed within APA to study the feasibility of standardizing the collection of mental and physical measurements. Since then numerous committees and even individual psychologists have offered recommendations. Kelley (1924, cited in Haney & Madaus, 1991) is said to have suggested that a test needed to have a reliability of .94 to be useful in evaluating individual accomplishment.

The published fruits of these various recommendations did not begin appearing until the middle of the present century, with the publication by APA in 1954 of the joint AERA-APA-NCME document *Technical Recommendations for Psychological Tests and Diagnostic Techniques* (APA, 1954). There were 160 guidelines arranged in six categories in this initial publication. In 1966, recommendations for psychological and educational tests and test usage were combined with the publication of *Standards for educational and psychological tests* (APA, 1966). The number of guidelines remained at 160 in this version, but ballooned to 240 with its revision in 1974 (APA, 1974). The latest version pared the number to the 180 mentioned above (APA, 1985).

The standards, and variations of them published by other organizations (e.g., American Association for Counseling and Development, 1978; National Association of School Psychologists, 1984) are used by the organizations to police their members. Sanctions are limited, with expulsion from membership being perhaps the most severe consequence for failing to uphold the standards. Less extreme measures include censure and public notices to the effect of these actions. The standards have also been used by the courts as a criterion of professional practice (Lerner, 1978).

Recommendations for New Standards

Considering recommendations for new standards in the area of assessment and measurement practices is greatly facilitated by the extensive work of others over the past 100 years. Certainly the cumulative wisdom of the giants in psychometric theory and practice provides a good context in which to consider change. In what follows, suggestions are made that can be supplementary to, and incorporated into existing standards. They are not meant as replacement or alternative suggestions. Moreover, they are offered as points for discussion, as a way of stimulating consideration of practice standards based on contemporary psychological science. It is hoped that joint committees and subcommittees of professional organizations might take these suggestions and add to, elaborate, or modify them to come up with new practice standards.

Recommendation 1: Recognize Subject Matter Differences

The present technical standards focus almost exclusively on classical latent trait models of assessment. There is an increasing body of evidence that different subject matters require altered conceptual and methodological approaches to the development and use of tests (Herson & Bellack, in press; Bollen & Lennox, 1991; Cone, 1988; Johnston & Pennypacker, 1993). For example, traits are defined in terms of observed differences in individuals' behavior. Differences in test behavior are used to infer the underlying construct. Variation is, therefore, essential to defining the subject matter initially. It then becomes essential to establishing whether tests of it are any good (Johnston & Pennypacker, 1980).

When behavior is the subject matter, the situation is fundamentally different. Behavior can be defined more or less absolutely, and does not depend on observed differences in test behavior for its existence. Unlike traits, for which there is no universally agreed upon definition, behavior is something about which agreement *can* be achieved. When dealing with behavior, the principles of measurement worked out in the physical sciences appear to have relevance. This is a measurement tradition fundamentally different from classical latent trait theory (Johnston & Pennypacker, 1980). It would be logical, therefore, that the procedures for test development, evaluation, and use would be somewhat different, as might the technical standards applied to these activities.

Bollen and Lennox (1991) recently called attention to problems with some of the conventional wisdom applied to test development. Most significant was their clarification of the difference between effects indicator and causal models underlying test construction, a distinction made earlier by Blalock (1964). Bollen and Lennox (1991) observed that the traditional latent trait approach assumes a model in which responses to items (indicators) on a test are determined by the latent trait. Associated parallel tests assumptions result in each item being viewed as interchangeable with every other, with all being equally trait determined. Conceptualized in this way, it is expected that tests will be homogeneous and measures of this homogeneity are appropriate ways of establishing something about the quality of the test. Alternative models of the construct being tapped by an assessment instrument exist, however, as was just discussed in terms of the trait-behavior distinction. For example, Bollen and Lennox (1991) discuss causal indicator models, in contrast to traditional effects indicator models. They also consider mixed models. In causal indicator models, test items are seen as determining the construct, rather than the reverse as in conventional latent trait theory. An example is a measure of socioeconomic status (SES). Components of scores on such an index often include income, job classification, years of education, and neighborhood of residence. As a person's income increases, it would be expected that SES would increase. The reverse is not logical, nor anticipated in the conceptualization of such a construct. Moreover, the components are not necessarily expected to be comparably related to the index score or to each other. As Bollen and Lennox (1991) point out, it is not clear what to expect concerning the internal consistency of such a measure. Again, as was true for different subject matters, alternative models of the underlying construct might have implications for test development, evaluation, and use procedures, as well as the technical standards applied to tests of the construct.

Recommendation 2: Recognize the Distinction between Accuracy, Reliability, and Validity

In keeping with acknowledged differences in test models and in the subject matter of tests, new standards can profit from recognizing and sharpening distinctions between basic measurement concepts. When latent traits are the focus, determining the quality of their measures relies on studying variation in scores on the measures. Thus, various forms of reliability and validity resolve to alternative ways of studying variability. This is logical, and quite necessary given the inherent use of variability to define the trait in the first place. We will come back to these more familiar psychometric concepts in a minute. First, let us focus on accuracy, a less familiar concept, and one not referenced in the current technical standards.

Accuracy. When the subject matter of assessment is "real" rather than hypothetical, there is the possibility of consensus concerning its definition. Consider the following examples: a child gets out of his/her seat or s/he does not; a person with borderline personality disorder threatens suicide or s/he does not; and one spouse hits the other or s/he does not. The occurrence of these events can be definitively established. If behavior is the focus of a test, and if behavior is viewed from a natural science perspective, the characteristics of measures worked out in the physical sciences would seem to be relevant (Johnston & Pennypacker, 1980). In such cases, the preeminent characteristic of measures is their accuracy. If scores on a test are controlled by objective topographic features and relevant dimensional quantities of the behavior of interest, the test may be said to be accurate. This quality of an instrument can be evaluated by comparing the scores it produces against an incontrovertible index of behavior occurrence. Its level of accuracy can then be provided along with other information documenting its adequacy as a measuring instrument. This is like the practice of providing data on the power and resolution of microscopes or the signal-to-noise ratios or percent total harmonic distortion of sound reproduction equipment in the physical sciences. Given the observance of phenomena with measures of known levels of accuracy, one can have associated levels of confidence in the nature of what is being observed.

Accuracy is established in a calibrating context, the precise characteristics of which are specified by the test developer. To establish accuracy one only need have an incontrovertible index against which to compare test observations and well-articulated rules/procedures for using the test. The index consists of a set of operations constituting a criterion of "truth," such as programming a light to flash with a certain frequency or a person to say complimentary things at a certain rate. If data from the test compare favorably with what is known to have been programmed, the test is said to be accurate. Similar accuracy levels can assumed for subsequent uses of the test provided such uses conform closely to the calibrating conditions. Of course, accuracy generalization is subject to empirical test just as any test characteristic would be. Different ways in which accuracy can be generalized include across scorers, times, settings, and alternative tests of the same behavior (Cone, 1988).

Reliability. Accuracy involves agreement between scores on a measure and an incontrovertible index. Reliability involves agreement between scores on highly similar, independent measures of the same thing, neither of which has the status of an incontrovertible index. The various forms of reliability are familiar. If scores obtained at one time are comparable to those obtained sometime later, we say the measure is temporally stable or has test-retest reliability. If scores on portions of a measure agree with each other, we say the measure is internally consistent. If different forms of the same test correlate with one another, we say they are comparable and speak of alternate form reliability and coefficients of equivalence. Cronbach and colleagues have subsumed these various types of consistency under the rubric of generalizability theory (Cronbach, Gleser, Nanda, & Rajaratnam, 1972).

When dealing with hypothetical constructs as the subject matter, reliability is important as a way of estimating the extent to which measures are error free. When dealing with behavior, accuracy replaces reliability as the preeminent characteristic of measures. This is because the extent to which scores are error free can be absolutely determined and does not need merely to be estimated. That is not to say reliability has no relevance for behavior measures. There is still the need to show their internal consistency and temporal stability, for example, though it is not necessarily a requirement that either or both be high.

Validity. When there is evidence supporting various types of inference from scores on tests we speak of validity. The existing standards are clear in emphasizing that it is not tests, per se that are valid or invalid, but rather the interpretations made from their scores. Behaviorally, validity can be seen as a value judgement reflecting the extent to which empirical and theoretical evidence support the classification of assessment instruments as discriminative for certain behavior of persons having contact with them (Cone, in press). The kinds of behavior might include judgments of whether the test looks appropriate for a particular use (face validity) or judgments of whether it is made up of stimuli calling for construct relevant responses (content validity). Other behavior for which tests might be discriminative include predictions from responses on the test to other types of responses, either concurrently available or to be available sometime in the future (criterion-related validity), or judgments of whether relationships entered into by scores on the test are consistent with theory (construct validity).

The present standards emphasize content, criterion-related, and construct validity. They are clear on the importance of showing a measure is, indeed, tapping the variable of interest. They also acknowledge this as a different activity from showing the measure's usefulness for various purposes. New standards would do well to recognize this distinction. Moreover, they would do well to require purveyors of new measures to show the measure does, indeed, represent the construct or behavior as they intend it. Further, evidence of this sort could be required before presenting evidence of the measure's usefulness. After all, it is fundamental to advancing psychology as a science that when relationships are shown between measures, we have confidence in the substance of the relationship. This is unclear unless appropriate steps have been taken to show that the measure truly represents the construct as intended. Conventionally, this process and that of pursuing construct validity occur concurrently. Problems arise with the concurrent approach, however, especially when research results are negative. Was the failure to find the expected relationship due to shortcomings in the test, the design of the study, or the theory relating the constructs in the first place? Interpretive clarity would be enhanced by recognizing two phases of the validation process: (a) representational, and (b) elaborative.

(a) representational validity: Representational validity involves showing the test really does measure the construct or behavior as the developer intends. When behavior is the subject matter, showing the test to be accurate is synonymous with establishing its representational validity. Examining the content or stimulus material making up the test is an important aspect of representational validity. The current standards refer to this as gathering evidence for the validity of the construct underlying the test by examining "the degree to which the sample of items, tasks, or questions on a test are representative of some defined universe or domain of content." (APA, 1985, p. 10). They go on to note that expert opinion should be considered in defining the construct being measured and in selecting content and "specifying the item format and scoring system" (p. 11). Messick (1994) views content validity as one of six aspects of a unified view of validity, noting that it "includes evidence of content relevance, representativeness, and technical quality" (p. 3).

Additional aspects of representational validity include showing that the new measure produces evidence agreeing with that of alternative ways of operationalizing the construct. Often referred to as convergent validity (Campbell & Fiske, 1959), the overriding interest is in showing the construct is more than the measure of it. This is a logical requirement when responses to test stimuli are viewed as "signs" (Goodenough, 1949) of some trait. If a test really represents the trait, it will correlate with other ways of assessing the same trait, and it will do so for reasons other than shared variance produced by a common method. For example, alternative ways of tapping moral knowledge (Hartshorne & May, 1928) would be expected to correlate. If they do not, there is difficulty concluding some underlying latent trait is determining performance on them. Showing that self-report measures of anxiety correlate with ratings by clinicians supports the inference that a common variable is being assessed, and is evidence of the representational validity of both measures.

Representational validity is advanced by showing a test correlates with others with which it should be associated. It is also advanced by showing its independence from measures of constructs with which it should not be associated. Campbell (1960; Campbell & Fiske, 1959) has identified certain pervasive characteristics from which new measures should be shown to have discriminant validity. The dual processes of convergent and discriminant validity, facilitated by multitrait-multimethod analyses, are akin to sharpening the definition of concepts by showing numerous "is" instances and numerous "is not" instances of the concept as well (Becker, Engelmann, & Thomas, 1971). Thus, we learn the concept "square" by viewing numerous examples of square, varying in size and color, and by contrasting squares with other shapes that are clearly not square.

The requirement to show convergent and discriminant validity for new measures is generally not controversial. There is some confusion, however, about Campbell and Fiske's (1959) original advice that convergence be shown between maximally different independent approaches (Pedhazur & Schmelkin, 1991). Nonetheless, it is reasonably likely that "maximally different" is not a characteristic of two self-report measures. Nor would it characterize comparisons of mother reports and father reports of some child behavior. Comparing self-report data with reports of others for the same construct would seem more in keeping with the spirit of Campbell and Fiske's (1959) recommendations, however, as these methods are likely to share less method variance than the preceding examples.

Similarly, confusion exists over criteria to use in showing discriminant validity. For example, one of Campbell's (1960) pervasive characteristics for which we already have good measures is the tendency to portray oneself in socially desirable ways. It is common for newly developed self-report measures to correlate with social desirability (SD), absent explicit efforts to minimize its influence in the scale construction process. When such a relationship exists, the scale's representational validity is compromised. Is it conscientiousness or social desirability that is being tapped, for example? General appreciation for this form of discriminant validity has led developers of new instruments to show the independence of scores on their scale and scores on a measure of social desirability. For example, Kumar and Beyerlein (1991) recently reported a scale to assess ingratiation in organizations. They showed correlations ranging from zero to .09 between individual scale items and total scores on a short version (Strahan & Gerbasi, 1972) of the Marlowe-Crowne social desirability scale. Unfortunately, for Kumar and Beyerlein, the Marlowe-Crowne Scale (Crowne & Marlowe, 1960) has been shown to assess something different from social desirability as defined by Edwards (1957). Indeed, the Marlowe-Crowne "need for approval" scale is more highly correlated with the Lie Scale of the *MMPI* (Edwards & Walsh, 1964). In factor analyses of multiple scales, the Edwards form of SD has been shown to load the large first principle component while the Marlowe-Crowne scale loads a third, much smaller factor, and one also loaded by the Lie Scale (Edwards & Walsh, 1964). Thus, revised standards might require test authors to show discriminant validity from the Edwards form of SD, and to recognize the distinction between SD on the one hand, and lying on the other.

A recent suggestion by Ozer and Reise (1994) following a cartographic analogy by Goldberg (1993a) relates to representational validity and the subvarieties of convergent and discriminant validity when personality measures are at issue. According to Goldberg (1993b, cited in Ozer & Reise,1994), the "big five" or five-factor model serves as a good taxonomy of personality characteristics. Because of the extensive empirical support for the model, Ozer and Reise (1994) suggest it be viewed as a "hierarchical coordinate system, for mapping important personality variables (p. 360)." Thus, purveyors of new personality measures might be required to locate them in the five-factor space, much as discoverers of new lands would be expected to locate them in terms of longitude and latitude. Before doing so, however, the "contrarian view" on the five-factor structure recently presented by Block (1995) should be consulted.

(b) elaborative validity: Once a test has been shown to represent the latent trait or behavior as its developer intended, one can begin to examine whether it has any theoretical or applied utility. That is, its validity can be elaborated. Validity elaboration is essentially the process of showing relationships between scores on the measure and scores on measures of other variables. Criterion-related validity is the most relevant concept of the current standards to this process. Though sometimes seen as crass empiricism and referred to as "psychotechnology" (Loevinger, 1957, p. 636), the concept can be profitably elevated to encompass any relationships between scores on a measure and scores on other measures of different variables. When viewed in this expanded way, criterion-related validity absorbs some of the activities typically subsumed under construct validity. This perspective defines criterion-related validity operationally and avoids the necessity of inferring whether its pursuer was more practically or theoretically driven.

By elaborating the validity of a test, we are clarifying its meaning or usefulness. When scores on the test relate to scores on some criterion, we say the test is useful as a predictor of the criterion. At the same time, we learn something about the nature of the construct or behavior being tapped by the test. Presumably our theory accommodates the relationship and is supported by it. In this way we are advancing construct validity, though it does not seem useful to call attention to construct validity as a separate process as the current standards do.

Messick (1994) argues convincingly that construct validity encompasses all of the activities traditionally viewed as different types of validity. In this regard he echoes the observation of Cronbach (1980) who questioned the logic of dividing validity into different types, saying it can all be subsumed under construct validity. This is eminently reasonable. Furthermore, construct validity can be expanded to include traditional reliability issues as well. For example, if the variable underlying scores on a test is viewed as a unidimensional latent trait, internal consistency is important. If the variable is seen as multidimensional, however, internal consistency is not clearly so relevant (Bollen & Lennox, 1991). In the first case, demonstrations of high coefficient alphas support the validity of the instrument as a measure of the construct. In the second case, high alphas fail to support construct validity. Similar arguments can be made for temporal stability demonstrations. Moreover, even the assessment method used can be selected to support the construct as it is understood by its originators. If subjective appraisals (e.g., "I feel sad.") are the focus, self-report or self-monitoring methods are the most construct appropriate. If behavior (e.g., praising one's boss in the presence of others) is the focus, rating-by-others or direct observation methods take precedence.

When construct validity is expanded this comprehensively, it becomes the entire process of arguing the evidence for a measure. In so doing, it loses its distinctiveness, and therefore its meaning. It becomes a substitute term for instrument development and refinement.

Distinguishing between representational and elaborative forms of validity is similar to the distinction between meaning and significance noted by operationists in reaction to Cronbach and Meehl's (1955) classic treatise on construct validity. Bechtoldt (1959) argued that the meaning of a concept is to be found in the operations that define it. Thus, a particular test is what is meant by a construct. The significance of the construct is established by the relationships into which scores on the test enter. All constructs can have meaning, though not all will have significance. It is not possible, however, for a construct to have significance without meaning. Representational validity is a broader concept than Bechtoldt's "meaning," extending beyond simply the operations comprising the test.

A final type of elaborative validity warranting explicit consideration in any set of new or revised standards is functional validity. This term encompasses incremental utility (Mischel, 1968) and treatment utility (Evans & Nelson, 1977; Hayes, Nelson, & Jarrett, 1987; Silva, 1993) or intervention validity (Cone, 1989). Functional validity relates to the value added by using the test. For example, incremental validity results when test use produces increased predictive accuracy over simple population base rates. Treatment utility results when outcomes from some form of intervention are shown to be better when the intervention is informed by test results than when it is not.

Recommendation 3: Require Representational Validity First

There are advantages to showing representational validity before moving to elaborative validity. When we know how adequately the test represents the object of assessment before we attempt to elaborate its meaning by showing relationships with other variables, it is easier to interpret negative results. The test can be eliminated from suspicion as the culprit when anticipated relationships are not forthcoming. For example, having demonstrated convergent and discriminant validity, we can interpret correlations as the result of "real" relationships between the constructs rather than worrying whether they resulted from the use of a common assessment methodology. Similarly, negative evidence can be more instructive if it results from measures that have passed appropriate representational validity tests. If so, and if the study has been conducted correctly, the substance of the theory generating the predicted relationships can be challenged.

Thus, revised standards might require purveyors of new instruments to show their representational validity and some degree of elaborative validity before submitting them for publication. This seems especially sensible in view of Comrey's (1988) observation that constructs are easy to invent, and successful measures of them relatively forthcoming. The plethora of new measures can be contained somewhat by requiring evidence of their usefulness before presenting them to the public.

Recommendation 4: Require Psychologists to Evaluate What they Do

This recommendation is more general than the previous three. In a sense it might be seen as foundational to specific test standards. This is the suggestion that psychologists be required to evaluate their effectiveness. Such a standard is foundational in that it focuses everyone practicing psychology on the very important assessment/measurement issues discussed in this paper and elsewhere. If psychologists evaluate what they do, they have to come under the control of test standards. The standards are no longer a set of guidelines to be avoided if one does not "do testing."

It is perhaps in this recommendation that testing standards overlap most with those for intervention or treatment. The recommendation may seem radical to some. It might be seen as unwarranted intrusion by a professional organization into the activities of its members. Afterall, what other profession or trade requires its members to determine the effectiveness of the services they offer? Certainly there is no requirement for such accountability in the present test standards. Nor is there such a requirement in the current ethical standards of the APA. Indeed, in Section 4, Therapy, where one might expect to see such a guideline if it existed, 33% of the standards deal with sexual intimacies with clients. There is not a single standard requiring the evaluation of what one does with clients, even the evaluation of whether sexual intimacies make any difference.

The ethical standards are not completely silent on the issue, however. They provide an opening for the consideration of an "accountability requirement" in

Standard 1.06 where it is stated that "psychologists rely on scientifically and professionally derived knowledge when making scientific or professional judgements or when engaging in scholarly or professional endeavors" (APA, 1992). It seems logically in keeping with this standard that professional judgements such as whether to change treatment in some way, terminate it, or not offer it at all be based on evidence from scientifically acceptable tests and measures. If psychologists are consistently monitoring changes in their clients (whether individual or corporate) using high quality measures in order to make informed professional judgements, they are simultaneously collecting the data to evaluate their effectiveness. It thus seems a relatively small step to require psychologists to evaluate what they do, at least at a conceptual level.

It might be tempting to argue that this particular recommendation has wandered afield of the customary focus of testing standards. There are assessment activities and there are treatment activities. It may make sense to require treatment providers to evaluate their effectiveness. Afterall, they hold themselves out as experts on change. The same cannot be said of assessors or testers. They do not claim to change individuals or organizations. What, therefore, constitutes an evaluation of their effectiveness? Would not a test developer satisfy the accountability standard by showing that s/he produced a high quality test, i.e., one that meets the customary psychometric criteria?

Several responses to such a question are worth considering. At a specific level, the previously mentioned elaborative validity concept of functional utility and its subcategories of incremental and treatment utility are relevant. What does the use of the test, assessment, or measurement activity contribute over and above what can be expected without it? Applied to the requirement that psychologists evaluate what they do, those of us involved in test activities would need to show that clients improve faster with than without the information provided by our efforts. For example, it would not be enough merely to show that we are good at assigning clients to psychopathological categories. We would have to show that the assignment mattered in terms of criteria relevant to the client's quality of life. When tests are used to determine the most appropriate form of intervention, their functional utility is shown if they add anything to the overall benefits derived from the intervention (Hayes et al., 1987). When used to monitor change over the course of intervention and to make strategic decisions about modifications in the treatment, the functional utility of the measuring procedure would be shown in a similar way, i.e., in terms of increments in benefits associated with the treatment.

Paul's (1969) ultimate question concerning the effectiveness of various forms of treatment seems applicable to assessment/measurement practices as well. What assessment procedure applied by whom to what client experiencing what problems will produce the greatest benefit for that client, and how will the use of the assessment procedure bring this about? It can be argued that psychologists have an ethical responsibility continually to be seeking answers to this question. The reference to Ethical Standard 1.06 (APA, 1992) above made clear the requirement to rely on scientifically and professionally derived knowledge when making scientific or professional judgments. It seems this standard provides the basis for both the recommendation that psychologists evaluate the effectiveness of what they do and that they strive continually to produce the best measures to use in this evaluation. The best measures would be ones having high levels of functional utility. Following this logic, the optimally ethical intervener would be doing dismantling analyses continuously and would be aware of whether any given aspect of the intervention, including its assessment and measurement aspects, had any functional relevance.

At a more general level, the purpose of testing programs is usually to accomplish a social benefit, e.g., improved manufacturing efficiency via the selection of the most appropriate employees; improved educational outcomes via the assignment of students to the most appropriate educational alternatives. The testing enterprise might be shown to be quite effective at doing these things, and therefore to have functional utility. This touches on what Messick (1994) refers to as the consequential or social impact of assessment. He notes the irony involved in the relative neglect of the social consequences of test use and interpretation over the years, given that the functional worth of tests has consistently been implied in validation efforts. Afterall, such efforts seek to determine whether tests do what they are supposed to do.

Messick (1994) views consequential validity quite broadly. It includes a test's criterion and functional utility, and goes beyond them to appraise the larger social impact of using the test. One might find a particular job selection procedure to be quite effective in securing employees who are quick at learning their jobs, dependable, and unusually loyal. The same procedure might select a disproportionate percentage of employees from a particular racial or gender group, having the adverse side effect of reducing opportunity for these groups.

It is not clear that testing standards can address the multiple social agenda of test users, however. In previous versions, such issues have been specifically exempted from inclusion for fairly obvious reasons. It might be that the best one can do in this area is acknowledge the importance of the concept, call attention to potential side effects that are known, and suggest the issuance of general consequential impact disclaimers. This might be roughly analogous to the disclaimers issued by manufacturers of many products in which the product itself is warranted against defects in workmanship, but consequential damages resulting from use of the faulty product are specifically excluded.

It would also be a daunting task to show the effectiveness of assessment/testing/ measuring practices with every client. Preliminary standards in this area might focus on the requirement that *developers* of measures show their incremental and functional utility before offering them to the public. *Users* of the measures might simply be required to show the tests they use do, indeed, meet such standards. In time, science and application will advance to the point where individual assessment activities can be routinely evaluated for their effectiveness. For the present, the requirement that psychologists evaluate what they do might be focused on intervention efforts. If so, perhaps this is a guideline best relegated to treatment practice standards. How one conducts such an evaluation might be included in testing standards, however, a recommendation to which we now turn.

Recommendation 5: Develop Standards Dealing with the Evaluation of Individual Treatment Activities

As the field of psychology moves more toward evaluating the effectiveness of individual practitioners, it needs guidelines governing the conduct of such evaluations. The present testing standards are silent in this area. The most relevant section of the standards is that dealing with program evaluation guidelines. The eight standards in this section focus specifically on the program, however, not on the individual participant, and aggregated data are used.

Standards focused more on the individual might include the requirement that change be shown pre to post intervention (or early to late) in appropriate measures of ultimate goals (Rosen & Proctor, 1981). Appropriate measures would be those that are the most direct (Cone, 1978), with the psychologist being expected to justify the use of less direct measures. Moreover, the pre/post (early/late) change would be assessed external to the treatment context. This recommendation is similar to Paul's (1969) suggestion that behavior modification procedures be shown to produce change pre to post in the client's presenting complaint outside of treatment. Appropriate measures would be ones for which the stability of scores in the absence of treatment were also known. Such knowledge makes it easier to interpret change over time.

While minimum standards would require summative assessment, document-ing the status of the client's presenting complaint by the most direct means external to the treatment context, additional recommendations would focus on formative evaluation. These might be considered secondary standards using the present rating system. They would deal with measurement requirements as distinct from assess-ment in that they focus on changes over the course of treatment rather than merely the status of the client at discrete points in time. The specific behavior or characteristics selected for ongoing monitoring would be ones that met Rosen and Proctor's (1981) criteria for instrumental goals. Changes in them would be expected to lead to changes in the ultimate goals or presenting complaints. Monitoring could take place inside or outside of the treatment context. Because the monitored targets are instrumental rather than ultimate goals, other relaxations of the directness requirement might be permitted as well.

Recommendation 6: Consider Specific Standards Covering Functional Assessment

When the subject matter of assessment is behavior, our interest is likely to be the functions the behavior serves. That is, we focus on environmental events antecedent to and following the behavior, with an eye toward discovering events functionally related to, or supporting it. Changes in these events lead to changes in the behavior, the hallmark of functional analysis or assessment. Functional analysis has a long history (e.g., Kanfer & Saslow, 1969; Lindsley, 1964), though its evolution as an assessment practice has been disappointing (Hayes & Follette, 1993).

Recent work indicates it is a viable form of assessment, however, and may become even more important in the future (see the special issue on "Functional analysis approaches to behavioral assessment and treatment." *Journal of Applied Behavior Analysis, 27*[2], 1994). For example, Durand and Crimmins (1988) developed an assessment instrument and formulated preliminary functional diagnostic categories for organizing intervention efforts for persons with severe behavior disorders. Hayes and Follette (1993) suggested a category termed "'emotional avoidance disorder' in which clients attempt to avoid particular negative emotions" (p. 185). They note several clinical problems speculated to be maintained by avoiding unpleasant emotions, e.g., phobic behavior to avoid anxiety, or substance abuse to avoid negative mental states. The use of such categories which bring together topographically diverse sets of behaviors having a common purpose might provide a powerful alternative to the currently popular practice of syndromal classification (American Psychiatric Association, 1994).

The design, evaluation, and use of instruments to assess the function(s) of behavior (e.g., *Motivation Assessment Scale* [MAS; Durand, 1990; Durand & Crimmins, 1988]; *Behavior-Environment Taxonomy of Aggression* [BETA; Fisher, unpublished] might benefit from testing standards composed specifically for them.

Slight differences will be needed in approaching the representational validity of functional measures, however. For example, when examining the content validity of a scale such as the MAS, where multiple dimensions (functions) are being tapped, two levels of content validity questions are involved. First, has the domain of all possible functions known to be relevant for a particular type of behavior been adequately sampled? Second, has the domain of all possible environmental events representative of a particular function been adequately sampled? When examining convergent validity the issue is the extent to which functions determined from instruments such as the MAS and BETA are the same as those identified from some other process (e.g., that proposed by Carr et al. [1994]).

Discriminant validity treats the extent to which the functions identified for a particular behavior are nonoverlapping with other possible functions. This can be a bit tricky as it is quite reasonable that a behavior might have multiple purposes. It may be necessary to specify the circumstances in which a behavior occurs along with its functions in order to evaluate the precision with which the latter are identified by a particular measure. A behavior would not be expected to serve both "attend to me" and "leave me alone" purposes under the same circumstances, for example, though it might have both functions at different times or places.

The verification or experimental phase of functional analysis provides the most direct assessment of behavior functions, just as direct observation measures provide the most direct assessment of the behaviors themselves. The use of either is limited by practical concerns, however, leading to the use of less direct, more practical assessment methods. Though existing examples of function measures have relied on interviews and ratings-by-others, it is conceivable that self-report measures could be developed rather easily as well. When they are, the same representational and elaborative validity evidence will be needed for them as we are discussing here. To preserve the spirit of functional analysis, however, standards might direct us away from a tendency to rely on easy measures. For example, the wording of one such standard might be that the "psychologist focuses on directly observable environmental or client conditions when describing antecedents to a particular response, minimizing inference as much as possible."

When function measures have been shown accurately to represent environmental events controlling behavior, attention can shift to elaborating their practical utility. An immediate question is likely to be the breadth of stimulus control over particular behaviors. How many functions will be reliably identified for a given behavior? A person described as exceptionally generous may be seen that way in numerous circumstances, for example, having experienced an association between giving and various forms of social response, self-talk, and even autonomic reactions.

Another "validity" question deals with response generalization, i.e., how much of a person's repertoire is under the control of certain environmental circumstances. A person described as a compulsive gambler is typically someone for whom the opportunity to place a bet is discriminative for a wide variety of behaviors involving getting money and making the wager. Similar observations have been made of persons addicted to heroin and other narcotics. Correlations between scales designed to tap many different functions for a particular behavior will provide evidence of breadth of stimulus control. Likewise, correlations between scales designed to identify the behaviors under the control of particular environmental events will provide evidence of the extent of response generalization. Both stimulus and response generalization would appear to be logical avenues for elaborating the validity of function measures. Ultimately, such measures must be exposed to and successfully negotiate tests of their intervention or treatment utility, to be sure. And, it is likely that modifications of this form of elaborative validity to make it more specific to functional analysis will be needed, just as was true for various types of representational validity.

Recommendation 7: Consider Standards Dealing with Idiographic Assessment Approaches

If psychologists are expected to evaluate their effectiveness and if their work involves individual clients, increased attention will undoubtedly focus on idiographic approaches to assessment. The final suggestion for revised testing standards is that they provide some guidance in this area. Space does not permit a full exploration of different conceptualizations of just what is meant by "idiographic," but there is reasonable agreement that it recognizes the uniqueness of a particular individual or organization. To borrow from Shontz (1965), the individual is seen as a "self-contained universe with its own laws."

Idiographic assessors are likely to view conventional, nomothetically derived tests as irrelevant, and to develop the "ultimately local" assessment instrument(s) to deal most directly with the issues confronting the individual client. A strong argument of proponents of idiographic approaches is that the prior formulation of concepts based on nomothetic research narrows one's focus when approaching the individual. The result can be the failure to consider important information falling outside this focus. Shapiro (1961) repeatedly warned of the dangers of such prior formulation. Indeed, a standard based on his warnings might be worded something like " psychologists approach the assessment of clients systematically, but maximally free of the traps of pre-conception." To assist in this, additional standards could deal with the selection of stimulus content for idiographic assessment devices. How should the initial item pool be developed, for example? Should this be an inductive process or a deductive one? How should either approach be implemented to produce the optimally representative item pool? What standards should govern the narrowing of the initial pool? How should one assess the client viz the stimulus content finally selected? How should the quality of the resulting instrument be determined? Is a "single-subject psychometrics" needed for guidance?

The present standards are avowedly directed toward general use tests, excluding local use ones. As we move toward holding practitioners more accountable for the quality of their work, however, they will need the tools to assess and improve on that quality. Standards focusing on idiographic or local use testing practices can assist greatly in this regard.

Summary and Recommendations

Existing technical standards for tests and testing have a long and noble history and reflect some of the best thinking of the giants in the field of measurement from both psychology and education. The recommendations made here respect this work and retain the present standards. They point to the strictly process focus of the standards, however, and argue for more attention to outcomes produced when using assessment and measurement procedures, including the effects of adhering to the standards themselves.

Specifically, it is recommended that new standards:
(1) Recognize that different subject matters might require modifications in standards.
(2) Make room for the concept of accuracy, and distinguish it from reliability and validity.
(3) Distinguish between representational and elaborative validity, and require purveyors of new measures to show the former and some evidence of the latter before publishing the measure.
(4) Require psychologists to evaluate what they do.
(5) Develop standards dealing with the process of that evaluation.
(6) Consider specific standards dealing with functional analysis.
(7) Include standards focusing on idiographic or local use assessment activities.

A joint committee of APA, AERA, and NCME is currently deliberating changes in the existing standards (DeAngelis, 1994). It would be important for other organizations with an interest in testing/assessing/measuring to identify that interest and attempt to influence the standards accordingly. At the same time, it can be recognized that the present volume is aimed at a larger purpose, i.e., the development of practice standards more generally. Thus, a parallel effort to influencing the Joint Committee could be the refinement of the above suggestions and their incorporation into a larger set of general practice guidelines. This could take place via the collaborative effort of a joint committee representing several organizations concerned with scientific practice standards, (e.g., APS, AAAPP, APA, AERA, NCME, SIOP). Such a committee could benefit from membership by technical assessment/measurement experts as well as experts in the use of testing procedures. Representatives of each type of use (e.g., classifying/describing/ diagnosing, understanding, predicting, controlling, monitoring) might be included. Perhaps the joint committee could be large enough to divide into subcommittees along type of use or some other dimension. The document resulting from the committee's work should be available in multi-media format, and should include cross-referencing to similar (e.g., APA's) testing standards, to ethical standards, and to other standards covering the scientific practice of psychology more generally, as are represented in this book.

References

American Association for Counseling and Development (AACD). (1978). Responsibilities of users of standardized tests. *Guidepost*, 5-8.

American Psychological Association, American Educational Research Association, & National Council on Measurements Used in Education. (1954). *Technical recommendations for psychological tests and diagnostic techniques.* Washington, D. C.: APA.

American Psychological Association, American Educational Research Association, & National Council on Measurements Used in Education. (1974). *Standards for educational and psychological tests.* Washington, D. C.: APA.

American Educational Research Association, American Psychological Association, & National Council on Measurement in Education. (1985). *Standards for educational and psychological testing.* Washington, D. C.: APA.

American Psychiatric Association. (1994). *Diagnostic and statistical manual of mental disorders* (4th ed.). Washington, D. C.: Author.

American Psychological Association. (1953). *Ethical standards of psychologists.* Washington, D. C.: Author.

American Psychological Association. (1966). *Standards for educational and psychological tests and manuals.* Washington, D. C.: Author.

American Psychological Association. (1992). *Ethical principles of psychologists and code of conduct.* Washington, D. C.: Author.

Bechtoldt, H. (1959). Construct validity: A critique. *American Psychologist, 14,* 619-629.

Becker, W. C., Engelmann, S., & Thomas, D. R. (1971). *Teaching: A course in applied psychology.* Chicago, IL: SRA.

Blalock, H. M. (1964). *Causal inferences in non experimental research.* Chapel Hill: University of North Carolina Press.

Block, J. (1995). A contrarian view of the five-factor approach to personality description. *Psychological Bulletin, 117,* 187-215.

Bollen, K., & Lennox, R. (1991). Conventional wisdom on measurement: A structural equation perspective. *Psychological Bulletin, 110,* 305-314.

Campbell, D. T. (1960). Recommendations for APA test standards regarding construct, trait and discriminant validity. *American Psychologist, 15,* 546-553.

Campbell, D. T., & Fiske, D. (1959). Convergent and discriminant validation by the multitrait-multimethod matrix. *Psychological Bulletin, 56,* 81-105.

Carr, E. G., Levin, L., McConnachie, G., Carlson, J. I., Kemp, D. C., & Smith, C. E. (1994). *Communication-based intervention for problem behavior.* Baltimore: Brookes.

Comrey, A. L. (1988). Factor analytic methods of scale development in personality and clinical psychology. *Journal of Consulting and Clinical Psychology, 56,* 754-761.

Cone, J. D. (1978). The Behavioral Assessment Grid (BAG): A conceptual framework and a taxonomy. *Behavior Therapy, 9,* 882-888.

Cone, J. D. (1988). Psychometric considerations and the multiple models of behavioral assessment. In A. S. Bellack & M. Hersen (Eds.), *Behavioral assessment: A practical handbook* (3rd ed.) (pp. 42-66). New York: Pergamon Press.

Cone, J. D. (1989). Is there utility for treatment utility? *American Psychologist, 44,* 1241-1242.

Cone, J. D. (in press). Psychometric considerations. In M. Hersen & A. S. Bellack (Eds.), *Behavioral assessment: A practical handbook* (4th ed.). Boston, MA: Allyn & Bacon.

Cronbach, L. J., Gleser, G. C., Nanda, H., & Rajaratnam, N. (1972). *The dependability of behavioral measurements.* New York: Wiley.

Cronbach, L. J. (1980). Validity on parole: How can we go straight? *New directions for testing and measurement, 5,* 99-108.

Cronbach, L. J. (1984). *Essentials of psychological testing* (4th ed.). New York: Harper & Row.

Cronbach, L. J. , & Meehl, P. E. (1955). Construct validity in psychological tests. *Psychological Bulletin, 52,* 281-302.

Crowne, D. P., & Marlowe, D. (1960). A new scale of social desirability independent of psychopathology. *Journal of Consulting Psychology, 24,* 349-354.

DeAngelis, T. (1994). APA and other groups revise testing standards. *The APA Monitor, 25*(6), 17.

Durand, V. M. (1990). The "aversives" debate is over: And now the work begins. *Journal of the Association for Persons with Severe Handicaps, 5,* 140-141.

Durand, V. M., & Crimmins, D. B. (1988). Identifying the variables maintaining self-injurious behavior. *Journal of Autism and Developmental Disorders, 18,* 99-117.

Edwards, A. L. (1957). *The social desirability variable in personality assessment and research.* New York: Dryden.

Edwards, A. L., & Walsh, J. A. (1964). Response sets in standard and experimental personality scales. *American Educational Research Journal, 1,* 52-61.

Evans, I. M., & Nelson, R. O. (1977). Assessment of child behavior problems. In A. R. Ciminero, K. S. Calhoun, & H. Adams (Eds.), *Handbook of behavioral assessment.* New York: Wiley.

Fisher, J. (1994). *The Behavior-Environment Taxonomy of Aggression (BETA).* Unpublished manuscript, Northern Illinois University, Dekalb, IL.

Goldberg, L. R. (1993a). The structure of phenotypic personality traits. *American Psychologist, 48,* 26-34.

Goldberg, L. R. (1993b). The structure of personality traits: Vertical and horizontal aspects. In D. C. Funder, R. Parke, C. Tomlinson-Keasey, & K. Widaman (Eds.), *Studying lives through time: Approaches to personality and development* (pp. 169-188). Washington, D. C.: APA.

Goodenough, F. L. (1949). *Mental testing; Its history, principles, and applications.* New York: Rinehart.

Haney, W., & Madaus, G. (1991). The evolution of ethical and technical standards for testing. In R. K. Hambleton & J. N. Zaal (Eds.), *Advances in educational and psychological testing: Theory and applications* (pp. 395-425). Boston, MA: Kluwer.

Haring, N. G. (1977). Measurement and evaluation procedures for programming with the severely and profoundly handicapped. In E. Sontag, J. Smith, & N. Certo (Eds.), *Educational programming for the severely and profoundly handicapped* (pp. 189-202). Reston, VA: CEC.

Hartshorne, H., & May, M. A. (1928). *Studies in the nature of character.* Vol. 1. *Studies in deceit.* New York: Macmillan.

Hayes, S. C., & Follette, W. C. (1993). The challenge faced by behavioral assessment. *European Journal of Psychological Assessment, 9,* 182-188.

Hayes, S. C., Nelson, R. O., & Jarrett, R. B. (1987). Treatment utility of assessment: A functional approach to evaluating the quality of assessment. *American Psychologist, 42,* 963-974.

Hersen, M., & Bellack, A. S. (Eds.). (in press). *Behavioral assessment: A practical handbook* (4th ed.). Boston, MA: Allyn & Bacon.

Johnston, J. M., & Pennypacker, H. S. (1980). *Strategies and tactics of human behavioral research.* Hillsdale, NJ: Erlbaum.

Johnston, J. M., & Pennypacker, H. S. (1993). *Strategies and tactics of behavioral research* (2nd ed.). Hillsdale, NJ: Erlbaum.

Kanfer, F. H., & Saslow, G. (1969). Behavioral diagnosis. In C. M. Franks (Ed.), *Behavior therapy: Appraisal and status* (pp. 417-444). New York: McGraw-Hill.

Kelley, T. (1924). *Statistical method.* New York: MacMillan.

Kumar, K., & Beyerlein, M. (1991). Construction and validation of an instrument for measuring ingratiatory behaviors in organizational settings. *Journal of Applied Psychology, 76,* 619-627.

Lerner, B. (1978). The Supreme Court and the APA, AERA, NCME test standards: Past references and future possibilities. *American Psychologist, 33,* 915-919.

Lindsley, O. R. (1964). Direct measurement and prosthesis of retarded behavior. *Journal of Education, 147,* 62-81.

Loevinger, J. (1957). Objective tests as instruments of psychological theory. [Monogr. No. 9]. *Psychological Reports, 3,* 635-694.

Messick, S. (1983). Assessment of children. In P. H. Mussen (Ed.), *Handbook of child psychology* (4th ed.) (pp. 477-526). New York: Wiley.

Messick, S. (1994). Foundations of validity: Meaning and consequences in psychological assessment. *European Journal of Psychological Assessment, 10,* 1-9.

Mischel, W. (1968). *Personality and assessment.* New York: Wiley.

National Association of School Psychologists (NASP). (1984). *Principles for professional ethics.* Washington, D. C.: Author.

Ozer, D. J., & Reise, S. P. (1994). Personality assessment. *Annual Review of Psychology, 45,* 357-388.

Paul, G. L. (1969). Behavior modification research: Design and tactics. In C. M. Franks (Ed.), *Behavior therapy: Appraisal and status* (pp. 29-62). New York: McGraw-Hill.

Pedhazur, E. J., & Schmelkin, L. P. (1991). *Measurement, design, and analysis: An integrated approach.* Hillsdale, N.J.: Erlbaum .

Rosen, A., & Proctor, E. K. (1981). Distinctions between treatment outcomes and their implications for treatment evaluation. *Journal of Consulting and Clinical Psychology, 49,* 418-425.

Shapiro, M. B. (1961). A method of measuring psychological changes specific to the individual psychiatric patient. *British Journal of Medical Psychology, 34,* 151-155.

Shontz, F. C. (1965). *Research methods in personality.* New York: Appleton-Century-Crofts.

Silva, F. (1993). *Psychometric foundations and behavioral assessment.* Newbury Park, CA: Sage.

Strahan, R., & Gerbasi, K. C. (1972). Short, homogeneous version of the Crown-Marlowe Social Desirability Scale. *Journal of Clinical Psychology, 28,* 191-193.

Discussion of Cone

Standards, Assessment, and the Realities of Practice

Robert F. Peterson
University of Nevada

Webster (1959), who seems to have the first and last word on everything, describes a standard as a "rule, criterion, or gauge." Standards develop as a discipline ages. There are few standards in a fledgling endeavor where no one approach has been shown to work better than any other. The maturation of psychology can be seen in it's lengthening list of ethical, scientific, and professional standards.

Scientific standards have many uses. They allow an evaluation of assessment, treatment, and other professional behaviors. They may also provide excuses. For example, a student may use a substandard procedure but nevertheless produce a good outcome. This success may result in overlooking the use of an unacceptable procedure. Similarly, a practitioner may follow an approved procedure yet produce an undesirable outcome. This also provides an excuse: accepted practices were utilized despite the negative result. For different reasons, standards can protect both professionals and the public.

Psychological Assessment

The interview remains the most frequent form of psychological assessment. Dissatisfaction with the subjectivity of this procedure however, led to the development of objective psychological tests. Because objectivity is the child of science, scientific standards have played a continuous role in test evolution. These standards, which include criteria for many different types of reliability and validity, have been revised and updated almost every decade for the past century. They now number in the hundreds.

Traditionally, assessment has focused on the characteristics of the individual and the measurement of personality, emotional, and intellectual traits. Clinicians have come to view the initial assessment of the individual as one of their most important professional responsibilities. But like all good things, assessment can be overdone.

Some years ago, the author held a job at a clinic for disturbed children. When a child was having trouble in school, particularly with reading or other academic subjects, he or she was referred for assessment. The child was first examined by a pediatrician for medical problems and a psychiatrist for emotional difficulties. Next, a psychologist evaluated the child's intellectual and behavioral characteristics. This examination was followed by an interview with a speech therapist who searched for language disorders. A nurse then reviewed the child's health status and a social worker scrutinized family relationships. Finally, the team educator probed for learning disorders. A variety of psychological tests were employed in these procedures.

The information was brought to a staff conference. Each member of the team presented his or her findings. At the end of the conference the presenting problem was summarized and confirmed: the child couldn't read, write, or do math well, and was misbehaving in class. The child was referred for treatment. By affirming that there was a problem the clinic staff felt they had done their job.

Affirmation alone, however, is not adequate. Confirmation of the problem and a static assessment of personal qualities seldom relieves discomfort or produces change. What is needed is a functional appraisal of how specific behaviors function in a given environmental context to produce the problem (Bijou & Peterson, 1971; Hayes, Nelson, & Jarrett, 1987). This appraisal provides a crucial link to treatment. The next step includes an evaluation the effects of the treatment. This call for psychologists to evaluate what they have done is not new. Because it is often forgotten or ignored, we need to be reminded of its importance on a regular basis. We thank John Cone for his reminder.

The recommendations just discussed are not often followed. The following example provides a second illustration. During the past five years the author spent over 750 therapy hours with patients from a multi-state, preferred provider organization (PPO). Before being referred for treatment, patients were initially screened by an intake coordinator over the telephone. This was the primary assessment. There was no requirement that psychological tests validate the need for treatment. In fact, any use of psychological tests by the clinician required special permission. The PPO did request that treatment plans and progress summaries be submitted on a periodic basis. Information on treatment progress was obtained through clinician reports. Although client satisfaction data were garnered through questionnaires and phone surveys, no formal (test) assessment of change was required at the end of therapy.

The approach taken by the PPO is the opposite of that of the child clinic. The clinic staff assessed every nook and cranny of the child but paid little attention to the environmental context of the problem and resulting treatment issues. Clinic staff were primarily concerned with demonstrating the thoroughness of their approach. In contrast, the PPO required far less evidence that there was indeed a disorder. In fact, nearly every eligible person who called the PPO complaining of a problem was subsequently referred for treatment (Anonymous, personal communication, February 15, 1995). They were reluctant to limit access to treatment and chose instead to control provider selection and length of treatment.

The approach taken by the (non-profit) child clinic over-utilized assessment while the PPO under-utilized assessment in order to minimize costs. The use of psychological tests will obviously add to costs in the short run. A long run view however, suggests that tests could provide objective data on many variables. These include client characteristics, presenting problems, the efficacy of screening procedures, appropriate treatment choice, and therapist effectiveness. In other words, the systematic administration of well chosen tests before and after treatment, could increase information about overall cost effectiveness at relatively little additional expense. Data would become more objective and more closely tied to established scientific standards. Such data would also provide a useful stimulus to researchers and test developers, as well as to those who market managed care.

Conflicts Between Standards and Practice

Standards often state that psychological tests and interventions are to be used "appropriately." This word indicates that tests and treatments are designed to be used in a particular way with a specific population. Therapists sometimes find that test standards and therapy protocols do not fit the realities of the current clinical situation. The question then becomes how detailed should a standard be? Certain procedures need to be carried out in a precise fashion in order to obtain a valid result. For example, both a subtest of an intelligence scale and a procedure for time-out need to be administered in a specific manner if the outcome is to be valid and useful.

There is an even greater problem when it comes to complex treatments such as those in psychotherapy. Detailed recommendations concerning what to say and when to say it may be awkward or impossible to follow in practice. Standards which involve a large number of rules, do not cover the current situation, or delineate therapist behaviors too precisely, may be ignored or partially followed. Assessment plays a critical role in such circumstances. How should therapist adherence be measured? How can the usefulness of a treatment protocol be evaluated? Does adherence to the manual mean that the treatment variable has been successfully manipulated (Waltz, Addis, Koerner, & Jacobson, 1993)? Problems such as these mark the frontier of psychological assessment.

Assessing treatment effectiveness is a difficult task. Standards are no different. Like treatments, they too are designed to influence behavior. For the profession to progress, we must subject our standards to the same kind of empirical scrutiny. Knowledge of how standards affect our own behavior will be another indication of the maturity of psychology and further increase our ability to serve the public.

References

Bijou, S. W., & Peterson, R. F. (1971). Functional analysis in the assessment of children. In P. McReynolds (Ed.), *Advances in psychological assessment*, Vol. II (pp. 63-78). Palo Alto, CA: Science and Behavior Books.

Hayes, S. C., Nelson, R. O., & Jarrett, R. B. (1987). The treatment utility of assessment: A functional approach to evaluating assessment quality. *American Psychologist, 42*, 963-974.

Waltz, J., Addis, M. E., Koerner, K., & Jacobson, N. S. (1993). Testing the integrity of a psychotherapy protocol: Assessment of adherence and competence. *Journal of Consulting and Clinical Psychology, 61*, 620-630.

Webster's new collegiate dictionary. (1959). Cambridge, MA: Merriam.

Chapter 11

Correcting Methodological Weaknesses in the Knowledge Base Used to Derive Practice Standards

William C. Follette
University of Nevada

In recent years there have been two important, yet sometimes conflicting influences in the evolution of practice standards. On one hand, there has been a strong push for psychologists to deliver treatments of demonstrated efficacy. On the other hand there is a large body of literature suggesting that most treatments are equivalent (e.g., Luborsky, Singer, & Luborsky, 1975). Despite many years of research and hundreds of published articles addressing treatment efficacy, our research strategies to date have failed to provide sufficiently clear data to convince the practitioner that there is necessarily a set of standards to follow that would yield clinically significant results.

There are several reasons for this state of affairs. First, there is little compelling in the empirical findings to date, that would grab the attention of the practitioner. The average effect sizes observed in meta-analyses are less than stunning. Comparing treatment to no treatment conditions, across therapies and problems, produces average effect sizes of about .6 to .8. Cohen (1988, pp. 23-26) describes the interpretation of these effect sizes as explaining about 8% to 14% of the variance in outcome as being attributable to treatment. It is difficult to claim that these values are so peremptorily large as to preclude practitioners from believing they can do better using ad hoc procedures.

Second, often the empirical findings seem irrelevant to readers. Many of the reasons have been given elsewhere (Barrom, Shadish, & Montgomery, 1988). However, the mantra of "it's an empirical question" seems have produced a line of research that is empirically driven, but only weakly, if at all, theoretically driven, and hence not as appealing to consumers of the literature as might be useful. For example, therapies become primary, and the client with a particular problem appear less important. While cognitive therapy for depression was originally appealing on both theoretical grounds and had initial empirical support, it has subsequently been extended to many other domains including the treatment of anxiety disorders (Beck, Emery, & Greenberg, 1985), marital distress (Beck, 1988), substance abuse (Beck & Emery, 1977), and personality disorders (Beck, Freeman, Pretzer, Davis, Fleming,

Ottaviani, et al., 1990) with less compelling theoretical justification. The extension to a variety of problems seems to have occurred by the following reasoning: "cognitive therapy worked for depression; perhaps it will work for personality disorders; it's an empirical question; let's see." These clinical problems may respond moderately to cognitive therapy, but it leaves therapists in somewhat of a conundrum. They are taught to engage in clinical assessment of the individual, diagnose, and implement a therapy that best helps the client. The client certainly wants to be seen as an individual. At the end of the process the therapist ends up giving the same form of therapy anyway. The treatment utility of assessment is not readily apparent (Hayes, Nelson, & Jarret, 1987), and the purpose of matching treatment to client problem becomes less obvious.

The purpose of this chapter is not to argue against empirically testing therapies, nor complain about the existence of broadly effective therapies. What is argued is that therapies are weakly tested, and outcome studies result in unimpressive effect size estimates, thus provide little basis for the practitioner to be convinced that there is sufficient reason to go through a treatment matching process. In this chapter a method of conducting, analyzing, and interpreting outcome studies is proposed to accomplish the following: 1) lead to stronger testing of theory based therapy and concomitantly reduce the number of clinical studies that are merely extensions of existing methods to new populations without regard to why and how they should work; 2) allow more information to result from the outcome studies with relatively little increase in cost or effort; 3) permit some estimate of the relative magnitude of nonspecific versus active components of a treatment; 4) allow estimates of benefit, if any, of matching clients with therapies; 5) lead treatment designers to identify theoretically derived active treatment components and optimize those components; and 6) blend the strengths of both single subject and group design methodologies to make stronger causal inferences and better answer the question of what individual characteristics matter in predicting response to treatment.

Background

The suggestions made in this chapter stem from a growing discontent with the slow pace of progress in the advancement of psychotherapy outcome research, and a disappointment in our inability to identify large effect sizes in adult outpatient problems. Some time ago Platt (1964) bemoaned the slow progress he observed in social science research. He proposed strong inference testing where competing theories were tested against each other and the losing theory discarded. While Hempel (1966) argued why such tests were not directly possible, it does seem necessary for researchers to be in closer contact with data in support (or not) of their theoretically derived treatments so they can better evaluate, refine, modify, or discard their models of why clinical problems persist and how they should be treated. What is proposed in this chapter presumes that having such data is valuable and will create an atmosphere where theory and treatment will evolve faster, even if not through strict Popperian falsificationism. The ideas in this paper are not entirely novel, but are intended to lead to outcome research that allows psychologists access to more useful data that may more meaningfully direct their behavior.

There are weaknesses in our understanding of what psychotherapy does and what aspects of therapy produce any observed effects. I have little interest in attributing improvements that occur during therapy to nonspecific (or more accurately, not specified) factors. Nonspecific factors may be important, but they take on meaning when they are transformed into more testable, functional concepts. Thus, part of the purpose of this chapter is to be able to distinguish occasions when identified active treatment components are operating from when some other unspecified facet of therapy might be responsible for change.

There are some scientific and cultural factors that place us in the position of believing that we should be adhering to certain practice standards on the one hand, and on the other hand debating whether therapy works (Smith, Glass, & Miller, 1980), whether or not professional or paraprofessional practitioners are comparable (Berman & Norton, 1985; Christensen & Jacobson, 1994), or whether therapist experience matters (Stein & Lambert, 1984). Without going into much detail, two of these influence are meta-analysis and the *Diagnostic and Statistical Manual* (DSM) system (American Psychiatric Association, 1994).

Meta-analysis as a methodology for maximizing and summarizing information from existing work is clearly an important and useful tool. The problem resulting from meta-analytic studies isn't a problem with the procedure. The problem is that the database for meta-analyses is flawed. In theory, meta-analysts can empirically code information about study characteristics that may compromise a conclusion and test whether the information is correlated with effect sizes. One can design very elaborate coding sheets to identify all sorts of potentially important variables that are associated with outcome. The problem is that the historical database that meta-analysts use does not contain all kinds of important study details that would useful. Without complete information going into the meta-analysis, conclusions seem to be uninteresting or misleading. It's not that they don't accurately summarize the literature. It's just that the literature itself is poor. Post hoc statistical control cannot make up for poor experimental work, or at least poor reporting, in the original research. If one takes the original Smith and Glass (1977) work as the start of the meta-analytic movement in applied psychology, then the first decade or so of subsequent work was most often conducted by methodologists and statisticians who were trying to find and agree upon ways of estimating effect sizes when such basic information as group means and standard deviations were missing. If that information is not commonly a part of the outcome literature, imagine how little other crucial information on experimental design and theory testing is missing. As meta-analysis has become established, researchers are now including more relevant information in their research reports, but I would submit much of the information I am going to describe subsequently is still missing from our current literature.

Meta-analysis has been useful and may become more so as the source literature improves. Meta-analytic studies have focused attention on the fact that there is an important unit of analysis problem in psychotherapy research. Subjects are units imbedded within larger units, the study site or investigator and are thus not independent observations. Since the initial investigators with an allegiance to the therapy often get the largest effect sizes, the importance of replications have been highlighted. Meta-analysis offers a way to test external validity by allowing us to look at the stability of effect sizes across settings and subject variables. Nevertheless, meta-analysis still cannot make a silk purse out of a sow's ear. Its real contribution is that it forces psychotherapy researchers to improve the quality of the data they gather and the questions they ask.

The second influence that I would submit has been for the worse is the *Diagnostic and Statistical Manual* (DSM) system. The DSM is putatively atheoretical, but its success as a useful scientific taxonomy rests on a faith that importing the medical model without including psychological theory will yield the same benefits for the study of psychopathology as it did for medicine. I don't think this is likely and have discussed this elsewhere (Follette, Houts, & Hayes, 1992). For the point I wish to make here, the liability of the DSM approach is that it has produced research based on diagnostic category designs. Persons (1986) thoughtfully critiqued this kind of design where individuals are assigned to conditions on the basis of (an explicitly atheoretical) diagnostic labels rather than on the basis of any functionally stated principle. Treatment groups in outcome studies are formed on the basis of symptoms rather than on how the symptoms came to be. Assignment of subjects is atheoretical. This entails the investigator believing either that all members of the group share a common etiology, a view almost no one actually asserts, or that treatments will work equally for everyone regardless of the etiology. The latter supposition also does not appear to be commonly held. Therefore, the result is that treatment effects are probably underestimated in diagnostic group designs. The standard "solution" to this problem is to get very homogeneous subjects, thus undermining the relevance of the results of controlled study that use participants unrepresentative of the clinical populations seen by practicing clinical psychologists. However, getting homogeneous subjects where subjects are selected on the basis of similar symptoms still does little to solve the problem of having subjects with many different causes for their problems unless one is willing to say that there is only a single way to get a particular symptom constellation. I am not.

Adopting diagnostic category designs and believing that the DSM system is a good representation of how to organize research leads to other problems as well. The medical model presumes one produces a diseased on undiseased state as the outcome. Thus measurement tends to be faced with floor effects that limit our ability to classify outcomes along dimensions other than normal or disordered. For example, there has been little attention paid to measuring treatment effects on psychological health rather than only on the level of pathology (Follette, Bach, & Follette, 1993).

There are several additional reasons why the kinds of outcomes studies commonly performed are bound to produce modest effects and will continue to provide weak support for the theoretical underpinnings of treatments when they are specified. The remainder of this paper is intended to offer a method of conducting outcome studies and interpreting results that improves on current practices.

Current Methods

Kazdin (1992) reviews some of the common clinical group design outcome study methods. I mention these because most of the suggestions I make subsequently can be readily adapted to fit each of these designs. One type of study is the treatment versus no treatment design where one is interested in knowing whether the treatment taken as a whole produces therapeutic change. Another type of study which usually follows the treatment versus no treatment study is a dismantling study. The goal is to determine which components of a treatment package are actually active or necessary. Another variation on this theme is the constructive strategy where components are added to existing treatments to see if they enhance outcome. Parametric studies are those in which the investigator modifies treatment parameters to study the effects on outcome. This may entail changing the number of sessions and comparing the results from the different length versions of the treatment. Another strategy is the comparative outcome study in which two or more different treatments are compared to determine which is most effective for a particular problem. The classic example is the NIMH collaborative research trial for depression (Elkin, Parloff, Hadley, & Autry, 1985). Often comparative outcome studies involve features of another design, the client-therapist variation strategy. In this design the investigator is interested in identifying what client or therapist characteristics are associated with differential outcomes. Finally, there are process studies were the researcher is interested in what happens within a session that may affect performance for that session. Sometimes process research is related to actual clinical outcome, though sometimes within session events are studied as ends unto themselves. Process-oriented therapies present interesting issues when considered in contrast to outcome-oriented therapies (Gold, 1995).

Traditional outcome studies, particularly those that preceded the publication of treatment manuals (e.g. Beck, Rush, Shaw, & Emery, 1979) possess a fundamental logic that is shown in Figure 1. This diagram assumes that the treatment is derived from some theory, an assumption that is often only loosely held when investigators are merely applying an existing therapy to a new clinical problem with only

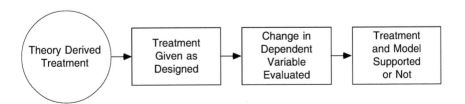

Figure 1. Historically common approach to interpreting outcome study results.

minimum regard about how the theory behind the original therapy applies to the new problem area.

The implication is that if the treatment is given and the dependent variable changes, then it is because the therapy was the cause, and therefore the model behind the therapy must be correct. When studies are analyzed in accordance with this model, there is the opportunity for many interpretive errors to occur. Except for the case where what look like treatment effects are actually due to outside influences unrecognized by the therapist (i.e. threats to internal validity), effect sizes are probably lower bound estimates of how effective treatment may actually be.

The obvious problem with considering the logic in Figure 1 is that one makes the assumption that the independent variable was manipulated as designed, that is, therapy is assumed to have been delivered as intended. Kazdin (1992) makes the point that it is important to assess whether one successfully manipulated the experimental variable of interest when interpreting outcomes. This results in our understanding outcomes in terms of the 2 x 2 table shown in Figure 2. If one actually examines the treatment integrity of the clinical interventions in relation to outcomes, one ends up with the two ostensibly interpretable cells in row one of the table. Cell 1 indicates that the therapy was successfully delivered and there was an observable difference in the outcome measures. This is presumably what the researcher hoped to find. The results in Cell 2 are less welcome but, in principle, interpretable as well. In this case, the therapy was administered successfully, but there were no identifiable changes in the dependent measures. If there were adequate statistical power, the simple interpretation is that the treatment was not effective for the sample studied. Cell 3 is one that is interesting and will be discussed later in another context. In this instance, therapy was not given as designed, and there was no treatment response. The members of this cell dilute the estimated treatment effectiveness if they are included in the final analyses. When cases fall into Cell 4,

Change in Dependent Variable(s)

		Yes	No
		IV+ / DV+ 1	IV+ / DV- 2
Intended Presentation of Independent Variable — Yes	Yes	IV+ / DV+ (1)	IV+ / DV- (2)
— No	No	IV- / DV+ (4)	IV- / DV- (3)

Figure 2. Interpreting outcome and treatment integrity simultaneously.

researchers must recognize that they cannot take credit for observed improvements. Treatment was not delivered as designed, but the clients in this cell improved. This cell is often interpreted as resulting from nontreatment related events, usually some threat to internal validity or are due perhaps to spontaneous remissions. Spontaneous remission could explain those who fall into Cell 1 as well and is one reason why no-treatment control groups are important when one begins to treat clinical problems where the course of the problem is not established.

Examining results in light of whether or not treatment was given as intended helps avoid contaminating effect size estimates which occurs if one includes the data from the bottom row of Figure 2. The remainder of this paper will argue that a finer grain analysis of outcomes studies is required in order to interpret the clinical importance of a particular therapy for a particular population.

An Alternative Proposal

The following argument depends on one agreeing that those who design interventions should have some model of how a therapy works in a particular instance. The delivery of therapy is how the researcher manipulates the independent variable, but the manipulation of the independent variable does not directly affect the dependent variable. The therapy is an environmental manipulation that produces a change in some mediating variable. It is the change in the mediating variable that therapy tries to produce with the expectation that there will be a resulting change in the dependent variable.

An example from the treatment of depression may help clarify the issue. When Beck et al. (1979) delivers cognitive therapy for depression, they do so using a model of depression that says depression is the result of certain kinds of cognitive errors. Treatment is designed to change these cognitive distortions which will then and (implicitly) only then result in the improvement of depressive symptoms (the dependent variable). Faithfully delivered cognitive therapy is the independent variable which is designed to improve defective cognitions, the mediating variable, which will finally result in changes in depressive symptoms, the dependent variable.

Mediating variables are those through which the independent variable is able to influence the dependent variable. The independent variable causes the mediator which, in turn, causes the observed change in the dependent variable. Mediating variables differ from moderator variables in that moderators affect the strength or perhaps the direction of the relationship between the independent and dependent variable, but they are not the means by which the influence occurs (Baron & Kenny, 1986). The potential importance of examining psychotherapy outcome studies in light of mediating mechanism using meta-analytic procedures has recently been underscored by Shadish and Sweeney (1991).

Therapy, then is based on a model of how symptoms come to exist or are maintained. Therapy is designed to affect the mediating variable directly which, in turn, produces a change in symptoms. When one conducts a therapy outcome study, there are three separate questions being asked simultaneously that need to be understood individually and in relation to each other. The questions are 1) is the therapy delivered as intended, i.e., is the independent variable successfully manipulated, 2) did the mediating variable change, and 3) did the dependent variable change? The argument can be extended to multiple treatment components (independent variables), mediating variables, and outcome measures (dependent variables). The logic for the simple case appears in Figure 3.

Appreciating that Figure 3 represents what is actually involved in theory derived treatment design requires that the results from outcome studies be analyzed much differently than they traditionally are. If a rather modest increase in the amount of data collected at regular intervals during therapy occurs, what one can learn from a particular study increases dramatically. If one takes the traditional approach to understanding what is asked in an outcome study as shown in Figure 1, the question asked is "What is the average effect of therapy X for condition Y?" If one takes the approach shown in Figure 2, the question becomes 'What is the average effect of therapy X, when properly given, on condition Y?" If one fully understands what is shown in Figure 3, data that bear on many questions can be gathered in a single study. Among those questions are 1) can the therapy be delivered as designed; 2) does the therapy, when delivered properly, actually affect the mediating mechanism on which the therapy is based; 3) is the degree to which one changes the mediating mechanism related to the magnitude of improvement in the dependent variable; 4) what is the magnitude of nonspecific (nonspecified) therapy effects; and 5) to what extent is therapy specific to those clients who show a deficit in the mediating variable?

Actually, more questions than these can be examined. For the following analysis to be useful it must be emphasized that the relationship between therapy,

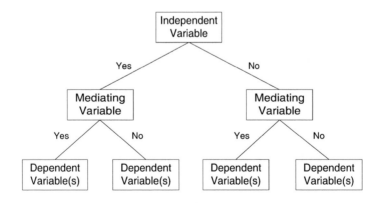

Figure 3. Factors to consider when evaluating theory derived outcome studies.

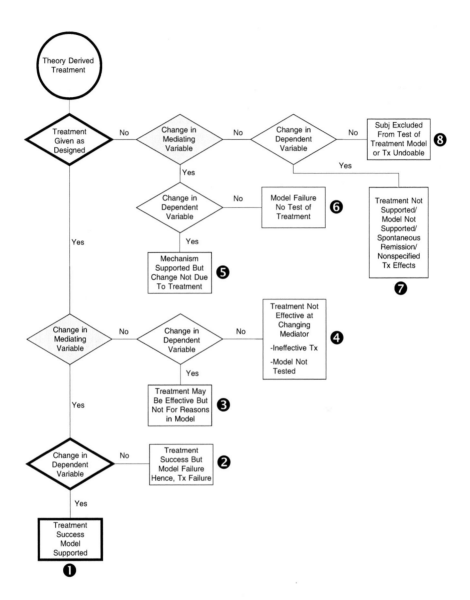

Figure 4. Logical model for interpreting individual outcome possibilities when evaluating theory derived outcome studies.

the mediating variables, and the dependent variables must be specified *prior* to when the study begins. If the treatment designer is not willing or able to say how therapy works, then the analysis is limited to the driest of empirical questions, and the following elaborations are not valid.

Let us now turn attention to Figure 4. This figure depicts how one would interpret results from outcome studies where the relationship between the independent variable (treatment), the mediating variable, and the dependent variable (outcome measure) is specified. To orient to the diagram, the heavily outlined portions of Path 1 are the same elements shown in Figure 1. The shaded decision boxes are where the mediating variables that were shown in Figure 3 are considered. The starting point of each path is the circle labeled "Theory Derived Treatment" which specifies the relationship between variables. To aid in relating the text to the figure, the terminal points of each logical outcome are numbered.

There are a few assumptions I have made when discussing this diagram. As these assumptions are changed, different things can be learned. For simplicity, I have assumed that the subjects in the study all show the problem with the mediating variable that the model assumes is the cause of the problem and which therapy is intended to redress. This assumption is much more optimistic than I think actually exists. I assume that the investigators gather data on this mediating variable at least before and after therapy, though preferably much more often than that during the course of treatment. I have also assumed that though the study tries to assure that therapy is given as intended, that in some cases, this will not be the case, but that data on the mediating variable and the dependent variable are still gathered. The assumption that treatment is not always faithfully delivered seems reasonable (e.g., Feldman, Caplinger, & Wodarski, 1983 as cited in Kazdin, 1992, p. 204]. Let us now turn out attention to the outcome paths enumerated in Figure 4.

Path 1. If our data indicate that we have delivered therapy properly and effected change in the mediating variable and observed a change in the dependent or outcome measures, the study has produced the hoped for result. This result supports both the soundness of the model of how to influence the problem (shown in the diagram as "Model Supported"), and indicates that therapy is successful in changing the mediating variable (shown as "Treatment Success"). Treatment is successful in changing the mediating variable which, in turn, brings about improvement in symptoms. The effect size observed for these subjects should be the largest observed in any path and represent the maximum response for the specific therapy tested. The degree to which the dependent variable changes can be further analyzed with respect to how clinically significant any observed improvement is (Jacobson, Follette, & Revensdorf, 1984).

Path 2. Following Path 2 begins to show how looking more closely at results actually provides important scientific information. In this case the treatment is successful at changing the mediating variable it was intended to impact. In this sense, treatment is successful. However, in spite of the fact that the mediating variable changed, the symptoms did not improve. In practical terms this looks like a treatment failure, but in fact, this is a model failure. Treatment did what it was designed to do. In this case, the scientist's understanding of the variable controlling the clinical phenomenon is at fault, not the treatment itself. If one didn't collect data showing that the mediating variable changed and the dependent variable did not, but merely that therapy was correctly given with no resulting clinical improvement, the treatment would be considered a failure for this class of subjects. I am not splitting hairs here. This is an important distinction that, if we do not make, slows down scientific progress and confuses our understanding of a particular theory derived therapy. In this case, there is nothing wrong with the therapy. The model reflecting the scientist's understanding is wrong. There is no sense in proceeding with refining therapy if the model isn't reconstructed first to identify what other mediating variable should be targeted for change. If one attends to the meaning of this result, it is as close to falsifying evidence as we can efficiently gather in a single study, though independent replications are still required. The therapist did what he or she was supposed to, the client changed in response to the therapy as intended, but the symptoms did not change. There is no sense in "blaming" the client for being resistant because the mediating variable did indeed change. There is no clear sense in which making this therapy stronger by, for example, extending the time of therapy, would be expected to produce a different outcome. The mediator changed, but it did not matter.

If one observes outcomes going down both paths 1 and 2, then it is possible that there is more than one source of the clinical problem that may require a different model and different intervention. That is, this outcome may suggest the need for an extended theory based typology. Almost all of these end points have multiple explanations that, if detailed in full, would make the discussion too difficult to follow. For example, it could be that the model is wrong even for those going down Path 1, and that changes in the mediating and dependent variables were either coincidental or both caused by an as yet not understood third variable.

Path 3. Now consider the case where a correctly delivered treatment does not change the postulated mediating mechanism, but the dependent measure changes anyway. In Figure 2, this would look like a true positive result and fall in Cell 1. In fact, this outcome tells the scientist that he or she does not understand how the therapy works, if it does at all. In this case the therapy, though given correctly, did not change the mediating variable that is supposed to result in clinical improvement. This result should be considered a model failure. The researcher cannot claim credit for improvements, at least not for the reason stated in the model that led to the development of the therapy in the first place.

The treatment may be effective, but not for the reasons initially believed. It may be that the treatment possesses active components, but they are different from what the treatment designer thought. In this case, the model would have to be reconsidered. This realization may result in the researcher considering how other mediating variables might be affected by this therapy. Therapy may be redesigned to better target other mediators that could produce stronger effects on the dependent variable. It is likely that the effect size in this case is smaller than it would be if the mechanism of change were better understood, though this is not necessarily the case. For example, some medications work for reasons that are not well understood. For example, why aspirin works for headaches was not understood for many years. While it seems likely that when the mechanisms are fully understood, better drugs can be designed specifically for that mechanism, it may be that aspirin will remain the drug of choice because it still optimally affects the causal mechanism once it is identified.

It is possible that results of Path 3 are due to spurious changes in the dependent variable. Other threats to internal validity may also explain these results, though these other causes of change would have to be working through mechanisms not yet understood since they were not associated with a change in the mediating variable.

Path 4. One has delivered therapy correctly but observed no change in the mediating or dependent variables. The researcher has to return to the drawing board. In this case, the treatment developer needs to produce a more effective means of changing the mediating variable. The therapy protocol needs to be improved in any number of ways such as extending treatment, or adding additional components, and so on. The model on which the therapy was based has not been compromised. It has not been tested. The treatment is ineffective but the model has yet to be directly tested. The test of the model most clearly occurs when one goes down path 1 or 2, though the falsificationists would say Path 2 informs us the most.

Path 5. Paths 5 through 8 involve the cases where therapy was not delivered as intended. Though careful researchers try to insure that treatment does get delivered as designed, this does not always happen. This occurrence is expensive in terms of time, money, and clients, and is generally unfortunate and unintended. This does not mean, though, that nothing can be learned from going down these paths.

In the case of Path 5, treatment was not delivered as intended but there was a change in the mediating and dependent variables. The first thing to notice is that the model is supported. However the change in the mediating occurred, it was associated with a change in the dependent variable. The researcher cannot appropriately attribute it to therapy per se. It may be that some portion of the therapy was given correctly and that portion may be all that is necessary. This may suggest therapy could be shortened, or whatever was given could be studied as possibly sufficient. Other outside influences, not related to therapy, may be responsible for the observed changes.

Path 6. In this case, treatment was not properly administered, but the mediating variable was observed to have changed. However, the dependent variable did not change. This result is also interesting. The treatment was never directly given so it cannot be presumed to have brought about the change in the mediating variable. Since it was not given properly, there is no reason to redesign it or call the treatment a failure. For some reason, though, the mediator changed with no observed change in the dependent variable. The model itself must be considered to have failed because the variable that should be responsible for change did, in fact, change as it was supposed to have, yet the dependent measure did not change. The investigator could increase his quality control or therapy delivery, but the question would be why would one expect that to help? In spite of inadequate therapy delivery, the mediator changed anyway, but there was no beneficial effect on the dependent variable. The researcher would have to come up with a reason why not to count this case as a model failure. More effective therapy delivery could not produce a better result on the mediator variable since it already changed. Results along this path suggest that the understanding of what mechanisms influence symptoms is not adequate. At the very least, the model needs to be examined, and in all likelihood, a new therapy that more efficiently targets changes in new mediators needs to be developed. All this is suggested even though the intended therapy was never actually delivered.

Path 7. At first inspection, Path 7 seems particularly troublesome. In many ways it is. Therapy was not given as intended, the mediator did not change, but the client improved. This is disconcerting, because the investigator has no reason to predict this outcome. Because the treatment was not properly given, it cannot be said to have been directly tested as a means of affecting the mediator (which did not change). However, since the client improved, it may be that the therapy as designed may not be specific (i.e. the only way to get improvement). Since the mediator variable did not change, the model is not supported since it would not predict clinical improvement in the absence of changes in the mediator variable.

However, by including information about the mediator variable, the investigator has potentially valuable information on two issues that are important in outcome research. First, one possible interpretation, though subject to criticism, is that this path represents data on the spontaneous remission rate of the clinical problem in cases where it is unknown. The logic would be that there is no other reason that the client should have improved. However, the only reasonable way to argue for spontaneous remission is to have a no-treatment control group.

This brings us to the second interpretation that is much more interesting. Path 7 can be interpreted as the effect due to the nonspecific treatment factors in the therapy. One of the great debates in outcome therapy studies is what constitutes a reasonable control group (Parloff, 1986; Wilkins, 1973; Wilkins, 1986). This (and Path 8) provides a very interesting estimate of the effect size due to nonactive treatment components, at least as defined by the treatment designer. In this case, whatever treatment response that was observed cannot be ascribed to the reason intended by the investigator. Yet therapy was delivered with the intention of being effective. The therapist should have supplied all the enthusiasm to this client as he or she did to any other client since the therapist was presumably trying to deliver the correct treatment. Thus clients have experienced a credible control condition complete with all the placebo effects one could ask for. For this to be the case, of course, the deviations in therapy delivery cannot be egregious such as not having held a sufficient number of session or similar kinds of problems. Assuming the therapist tried but didn't quite meet quality standards and didn't manage to alter the mediating variable, this is a very interesting control condition. It is especially interesting in cases where there are ethical concerns about having a wait-list control group where significant morbidity or mortality may occur. The trouble is, one cannot know ahead of time whether anyone will go down this path.

If the researcher wanted to know the incremental validity of the properly administered treatment when it actually changed the mediating variable, he or she could take the combined effect sizes of paths 1 and 2 and subtract the combined effect sizes of paths 7 and 8. Different combinations of paths could yield other useful effect size estimates such as one bearing on the strength of the relationship between the mediating variable and dependent measure.

Path 8. In the case of subjects ending up without having received the intended therapy, showing no changes in the mediating variable, and then no subsequent change in the dependent measure, there are a couple of options for how to interpret the results. An important option is to combine these results with those who went down Path 7 to form the important control group to test credible nonspecific treatment effects (see above). Another option is to exclude the subjects from at least one set of analyses. These subjects are neither tests of the treatment nor do they speak to the validity of the underlying model. If the number of subjects who follow paths 5 through 8 is a very high proportion of the total subjects in the study, then the investigator has to consider whether the treatment may be too hard to train to be practical, or that the study may not be replicable.

If one contrasts the information available from analyzing data using the procedures detailed in Figure 4 versus that in Figure 1, the difference is huge. The traditional study lumps everyone in all pathways together and contrasts that with a control group in order to get an estimate of therapy efficacy. The more sophisticated researchers (who can afford to do so) may discard paths 5 through 8 before making their comparison. However, in both cases, studying all the available pathways provides important information about nonspecific effects and the validity of the model underlying the development of the treatment in the first place. Using this analytic strategy, there is useful information provided by each study participant, albeit some is more useful than others.

This kind of analysis begins to shed light on questions of great relevance to both scientists and practitioners. Responders and nonresponders can be studied in light of whether the underlying treatment model is problematic, the treatment itself is ineffective, or whether there may be a need to understand that topographically similar clinical problems may have very different etiologies and require specific assessment leading to different interventions. Earlier in the paper I said that meta-analyses often concluded that most treatments produced comparable results, most of which were quite modest. By studying the results of paths 1 and 2 one can get information on the effect sizes one might expect for clients with a particular clinical problem due to an identified mediating mechanism. I believe these effect sizes will be larger than those from combining paths 1 through 4 (or all 8 in the worst case).

Other Issues

It is necessary to understand that the subjects who wind up at each of the terminal nodes of the diagram in Figure 4, cannot be presumed to be comparable. There may be a variety of reasons why subjects end up where they did. For instance, if a client did not receive treatment as designed, and did not show a change in the mediating variable and dependent variable, one cannot assume that had the client received the intended treatment they would have responded favorably. We cannot assume that subjects reached a particular terminus for random reasons. It may well be that subjects were not equivalent when the study began and those pre-existing factors dictated or interacted with experimental conditions to produce the observed results. It is even possible that how one ends up at a particular outcome has nothing to do with treatment at all, but is due to some as yet unidentified variable(s).

What is being proposed is a way to take a closer, theory-driven look at outcome that makes use of individual variability in response to treatment to aid in theory and therapy development. How this information is used depends on the sophistication and probity of the scientist. It would not be legitimate to simply eliminate all subjects who did not end up down either paths 1 or 2 from any analysis that is used to create an estimate of overall effect size for anyone assigned to a particular treatment. Such an estimate would require comparing all subjects who were initially intended to be exposed to the treatment to those in the control condition[1]. The proposed partitioning of results does provide the basis for understanding outcomes better than just considering overall group statistics. How data are reported is crucial to maintaining the integrity of the literature. Should researchers find this way of understanding and reporting data useful, it is incumbent on them to report the outcomes for all subjects so that interpretation of the results for any particular pathway can be seen in the larger context of entire sample. With appropriate qualifications and controls, it is possible to use this more detailed analysis to build research programs that could evolve more quickly than they currently do. This depends on the ability of the scientist to state the causal model a priori and then adequately measure the independent, mediating, and dependent variables appropriately. This is no small feat.

The reader has certainly noticed by now that the analysis does not deal with attrition as a possible outcome. I have not done so merely to keep an already complicated discussion as simple as possible. One can add attrition as an outcome and determine how it is related to changes in the mediating and dependent variables. Attrition remains a significant problem in interpreting outcome data. Adding information about when attrition occurs and its relationship to treatment delivery and change might provide useful information for treatment innovation. A more detailed discussion of this issue must occur elsewhere.

Should one include subjects who do not show a problem with the mediating variable into the study at all? It depends on how one understands therapy to work. If one believes that therapies have specific effects, then including these subjects would give the researcher an estimate of the magnitude of nonspecific treatment effects, but one would not predict substantial improvements for these subjects. This type of study is sometimes considered using aptitude-treatment-interaction (ATI) designs (Cronbach & Snow, 1977; Shoham & Rohrbaugh, 1994). Studies such as these would help the clinician decide how important it might be to conduct an assessment to identify vulnerabilities in the mediating variables, and what benefit there might be to delivering a treatment targeted at the particular problem with the mediating variable. One of the advantages of adding the information on the specific role of the mediating variable in understanding outcome is that it allows for a more formal, quantitative decision making procedure for treatment planning purposes (Sax, Blatt, Higgins, & Marton, 1988). To better evaluate the importance of the mediating variable, it is necessary to have variance in that variable, thus including subjects without a problem in the mediating variable makes logical and statistical sense.

Typical controlled trials now use multi-component treatment manuals that specify what happens in each session. If there are some sessions planned to alter a mediating variable that does not need changing, then those sessions should be irrelevant and add little to overall improvement. They could be replaced by other sessions to address remaining clinically relevant factors. Though the importance of having replicable treatments is obvious, there is no reason why the manuals cannot have assessment components evaluating the status of the mediating variables. Further, treatment manuals should provide for a therapy component to last until a change in the mediator occurs or until a predefined limit on the number of session occurs that indicates the treatment is ineffective at altering the mediator variable.

Studies that have compared structured versus flexible treatment delivery have suggested that allowing clinicians to use their own intuition about what to treat does not produce as good a result as when they must thoroughly cover a broader spectrum of treatment components in a more structured way (e.g., Jacobson, Schmaling, Holtzworth-Munroe, Katt, Wood, & Follette, 1989). What is lacking in these studies is any assurance that the clinicians were accurately assessing the status of the mediating variable therapy was intended to affect when they chose to emphasize a specific treatment component. The logic tree shown above would indicate whether a therapy that had specific active components should continue to be delivered as long as the mediating variable remained a problem.

Conclusion

If studies were analyzed as suggested, outcome studies and traditional therapy might be done differently. Specifically, if therapists gathered ongoing data on the status of the mediating variable and the dependent variable at regular intervals during treatment, one would know when a sufficient dose of therapy had been given to change the mediator. If data were repeatedly gathered on the dependent variable as well, then the time course of the change process could be studied. Assuming one gathered these data on all subjects, one would have several replications across subjects in a study, and appealing evidence of causality if changes in the mediator variable reliably occurred in response to identifiable treatment elements and preceded changes in the dependent variable. Treatment decisions could be made on the basis of if the therapy targeted the right problems, and whether the client was responding.

I have proposed that outcome studies could yield a great deal more information than is currently the case if investigators would specify how treatment is supposed to effect change in the variables that mediate change in the clinical problem. The results would bring researchers into better contact with data that would support or challenge their understanding of the change process. It would be possible to better estimate effect sizes under conditions where the therapy actually was appropriate and affected the mediating variable. Applied clinical psychology seems to advance more slowly than necessary, and it produces fewer clinically significant effects than is desirable. Disaggregating results as shown above could mean that researchers can learn more from individual clinical trials. *This in no way reduces the need for independent replications*, but it does potentially speed the evolution of models of the origins and maintenance of clinically relevant problems and the design of therapies to address those problems.

What is the benefit of this type of approach where, in addition to any standard group statistical analysis, the data can be broken down at the individual level for more sophisticated frequency analyses in ways that illuminate our understanding of both the treatment and the underlying model? As I have already said, it places the researcher in closer contact with informative data that may speed the rejection or evolution of therapies and models of clinical problems. Beyond that benefit, clearer effect size estimates can emerge under more clearly interpretable conditions. At that point, the practitioner interested in delivering the most effective intervention to the right person for the right problem may actually find data indicating that following properly established practice guidelines will clearly and convincingly help his or her clients.

References

American Psychiatric Association. (1994). *Diagnostic and statistical manual of mental disorders* (4th ed.). Washington, DC: American Psychiatric Association.

Baron, R. M., & Kenny, D. A. (1986). The moderator-mediator variable distinction in social psychological research: Conceptual, strategic, and statistical considerations. *Journal of Personality and Social Psychology, 51*, 1173-1182.

Barrom, C. P., Shadish, W. R., & Montgomery, L. M. (1988). PhDs, PsyDs, and real-world constraints on scholarly activity: Another look at the Boulder model. *Professional Psychology: Research and Practice, 19*, 93-101.

Beck, A. T. (1988). *Love is never enough: How couples can overcome misunderstanding, resolve conflicts, and solve relationship problems through cognitive therapy*. New York: Harper & Row.

Beck, A. T., & Emery, G. (1977). *Cognitive therapy of substance abuse*. Philadelphia: Center for Cognitive Therapy.

Beck, A. T., Emery, G., & Greenberg, R. L. (1985). *Anxiety disorders and phobias: A cognitive perspective*. New York: Basic Books.

Beck, A. T., Freeman, A., Pretzer, J., Davis, D., Fleming, B., Ottaviani, R., Beck, J., Simon, K. M., Padesky, C., Meyer, J., & Trexler, L. (1990). *Cognitive therapy for personality disorders*. New York: Guilford.

Beck, A. T., Rush, A. J., Shaw, B. F., & Emery, G. (1979). *Cognitive therapy of depression.* New York: Guilford.

Berman, J. S., & Norton, N. C. (1985). Does professional training make a therapist more effective? *Psychological Bulletin, 98,* 401-406.

Christensen, A., & Jacobson, N. S. (1994). Who (or what) can do psychotherapy: The status and challenge of nonprofessional therapies. *Psychological Science, 5,* 8-14.

Cohen, J. (1988). *Statistical power analysis for the behavioral sciences* (2nd ed.). Hillsdale, NJ: Lawrence Erlbaum Associates.

Cronbach, L. J., & Snow, R. E. (1977). *Aptitudes and instructional methods: A handbook for research on interactions.* New York: Irvington.

Elkin, I. E., Parloff, M. B., Hadley, S. W., & Autry, J. H. (1985). NIMH treatment of depression collaborative research program: Background and research plan. *Archives of General Psychiatry, 42,* 305-316.

Feldman, R. A., Caplinger, T. E., & Wodarski, J. S. (1983). *The St. Louis conundrum: The effective treatment of antisocial youths.* Englewood Cliffs, NJ: Prentice-Hall.

Follette, W. C., Bach, P. A., & Follette, V. M. (1993). A behavior analytic view of psychological health. *The Behavior Analyst, 16,* 303-316.

Follette, W. C., Houts, A. C., & Hayes, S. C. (1992). Behavior therapy and the new medical model. *Behavioral Assessment, 14,* 323-343.

Gold, J. R. (1995). The place of process-oriented psychotherapies in an outcome-oriented psychology and society. *Applied and Preventive Psychology, 4,* 61-74.

Hayes, S. C., Nelson, R. O., & Jarret, R. (1987). Treatment utility of assessment: A functional approach to evaluating quality of assessment. *American Psychologist, 42,* 963-974.

Hempel, C. G. (1966). *Philosophy of natural science.* Englewood Cliffs, NJ: Prentice-Hall, Inc.

Jacobson, N. S., Follette, W. C., & Revensdorf, D. (1984). Psychotherapy outcome research: Methods for reporting variability and evaluating clinical significance. *Behavior Therapy, 15,* 336-352.

Jacobson, N. S., Schmaling, K. B., Holtzworth-Munroe, A., Katt, J. L., Wood, L. F., & Follette, V. M. (1989). Research-structured vs. clinically flexible versions of social learning-based marital therapy. *Behaviour Research and Therapy, 27,* 173-180.

Kazdin, A. E. (1992). *Research design in clinical psychology* (2nd edition). New York: Macmillan Publishing Co.

Luborsky, L., Singer, B., & Luborsky, L. (1975). Comparative studies of psychotherapies: Is it true that "Everyone has won and all must have prizes"? *Archives of General Psychiatry, 32,* 995-1008.

Nowak, R. (1994). Problems in clinical trials go far beyond misconduct. *Science, 264,* 1538-1541.

Parloff, M. B. (1986). Placebo controls in psychotherapy research: A sine qua non or a placebo for research. *Journal of Consulting and Clinical Psychology, 54,* 79-87.

Persons, J. B. (1986). The advantages of studying psychological phenomena rather than psychiatric diagnoses. *American Psychologist, 41*, 1252-1260.

Platt, J. (1964). Strong inference. *Science, 146*, 347-353.

Shadish, W. R., & Sweeney, R. B. (1991). Mediators and moderators in meta-analysis: There's a reason why we don't let dodo birds tell us which psychotherapies should have prizes. *Journal of Consulting and Clinical Psychology, 59*, 883-893.

Shoham, V., & Rohrbaugh, M. (1994). Aptitude x treatment interaction (ATI) research: Sharpening the focus, widening the lens. In M. Aveline & D. A. Shapiro (Eds.), *Research foundations for psychotherapy practice*. New York: John Wiley and Sons, Inc.

Smith, M. L., & Glass, G. V. (1977). Meta-analysis of psychotherapy outcome studies. *American Psychologist, 32*, 752-760.

Smith, M. L., Glass, G. V., & Miller, T. I. (1980). *The benefits of psychotherapy*. Baltimore: Johns Hopkins University Press.

Sox, H., C, Jr., Blatt, M. A., Higgins, M. C., & Marton, K. I. (1988). *Medical decision making*. Boston: Butterworths.

Stein, D., & Lambert, M. J. (1984). On the relationship between therapist experience and psychotherapy outcome. *Clinical Psychology Review, 4*, 127-142.

Wilkins, W. (1973). Expectancy of therapeutic gain: An empirical and conceptual critique. *Journal of Consulting and Clinical Psychology, 40*, 69-77.

Wilkins, W. (1986). Placebo problems in psychotherapy research: Social-psychological alternatives to chemotherapy concepts. *American Psychologist, 41*, 551-556.

Footnote

1. I would like to thank Robyn Dawes for emphasizing this point to me during discussion of this paper and subsequently on the SSCPNET where he cited Nowak (1994) for examples of data editing problems in clinical trials.

Discussion of Follette

Attending to Findings

Logan Wright
Central Oklahoma University

Dr. Follette's statement is well thought out, and lends an important sense of balance to this book. Without his comments, I am not sure that the various authors would have attended properly to the fact that even the best, currently available scientific information regarding psychological procedures still leaves us with a level of knowledge which is extremely primitive.

The notion that we may be ready to advance to a new plateau of inquiry regarding effective psychotherapy is appealing. As described by Follette, this new plateau might be termed the "parceling out" or "more molecular" stage. The evidence is now reasonably definitive that, *as a group*, psychotherapists are effective, and *as a group* patients seem to benefit from treatment. We also know that some procedures are better than other. However, the difference between treated and untreated groups is minimal, and a significant number of therapy recipients either do not improve more than might be expected via spontaneous recovery, or their condition appears to worsen because of therapy.

I concur with Follette's suggestion that we focus on *why* psychotherapy works or fails to do so in a more molecular sense. We need to know which therapy is effective for which types of patients with which kinds of disorders. Meta-analysis, one of our newest scientific companions, may now become less of a friend. The problem, of course, is not only GIGO ("garbage in/garbage out"), but also that this method provides only universal and not specific information. As Follette points out; "meta-analysis is the ultimate aggregation, which distorts information about specific variables." What about individuals who fall outside the range of the hypothetical average patient, receiving the hypothetically average version of a procedure, for a disorder which represents the least mean squares difference from the average problem? Answers to these concerns will come only when we advance to the next plateau of inquiry. Follette has provided a path to that plateau.

Advancement beyond the current state of the art will also require research involving more homogeneous samples as regards patient demographics and patients' disorders. It may not be a mere coincidence that the Chambless list involves procedures which are effective with disorders which, for the most part do not correspond to DSM categories. It will also require greater reliance on treatment manuals, which should aid in imposing more standardization on our methods of intervention.

The above not withstanding, I wish that methodological softness in our current research were our biggest overall problem. Sadly, however, it is not. Should we ever reach the point when we no longer violate a single statistical assumption and/or when (as we already have to a limited extent) we can demonstrate that certain procedures are unequivocally superior, we will still have to face why so few providers pay attention to research findings. As Beutler, Williams and Wakefield (1993) have previously pointed out, there exists a correlation approximating -1.00 between the scientific quality of information, and how much that information impacts the practice of hands-on providers.

Finally, it is good that Follette mentioned the DSMs. These documents—though viewed by many medical-model-inclined individuals as involving entities—actually often represent very poor, non-specific constructs. The DSM categories may constitute an on going source of inertia to both scientific progress and patient well being. In the future, we may be continuously pressured to utilize labels, and to research flawed quasi-disorders. Outcome will be defined by whether the patient is more or less ingrained within a heterogeneous, non-reliable, and non-valid conceptual category. To participate in this process may not only retard the progress of psychological science, but it might also involve us, inadvertently, in procedures/processes that have a significant iatrogenic potential. An unavoidable component of the standards setting process may be to force the issue, that is, to demand a dialogue between those of us involved in the FDA-like effort and those involved in the development of future DSMs.

Reference

Beutler, L. E. Williams, R. E., & Wakefield, P. J. (1993). Obstacles to disseminating applied psychological science. *Applied and Preventive Psychology, 2,* 53-58.

Chapter 12

The Relevance of Psychological Theories to Standards of Practice

Henry E. Adams
University of Georgia, Athens

Before I can properly address the issue of theories in applied applications, I must first evaluate the nature of theories in psychology. I do not mean to embark on a scholarly journey into the theoretical and philosophical basis and parameters of theories but want to examine theories in a practical, common sense manner which may not always be completely accurate but allows us to consider the issue of whether theories are useful in practical applications or clinical practice and should be consider in standards of intervention.

Types of Psychological Theories

A theory is a series of two or more constructs or abstractions which have been hypothesized, assumed, or even demonstrated to bear a relationship to one another. In other words, theories are ways of thinking about phenomena. Psychology is the science of behavior. Thus, when we talk about psychological theories, we are referring to explanations of behavior. Theories vary greatly in psychology and I would like to focus on three major characteristics of theories. First, theories may be broad band or narrow band. The broad band theories in psychology are those which attempt to explain all of human behavior. Two examples are Freud's psychoanalytic theory and Skinner's radical behaviorism. With these theories any pattern of behavior that you are describing will have an explanation. In other words, broad band theories are comprehensive explanation of behavior. The narrow band or miniature theories usually restrict their explanation to specific patterns of behavior such as anxiety, depression, schizophrenia or similar specific topics. These theories are often eloquent, well delineated explanations of a restricted range of behavior which appear in Journals such as Psychological Review. A recent example is the very intriguing explanation of the interaction of nature and nurture by Bronfenbrenner and Ceci (1994). This model or theory gives a very interesting, novel explanation of how heredity and environment interact.

Second, theories may be rational or empirical. The dictionary states that rationalism is the belief that reason is, in itself, a source of knowledge superior to and independent of sense perception. Rational theories of behavior develop from intuition, experience, or other armchair tactics. Empirical theories develop from research and are data driven. For example, psychanalysis is a broad band, rational theory. The theory of "recovered memories of childhood sexual abuse" is a narrow band, rational theory. Skinner's radical behaviorism is a broad band, empirical theory which developed initially from his animal research. Seligman's (1974) "learned helplessness" theory of depression and later modifications is a narrow band, empirical theory developed from laboratory research.

Third, the source of these theories can vary greatly. While some theories develop from research activities, many develop from therapeutic activities, particularly psychotherapy. This is often the case with psychodynamic, humanistic, and medical model theories. I always find this fact amazing. Can we determine the nature of schizophrenia, depression, personality disorder or even normal behavior by treating these disorders? Does the fact that Freud treated hysteria mean that he understands hysteria and maybe even normal behavior? Does the fact that schizophrenia responds to phenothiazine mean that schizophrenia is a biological disorder and we now understand it? Does knowing that penicillin cures paresis give us a theoretical explanation of syphilis? I do not think so! I think that in order to intervene effectively you must first understand the nature of the disorder and then devise treatment procedures. This strategy appears to be most effective to me and the other way around rarely works. Clinical psychology, in particular, has been infested with "so-called" knowledge gained from psychotherapeutic sessions, a situation not highly conducive to advancing knowledge about human behavior nor to generating intervention techniques which are effective. The statement "in my clinical experience ..." invariable produces nausea in my case. Most of our highly effective treatment procedures have developed from applied, clinical research where there is some understanding of the disorder and treatment procedures are designed based on that knowledge.

The Advantages and Disadvantages of Theories

How are theories useful to scientists, practitioners, the public and policy makers? First and foremost, theories organize massive amounts of data into a cohesive whole which makes sense. In other words, they allow us to think about what all these facts and data mean. Second, a good theory has implications, usually for further research, which elaborates knowledge or suggests an alternate theory. Third, they are heuristic devises which stimulate our creativity and research as well as make us happy.

There are some real down sides to theories as well. This is particularly true of broad band theories which explain all aspects of human behavior. A theory which explains everything explains nothing. Another major problem with these theories is that, as Platt (1964) stated, we become attached to them and develop a commitment to them. When this happens, we almost unwittingly begin to press the facts to fit the theory rather than modifying the theory to fit the facts. Let me give you the essence of this problem, as described by Platt (1964) and discussed by me in my article on "the pernicious effects of theoretical orientations" (Adams, 1984).

Table 1

Characteristics of Charismatic Theories

Characteristic	*Example 1*	*Example 2*
1. The Great Man	Freud	Skinner
2. A single hypothesis	Unconscious motivation	Behavior is learned
3. The club of dependents	Psychoanalysts	Radical Behaviorists
4. The vendetta	Jung, Horney, et al	Cognitive and Biological Types
5. The all encompassing theory that can not falsified	"Psychoanalysis is a method of studying man"	"But Skinner did consider biology"

As shown in Table 1, many of these theories are proposed by charismatic persons such as Freud, Skinner, Rogers or similar individuals who capture the profession and public "fancy". Second, they usually propose an explanation of behavior based on a single unifying principle or assumption. With Freud it was unconscious motivation particularly psychosexual conflict. With Skinner, it was the assumption that all important behavior is learned. As these theorists gain the attention of the profession and the public they soon attract disciples who spread the word and bond with one another. However, "fads" fade and soon the critical critiques begin to occur. This starts the vendetta where the disciples or "true believers" rush to defend the truth. An example of this is the legendary quarrels of Freud and his disciples with other psychodynamic types such as Jung and Adler who broke away from classic psychoanalysis. Even in a theory which developed from data and research such as radical behaviorism there are similar reactions. The current distress among Skinnerians caused by the growing interest in cognitive and biological theories is an example. I recently reviewed an article where one of Skinner's disciples was vigorously denying that Skinner ignored biological variables. He had carefully searched Skinner's writing to illustrated his point. This reminds me of Biblical scholars searching the Bible to make their points. The bottom line is that if you have faith, these theories are impossible to falsify. The theory is more important than the data and when this happens, we are in big trouble as searchers for the truth.

Over the last 50 years or so we have witnessed how public and professional interests have shifted, from psychoanalysis to behaviorism and now cognitive and biological approaches. An interesting fact is that while these theories wan in popularity they never disappear. As Brendan Maher once stated, "New theories often enter the fray but I have never seen one withdraw from the battlefield in defeat".

What does this mean for the science of psychology and its practical applications? I think Kuhn (1971) was right when he discussed "normal science" as broadening the scope of an explanatory theory and paradigms shifts as the overthrow of an old formerly popular theory with a new theory. These shifts are easy to observed in psychology. We are currently in a shift from the behavioral paradigm to biological and cognitive paradigms. I do not necessarily agree with Kuhn's other notions such as scientific advancement is a matter of social change rather than an accumulation of data, if that is what he meant.

Nevertheless, I do think that, on occasions, the "fads" or paradigms have contributed greatly to our knowledge. While behaviorism is no longer the current "fad", the contribution of this movement and of Skinner is truly impressive. What we know clinically as compared to what we knew 10 or 20 years ago is awesome. Scientific psychology is developing impressive data bases. There is little doubt that we are moving from what some have referred to as a pre-paradigmatic to a paradigmatic stage of science.

Nevertheless, there are negative aspects of theories. If we look at theories in terms of how they impact psychology and the public and analyze this impact carefully, some of the results are often distressing. In order to examine this issue we must differentiate between pure and applied science because the impact of pure science is often quite different than the impact of applied science. The function of pure science is to provide the necessary information for applied scientists to achieve their goals. I know that some pure scientists claim that research is a purely intellectual pursuit of knowledge but they often provide the knowledge for the development of some great applications. I disagree with psychologists who say basic science never contributes to our impressive clinical interventions. Where would behavior therapy be if we had not stolen all those great ideas from those guys who spent most of their lives in rat labs.

Clinical versus Scientific Theories

Unfortunately, not all clinicians and applied types use scientific knowledge to generate their theories. Many clinical theories ignore scientific knowledge completely. Practitioners do not often spend time searching the literature for scientific knowledge that might solve their problems. Instead, they rely on intuition and their clinical experience. Much to my dismay, I find that the clinically based theories have as much or ever more impact on the public than scientific theories. Data based theories are dull and often difficult to understand. They bore the public. In any case, I would like to further discuss the impact of these theories on professional education and public policy.

Impact of Theories on Education

By "education," I am referring to the education of applied and clinical psychologists, a topic particularly timely with the Education and Training Board of the American Psychological Association currently revising their standards of professional education. The impact of theories on models of training in professional education is tremendous. While training in science and scientific methods is supposedly required in all graduate programs, the primary agenda of most programs is the indoctrination of students in a particular theoretical orientation held by the majority of the faculty. Thus, prospective students look for programs which are humanistic, psychodynamic, behavioral and are either research or clinically oriented. Furthermore, the faculty advertise themselves in a similar manner.

Even worse, there is a whole group of psychologists who are afraid that graduate students may be exposed to much research or a research emphasis in these programs. The fear of research contradicting popular theories and practice among private practitioners was the prime motive for the development of professional schools of psychology. The claim that professional schools were developed to insure students received adequate clinical training is silly in terms of the facts. How can a professional program that accepts as many 10 time the number of students as a university program with half the number of faculty members, most of them part time, do a better job of clinical training and supervision, which is very time intensive? In addition, there is no evidence that students graduating from professional schools are better clinicians. I would insist, however, that science practitioner programs not ignore the clinical training of their students. Faculty in these programs should do clinical work, model clinical skills and supervise the clinical training of their students. If you only want to do research do not train clinical graduate students.

The professional, free-standing schools for applied and clinical psychologists are rapidly becoming a disaster for the whole field of clinical practice. Contrary to their claims, we do not, repeat, do not need to train more clinicians. Recent graduates of clinical psychology are already literally stumbling over one another. The California Schools of Professional Psychology, by themselves, are probably training more clinical psychologists than all the university based programs put together. What we do need is better trained clinicians. They need to be better in research, in research methodology, and have a greater exposure to first rate research psychologists who are found only in major universities and medical schools. Our students need more, not less research emphasis. They need to know how to be critical of theories and clinical lore. Last but not least, they need to know how to **THINK**. These traits can only be developed by a thorough exposure to science.

The Evaluation of Training Programs

The position of the American Psychological Association is that a graduate program should be judged only in terms of their training model or theoretical position, a political stance guaranteed to insure mediocrity. If the model is phrenology and their students do a good job of reading "bumps" on the head as well as having their four courses in content areas, a couple of statistics course, and an ethics course should the program be accredited? If the history of the E & T Board is any indication the program probably would be approved. I hope that if the American Psychological Society becomes involved in accreditation they do not repeat this stupidity. First and foremost, a student should trained as a psychologist and as a scientist. They can then be trained as a clinician or practitioner.

The practice of encouraging theoretical orientations also encourages ignorance because theoretical orientations value theories not data. Psychologists should drop any encouragement of loyalty to any theory except science. Why is it necessary for us to describe ourselves psychodynamic, non-directive, behavioral, or cognitive therapists? Are there no clinical psychologists left? We are clinical psychologists and we should use the effective tools of our trade regardless of the origin of the technique. Further, we should acknowledge and demand our colleagues to acknowledge that clinical and applied psychology is the application of the science of psychology. You can not train basic and applied scientists in trade or vocational schools such as professional schools of psychology. We must revise our standards of training of clinical and applied psychologists to eliminate the trade school, guild mentality of professional training.

A failure to train applied and clinical psychologists as scientists has and can result in the public being exposed to misleading information and claims. These claims, often seen on television "talk" shows, are frequently distorted, erroneous, or occasionally amusing. For example, one clinical psychologist has specialized in the treatment of persons abducted and sexually abused by aliens (Fiore, 1989). I am not exaggerating, there real problems with the public being given misinformation about the nature of human behavior and intervention techniques. Even the Public Interest Directorate of APA circulated a pamphlet entitled "How to chose a psychotherapist" where the characterization of behavior and cognitive therapists as compared to psychodynamic therapists was unfavorable and inaccurate. This is another case where theory or theoretical orientation results in the public being misinformed. Is this the type of activity the profession wants to adopt as its standards of care? I happen to agree with Richard McFall's position that only empirically proven therapies should be taught in clinical psychology training programs. One day, psychologists are going to be faced with a pure food and drug law. We are going to have to prove what we claim. Otherwise, the public and insurance companies will not pay.

Empirically-Based Treatments

There is another side to this story. In the last 10 or 20 years, clinical psychology has not only developed new intervention techniques, we have shown some of them to be quite effective. Table 2 shows some of these effective interventions developed by clinical researchers. There is some good research documenting the effectiveness of these tactics with a variety of disorders. Barlow's (1994) recent review article in *Clinical Psychology* is one example. APA has appointed a Task Force on Psychological

Table 2

Effective Interventions

Disorder	*Technique*	*Major Investigators*
Simple Phobias, Social Phobias, GAD	Systematic Desensitization, Flooding	Wolpe, Paul and others
Panic Disorders	Complex Behavioral	Barlow and others
OCD	Response Prevention, Flooding	Meyer, Foa
Borderline PD	Complex Behavioral	Linehan
Depression	Cognitive and Behavioral	Beck, Lewinsohn
Addictions	Social drinking, Relapse Prevention	Sobels, Marlatt
PTSD	Exposure, Flooding	Keene and others
Chronic Schizophrenia	Complex Token Programs	Paul and others

A variety of other programs and techniques, some not fully evaluated.

Interventions guidelines. Hopefully, they will acknowledge some of these advancements.

I do not trust APA, however. APA is a political organization and I do not trust politicians. I blame APA for free-standing professional schools, for blocking Divisions 12 from defining clinical psychology and allowing the Practice Directorate to do so, for giving psychology away (often to idiots), for protecting members engaged in questionable assessment and treatment techniques so that they can collect third party payment, and for slandering a good candidate for President in 1994. Science is not perceived as a window dressing for APA it is only a window dressing (Seligman, 1994). APA's main agenda is "Political Correctness" and a majority vote for their policies. Scientists and science practitioners are only needed by APA to satisfy the public and Congress. APA attempts to placate scientists so that we will not complain but our values are largely and sometimes openly ignored. APA has become a guild organization and science plays a minor role. There is really no solution to this dilemma because scientists are in a minority in APA. Hopefully, APS will not follow in these footsteps.

Let's hope that my misgivings are wrong and these positive efforts will not be undermined. In the future, we may be able to say that if you have this type of problem you need this type of treatment and have this probability of getting better. We have come a long way in devising and evaluating new as well as exiting treatment procedures. It is this type of research documentation that third party payers and the public want, not theory nor rhetoric. The "cream will rise to the top" in the long run and questionable clinical techniques such as biofeedback may be used by private practitioners but they will not receive third party payment.

There is another interesting characteristic of these effective treatment procedures. While the majority of them have developed from behavioral or cognitive approaches, some of them, such as the Barlow approach to anxiety disorders and Linehan's program for borderline personality disorders, have incorporated cognitive, behavioral and biological components. This is relevant to the development to new theories of psychopathology and intervention. The more useful theories will incorporate cognitive, biological and behavioral variables rather than adhering to a single theoretical position which emphasizes only one of the three.

Impact of Theories on Policy

Another major impact of theories is on policies by the government and the legal system. We do have a great deal to offer these agencies in some specific areas. While I question whether APA should be involved in some political issue such as abortion, there are some areas where we have data and expertise. For example, with AIDS prevention we have a great deal of information which might be helpful in preventing this devastating disorder. Another example is the Ceci and Bruck (1993) *Psychological Bulletin* article on the suggestibility of child witnesses. This is an impressive document which is going to be extremely important to the courts in child sexual abuse cases. A further recent example is the Bronfenbrenner and Ceci (1994) description of a bioecological model of the interaction of nature and nurture. The increasingly popular belief by some of our conservative politicians that biology is destiny directly threatens some very good programs such as Head Start as well as other poverty programs. The Bronfenbrenner-Ceci model emphasizes that environmental factors, particularly in the first years of life, facilitates the realization of innate, genetic potential. Because of providing a supportive environment , unrealized genetic endowment may be actualized by programs such as Head Start. Newt, we may not need those orphans homes. Our models and mini-theories often have direct implications for public policy and planning. Psychology does has a lot to offer the public.

Unfortunately, the implications of data and theories are often ignored. For example, one of the best documented treatment program for treatment of chronic mental patients is the social learning program developed by Gordon Paul and his students (Paul & Lenz, 1977). It has been largely ignored. The fact that we have good treatment programs and good information for public policy does not mean they will be utilized. The public still prefer Oprah and Donahue for their psychological information. Private practitioners are still largely doing "talk therapies" with a variety of disorders although more effective techniques are available. What can we do? We have got to become more abrasive and more aggressive in informing the public about sense and nonsense in psychology as well as forcing our private practice colleagues to update their skills.

Theories and Standards of Care

What role should theories play in scientific standards of care? Do we need to promote a particular theory of intervention in order for the public to know why we are using that technique? I do not think so. I know at one time you could discuss psychology and psychological treatment with your bartender and he knew as much about these topics as you did. Psychology has changed. We are moving from literature or science fiction to becoming a real science. I have difficulty understanding some of the data and theories of current psychological scientists, particularly the cognitive and biological researchers. The bartender would not attempt to discuss physics with a nuclear scientists and he can no longer discuss psychological science in a meaningful fashion. This is the price psychologists pay in moving from folklore to science. The public is generally not capable of understanding our more recent theories and models.

The role theories should play in standards of care is that they should instigate the development of more effective treatment techniques. If it can then be demonstrated that a technique is effective for a particular disorder or problem, then the procedure should be introduced perhaps even described to the public. Standards of care should be concerned with what percentage of patients with a specific disorder is cured or improved when treated with a specific technique. While the logic of the procedure may be explained to the public, they do not need to be indoctrinated in a particular theoretical orientation. What can we say when the theory is proved inaccurate and it will be! That is the nature of good theories. They do not survive. The public does not need to know our thinking. They are not psychologists. They need our products.

The Kinds of Theories We Need

In closing, I have several suggestions about theories. First, we do not need another broad band theory that explains all of human behavior, particularly one developed from intuition or armchair theorizing. We do not need another great man with an all inclusive theory whether the theory is data or clinically based. What we do need is small theories which are data based, can be disproved, and address specific aspects of human behavior. We must stop valuing theories and theoretical orientation because they blind us and cause us to be ignorant. We should value data and facts. Theories are nice, useful tools. Theories serve the function of stimulating us to do research which yields data causing us to revise our theories or discard them for better ones. Like tools, theories wear out. By discarding or modifying theories as data accumulates we can more closely approximate the nature of the universe. A useful theory is one which is well documented and has practical implications for public problems and policies. Nevertheless, they are subject to replacement by better ones.

In the last 10 or 20 years, we have come a very long way. We are becoming a profession which has a lot to offer the public. We need to avoid the pitfalls of theoretical and guild commitments because we still have a lot more to learn. With a commitment to science and the scientist practitioner model we may achieve these goals.

References

Adams, H. E. (1984). The pernicious effects of theoretical orientations in clinical psychology. *The Clinical Psychologist, 37*, 90-94.

Barlow, D. H. (1994). Psychological interventions in the era of managed competition. *Clinical Psychology: Science and Practice, 1*, 109-122.

Bronfenbrenner, U., & Ceci, S. J. (1994). Nature-nature reconceptualized in developmental perspective: A bioecological model. *Psychological Review, 101*, 568-586.

Ceci, S. J., & Bruck, M. (1993). Suggestibility of the child witness: A historical review and synthesis. *Psychological Bulletin, 113*, 403-439.

Fiore, E. (1989). *Encounters: Psychologist reveals case studies of contact with extraterrestrials.* New York: Doubleday.

Kuhn, T. S. (1971). The *structure of scientific revolutions* (2nd ed.). Chicago: University of Chicago Press.

Mineka, S. (1994). Presidential perspectives. *Clinical Science*, Newsletter, Fall, 1994.

Paul, G. L., & Lenz, R. J. (1977). *Psychosocial treatment of chronic mental patients: Milieu versus social learning programs.* Cambridge, MA: Harvard University Press.

Platt, J. R. (1964). Strong inference. *Science, 146*, 347-353.

Seligman, M. (1994). APA in crises: Scientists alienated by election. *The Clinical Psychologist, 47*(3), 2-3.

Seligman, M. E. P. (1974). Depression and learned helplessness. In R. J. Friedman & M. M. Katz (Eds.), *The psychology of depression: Contemporary theory and research.* Washington, D.C.: Winston-Wiley.

Discussion of Adams

Science, Theory, and Practice

Patrick M. Ghezzi
University of Nevada

Unraveling the issues pertaining to the relationship between psychological theory and standards of clinical intervention is much like trying to separate milk from its mix with this morning's coffee; once mixed, they will never unmix again. Professor Adams' remarks likewise remind us of how very difficult it is to uncouple science, theory, and practice. His remarks expose as well how the difficulty is compounded when culture and personality enters the mix.

There may be no way to unravel the issues that Adams raises. My general purpose therefore is not to try, but to try instead to draw out of his remarks some basic assumptions which we can all agree upon. When we agree among ourselves on fundamentals, we begin to take on the character of an authentic profession, capable of articulating itself to itself and to the rest of society.

Science

The light that science casts on nature differs significantly from all other ways of seeing. Regularity, uniformity, and lawfulness are both presumed and sought, with the latter taking place in a culture that values knowledge derived from careful observation and precise measurement, and that insists on scrutinizing every fact, statement, explanation, and conclusion that is offered.

But science is more than knowledge, order, and relentless self-examination. Ultimately, it is about controlling nature. In some cases, for example, astronomy, the control is entirely intellectual, while in others, it is closer to home, where the battle for control over the physical and social environment can take on life and death proportions, as in medicine. Indeed, owing to the triumph of scientific practice, the old view of science as a means of *knowing* the world has given way to the modern view that science is also a way of *changing* the world (Russell, 1961).

Theory

It is a truism among contemporary philosophers of science that all observation is more or less shaded by assumption and expectation. This is not meant as an indictment against science and scientists, but rather as a caution to not presume that our observations are "pure" or our established methodologies unassailable (cf. Hanson, 1969). The upshot of this is that all our observations and descriptions of nature are made in light of theory, and that the burden is ours to not only remain alert to the impact that this has on science, but also to recognize and evaluate the arbitrary elements in our constructions of the world.

That said, what is theory? A dictionary definition might read something like this: *A coherent group of general propositions used as principles of explanation for a class of phenomena.* Taking a behavioral perspective (read: theory) on psychology (Bijou, 1993; Kantor & Smith, 1975; Skinner, 1953), we shall take a moment to elaborate upon several key concepts in this definition.

The *phenomena* dealt with are observable environment-behavior interactions. Critical to understanding psychological phenomena is the idea that behavior cannot be understood without reference to a stimulating environment, and that the environment cannot be understood without reference to a responding organism. This is what is meant when we talk about a *functional* point of view.

General propositions take advantage of all the definitions, terms, concepts, and principles that comprise the main body of behavioral psychology. Their source derives primarily from research on individual organisms in laboratory and quasi-laboratory environments. Evolving out of that research are propositions or statements about functional relationships which manifest a greater degree of generality than does the evidence on which they are based (cf. Sidman, 1960).

Explanation is achieved whenever a psychological event is related to the factors involved in its occurrence. On this view, explanation amounts to a description of a functional relationship between behavior and its controlling variables. Indeed, if we know the cluster of variables that are involved in the occurrence of an event, then we should be able to not only predict it, but also to bring the event about.

Coherence is a concept that unites all the elements in our interpretation of theory. That is, we maintain a coherent perspective on psychological events when a) observation remains functional and at the level of environment-behavior interaction, b) general propositions are based on principles derived from a functional analysis of behavior, and c) explanation centers on identifying functional relationships.

Practice

The goals for the practice of psychology are two-fold: prevention and remediation. The means for achieving those goals center on prediction and control. In the case of prevention, the ideal is to ensure that a problem does not arise, or if one does, to contain its intensity, duration, metastasis, etc. How we are able to do that is a matter, first, of anticipating what problem will arise given certain conditions, and second, of altering those conditions to the point where the problem is either avoided or curtailed. Poverty is a good example. Where marginal living conditions restrict a child's developmental opportunities, there exist compensatory programs designed to prevent or curtail retardation by stimulating intellectual, emotional, and social growth (see Bijou, 1983).

Remediation likewise is based on prediction and control. For example, in behavior therapy the selection of an intervention is made in light of a prediction regarding how effective that intervention will be in controlling an individual's problem. A prediction of this sort has many sources, but none are more important than the empirical evidence documenting the conditions under which an intervention is most likely to be effective.

In turning to a body of research, the usual course of action is to critically review the relevant studies, and to base decisions on the evidence examined. But decisions cannot now be based on empirical grounds alone, because much of what is empirical in applied psychology is fraught with questionable assumptions and theoretical ambiguity. Predictions based on the "strength" of that sort of research are not likely to be very meaningful, and may in fact lead to harm.

On what basis, then, are we to discriminate "good" from "not so good" applied research? One way to approach this question is from a logical standpoint. If a given intervention is based on the effective application of well-substantiated psychological principles and techniques, then *logically* it should not fail to produce large and lasting results. Likewise, in medicine the assurance *on logical grounds* is that if competent personnel are guided by sound medical principles and techniques, benefits will accrue to those who are treated.

A final comment is in order concerning what we mean, and do not mean, by well-substantiated psychological principles, and by their effective application. By well-substantiated principles we do not mean formulations with vague and meaningless referents, like intelligence, aptitude, and the like. Neither are we referring to formulations involving concepts and relationships based on metaphors and principles borrowed from other sciences (e.g., the person conceptualized as a computer). Nor are we referring to formulations based on response averages which are in turn related to mystical inner personality determiners. What we do mean by well-substantiated psychological principles are those which derive from a) an articulated philosophy of science (Kantor, 1981; Skinner, 1974), b) a general theory of behavior (Bijou, 1993; Skinner, 1953), c) a core research methodology (Sidman, 1960; Barlow, Hayes, & Nelson, 1984), and d) research findings that have been replicated enough to give us confidence in their generality. Unfortunately, psychology, in its preparadigmatic state, has relatively few well-substantiated principles as here conceived, a fact that contributes to the marginal effectiveness to date of many applied programs.

As to the effective application of well-substantiated psychological principles, three questions can be raised: Are we applying all the principles? Are we applying all of them broadly? Are we applying all of them thoroughly and appropriately? The answer to each question is, probably not, and here again is a circumstance that militates against more effective practices.

A fitting conclusion to this commentary is provided by Leonardo de Vinci, who wrote, "Those who fall in love with practice without science are like a sailor who enters a ship without a helm or a compass, and who never can be certain whither he is going." On this, at least, we can all agree.

References

Barlow, D. H., Hayes, S. C., & Nelson, R. O. (1984). *The scientist-practitioner: Research and accountability in clinical and applied settings.* Needham Heights, MS: Allyn & Bacon.

Bijou, S. W. (1983). The prevention of mild and moderate retarded development. In F. J. Menolascino, R. Neman, & J. A. Stark (Eds.), *Curative aspects of mental retardation: Biomedical and behavioral advances* (pp. 223-241). Baltimore, MD: Brookes.

Bijou, S. W. (1993). *Behavior analysis of child development.* Reno, NV: Context Press.

Hanson, N. R. (1969). *Perception and discovery: An introduction to scientific inquiry.* San Francisco, CA: Freeman, Cooper, & Co.

Kantor, J. R. (1981). *Interbehavioral philosophy.* Chicago, IL: The Principia Press.

Kantor, J. R., & Smith, N. W. (1975). *The science of psychology: An interbehavioral survey.* Chicago, IL: The Principia Press.

Russell, B. (1961). Science and values. In R. E. Egner & L. E. Denonn (Eds.), *The basic writings of Bertrand Russell* (pp. 635-646). New York, NY: Touchstone Books.

Skinner, B. F. (1953). *Science and human behavior.* New York, NY: Macmillan.

Skinner, B. F. (1974). *About behaviorism.* New York, NY: Vintage Books.

Sidman, M. (1960). *Tactics of scientific research: Evaluating experimental research in psychology.* New York, NY: Basic Books.

Chapter 13

The Implications of Diversity for Scientific Standards of Practice

Stanley Sue
University of California, Los Angeles

The principle that scientific standards should underlie clinical practice is widely accepted. Nevertheless, as we contemplate the application of scientific standards to practice with diverse populations, a number of important and interesting policy, practice, research, and political issues arise.

1. Research and policy dilemmas: Is there any evidence that psychotherapy is effective with ethnic minority populations? Should we offer psychotherapy even if effectiveness has not been demonstrated? Should policy and practices be strictly guided by research findings? How far do we go in adopting the "whatever works" philosophy? Can standards be culturally biased?

2. Socio-political issues: Is ethnic matching of therapist and client a form of segregation? Should we offer specialized ethnic specific services to targeted groups or should ethnic specific services be avoided? If therapists are not competently trained to work with diverse populations, should their practice be limited?

3. Implications for practice and research: What kinds of therapist or treatment characteristics are associated with effectiveness in the provision of services to ethnic populations? Aside from the need to study growing ethnic minority populations in society, are there good reasons to conduct diversity research? That is, in what ways can diversity research enhance our activities as scientists and practitioners?

In trying to address these questions, I have no magical insights into the solutions. In fact, I shall try to raise questions and draw implications rather than to provide answers. Let me begin by indicating my particular diversity focus. Diversity can obviously be framed in a variety of terms—ethnicity, gender, social class, sexual orientation, or other human characteristics. I shall confine my comments to ethnic minority populations with the assumption that many of the issues that will be mentioned are applicable to other diverse populations. Rather than to spend time trying to define ethnicity, culture, and minority groups, I want to get to the heart of the chapter and address the policy, socio-political, and research issues.

Research and Policy Dilemmas

Empirical Evidence

Is psychotherapy effective with members of ethnic minority groups? The fact of the matter is that there is not much of a scientific base for demonstrating positive treatment outcomes among diverse client populations. The paucity and state of treatment outcome studies on ethnic minorities make it difficult to draw any definitive conclusions about the effectiveness of psychotherapy with ethnic minorities.

Not counting analogue investigations, I know of no studies that meet basic conditions, or even most of the basic conditions, important for demonstrating treatment efficacy—namely, research in which (a) pre- and post treatment outcomes are assessed for clients from one or more ethnic group(s), (b) random assignment and control groups (e.g., no treatment, attention-placebo, or different ethnic groups matched on demographic characteristics other than ethnicity, etc.) are used when appropriate, (c) type of treatment and ethnicity are crossed when comparisons of outcomes by ethnicity and treatment are made, (d) multiple, culturally cross-validated assessment instruments are employed, (e) outcomes are assessed over time, and (f) findings are replicated.

Reviews of the literature on the effectiveness of psychotherapy with ethnic minorities—largely African Americans—have yielded different conclusions. Sattler (1977) generally concluded that African Americans did not differ from Whites in treatment outcomes. On the other hand, Griffith and Jones (1978) believed that evidence indicated that clients' race did have an effect on psychotherapy outcomes. Others took a more moderate position. Parloff, Waskow, and Wolfe (1978) felt that the paucity of treatment outcome studies on African Americans did not permit conclusions to be drawn, a point supported in the reviews by Abramowitz and Murray (1983) and Sue, Zane, and Young (1994). Because reviews of the literature are available, I shall only mention some of the research in passing. Some of my own work are discussed in more detail because policy issues have arisen from them.

Some studies have demonstrated no treatment outcome differences in the case of African American and White clients (Jones, 1978; 1982; Lerner, 1972); high rates of premature termination on the part of ethnic minority clients (Sue, 1977); poorer outcomes among ethnic minorities than Whites in drug treatment programs (Brown, Joe, & Thompson, 1985; Query, 1985); less positive posttreatment change among African American than White clients (Sue, Fujino, Hu, Takeuchi, & Zane, 1991); and more favorable outcomes among treated rather than control groups of Latino boys (Szapocznik et al., 1989). Conclusions are difficult to draw, given the inconsistencies in the findings from these studies and the fact that researchers examining treatment outcomes for ethnics have had to rely on less-than-rigorous studies, approximations of true outcome studies, theoretical and conceptual arguments, anecdotes and case examples, and research primarily conducted on African Americans.

Cultural Interventions

Rather than to address the broader question of whether psychotherapy is effective, some investigations have examined whether culturally sensitive interventions have an influence on clients. The interventions include improving the accessibility of services to ethnic minorities (e.g. by providing flexible hours, placing the treatment facility in the Latino communities), and employing bicultural/bilingual staff. They may also involve the selection, modification, or development of therapies that consider the cultural customs, values, and beliefs of clients (e.g. involving indigenous healers or religious leaders in the community in treatment, increasing participation of family members in treatment, etc.) Research suggests that these treatment may increase service utilization, length of treatment, client's satisfaction with treatment, and therapy outcomes, and decrease premature termination of treatment (Rogler, Malgady, & Rodriguez, 1989; Sue, Zane, & Young, 1994; Szapocznik et al., 1989).

One study has tried to link changes in the mental health system to utilization and premature termination patterns of ethnic minority clients. O'Sullivan, Peterson, Cox, and Kirkeby (1989) studied the status and situation of ethnic clients in the Seattle mental health system. They noted that the system had made special efforts to hire ethnic providers, create ethnic-specific services, and establish innovative and culturally-consistent treatment modalities. Using some of the same variables reported in an earlier study (Sue, 1977), they found that the situation had improved considerably from that found in the earlier study. Ethnic minority groups for the most part were no longer underutilizing services; their dropout rates had been reduced and were not much different from that of Whites. O'Sullivan and his colleagues attributed the changes to the increasing cultural responsiveness of the system to underserved populations.

The work of O'Sullivan and his colleagues is certainly encouraging, in that our mental health systems have perhaps become more effective and culturally-appropriate for diverse groups. However, their conclusions were based on a temporal relationship: "Culturally-responsive" features were introduced and ethnic minority groups seemed to fare well. Some of our own research (Sue, Fujino, Hu, Takeuchi, & Zane, 1991) was intended to more directly test the association between culturally-responsive strategies and treatment outcomes. Our study was based on thousands of African American, Asian American, Mexican American, and White clients seen in the Los Angeles County Mental Health System from 1983-1988. It was intended to examine utilization rates, dropout rates (after one session), and treatment outcomes (using pre-and post-treatment Global Assessment Scale scores). Furthermore, we wanted to find out if therapist-client matches in ethnicity and language (a presumed culturally-responsive feature) would be associated with less dropping out and more favorable treatment outcomes. Results indicated that Asian Americans and Mexican Americans tend to underutilize services in comparison with their populations, while African Americans tend to overutilize services. Moreover, dropout rates for ethnic clients were higher (in the case of African Americans) and lower (in the case of Asian Americans) than for Whites. Interestingly, Asian Americans–especially those who are unacculturated–generally fared better when they saw a therapist who was matched ethnically and linguistically. Similar effects were found for Mexican Americans, although the effects were less dramatic. However, ethnic and language matches were not significantly related to dropping out or outcomes for African Americans and Whites. We do not know why matching is related to outcomes for some groups but not others. The importance of ethnic match may depend heavily on the acculturation level or ethnic-cultural identity of clients. For some clients in the same ethnic minority group, match may be quite important. We do know that ethnic or language matches do not ensure cultural matches which may be of major importance.

We have also examined the outcomes received by ethnic minority clients who use either ethnic-specific services or mainstream services (Takeuchi, Sue, & Yeh, in press). The study compared the return rates, length of treatment, and treatment outcome of ethnic minority adults who received services from ethnic-specific or mainstream programs. The sample consisted of 1516 African Americans, 1888 Asian Americans, and 1306 Mexican Americans who used one of 36 predominantly White (mainstream) or 18 ethnic-specific mental health centers in Los Angeles County over a six year period. Predictor variables included type of program (ethnic-specific vs. mainstream), disorder, ethnic match (whether or not clients had a therapist of the same ethnicity), gender, age, and Medi-Cal eligibility. The criterion variables were return after one session, total number of sessions, and treatment outcome. The results indicated that ethnic clients who attend ethnic-specific programs stay in the programs longer than those using mainstream services. The findings were less clear-cut when treatment outcome was examined.

Some studies have demonstrated the value of pretherapy programs that orient culturally-diverse clients to psychotherapy–how it works, what to expect and do, etc. For example, Acosta, Yamamoto, Evans, and Skilbeck (1983) exposed one group of clients to slides, audiotapes, or videotapes to help orient clients to psychotherapy; another group of clients was given a program that was neutral with regard to psychotherapy. Knowledge of and attitudes toward psychotherapy were assessed before and after the programs. Results indicated that exposure to the orientation program increased knowledge and favorable attitudes toward psychotherapy. Therapist orientation programs have also been devised to orient therapists who are working with ethnic minority clients. Reviews of these client and therapist orientation programs have been favorable (see Jones & Matsumoto, 1982).

Let me summarize some of the major findings. First, the quality and quantity of psychotherapy outcome research with ethnic minority clients are problematic. Conclusions cannot be drawn with great confidence. Second, relatively high rates of dropping out from treatment are observed among some ethnic minority groups, especially African Americans. Third, most comparative studies reveal that treatment outcomes for ethnic clients are either the same as, or poorer, than for Whites. No study has demonstrated superior outcomes for ethnics. Ethnic minorities tended at best to have similar treatment outcomes to White Americans. Fourth, the effectiveness of psychotherapy is complex, requiring more than an affirmative or negative response. If we put aside the subtleties and complexity involved in the question of overall effectiveness, we have some reason to believe that certain conditions are related to effectiveness: Ethnic similarity for clients and therapists of some ethnic minority groups; the use of some culturally responsive forms of treatment; pretherapy intervention with ethnic clients; and the training of therapists to specifically work with members of culturally diverse groups. The most meaningful research, therefore, deals with conditions of effectiveness rather than with attempts to answer the effectiveness question in general. In actuality, the research on culturally-responsive forms of treatment attempts to identify those culturally-derived practices that are beneficial.

Most critics of psychotherapy with ethnic groups do not challenge the value of psychotherapy or psychological interventions. What they often challenge is the outcomes of psychotherapy when traditional psychotherapeutic practices do not consider the culture and minority group experiences of ethnic minority clients. Some may also advocate for prevention and social, political, and economic changes rather than psychotherapy. Nevertheless, few critics would argue that psychotherapy cannot be effective with ethnic minority group clients.

Policy/Psychotherapy Issues

Given the state of our knowledge, should we offer psychotherapy even if effectiveness has not been demonstrated? Should we use treatments if they have not been tested with ethnic minority populations? If we are serious about basing treatment on research findings, what should we do in terms of treatment, if not enough research has been conducted to permit conclusions to be drawn with respect to psychotherapy and assessment with ethnic minority clients? This leads to other questions. Is the lack of evidence over effectiveness attributable to the lack of good research (i.e., if good research were available, effectiveness would be apparent) or to the actual ineffectiveness of treatment? What alternatives are there to psychotherapy?

I raise these questions, not because I have answers but because the science and profession of psychology must address them. However, it does seem to me that we cannot wait for research to always provide answers as to what we should do. As argued in a previous paper (Sue, 1992), I know that many investigators believe that before taking a stance on policy and public interest issues, we should have substantial research justification. Their position is that advocating for programs and policies in the absence of a strong research foundation is irrational and may lead to poor policies and programs. Others, who feel the urgency of addressing public needs for programs and solutions to problems, point out that "Rome may burn while researchers fiddle away."

There is not much disagreement over the critical importance of using research to guide policies and practices. But should we practice or perform treatment in the absence of definitive research findings? Doing so could result in practices that are driven by emotions rather than reason, or opinion rather than fact. However, what should be done if there are urgent needs for which solutions have not been well researched? Do we suspend actions? This is the case for ethnic minorities for whom no rigorous studies have examined treatment outcomes. Furthermore, what should be done if there are legitimate debates over the conclusiveness of research findings? Smith (1990) maintains that research data on issues are seldom conclusive, and judgements differ as to the threshold for research findings that are considered "definitive."

In addition, it is erroneous to believe that policies and practices are adopted only after solid research justification is available. They may be established because of ethical-moral issues, public opinion, cultural practices, and political considerations. There are also many examples in which convergent and substantial research evidence pointing to a specific course of action exists; yet, the action has failed to be adopted. For example, research has consistently shown that alternative programs for persons with mental disorders are often as effective, and yet less expensive, as traditional forms of care in mental hospitals (Fairweather, 1980; Kiesler, 1982). However, decision-makers as well as the public have failed to implement such alternative care systems. (In my more cynical moments, I believe that human beings have not biologically evolved to the point where decisions can be guided primarily by rational and empirical thinking and where violence and aggression can be avoided.)

As noted in my previous paper (Sue, 1992), perhaps in our debate over whether or not solid data should precede policy recommendations, we have neglected the fact that research is important in all phases of the policy making or maintaining process. This fact implies that the important issue is the intertwining of research with policy and practice, not which comes first. Sometimes, policies and practices may be established for any of a variety of reasons. Research is then initiated to test the outcomes, and the policies and practices are modified or new and often untested practices develop, which are then subjected to research. Thus, the initiation of new and untested therapies and practices can be encouraged without abandoning science. In our bid to link scientific standards to practice, let us not become so single minded that we fail to deal with the consequences of the limitations in our knowledge concerning effective treatments and the fact that the needs of the public may have to be addressed even if our knowledge is limited.

Let me raise some other issues. How far do we go in "what works" philosophy? If we find through our research that certain procedures work with some ethnic minority clients, should we employ the procedures even if they involve spiritualism, faith healing, satanism, or deception? The question is not absurd. I have spent considerable time in various Asian countries. While in Singapore, I was informed by mental health workers that some individuals develop a culture bound syndrome in which hysterical symptoms appear. The afflicted individuals attribute the symptoms to spirits that invade the body after a person has stepped on the "wrong" piece of earth. I asked some of the Western trained psychiatrists how they treat persons with the disorder. Although they did not believe in the cultural explanation involving spirits, they nevertheless provided treatment (as explained to clients) intended to "rid the body of the spirits" as well as western psychotherapy. Lefley and Bestman (1984) describe their work with different ethnic groups in Miami where mental health professionals collaborate with folk healers or spiritualists who may perform exorcisms. Assuming that one does not believe in spiritual healing (i.e., believe in the supernational explanation for the outcome), is there anything unethical, dishonest, or disturbing about pretending in front of the client to believe in such treatment?

Finally, can standards be culturally biased? Let me provide some examples of where guidelines and standards appear to have differential cultural implications. In the U.S., we have child abuse laws that help us to determine if adults are acting inappropriately with children. An assumption underlying these laws is that children have certain human rights. In other cultures, the assumption is considerably weaker. Traditionally, in certain Asian cultures, children have very little rights and parents are expected to have much greater freedom in how they treat and discipline children. Some cases have occurred where Asian American parents who been accused of child abuse maintain that it is their right to treat their children as they see fit. As another example in which standards of practice have different cultural implications we can examine guidelines for the providers of care. Guidelines often discourage the receiving of gifts from clients and the development of personal relationships between therapists and clients. Accepting gifts and forming personal relationships can undermine the professional relationship. Yet, the professional and personal roles are often blurred in other cultures. For example, in Chinese culture, clients often give physicians or other service providers expensive or inexpensive gifts as tokens of appreciation or as an encouraged cultural practice. They may also invite the provider to family gatherings as a respected friend or expect the provider to act as a family advisor. If the provider refuses gifts or maintains a formal and distant relationship, clients may lose face and feel rejected.

By raising all of these issues, I am not trying to deemphasize the role of science in practice. For too long, practice has proceeded without research guidance. What I am saying is that perhaps our ideals are now advancing ahead of reality, and issues concerning science and practice cannot be approached in a naive fashion.

Socio-Political Issues

In dealing with ethnic minority issues, research and practice are not just scientific or value-free ventures. There are consequences or side effects to nearly every course of action we can take, because of the history of race relations. There is no question that ethnic minority issues have been controversial. They are attributable to the concepts of ethnicity and minority group status. Differences in ethnicity often results in cultural value clashes, while minority group refers to a status in society—a status accompanied by prejudice and discrimination. The two are often confounded. Differences between ethnic groups are often erroneously attributed to cultural factors and visa versa. For example, traditional Chinese values are often compared with Western values in order to explain why Chinese Americans may be more likely to show certain attitudinal or personality differences from White Americans. In essence, the two cultures are conceptualized as being orthogonal or independent variables. In reality, the two are interactive and not independent. That is, Chinese Americans have had a long history in the U.S. As members of a minority group who have experienced prejudice and discrimination, their attitudes and behaviors may be a product not only of Chinese culture but also of the history and experiences in this country. Because of this history, research and treatment involving ethnic minorities are embedded in larger issues regarding segregation, discrimination and inequalities, cultural biases, stereotyping, and political correctness. Kenneth Clark (1972) argued that the mental health profession has not been immune to the forces of racism in society and that racism may be reflected in processes such as diagnosis, assessment, and treatment. These two concepts-- ethnicity and minority group status—help to differentiate ethnic minority research from cross-cultural research. The former is more likely to involve the two concepts while the latter is primarily concerned with ethnicity. The two concepts also explain why debates over diversity and psychotherapy are far more intense than debates over, say, schizophrenia and psychotherapy.

Moreover, research on ethnic minority groups, especially those that have policy implications, often generate unexpected issues. Our work on psychotherapy and treatment also created controversies. Let me indicate some of the consequences of involvement with ethnic minority issues and then raise some dilemmas for consideration.

An unexpected controversy occurred just a few months ago. One of our early studies (Sue, 1977) indicated that ethnic minority clients tended to drop out of treatment rather quickly. This led us to examine whether drop out rates were lower when clients saw therapists of the same ethnicity (Sue et al., 1991). The findings were clear in that ethnic match was associated with lower drop out rates. We felt that ethnic match was therefore beneficial. However, ethnic matches were also associated with more treatment sessions. When I presented the results of the study at a meeting with directors of NIMH funded ethnic minority research centers in 1994, James Jackson, a close friend of mine who directs the African American Mental Health Center at the University of Michigan, brought up an interesting point. He noted that the greater number of sessions, the costlier the treatment. Therefore, the association between ethnic match and increased numbers of treatment sessions could be used to argue against matching because match appears to increase the cost of treatment. This is a particular problem because superior outcomes for ethnically matched dyads could not be demonstrated in a clear manner. That is, the outcome measure was rather weak and ethnic match and treatment outcome were related only for certain, and not all, groups. Other dilemmas are also apparent in the following situations:

1. Several years ago, the Committee on Psychological Tests and Assessment was reviewing guidelines on assessment and sought input from various APA divisions and governance agencies. In attempting to see that assessment procedures would not

be culturally-biased against ethnic minorities, the Committee dealt with a proposal indicating that if clinicians were not competent to conduct a psychological evaluation of an ethnic minority client—presumably because of cultural unfamiliarity—they should avoid making an assessment. One can imagine a similar proposal concerning psychotherapy—that clinicians whose competence with ethnic clients is in question should not provide clinical services. Obviously, it would be inappropriate to subject ethnic minority clients to inadequate services. On the other hand, in the attempts to see that clients are not given inappropriate services, I raised several questions. If the proposal is adopted, what would prevent clinicians from discriminating against ethnic clients? Who is going to serve ethnics? Don't we have the responsibility not only to decline from providing services to which we are not qualified but also to see that services are available to all? In the attempt to be culturally-responsive, a more fundamental issue concerning the availability and accessibility of services was overlooked. It seemed to me that while the underlying principle was appropriate, detrimental side effects could follow. In practice, we needed to also specify, and to have available, services for the entire population.

2. In advocating for mental health services for diverse populations, I recommended that ethnic specific services be created (see Sue, 1992). This recommendation involved the creation of mental health programs/centers or sections of hospitals that would specifically serve targeted ethnic minority populations. The recommendation made sense to me because in some communities there was a heavy concentration of members of a particular ethnic group. Having services that could cater to this group—e.g., bilingual/bicultural service providers, notices and announcements written in the ethnic language of the group, an atmosphere ethnically-consistent with the community, etc.—seemed important. However, some argued that ethnic specific services would perpetuate segregation and rather than having special services for ethnic minorities, the mental health system should be designed to effectively serve all groups (Kramer, 1984). In principle, I agreed with the need for integrated services. However, I did not believe that in the near future, this goal could be attained, given patterns of ethnic residential segregation and lack of research over the effectiveness of services for all populations.

3. Ethnic matching of therapists and clients has also provoked much discussion. As mentioned previously, our studies revealed that ethnic match may be beneficial for some kinds of clients. The findings bolstered the fact that ethnic diversification of service providers is important, in order for clients to find ethnically similar therapists. However, they also raised unanticipated issues. For example, after I gave a talk on the research at the 1994 Congress meeting of the International Association of Applied Psychology in Spain, a member of the audience informed me that some in South Africa were using my research to justify having "Whites taking care of Whites and Blacks taking care of Blacks." Again, I was confronted with the segregation issue. My position is not that ethnic match should always take place, that ethnic mismatches cannot be beneficial, or that individuals cannot be trained to effectively work with diverse client populations. Rather, our mental health ideals

have implicitly promoted freedom of choice in the matching of therapist and treatment approach with the client. Such choices are often based on client perceptions of the therapist's effectiveness, rapport, and understanding. I believe that matching and ethnic-specific services are consistent with freedom of choice and effectiveness of treatment. If clients need or want therapists of the same ethnicity, such therapists should be available.

4. The outcomes of research findings have often created problems and dilemmas. Our Seattle project (Sue, 1977) found a high drop out rate for ethnic minority clients undergoing treatment, We felt that services were not meeting the needs of ethnic minority clients. After some of the results were published, and without our knowledge, the National Institute of Mental Health, which funded our research, contacted the Washington State Department of Social and Health Services (DSHS) in order to express its deep concern over the inequities in service delivery that were demonstrated by our project. Reacting to this concern, DSHS apparently became worried over the possible adverse public reaction to the findings and over the criticisms from NIMH which could jeopardize future State funding opportunities from NIMH. It then challenged the validity of the findings by arguing that one of the 17 mental health facilities included in the study might not have provided accurate data. Thus the State raised some doubt over the validity of the data that it had supplied us.

Again, these events occurred without my knowledge. It was not until I was asked by the Washington State Psychological Association to testify at a senate subcommittee hearing that the controversy was explained to me. In preparation for the hearing, I reanalyzed the data. By excluding from the reanalysis the one facility in question, we found that our original conclusions were valid. Even though I was gratified that the findings did not essentially change, I had strong and mixed feelings over the situation. I wanted to use the findings to find out what the status was of various ethnic minority clients who used mental health services and to make policy and practice recommendations in order to improve services. However, in the process, the State of Washington was being singled out for criticism. I was concerned that the State was being subjected to criticism when other states and systems were encountering similar problems in responding to ethnic minority populations. Then too, the State had provided us with the data as a cooperative research partner and as a goodwill gesture (at our request). Given our experience, I was worried that other states and mental health systems programs might be reluctant to allow researchers access to their data, which could be used to criticize their mental health practices.

Fortunately, two positive outcomes emerged after my testimony. First, officials from the State indicated their concern over the delivery of services to all clients and told me that they would be willing to collaborate on research in the future. Secondly, over the years, the State made some firm commitments to offer culturally-responsive services. It then conducted a follow-up investigation of our Seattle project. The study found that the high dropout rates for ethnic minority clients had now been reduced and that the mental health system had hired more ethnic minority service providers, created more ethnic specific services, and established other innovative programs to serve ethnics (O'Sullivan, Petersen, Cox, & Kirkeby, 1989).

The point I am making is that as scientists whose works have practice and policy implications, we must be cognizant of the potential dilemmas that may well emerge when dealing with diversity issues. We must prepare ourselves for several circumstances when bringing research to bear on these issues. First, the complexity of issues must be recognized. Many of our actions that are based on research have side effects, so that actions to promote multi-culturalism may be beneficial at one level but harmful at another level. Second, it may not be possible to avoid the side effects of programs and policies that we undertake. In this case, there must be conscious and deliberate decision-making that considers costs, benefits, principles, realities, and ultimate goals that we have with respect to diversity. It is through this process of deliberation that a more coherent approach to diversity can emerge. Third, conflicts often cannot be avoided when we attempt to apply scientific standards to clinical practice. Fourth, cultural diversity is the nature of human beings, and it should be the nature of our science and practice of psychology.

Implications for Psychotherapy and Research

Psychotherapy

We must provide effective services to ethnic minority groups. In view of the fact that little empirical evidence exists concerning the effectiveness of treatment and the conditions that promote positive outcomes among ethnic minority clients, it would be unwise to set precise guidelines on how to conduct psychotherapy with these clients. Nevertheless, we can hypothesize, or speculate on, general processes or conditions that may be important. First, ethnicity, culture, and minority group status are important concepts for psychotherapists who work with ethnic minority clients. The available evidence suggests that therapists should be prepared to deal with these concepts and issues with their clients. Cultural issues may not be salient to all ethnic clients in all situations. Nevertheless, therapists who are uncomfortable with cultural issues are limited when their clients raise ethnically pertinent topics in therapy. Therapists should become knowledgeable about the cultural background of ethnic clients and be adept at working in cross-cultural situations.

Second, having available a therapist of the same ethnicity as the client may be advantageous. While ethnic matches are not necessary for positive outcomes, there are times in which certain clients may prefer or work better with an ethnically-similar therapist. Having bilingual and bicultural therapists is vital to those clients who are recent immigrants and who are not fully proficient in English. The problem is that ethnic clients often have little choice, unless we have available more ethnic minority, bilingual, and bicultural therapists.

Third, therapists who are unfamiliar with the cultural backgrounds of their clients may want to consult with mental health professionals who are knowledgeable of the clients' culture. Receiving training in working with culturally-diverse clients is also recommended. It is difficult to be fully proficient in working with many diverse groups. Assistance should be sought in the assessment or treatment of any client whose cultural background or lifestyle is unfamiliar to the therapist or markedly different from that of the therapist.

Fourth, culture-specific treatment should be available to ethnic clients, especially those who are unacculturated or who hold very traditional ethnic values that are discrepant from Western values. As mentioned previously, many researchers have argued that such treatment is valuable and beneficial.

Fifth, for clients who are unfamiliar with Western psychotherapy, some sort of pretherapy intervention may be important. Before therapy, clients should receive some knowledge of what psychotherapy is, what roles clients and therapists adopt, what to expect in treatment, and how treatment can affect mental disorders. Similarly, efforts should be made to educate community groups on how to recognize emotional disturbance, what do with someone who is disturbed, what mental health services are, and how to use services. Issues of confidentiality, client rights, etc., should also be presented to the community. These strategies increase the likelihood that ethnic clients will better understand treatment and will reduce feelings of strangeness in the role of a client.

Research

The greatest obstacle to having science play a major role in determining psychological practice with ethnic minority populations is the lack of research rather than the lack of appreciation for science. As mentioned earlier, not a single rigorous study exists that convincingly demonstrates the efficacy of psychotherapy with these populations; while inferences can be drawn about the conditions that promote psychotherapeutic effectiveness, little programmatic research is available. Furthermore, few studies have examined the cross-cultural validity of assessment measures. In the absence of research on ethnic minority populations, practice and recommendations for therapists and assessors have been guided by folk wisdom, intuition, experiences, and "best guesses."

Despite the lack of research, ethnic and cross-cultural research is important not only to guide practice but also to enhance science. Let me try to indicate what can be accomplished by ethnic minority/cross-cultural research.

1. Cross-cultural and ethnic research is invaluable in improving research designs and in testing the generality of theories. Cross-cultural research can be used to increase the range of variables of interest. For example, if one wanted to study the personality variable of collectivism versus individualism, a greater range on the variable can be achieved if the study were conducted among both individualistic (e.g., American) and collectivistic (e.g., Taiwan) societies. In addition, a researcher who conducts research in different societies can establish the validity of the theory for human beings (and not simply for one's own culture), as noted by Triandis and Brislin (1984). For example, some researchers have identified five, orthogonal personality factors (i.e., the Big Five) that have been consistently found to underlie

personality attributes in research spanning more than half a century, primarily in the U.S. (Wiggins & Picus, 1989). Is the Big Five germane to non-Western cultures? Bond and Yang (1990) have found some evidence that the Big Five is applicable in Chinese culture but also that some differences are apparent between the Big Five and the underlying personality factors in Chinese culture. What is interesting to explore is whether there are personality dimensions in other cultures that are more salient than those in the Big Five. For example, Zane (1991) has developed a measure of loss of face which is a very important construct in Chinese cultures. Loss of face is the threat to, or loss of, one's social integrity. Zane is studying whether this personality variable—loss of face—can supplant any of the ones in the Big Five in term of saliency for the Chinese. If so, then the Big Five is not universal in its saliency.

2. Limitations in our practices can be determined. Traditionally, western psychologists have studied the efficacy of different treatments on the same population or the efficacy of one treatment with diagnostically different clients. Strangely, we have largely failed to study the effectiveness of treatment with different ethnic populations; and yet, such studies are needed to demonstrate the generality of treatment effects and the potency of the treatment. Instead of always comparing different treatments on similar populations, we should also use one treatment and test different populations. Why have we not done this?

3. A related point is the need to study individual differences and heterogeneity among members of ethnic minority groups. For example, our work previously cited have demonstrated that the effects of matching the ethnicity of therapists and clients depend on individual difference variables. Research on individual differences can address the question of whether there universals in psychotherapy. That is, what psychotherapy principles, tactics, or processes appear to effectively cross cultures?

4. The principles that govern diversity and its effects should be studied. What aspects of culture is important in psychotherapy? We can assume that some cultural features are more important than others in psychotherapy. For example, we have hypothesized (and are now testing) that how a client conceptualizes mental disorders, what goals are deemed appropriate, and what means are used to resolve problems are especially important in the therapeutic relationship. By trying to determine the underlying principles, we can determine what aspects of culture are important for the clinician to consider.

In this chapter, I have tried to indicate some of the diversity or ethnic implications that emerge when we try to link scientific standards to clinical practice. There is no question that practice should be guided by research. My plea is that we conduct more ethnic research so that a meaningful relationship between science and practice can be achieved and that we become aware of, and deal with, controversies that inevitably arise whenever ethnicity is discussed.

References

Abramowitz, S. I., & Murray, J. (1983). Race effects in psychotherapy. In J. Murray & P. Abramson (Eds.), *Bias in psychotherapy* (pp. 215-255). New York: Praeger.

Acosta, F. X., Yamamoto, J., Evans, L. A., & Skilbeck, W. M. (1983). Preparing low-income Hispanic, Black, and White patients for psychotherapy: Evaluation of a new orientation program. *Journal of Clinical Psychology, 39,* 872-877.

Brown, B. S., Joe, G. W., & Thompson, P. (1985). Minority group status and treatment retention. *International Journal of the Addictions, 20,* 319-335.

Cattell, R. B. (1947). Confirmation and clarification of primary personality traits. *Psychometrika, 42,* 402-421.

Clark, K. B. (1972). Foreword. In A. Thomas & S. Sillen (Eds.), *Racism and psychiatry.* New York: Brunner/Mazel.

Fairweather, G. W. (Ed.). (1980). *The Fairweather lodge: A twenty-five year retrospective.* San Francisco: Jossey-Bass.

Griffith, M. S., & Jones, E. E. (1978). Race and psychotherapy: Changing perspectives. In J. H. Masserman (Ed.), *Current Psychiatric Therapies: Vol. 18* (pp. 225-235). New York: Grune and Stratton.

Jones, E. E. (1978). Effects of race on psychotherapy process and outcome: An exploratory investigation. *Psychotherapy: Theory, Research, and Practice, 15,* 226-236.

Jones, E. E. (1982). Psychotherapists' impressions of treatment outcome as a function of race. *Journal of Clinical Psychology, 38,* 722-731.

Jones, E. E., & Matsumoto, D. R. (1982). Psychotherapy with the undeserved. In L. Snowden (Ed.), *Services to the underserved* (pp. 207-228). Los Angeles, CA: Sage Publications.

Kiesler, C. A. (1982). Mental hospitals and alternative care: Non-institutionalization as a potential public policy for mental patients. *American Psychologist, 37,* 349-360.

Kramer, B. M. (1984). Community mental health in a dual society. In S. Sue & T. Moore, (Eds.), *The pluralistic society: A community mental health perspective* (pp. 54-262). New York: Human Sciences Press.

Lefley, H. P., & Bestman, E. W. (1984). Community mental health and minority: A multi-ethnic approach. In S. Sue & T. Moore (Eds.), *The pluralistic society: A community mental health perspective* (pp. 116-148). NY: Human Sciences Press.

Lerner, B. (1972). *Therapy in the ghetto: Political impotence and personal disintegration.* Baltimore: The Johns Hopkins University Press.

O'Sullivan, M. J., Peterson, P. D., Cox, G. B., & Kirkeby, J. (1989). Ethnic populations: Community mental health services ten years later. *American Journal of Community Psychology, 17,* 17-30.

Parloff, M. B., Waskow, I. E., & Wolfe, B. E. (1978). Research on therapist variables in relation to process and outcome. In S. L. Garfield & A. E. Bergin (Eds.), *Handbook of psychotherapy and behavior change: An empirical analysis* (2nd ed.) (pp. 233-282). New York: Wiley.

Query, J. M. N. (1985). Comparative admission and follow-up study of American Indians and Whites in a youth chemical dependency unit on the North Central Plains. *The International Journal of the Addictions, 20,* 489-502.

Rogler, L. H., Malgady, R. G., & Rodriguez, O. (1989). *Hispanics and mental health: A framework for research*. Malabar, FL: Krieger Publishing Company.

Sattler, J. M. (1977). The effects of therapist-client racial similarity. In A. S. Gurman & A. M. Razin (Eds.), *Effective psychotherapy: A handbook of research* (pp. 252-290). Elmsford, NY: Pergamon.

Smith, M. B. (1990). What have we done? What can we do? *American Psychologist, 45*, 530-536.

Sue, S. (1977). Community mental health services to minority groups: Some optimism, some pessimism. *American Psychologist, 32*, 616-624.

Sue, S. (1992). Ethnicity and mental health: Research and policy issues. *Journal of Social Issues, 48*, 187-205.

Sue, S., Fujino, D. C., Hu, L. T., Takeuchi, D. T., & Zane, N. W. S. (1991). Community mental health services for ethnic minority groups: A test of the cultural responsiveness hypothesis. *Journal of Consulting and Clinical Psychology, 59*, 533-540.

Sue, S., Zane, N. W. S., & Young, K. (1994). Research on psychotherapy with culturally diverse populations. In A. E. Bergin & S. L. Garfield (Eds.), *Handbook of psychotherapy and behavior change, 4th edition* (pp. 783-820). NY: Wiley & Sons.

Szapocznik, J., Rio, A., Murray, E., Cohen, R., Scopetta, M., Rivas-Vazquez, A., Hervis, O., Posada, V., & Kurtines, W. (1989). Structural family versus psychodynamic child therapy for problematic Hispanic boys. *Journal of Counseling and Clinical Psychology, 57*, 571-578.

Triandis, H. C., & Brislin, R. W. (1984). Cross-cultural psychology. *American Psychologist, 39*, 1006-1016.

Wiggins, J. S., & Picus, A. L. (1989). Conceptions of personality disorders and dimensions of personality. *Psychological Assessment: A Journal of Consulting and Clinical Psychology, 1*, 305-316.

Yang, K., & Bond, M. H. (1990). Exploring implicit personality theories with indigenous or imported constructs: The Chinese case. *Journal of Personality and Social Psychology, 58*, 1087-1095.

Zane, N. W. S. (1991, August). *An empirical examination of loss of face among Asian Americans*. A paper presented at the 99th annual convention of the American Psychological Association, San Francisco, CA.

Footnote

The writing of this paper was supported by NIMH Grant R01 MH44331.

Discussion of Sue

The Difficulties, and Importance, of Applying Scientific Standards to Clinical Practice with Diverse Populations

Alan E. Fruzzetti
University of Nevada

Epidemiological and treatment utilization studies have consistently demonstrated that people of lower socio-economic status (SES), older age, and from ethnic, cultural and language minority groups receive fewer psychological services than younger, middle-class or affluent, English-speaking white Americans (e.g., Hough, Landsverk, Karno, Burnam, Timbers, Escobar, & Regier, 1987; Shapiro, Skinner, Kessler, Von Korff, German, Tischler, Leaf, Benham, Cottler, & Regier, 1984). Stanley Sue (1988; this volume) has discussed many of the issues that make finding treatments with established efficacy for these populations a complex process. In the struggle to make effective services more accessible to underserved and diverse populations, several potentially damaging assumptions about the applicability of services to these groups are possible. This chapter will highlight some of the problematic issues affecting the application of scientific standards to clinical practice with diverse populations, and discuss why such standards are nevertheless essential.

The Pitfalls of Proxy Variables

Social scientists have a history of using proxy variables, or substitute variables, in statistical prediction equations when the variable of theoretical interest is difficult to measure or would confound an experimental procedure. The use of proxy variables is problematic because they introduce both random and systematic errors into statistical analyses and often lead to serious misinterpretations of statistical findings (Pedhazur & Schmelkin, 1991).

Problems in using proxy variables are especially relevant in the present discussion because ethnic minority group membership itself is often used as a proxy for specific cultural practices, and for concomitant psychological factors associated with those practices. So little research has investigated the *psychological* factors associated with cultural practices specific to ethnic minority, class, and other group memberships that researchers often have made conclusions that group membership per se is responsible for statistically significant group differences. However, psychological factors and cultural practices, not group membership, are more usefully defined to be "causes" of psychological phenomena than proxy variables (Persons, 1986).

This distinction is important for several reasons. First, when one treatment is found to be more effective with one group (e.g., age, ethnic minority, SES) than another, these differences are typically in degrees of effectiveness. That is, some members of both groups in question benefit, some do not; perhaps the proportions differ. Although it may be tempting to conclude (and often is) that "one treatment is more effective for group x," a more accurate statement would be that "more members of group x benefited." The difference between the two statements is that, presumably, cultural and psychological factors more associated with outcome are more prevalent in group x. Because we seldom know what these factors are, we often mistakenly attribute differences simply to the proxy variable, group membership itself.

The reality is that very few studies of psychological services examine diverse groups specifically. And even those studies that are heterogeneous with respect to age, ethnic minority status, SES or other diversity factors, have insufficient non-majority participants to be able to parse the data to ascertain what psychological and cultural factors associated with group status (if any) mediate outcome. It is impractical, of course, to require that every definitive set of studies performed on majority clients (there are few enough of these) be replicated with every minority group, and combination of groups (elderly/poor/English-speaking Hispanics, elderly/middle-class/English-speaking Hispanics, elderly/poor/Spanish-speaking Hispanics, etc.). Yet there may be hazards in establishing standards of practice that do not take psychological and cultural factors associated with group membership into account.

Thus, it is essential to decide both where to allocate resources to demonstrate efficacy and how to decide whether (or, when) to generalize results obtained with one population to another. In simple terms, the generalization answer can be conservative or liberal. The conservative interpretation would be something like: "If the data are not conclusive about effectiveness with a given population, assume this group is dissimilar and treatment is to be considered ineffective until proven otherwise." Of course, a liberal approach to generalization might suggest: "If there are no conclusive data about efficacy (or inefficacy) with a given population, assume the population is similar to that already studied and assume similar efficacy." Both of these approaches and assumptions can lead to serious problems, which are discussed next.

Problems in Assuming Similarity

There are two main problems that could result if we were to assume (until proven otherwise) that all psychological practice standards established with majority populations automatically generalize to more diverse populations. First, and most obvious, is that real cultural practice differences related to outcome could actually exist. Not only would this be culturally insensitive, it would likely result in poorer outcomes overall among those from different populations. If there are, in fact, psychological differences related to cultural practices (and hence group memberships), problematic mismatching of treatment to client would occur, with characteristically poorer results (Brickman, Rabinowitz, Karuza, Coates, Cohn, & Kidder, 1982; Sue, Fujino, Hu, Takeuchi, & Zane, 1991).

A more subtle result of the assumptions of similarity and generalizability might be the further marginalization of research with and on members of diverse populations. That is, if we assume homogeneity there may be less incentive to study applications with non-majority populations. Given the existing paucity of research with ethnic minority, low SES, elderly, and non-English speaking populations, this would be a terrible (and difficult to recognize) result.

Problems in Assuming Dissimilarity

Perhaps even greater problems could result if we assumed that research findings obtained with one population would not generalize and apply to other populations. The immediate impact would be to severely limit the number of psychological services of "demonstrated" efficacy with diverse populations. Even among those treatments where a whole series of studies support efficacy, a tiny number of these confirm efficacy differentially according to ethnic minority, language, class, or age status. Because of the homogeneity requirements of most large group studies, diversity is often limited or excluded a priori. Only those who fit the "typical" profile of study participants would be eligible for a treatment with demonstrated effectiveness under this assumption.

In the current social and political climate of budget-cutting and limits on growth of services, such a system could lead to further de facto exclusion from services for many whose needs are already less likely to get met. The "lack" of treatments with demonstrated efficacy could simply justify further reductions in needed (and perhaps, indeed, effective) psychological services.

Without sound theoretical or scientific reasons to assume research findings do not generalize, many resources could be wasted. For example, many programs with demonstrated efficacy have sought ways to make services accessible to those in need. Often, this has focused exclusively on redressing factors related to poverty and lack of education, and likely could apply to *any* economically disadvantaged group, irrespective of other diversity issues. Thus, tested programs that were developed to serve the needs of low SES members of one ethnic minority group could be readily applicable to anyone in low SES groups (e.g., Hatch & Paradis, 1993).

If we 1) assume that research results with traditional populations do not generalize to diverse populations, 2) realize that the number of possible combinations of group membership is quite large, and 3) recognize that funding (and perhaps interest) for multiple replications with different populations is not readily available, this may lead to another problem: we may conclude that it is not necessary to demonstrate efficacy at all with minority populations. This would represent, of course, a new kind of racism (and classism, ageism, etc.) wherein a double standard is created. That is, for majority populations, demonstrated efficacy would be required. For others it might be written off as "impractical." If practice standards are a good thing they should be applied to services for everyone.

Recommendations

Lest the preceding sections seem contradictory (problems with assuming similarity, problems with assuming dissimilarity), it may be useful to delineate several synthesizing recommendations for applying practice standards to psychological services with diverse populations.

1) Research psychologists should put more emphasis on the hard work of separating out what psychological factors are associated with cultural practices in different ethnic minority, social class, and age groups. This will help us determine when (and if) practices with established efficacy in one group are *likely* to transfer to members of another group at about the same rate. This type of work will help eliminate the guesswork, and pseudoscience, in transferring research findings from one group to another, and reduce our reliance on proxy variables. In this sense, good science will lead to good practice.

2) With cultural sensitivity, we should determine whether certain active factors in treatment programs are very likely to be antithetical to cultural practices (and, hence, common psychological factors) in given groups. This will assist in deciding when to assume dissimilarity of application across groups.

3) Beware the hegemony of group statistics. In the context of the above recommendations, we should be able to rely less on group status and more on an individual assessment of needs. Although group statistics provide an essential piece in establishing what are good psychological practices, we do not typically treat groups: we treat individuals. If we do a good job assessing what an individual needs (or couple, family, etc.), what cultural practices are important for that person, and what psychological processes are relevant to those cultural practices, we are likely to choose appropriate treatment practices. Thus, when we are able to establish practice standards they will direct us to indications and contraindications, some of which may relate to psychological factors related to cultural practices that are differentially prevalent across diverse population groups.

References

Brickman, P., Rabinowitz, V. C., Karuza, J., Coates, D., Cohn, E., & Kidder, L. (1982). Models of helping and coping. *American Psychologist, 37*, 368-384.

Hatch, M. L., & Paradis, C. (1993). Panic disorder with agoraphobia: A focus on group treatment with African Americans. *The Behavior Therapist, 16*, 240-241.

Hough, R. L., Landsverk, J. A., Karno, M., Burnam, M. A., Timbers, D. M. Escobar, J. I., & Regier, D. A. (1987). Utilization of health and mental health services by Los Angeles Mexican Americans and non-Hispanic Whites. *Archives of General Psychiatry, 44*, 702-709.

Pedhazur, E. J., & Schmelkin, L. P. (1991). *Measurement, design, and analysis: An integrated approach.* Hillsdale, NJ: Lawrence Erlbaum Associates.

Persons, J. B. (1986). The advantages of studying psychological phenomena rather than psychiatric diagnoses. *American Psychologist, 41,* 1252-1260.

Shapiro, S., Skinner, E. A., Kesler, L. G., Von Korff, M., German, P. S., Tischler, G. L., Leaf, P. J., Benham, L., Cottler, L. K., & Regier, D. A. (1984). Utilization of health and mental health services: Three epidemiological catchment area sites. *Archives of General Psychiatry, 41,* 971-978.

Sue, S. (1988). Psychotherapeutic services for ethnic minorities: Two decades of research findings. *American Psychologist, 43,* 301-308.

Sue, S., Fujino, D. C., Hu, L., Takeuchi, D. T., & Zane, N. W. S. (1991). Community mental health services for ethnic minority groups: A test of the cultural responsiveness hypothesis. *Journal of Consulting and Clinical Psychology, 59,* 533-540.